BITTER HARVEST

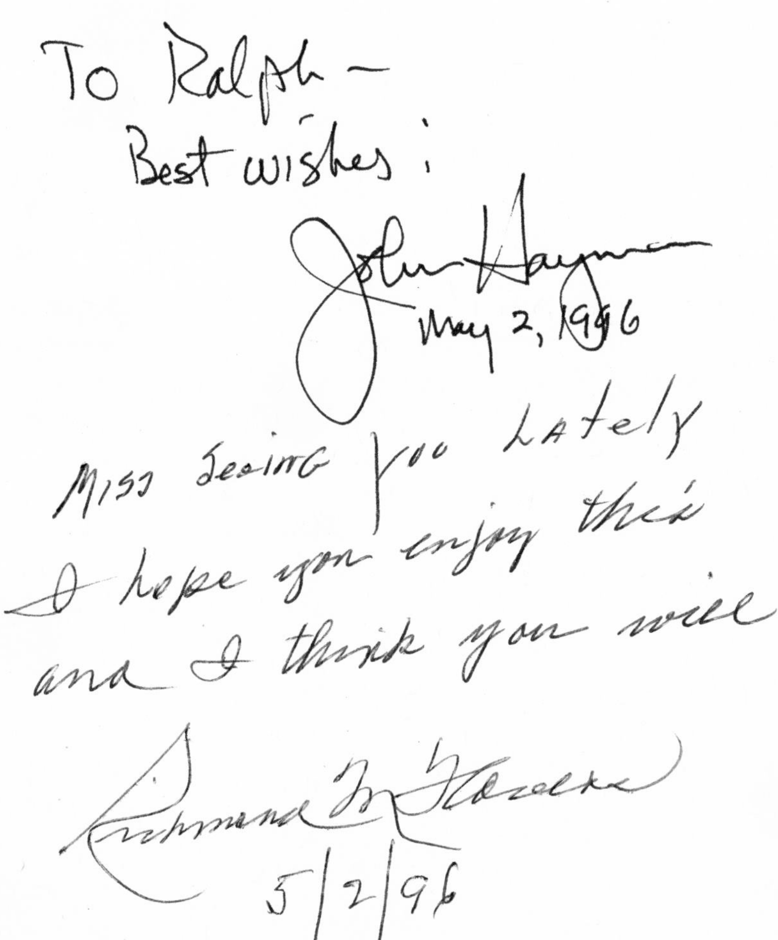

To Ralph —
Best wishes:
May 2, 1996
Miss seeing you lately
I hope you enjoy this
and I think you will
5/2/96

BITTER HARVEST

Richmond Flowers and the Civil Rights Revolution

JOHN HAYMAN

WITH A FOREWORD BY
PRESIDENT JIMMY CARTER

Black Belt Press
Montgomery

The Black Belt Press
P.O. Box 551
Montgomery, AL 36101

 Published in the United States by the Black Belt Press, a division of the Black Belt Communications Group, Inc., Montgomery, Alabama.

Cataloging-in-Publication Data

Hayman, John, 1929–
Bitter harvest : Richmond Flowers and the civil rights revolution / by John Hayman.
p. cm.
ISBN 1-881320-46-4
1. Flowers, Richmond, 1918– . 2. Politicians—Alabama—Biography. 3. Civil rights—Alabama—History—20th century. I. Title.

CIP

BOOK DESIGN BY RANDALL WILLIAMS

The Black Belt, defined by its dark, rich soil, stretches across central Alabama. It was the heart of the cotton belt. It was and is a place of great beauty, of extreme wealth and grinding poverty, of pain and joy. Here we take our stand, listening to the past, looking to the future.

Comments on *Bitter Harvest*

"In retrospect, history seems and reads very differently from the day-to-day political rhetoric one recalls. I shall enjoy taking another look at a fellow Alabamian's stand for his firm beliefs in the sixties. Perhaps it's time to meet the man."

—Fob James, Governor of Alabama

"One of Alabama's most fascinating political figures is former Attorney General Richmond Flowers. This book about his life and public service presents a new perspective on the volatile politics of the civil rights era in Alabama."

—Albert Brewer, Former Governor of Alabama

"This book is a true account of the life of Richmond Flowers, a champion of equal rights in the 1960s. In the 1966 governor's race, Flowers received approximately 90-95 percent of the black vote. Sadly, contrasted with 1996, there were not enough black voters in Alabama for this to make a difference."

—Jesse J. Lewis, first black appointee to former Governor George Wallace's cabinet

"While the author describes Flowers as a visionary leader trying to do the right thing during the most intense and emotionally-charged days of the civil rights movement, he does not ignore the shortcomings and failures of his subject . . . Richmond Flowers advocated a moderate course in the face of strong and often violent resistance to change. He ultimately paid a steep price for trying to counter the prevailing political sentiment of the era."

—Howell Heflin, United States Senator

"Looking back, it seems I had the heart of a wildcat during my political career. I was mauled and tattered many a time, but I always came fighting back. If I felt a cause was right, I rushed in whatever the odds. Bitter Harvest is a full and fair account of that struggle. I heartily endorse it because it tells the truth about my life and because it includes an interesting account on the civil rights struggle in the Deep South."

—Richmond Flowers

Contents

Foreword

I am honored to write this foreword to this biography of Richmond Flowers.

At some point in our lives, most of us wonder what we would do when faced with a great moral dilemma and forced to choose between doing what we know is right and doing what is expedient for ourselves and our family.

During the height of the civil rights movement, many good white Southerners made expedient decisions which they could rationalize and the rest of us could easily understand. When confronted with that same hard choice, Richmond Flowers made tough, uncompromising decisions which cost him not only his political career but jeopardized his brilliant legal career in Alabama and the South.

I am pleased that someone has now documented the life and courage of this good man. Richmond Flowers's story should not be lost to the generation of Southerners who lived through the civil rights struggle nor to their children or grandchildren. The lessons of great personal courage in the political life of our country are precious and far too rare to go unrecorded and unappreciated.

I am glad that this important book about this good Southerner has been written.

Jimmy Carter

Preface

Bitter Harvest traces the development of Richmond Flowers, a colorful politician from Dothan, Alabama, who was attorney general of his state during the first administration of George Wallace. Flowers began his career in 1946 as a traditional segregationist, but as attorney general he fought bitterly with Governor Wallace in trying to uphold the Constitution and the law. The text interweaves his story and that of the civil rights movement of the 1950s and 1960s.

The book is intended for the general reader who is interested in the history of civil rights and the people involved in the struggle. It was a time of great political and social drama. The civil rights movement brought fundamental change in race relations in the United States, which was sorely needed, but it also set the stage for the problems faced today. The search for equal rights and equal opportunities continues.

This is not an attempt to write "official history" of the type that professors of the subject would write and discuss at their professional meetings. I acknowledge to historians that I am not a member of their order and have not paid my dues to it. My effort, rather, is to tell an important story honestly, in a way which is as fair to all as I am capable of making it. I have also done my best to make it interesting and readable.

In 1966, when I was a young man in my flaming liberal stage, I lived in Denver, Colorado, and I was very proud of the fact that Richmond Flowers was making a strong race for governor of Alabama. I had grown up in Alabama, so it was a pleasure to see a nationally respected politician doing so well in a state dominated by George Wallace and his race-baiting friends.

Some twenty-five years later, and considerably more pragmatic in my views, I took on the task of organizing an academic computer science program at Wallace Community College in Dothan, Alabama. I was surprised to find my old idol on the faculty. When Richmond and I were introduced, I said, "You were my hero in civil rights days, and I really pulled for you in the 1966 race." Richmond liked that, of course. Almost immediately we became friends, and we used to sit around with some other faculty members, drink coffee, and talk about the world's problems.

In 1987 I was thinking of retiring, and I decided that in my new life I would like to focus on writing. One day I was talking about this, and I said to Richmond, "I'd like to write a book about you. Will you cooperate?" He thought that was an absolutely marvelous idea, and he cooperated fully in every way he was asked.

There were literally hundreds of hours of interviewing, beginning in 1988, which resulted in some 800 pages of printed material. Richmond patiently sat through all of this and offered suggestions when asked. As the text was being produced, he reviewed it for factual errors, but he never once objected to an author's judgment or editorial comment, whether favorable to him or not.

I make no pretense of being totally objective in this book. Richmond Flowers is a friend and a person whom I admire very much. I did my best to be honest and to tell the story as it occurred. I discovered, as I inevitably would, that there were warts and blemishes on my subject. Richmond is a human being, like the rest of us, with his share of faults. But, as it says in the text, in a critical period in the civil rights struggle, he stood on principle even though he knew the danger his stand posed in Alabama politics. This was an act of great courage which cost him his political career.

A substantial amount of library research was required to produce the text. I made considerable use of the Sterne Library at the University of Alabama in Birmingham. Court reports and other legal matters were researched at the library of the Cumberland School of Law at Samford University. The staff there was very gracious in helping a neophyte find things. The majority of the research was done at the Birmingham Public Library, with its complete newspaper and journal files and its excellent Linn-Henley Research Center on Southern History.

I am in debt to a number of people for helping to get this book finished. The greatest debt is to my wife, Clara Ruth Hayman. She did so much, in fact, that listing my name alone on the cover is shameful. She could, with considerable merit, claim to be a co-author. Clara Ruth helped significantly with the interviewing. I was very busy at the time holding down a full-time job at the college and trying to run a consulting business. But for her contribution, the work would have taken years longer.

Clara Ruth read all of the material as I produced it and was my severest critic (though always a sympathetic one). Often, though I hated to admit it, she was right. Her help in this regard was invaluable. She developed her own thoughts about what happened and how it ought to be presented, and she shared these with me. The chance to discuss matters with an intelligent, knowledgeable, and interested other is, of course, a great help in sorting things through and developing one's own broad conceptions.

Three other people read the material section by section as I produced it. These were Dr. John K. Folmar, professor of Southern history at California University of Pennsylvania; Dr. John Woodham, professor of history at Troy State University at Dothan; and my daughter, Rebecca Hayman, who is a special education teacher in the Atlanta area. Drs. Folmar and Woodham read primarily to check historical accuracy, and they were insightful, generous with their time, and very helpful. Rebecca read as an interested layperson. She asked questions when she did not understand something and made other comments on such matters as readability and presentation. I owe a great debt to all three of these readers.

John Woodham, whom I hardly knew when the project started, went far beyond the call of duty. He caught many factual errors, chided me gently when I made a questionable interpretation, and assured me this was a worthy project at those times I became discouraged. John says that, to the best of his knowledge, he has read every book on Alabama history ever published, and this reservoir of information was placed at my disposal. John was a real friend.

Dr. Joseph Brzeinski, former superintendent of the Denver public schools and an old friend, read the complete manuscript twice, after I completed the first version and after a major revision. A voracious reader with broad interests, Dr. Brzeinski approached the matter as an interested non-Southerner. He made extensive comments and suggestions, and he, too, made a major contribution. He has my sincere gratitude.

Malcolm MacDonald, former director of the University of Alabama Press, read the manuscript and made a number of valuable suggestions. He arranged for a history professor unknown to me to review the manuscript, and the result was an excellent critique with a number of very useful suggestions.

I am also greatly indebted to Mrs. Lucille Howard, a Birmingham neighbor, who tried to teach me some English many years ago at Jemison (Alabama) High School. I did not want to suffer criticism because of historical errors, and by the time the manuscript was completed I felt comfortable about this because three Southern-history professors had reviewed it. My next concern was grammar, spelling, consistency, and writing style. Mrs. Howard read the manuscript with an eye to these matters, and she saved me some embarrassment at several points. How often can you renew a pupil-teacher relationship with one of your favorite high school teachers after you are on Social Security?

Finally, I owe a great debt to Randall Williams, publisher of Black Belt Press. Randall, with his colleague Ashley Gordon, handled the reviewing and editing for Black Belt, and they were thorough, professional, and supportive. Black Belt Press contributes significantly to the state of Alabama and the South by preserving important historical matters. I feel fortunate to be associated with the press.

John Hayman

BITTER HARVEST

Prologue

The attorney general of Alabama, serving as prosecutor in the 1965 trial for murder of an Episcopal theological student, was spat upon and cursed as he entered the courthouse in the Black Belt town of Hayneville. He had to have a police escort to get in and out of the building. The student had been shot in a downtown street in broad daylight after being jailed for participating in a civil rights demonstration. In the trial, one of the jurors questioned a witness, a Catholic priest who had also been shot: "Preacher, let me ask you something. Did you kiss that little nigger gal in the mouth?" And when the priest answered no, the questioner said, amidst laughter from the remainder of the jury, "That ain't what we heered down here."

The police commissioner of Birmingham, after using powerful fire hoses to beat down black participants in a 1963 civil rights march led by Martin Luther King, Jr., turned dogs loose on them. When asked by a reporter from the national media why he used the dogs after the fire hoses had stopped the march, he said, "I had to wash them niggers off before the dogs would bite them."

How could such things happen in the United States of America in the second half of the twentieth century? The country had just fought a world war for the stated purpose of defending freedom, and it was in a desperate international struggle fighting despotism as leader of the "free world." How could people profess such strong dedication to an idea and at the same time completely ignore its implications in a key area of their own behavior?

The civil rights revolution brought the people of the South face-to-face again with hard contradictions of the past—the contradictions between living in a country founded on belief in the natural rights of "all men" and legal denial of basic rights to some, between the precepts of their Christian faith and their treatment of blacks. Ancient customs and prerogative again seemed at stake to Southerners. In parts of the South, the people hesitated in confusion and indecision, and events swept past them. For a time, they allowed some of the worst elements in themselves and in their society to take command. In the end, they paid a heavy price.

A few chose to take a public stand for moderation, however, and among the most conspicuous was Richmond McDavid Flowers, the man elected attorney general of Alabama in 1962. A likable storyteller who had served one term in the state senate, Flowers came into office promising like the rest to support the "Southern Way of Life" and to send the Yankees a message. He did not seem the stuff of which heroes (or martyrs) are made. But faced with the choice of upholding the law or of taking the popular course, he chose to uphold the law. Events thereafter made him a central figure in the most violent years of the civil rights revolution.

Richmond Flowers was elected attorney general at the same time that George Wallace won his first term as governor. The two had been law-school classmates and friends. Flowers's attempts to follow a moderate course soon put them in direct conflict, however, and they fought bitterly on civil rights issues. This confrontation received wide publicity, and Flowers was soon recognized as the most prominent enemy of "Wallaceism" in Alabama.

Upholding the law, a responsibility of the attorney general, was very difficult during the most bitter phase of the civil rights struggle. Juries would refuse to convict persons clearly guilty of assault and even murder. On several occasions, when it seemed that the most heinous crimes might go unpunished, Flowers stepped in and prosecuted the case himself. In these situations, he was seen by most local people as the enemy, part of the outside group attempting to interfere in long-established customs and to force change, and he found himself roundly disliked and even in physical danger.

As Wallace fanned the flames of discord and Flowers's moderate stand became more unpopular, the attorney general's advisors warned him that he was risking his political career. His reply was that he could not live with himself and do other than what he thought was right. Flowers continued his stand, and ultimately, this display of courage cost him his political career.

Richmond Flowers ran for governor in the 1966 Democratic primary, and in doing so, he went against the express desires of President Lyndon Johnson and the national Democratic party, who favored another candidate. He openly campaigned among blacks, the first candidate for statewide office in almost a century to do so, and in spite of winning about 90 percent of the black vote, he was soundly defeated by Lurleen Wallace. Lurleen was standing in for George, who by the state constitution could not succeed himself. In his race, Richmond Flowers had subverted the strategy of the national Democratic party; in the eyes of its leaders, he was not only the sworn enemy of George Wallace, he was a politically dangerous and unreliable man. Shortly after his 1966 defeat, the federal government brought him to trial on obscure charges of conspiracy to commit extortion during his term as attorney general. Though never accused of seeking personal gain, he was convicted by a hostile jury and served a term in prison. The section of the Hobbs Act under which he was convicted was later declared unconstitutional because of vagueness. Afterward, Flowers was given a full pardon by President Carter and restored to the bar, but his political career had been destroyed.

Richmond Flowers grew up in an atmosphere of privilege, and he acknowledges that he took segregation to be the natural order of things. Originally, he was not a reformer, and his position in the civil rights struggle developed primarily as a reaction to the outrageous lawlessness of forces represented and focused by George Wallace. The "liberal" label was pinned on Flowers by outsiders searching for a counter to Wallace's antihero. At most, he was a moderate progressive who took seriously his oath to uphold the law, even if it meant surrendering a degree of privilege and adapting to new ways.

When the crisis broke after the U.S. Supreme Court's *Brown* decision in 1954, Governor James E. Folsom attempted to steer a moderate course, but tragically he failed. Hard liners won control and went down the path of lawlessness and crudeness. Perhaps no one else could have been elected in Alabama at that time. Except for Mississippi, however, surrounding states made the change to integration with more grace, dignity, and human understanding, and one reason, it appears, was more insightful leadership.

This book is about Richmond Flowers, a colorful and interesting personality, who tried to provide alternative leadership to his state and who failed in the process. The book places his effort in context against the background of the civil rights revolution of the 1950s and 1960s. It highlights a group in Alabama, not widely reported nor recognized, which tried during the civil rights revolution to keep order and to do what it knew was right in redressing old wrongs. This group failed and the forces of reaction prevailed. The result was a bitter harvest, both personally for Richmond Flowers and economically and culturally for Alabama and other Deep South states which took a posture of bitter resistance.

1

Antecedents: The Evolution of Race Relations and Politics In the Post-Civil War South

The events which helped define Richmond Flowers's term as attorney general and his stance in the civil rights struggles of the 1950s and 1960s trace their origins to the Civil War and its aftermath. The war began with the single goal of preserving the union. As it progressed, a second goal of freeing the slaves was added, and finally, near its end, the goal of achieving full citizenship for black Americans was added.[1]

The first two goals were met with the North's victory, and achieving full citizenship for black Americans remained a strong focus of those in power in Washington after the war ended. The Fourteenth and Fifteenth Amendments to the U.S. Constitution, the Civil Rights Bills of 1866 and 1875, and the Reconstruction Act of 1867 were intended to establish the necessary legal machinery.

As historian Avery Craven points out, however, great difficulties were encountered in pursuing the goal of full citizenship. White Southerners were more intransigent and resourceful in their resistance than expected, the Freedmen's Bureaus, set up to do the job, were mostly ineffective, and the nation grew tried of the effort.[2] The problems were finally "pushed aside and the effort at solution left to a future generation."[3]

Reconstruction. The South was in utter chaos when the war ended. Its economic and social systems had been destroyed and had to be rebuilt. The former slaves were now free, and new racial relationships had to be established. President Andrew Johnson tried to let the Southerners themselves undertake these tasks, and they turned naturally to their experienced leaders, who tried to proceed with as little change as possible. Radical Republicans did not like the results, and after gaining control of Congress in 1866, they took charge, many harboring motives of revenge and punishment. The stated purposes of "Reconstruction," the movement the radicals set in motion, were achieving equality for all citizens in the former Confederate states and bringing these states, thus reformed, back into the Union. Another purpose, which produced a major reaction later, was building a dominant Republican party in the South, partly through capturing and holding the black vote.[4]

Reconstruction began with military occupation of the former Confederate states and with military government run by outsiders. This approach greatly rankled and embittered local white inhabitants, who felt that they were being deliberately insulted and deprived of their freedom. Bitterness and resentment increased as the occupiers encouraged black participation in government. Former slaves voted and held office, while many whites were still disfranchised. One effect was irrational fear of black dominance.

White Southerners believed they had to "redeem" their lives and their governments by restoring local control and white supremacy, and they set out to do this by whatever means they found necessary, including terrorism and murder.[5] Redeemer leaders spoke of restoration of the past, but Woodward notes that those who actually took control were in the main middle-class conservatives who had little connection with the old planter regimes.[6] To them, the South represented new opportunities for industrialization, railroad development, and commercial enterprise.[7]

Beginning with Virginia in 1869, the Southern states were redeemed one-by-one by the conservatives and lost to Republican control. In white Southern minds, redemption of their self respect and destiny became associated with Democrats being solidly in control. Reconstruction ended formally in 1877, through bargaining associated with the contested 1876 presidential election, and it ended in failure, with black citizens generally abandoned and forgotten.[8]

Reconstruction failed for several reasons. Probably the most important was that the great majority of white Americans agreed with Southerners that blacks were inferior.[9] A second reason it failed was the absence of effective land reform. Newly freed blacks were left without real property and with no way to make a living, rendering them subject to economic pressures of their white employers.[10] Reconstruction also failed because the people of the country were ready to put noble purposes behind. Their "enthusiasm for social justice gave way to enthusiasm for big business."[11] The Republicans had become the party of vested interests and big business in the North. They abandoned their black policy in the South and formed an alliance with conservative Southern Democrats.[12] This alliance lasted off and on through the civil rights revolution of the 1950s and 1960s, and it continues today.

From this period came the myth of Reconstruction, which influenced Southern thinking for generations. According to this view, a broken and helpless South was turned over to "Negro-carpetbag-scalawag" rule.[13] "In a grotesque carnival of corruption," the myth goes, "they diverted fabulous amounts of public funds to private use. All the while, they incited the blacks to such extremes of self-assertion as to destroy the harmonious relations that would otherwise have prevailed between the former masters and the former slaves."[14] The Southerners were forced to wage a noble fight for freedom.[15]

Much of this has been challenged by recent historians.[16] Republican radical rule lasted an average of only three and one-half years, and it did not have time to effect major change. Further, the notion that black rule was imposed or was ever imminent has been shown by hard evidence to be fictional.[17] It was the Redeemers, in fact, who laid the lasting foundations in matters of race, politics, economics, and law in the South.[18]

Reconstruction was, nevertheless, a traumatic time for whites, a time of extremely bitter feelings which lasted and had to be rationalized. Its realities included hard material circumstances in a shattered economy,[19] humiliation under military occupation, and the great insecurity of a destroyed social system.

Williamson refers to this period as the "nadir of the Southern white."[20] In time, the facts were embellished and the story broadened, and the resulting myth of Reconstruction was believed. This myth adversely affected the course of activities in the South for decades, and it was still potent a hundred years later when the unfinished business of the Civil War again took center stage.

The New South Era. After 1877, when Reconstruction had ended and conservative white Democrats were firmly in control, the former Confederate states entered what is called the "New South Era."[21] According to Ayers, this era, which lasted until approximately the turn of the century, was a time of instability and rapid evolution, of "continual redefinition and renegotiation, of unintended and unanticipated consequences, of unresolved tensions."[22]

The 1870s had been a decade of hard times, as the South and the nation suffered a series of depressions. Industrial development, which was desperately needed in the South, was very slow. The 1880s were more prosperous, however, and Southern leaders were able to focus on economic progress. The key industries which began to take shape included cotton gins, cottonseed-oil, textiles, sawmills, turpentine, tobacco, mining, and iron.[23] The South built railroads, a key to economic growth during this period, faster than the nation as a whole. The routes of the new railroads were a major determiner of the location and success of new towns.

Lumbering became the largest Southern industry, and great tracts of land in Alabama, Arkansas, Florida, Louisiana, and Mississippi were sold to lumber interests. Over two-thirds of these, however, went to owners from Chicago, Michigan, and Wisconsin. Except for textiles, most of the capital for industrial expansion came from outsiders, largely in the North. The Southerners do the work, said a local observer. "They get the tuberculosis, and the Northern owners get the profits."[24]

New towns and cities sprang up all over the region, and many of the larger ones became centers of trade. Dothan, Alabama, Richmond Flowers's home town, was one of these. The new towns and cities were the home of a bright and ambitious group of Southern entrepreneurs who saw opportunity in the evolving situation. Birmingham, which was incorporated in 1871, experienced great growth in the 1880s as a center of iron production and was seen as the "dreamed-of Southern industrial city."[25]

The prevailing economic philosophy among the new class of political leaders and businessmen was *laissez faire*, the belief that industry and commerce could prosper most if regulated least. They believed in a natural order, a social Darwinism, in which the worthy prospered and the rest got what they deserved.[26]

Despite the growth of the towns and economic progress in certain areas, the South in general continued to suffer extreme poverty.[27] Agriculture remained the occupation of the great majority, and the plight of the farmers grew steadily worse through the era.[28] Most depended on a single crop, cotton, and the fact that more and more people grew cotton caused a progressive decline in return from it. Cotton prices fell in 1890 and 1891 to their lowest level in thirty years.

A large proportion of blacks and many poor whites owned no land, while the owners of small tracts had difficulty holding onto their property because they were forced to take out liens to buy seed and other necessities.[29] A system evolved in which the land of a relatively few owners was worked by tenant farmers, renters, and agricultural laborers, all of whom were vulnerable to economic intimidation. The number of people in sharecropping increased rapidly. Most of the landowners were white, and most of the tenant farmers were black.[30] Ayers speaks of their "debilitating poverty" and of "material standards below those of their grandparents."[31]

Politics in the New South Era. In politics, the New South era was marked by the consolidation of Democratic control, with its themes of white dominance and white supremacy.[32] Southern Democrats propagated the notion that anyone opposing them was a traitor to their race and to memories of the "Lost Cause." The Democrats claimed to be the enemies of Reconstruction and everything it implied in the Southern mind, including Republican control, Northern meddling, and the possibility of black ascendance and domination.[33] The Democrats meant to maintain control by any means necessary, and their tactics included economic intimidation of blacks, blatant registration and voting fraud, and even murder and other forms of extreme violence.[34] Republican voting strength steadily diminished under this attack.

In the Democratic party, an internal struggle pitted the Black Belt planters, who adhered to old loyalties and privileges, against the new industrialists and hill people. At issue was who would control political processes and the patronage and economic payoff which resulted. Black Belt counties claimed heavy representation in state legislatures and congressional elections by counting all residents when they determined population, but they greatly restricted voting so that whites maintained a solid majority at the polls. White supremacy was not the question, but which whites were to be supreme.

The Evolution of Race Relations. Relationships between the races evolved slowly. Most Southern whites, consistent with their upbringing and their defense of slavery, believed deeply that the blacks were an inferior race. They thought it essential, for the good of society, to keep blacks subjugated, to maintain white supremacy, to assure their own "purity," and to guarantee all of this by controlling government. "Place" was an important concept to white Southerners, and one of their struggles through this period of change was to define the "place" of blacks.[35] More and more restrictions were slowly placed on black citizens as the attempt to define place proceeded.

The idea of segregation, as systematic racial separation, began with seating on railroad cars.[36] Tennessee passed the first statewide law requiring segregated seating in passenger trains in 1881. Other Southern states followed, and by 1891, all but Virginia and the Carolinas had such laws.

A move toward disfranchisement, legally denying blacks the vote, began in the late 1880s. Black votes were central to Republican hopes, and if a way could be found to bar them, Democrats would have uncontested control. Florida Democrats got a voter registration law passed in 1887. Disfranchisement gained momentum with the adoption of the secret ballot in Tennessee in 1888. Other Southern states followed with such devices as the poll tax, a property requirement, and a grandfather clause which exempted from the literacy and property tests those who were entitled to vote on January 1, 1867, plus their sons and grandsons.

Historians point to the decade of the 1890s as the critical period in the development of black-white relationships in the South after the Civil War.[37] Williamson states that "radicals," who were intent on total separation of the races, by legal and other means, gradually gained ascendance in Southern politics after 1889 and held it until about 1915.[38]

Mississippi Democrats led the way by rewriting their state constitution in 1890. This document provided that voters had to be registered by state-appointed officers and that only registered voters could hold office. A potential voter had to prove he had lived in the state at least two years and in his district at least one, and he had to be on record as having paid all taxes for the last two years. He had to be able to read any section of the state constitution or to prove he understood a section when it was read to him. The judgment as to understanding was made by the state-appointed registrars.[39]

Following the Mississippi model, other Southern states followed the radical approach with "segregation" constitutions, constitutional amendments, or laws. The Alabama constitution, approved in 1901, required the segregation of the races in housing, public facilities, and education. The U.S. Supreme Court augmented the move toward legal separation with its 1896 *Plessy* decision, which established the separate but equal doctrine as constitutional. In 1898, the Court upheld the Mississippi model by ruling that poll taxes and literacy tests did not violate the Fifteenth Amendment. White supremacy had become an open principle of the Democrats by this time.

The racial codes which emerged from all of this were insulting, humiliating, and degrading to black citizens. According to custom, the two races did not shake hands, walk together, or fraternize in public. Black men removed their hats in public places reserved for whites, while whites did not remove their hats even in black homes.[40] White violence toward blacks, because of some real or imaginary breach of the racial code, increased, and racial tensions grew. Lynching, an effective way to terrorize blacks into submission, increased and often went unpunished.[41]

The 1890s began with a depression which by 1893 had become the most severe of the nineteenth century. The resulting hard times boosted the radical cause. People found themselves in deep economic trouble, for causes beyond themselves which they did not understand. They needed to identify a reason for their misfortune, and they turned to recognized leaders for explanation and for new approaches which might improve things. Also, competition between blacks and poor whites for jobs during this period of economic distress caused great animosity and played into radical hands.[42]

The hard times also gave a boost to the People's party, popularly called the "Populists," which emerged from earlier efforts of farmers and other agrarian and labor interests to organize and fight for their own interests. The party's power increased rapidly as bad times continued. The Populist party included blacks and whites in its membership, and it strove for political union (though pointedly not social union) of the races.[43] The party ran strong campaigns in the presidential election of 1892 and the off-year elections of 1894. Times had improved by 1896, however, and the Populists faded.

The leaders of Populism were opposed to the elaborate structure of protective tariffs the Republicans in Washington had erected, to railroad subsidies, and to banking privileges.[44] They advocated unlimited coinage of gold and silver to ease the cash shortage and help farmers pay debts, a system of central storage so that farmers could store crops and get better prices, the elimination of convict leasing, and denunciation of lynching.

The Populists failed to gain permanent power, but they contributed important issues to the two major parties, and they made an impact by including blacks in their activities and espousing notions of justice and equality in financial and political areas. The threat the Populists posed to the entrenched Democrats undoubtedly strengthened radical resolve and accelerated the movement toward separation.

The South at the Turn of the Century. The integration of the South into the economy and mass culture of the nation accelerated in the late 1890s. For all the changes, however, the region as a whole remained a backwater. It still lagged far behind the rest of the country in literacy and school attendance.[45] Its average income was about half that of the nation as a whole. A Northern minister visiting the South at the turn of the century wrote that, "as soon as one gets away from the towns and ventures himself into the barren wastes of the unredeemed country about, the wretchedness is pathetic and the poverty colossal."[46]

By the turn of the century, the North in effect had become an active partner in subjugating blacks. The South enjoyed the gratitude of the rest of the nation for its enthusiastic aid in the Spanish-American War in 1898. The war kindled a spirit of reconciliation among white men, North and South, and a spirit of disdain for "colored" people.[47]

Reconstruction and the New South era had resulted in the one-party system, Democratic white supremacy rule, a hands-off policy by the federal government on civil rights issues, and the legacy of violence and fraud in dealing with issues perceived to have racial overtones. A "Cult of the Confederacy," which romanticized and glorified the Lost Cause and which perpetuated the myth of Reconstruction, reached its height and was used to maintain loyalty to the one-party system. By

1900, radical Democrats were well on their way to establishing rigid segregation and disfranchisement of blacks and of "profoundly" separating black citizens from the dominant society.[48]

The prevailing view among most whites, including the intellectual and financial elite, was voiced by the editor of the New Orleans *Picayune*. He wrote to a friend, "The only condition under which the two races can co-exist peacefully is that in which the superior race shall control and the inferior race shall obey."[49]

Radicalism reached its height about 1907.[50] The "place" of blacks, defined in the most restrictive way, was set, and it prevailed for the next fifty years. The difficult task of assuring full and equal rights for all citizens had not only been postponed, it had been made considerably more difficult. A half century later, the issue would resurface, with a heavy price for past failures. Williamson points out the need to recognize that the radicals in the 1890s and early 1900s were not consciously evil but were an integral part of Southern culture at that time.[51] They were "children of their age, bound by its assumptions."[52] However mistaken they may have been, they honestly thought that what they were doing was right and for the best,[53] a poignant consideration as the twenty-first century approaches and the problem remains unsolved.

2

Birth and Background

November 11, 1918

November 11, 1918, was one of the most significant dates in the twentieth century, marking the official end of World War I, among the most terrible of all wars. The United States and its Allied partners were victorious, and it was a day for rejoicing.

Like most other citizens, people in Dothan, Alabama, felt great exhilaration, and they began a noisy celebration at eleven a.m. when the armistice was announced. Little Paul Flowers knew that something great was happening.

As younger brother Richmond tells it, "My birth was a little colorful in the fact that I was born November 11, 1918, at eleven o'clock in the morning. Right on the hour of the Armistice. My brother Paul was in the front yard making mud pies, as kids used to do. He said the fire whistles blew, and people began to shoot shotguns up in the air, and all sorts of bells were ringing. And old Dr. Green, who lived just two doors from us, came walking out of the house and said, 'Well, Paul, you got a new little brother.' Paul said it never occurred to him, being a little over three years old, that all the celebrating was not the natural behavior when all little brothers came in."

Richmond McDavid Flowers was the fourth son of John Jefferson and Ila McDavid Flowers. His older brothers were John Jefferson, born in 1905, James Drury, born in 1910, and Paul Rutledge, born in 1915.

At the time of Richmond's birth, his father was forty years old.

Dothan was a small, country town in 1918, and the Flowers were one of its prominent families. Dothan, located in the southeast corner of Alabama, had been incorporated in 1885, only thirty-three years before. It was the commercial center of the "Wiregrass," an area known for sandy soil, piney woods, and small farms. Dothan was county seat of Houston County, some 28 percent of the population of which was black, compared to 39 percent for the state as a whole.

Family

The Flowers family traces its beginnings in North America to the early seventeenth century.

According to Richmond, "We all came from an old English sea captain, John Flowers. My mother was Scotch Irish. My father's family settled originally in Virginia. They came into South Carolina and stayed about two generations. One generation moved to Georgia and the other swung towards the west. Then the Georgia group came on into Alabama."

The financial standing of Richmond's immediate family was established by his great-grandfather, William Hampton Flowers. William Hampton was born in South Carolina in 1813, the son of a Methodist-Episcopal minister who made his main living by farming. The family moved to Georgia in 1826. William Hampton married in 1837 and moved his family to Butler County, Alabama, in 1857. He is described in the *Flowers Chronicles* as a poor man at this time.[1]

He set up farming, and after a chance meeting with John T. Milner, later one of the founders of Birmingham, William Hampton was hired to fulfill some large contracts with the Louisville and Nashville (L&N) railroad for cross-ties. Milner was impressed, and after the Civil War, he built a sawmill at Bolling and put William Hampton in charge. It thrived from the beginning, and in 1873, William Hampton and his oldest son bought a half interest. The mill and its facilities were then valued at $19,000. By the end of 1895, the year of William Hampton's death, the mill at Bolling had paid about $800,000 in cash dividends and was valued at $400,000. This established the family fortune of William Hampton's branch of the Flowers family.

Richmond's grandfather, James Drury Flowers, was the fifth of twelve children of William Hampton Flowers. He was born in Fayette County, Georgia, in 1844, and he moved with his family to Alabama in 1857.

He was drafted as a private in the Confederate Army and fought in several battles, including Missionary Ridge, other fighting around Chattanooga, and the Battle of Atlanta. "My father never failed to mention the fact," said Richmond, "that his father, one of four brothers, was the only one that wasn't able to pay the $400 which they could pay and be exempt. His three older brothers did. My grandfather always told the story, and my father repeated it many times, that when he left he told his wife, 'Emma, we're fighting a wrong cause; the Union should be preserved.'"

Richmond's grandfather was captured during the Battle of Nashville in 1864 and sent to prison at Camp Douglas, Illinois. "When the war ended, they took him back and freed him, and he didn't have a nickel in his pocket. That's the way they freed the prisoners; they took them back to where they captured them." He walked home. He made his way by working a few days, building up strength and getting some food, and walking until his strength gave out. The trip home took more than a year. "His family had heard that he was a prisoner," Richmond remembers, "but they hadn't heard that he'd been freed. His wife didn't have any idea where he was."

After the war, James Drury joined the family lumber business and served later as plant superintendent. The family closed the Bolling mill in 1900 because the timber supply in the area was exhausted. They moved to Dothan and opened two new mills nearby in Georgia. The mill in Jakin was called the Flowers Lumber Company, and James Drury was its president.

James Drury Flowers is described in the *Flowers Chronicles* as a hard worker and shrewd businessman who loved to make money.[2] He accumulated a "comfortable" fortune. He was a strong member of the Methodist Church who prided himself on forty-four years of Sunday School attendance without missing a Sunday. He died in 1924.

William Hampton and James Drury Flowers can be seen as prototypical of the "new" Southerner who emerged in the last years of the nineteenth century. They were not from the old landowning class. They took advantage of new commercial opportunities available as the South emerged from Reconstruction, and by their efforts they built substantial fortunes.

John Jefferson Flowers, James Drury's third son and Richmond's father, was born in Bolling, Alabama, in 1878. He received a degree in electrical and mechanical engineering from Alabama Polytechnic Institute (now Auburn University) in 1900. "The two majors were combined at that time," Richmond says, "because, according to my father, that's all they knew about." The fact that he could attend and graduate from college shows the financial strength of the family before their move to Dothan. John Jefferson married Ila McDavid of Jakin, Georgia, in 1903.

"My father came here, age twenty-two, and the first thing he did was to work as the superintendent of the Light and Water Plant. He worked for $60 a month a couple of months and asked for a raise, and old man Keeton, who was on the commission, told him, 'Why hell no, you're making more than you're worth now.'

"He quit and opened up a machine shop. He and his brother operated the machine shop very successfully until one day a lathe slung off, went right by his head and cut its way through an eight-inch brick wall. He said he could feel the wind as it went by his head. He said 'I had a wife and a couple of children, and I figured I best get out of that business.'

"So he sold his mill, bought an ice plant, and went into business selling coal and ice. They'd unload his coal up at the railroad, and he'd stand around there and breathe coal dust, and he would walk in and out of the freeze room at the plant. He was a chronic asthmatic, and between the coal dust and the freeze room, his lungs just couldn't stand it."

"He sold the ice plant, and he then made probably the best money that he ever made doing what the old timers called 'traffic and trade.' He'd just buy and sell things. He loved to fool with farmland. He would buy a little piece of farmland, build it up, fence it good, improve the house, and sell it, and make a nice bit of money."

The Flowers family solidified their position in Dothan by purchasing the Malone Mortgage Company in 1916, when John Jefferson was thirty-eight. They restructured it, and chartered it as the Dothan Bank and Trust Company. John J. Flowers became the first vice-president of the bank, and he later served as president and as chairman of the board. Subsequently, three generations of Flowers had careers in banking.

In 1972, Dothan Bank and Trust Company was sold by the Flowers family to First Alabama Bank.

Richmond remembers his father as a domineering, rather distant person. "My respect for him was mostly fear because he was so demanding. He was never a warm buddy to me. Me being the baby, there was a big spread, you see. He was forty years old when I was born. By the time I got up, he was in his fifties. He wasn't ready to hunt and fish and hike and ride bicycles with the boys, and so forth. He had with my brothers, but he didn't with me.

"One time, to get him started, I said to him, 'I know you love me just as much as you do any of your boys. There's no doubt about that, but when I think of the births—1905, 1910, 1915, and 1918—I wonder was I exactly planned for?' He said, 'You certainly were. I was going to try one more time to have a girl and the train done blowed for the station.' You know when they say the 'train done blowed for the station,' it takes people back in train days to know what a whistle stop is and what it means. It means, if you've got some business you better get it out there; otherwise, I'm gone."

Richmond's father was a teetotaler. "He was so of the old school. His father before him was a teetotaler, and he was a teetotaler, and 'never will a drop of that stuff cross my lips.' He had a couple of nephews that hit the skids, and that broke their father's heart. He just wouldn't touch it.

Richmond speaks of his mother as "the most influential person in my life. She was born and raised right outside of Milton, Florida, in a little community called McDavid. It's still there. Her mother died when she was twelve years old. Her father's name was John McDavid, and he was a very beloved man. My father knew him real well because he was also in the lumber business.

"Mother's father died, and she went to live in Jakin, Georgia, with her older sister, who had married my father's brother. She was very close to the Flowers family when she was growing up. My father always laughed that when he told his father he was going to marry Ila he was told, 'Well, son, you're marrying your sister.'" Richmond's father and two of his sisters had a triple wedding, on November 25, 1903.

Richmond remembers his mother as a good disciplinarian who had great influence in the family. "My father thought he was running his business and running the family, but he wasn't. She let him think he was in charge. I guess she had learned to take care of herself, given the death of her mother and her father, and having to go live with someone else. There's no doubt that she was the most influential person in my life. I had deep devotion for her. She got ten to one more out of me than my father did. She worked me. I thought we were buddies, and that I was making half the decision. She was doing it. She was directing me all the time. He was the old-time patriarch. 'Here, boy, this is the way it's going to be done.' She would never do it that way. She'd convince you that you wanted to do it that way first, then tell you why you wanted it that way. Oh, she was great."

Richmond's mother was active in community affairs, especially as a young woman. "She was ever the typical banker's wife. She was organizer and one of the charter members of the New Century Club. She had the church circle, and she did her welfare work. She was on the child welfare board."

When asked why his mother was such an influence on him, Richmond answered, "I don't know unless I was just what we used to call a 'Mama's boy.' I was always right under her apron strings; I was tied to her apron strings. She never worked. My father didn't want her to work. He wanted her to look after the children, and she did. All day long, I was asking 'Mother, Mother, can I do this, can I do that?' When my father would lay down a rule, he never explained it to me. I'd go ask Mother why. She would explain it to me, and she could make it make sense. My mother's influence is solely responsible for my easygoing personality and my love of and ability to get along with people."

John J. Flowers died in 1957, at age seventy-nine, and his widow, Ila Flowers, died in 1970 at age eighty-eight.

The Flowers family was prominent from its first arrival in Dothan's early days in 1900, and it continues in a position of high prominence today. Financial success was one reason, of course, but Richmond believes that longevity is also important. "The Flowers are so prominent in Dothan," he says, "because there's so many of them that stayed here."

Dothan and the Wiregrass

Dothan is in the southeast corner of Alabama, 15 miles north of the Alabama-Florida line, 20 miles west of the Alabama-Georgia line, and

100 miles southeast of Montgomery. It is in the "Wiregrass" region, whose name derived from a particular type of indigenous grass, now almost extinct. It was one of the new towns which sprang up in the New South era.

In the years immediately after the Civil War, the region was an isolated, lonely, piney-woods country, whose sandy soil was thought to be unproductive. The Wiregrass had no transportation connection with the rest of the state, and it was very sparsely populated.

Poplar Spring, a small settlement where Dothan is now located, was established about 1858. It was at a crossroads of what had originally been Indian trails, and it was the site of a spring which offered water to settlers and other travelers passing through. Later, after the area was safe from Indian attacks, major stagecoach routes intersected there.[3] The settlement grew slowly.

During the late 1870s and early eighties, turpentine men came, mostly from Georgia, and turpentining began developing as an important industry in the region. Then came lumbermen, who cut trees and shipped them south to Florida on the rivers. About this time, the soil was found to be more productive than originally thought, particularly with the addition of small quantities of fertilizer.

The removal of forests and the cheapness of the land and its high productivity attracted small farmers. They were poor men, from areas whose soil had been exhausted, "with not much of anything but children, dogs, and hope. All they had came in their wagons, and some barely had a wagon."[4] Most homesteaded.

In 1880, a church was established at Poplar Spring. The community began to thrive, and it was incorporated in 1885 as Dothan, a name taken from Genesis 37:17. A new name had to be chosen because there was already a post office named Poplar Spring. Several leading citizens with commercial interests worked with persistence and foresight for the routing of a railroad through Dothan.

They succeeded in 1890 as the Alabama Midland Railroad (later the Atlantic Coast Line) was completed from Montgomery through the heart of the Wiregrass country to Bainbridge, Georgia. Before the turn of the century, the Central of Georgia and the Louisville and Nashville constructed lines through the region. The new transportation facilities gave great impetus to agriculture and the lumber industry in the Wiregrass.

Dothan experienced a boom in the 1890s with the coming of the railroad. Many of the town's leaders moved in at this time. One of the most colorful was Joseph "Buck" Baker, a self-made farmer and businessman who settled in Dothan in 1889. He served as mayor and was later the subject of *Devil Make a Third*, a 1948 novel that received national attention. James R. Crawford, Richmond's great-uncle, moved the same year and organized the First Bank of Dothan, of which he was president. Crawford was credited with saving the cotton gin, one of Dothan's "great industries," from destruction.[5]

This was the time the early fortunes were made in Dothan. Baker and the others got the land, established key businesses, and successfully developed Dothan as a regional center. There was much discussion in the newspapers of Alabama at this time about the prosperous farmers in the Wiregrass and the area's growth. The population of Dothan was listed as 247 in 1889, just as the boom began, and it had grown to 3,275 in 1900. It was about 7,000 in 1910 and 10,000 in 1920. Houston County, with Dothan as county seat, was created in 1903 from land formerly in Dale, Geneva, and Henry counties.

One key to the background of Richmond Flowers is that development in the Wiregrass and in Dothan did not occur until well after the end of the Civil War and Reconstruction. The area did not have the rich black soil thought to be needed for cotton plantations and for a slave economy. It was not part of the "Old South," with its glorification of the Lost Cause. It put the romantic notions of leisure and chivalry behind, and it offered new opportunities to those who had the necessary drive, intelligence, and acumen.

It was like north Alabama in this regard. The population was mostly yeoman farmers, who traditionally felt a certain animosity toward the former slave-holding "betters," the plantation owners who considered themselves high society and naturally endowed to rule. The percentage of blacks was considerably smaller than for the state as a whole. There was always some Republican voting in these areas.

Richmond Flowers remembers Dothan as an almost ideal small town in which to grow up. "Dothan really was a delightful town. When I was big enough to talk about census and to know what it all meant, they were claiming that Dothan had 16,000 people, and my father said, 'Hmmmm, I hope they don't have to answer to the Master for that lie.

There ain't no 16,000 people here.' They were blowing things up. It was a typical small Southern country town.

"I think that my neighborhood was just like that in *To Kill a Mockingbird*. It was a real quaint small town where everybody knew everybody. When I went to school I'd walk right out in the middle of the street. There weren't any cars; nobody was going to run over you.

"Our barber, who ran the big barber shop downtown, lived right next door. Behind us, in the house that backed up to us and faced the next street, was the probate judge. The druggist lived diagonally across the street. Next to our house was a vacant lot, and next to it was the biggest lawyer in town, old man Burt Farmer, who sired all these Farmer children around here.

"Next to him was Dr. Green, our family doctor. Every time one of us children got sick, he'd come by in the morning and when he went home for dinner. We all had dinner in the middle of the day and not at night. We had breakfast, dinner, and supper. I've always said that, if I could pick a guitar, I'd write me a song, 'We Still Eat Supper To My House.'

"My grandfather was one block away. We lived on a corner, and he lived one door beyond the next corner. My Aunt Crawford with her four boys lived one block away. In every house except one or two, there were some kids. So it was a neighborhood full of kids.

"To show what a great town Dothan was, let me tell you about my Uncle Crawford, who got to having these weak spells in his old age. He could feel them coming on. 'I'd get this weakness,' he said, 'and the next thing I'd get dizzy, and then I'd begin to stumble.' When he'd feel that thing coming on, he'd just sit down right in the middle of the street or lean up against a building. 'I'm going to fall if I don't,' he said, and he would lean his head back. Somebody'd ask, 'Hey, Mr. Crawford, you got a weak spell?' 'Yeah.' 'Wait just a minute, I'll go get my car.' Anybody in the town would go get their car, because they knew where his son's office was. They'd take him up there. He'd stretch out on a couch in the back, and he'd be all right after a while."

Richmond remembers that few people in Dothan traveled very much in those days. "The area was extremely rural, and most people stayed in the same place," he says. "Most everyone would take some type of vacation in the summer, and that's about all the traveling you ever heard of. Everybody stayed around, and everybody knew everybody's business."

Dothan, he recalls, had typical small town values. This, in his opinion, was very influential in his development. "As a small boy, I didn't know any bad guys. Every now and then, if I went downtown I might see a man who would drink too much. But that was his general reputation in the community. They were just country folk, and nobody divorced. That was something you read about in books—men running around. It was just a very quaint, quiet, little country community.

"You can imagine in a town like that churches were very influential. The Flowers belonged to the old Foster Street Methodist Church, which was in the middle of downtown. The Malones all belonged to the Baptist Church. The Carmichaels and a lot of the Farmers belonged to the Baptist Church, but then a lot of them went to the Presbyterian Church. The Methodist church was a block and a half, the Presbyterian church was one block, and the Baptist church was two blocks. And across the street, diagonally, was the Catholic church. It was just a very small Catholic church—hmmm, hmmmm, they were sort of suspect in those days! "

Politics and Race in Alabama At Richmond Flowers's Birth

At the time of Richmond Flowers's birth, the dominant political view in Alabama was Progressivism, which came as the New South era ended and which was in part a response to the abuses which fueled the Populist uprising. Progressivism was a broad series of reforms which seemed a middle way between reactionary diehards and Populist radicals.[6]

Much was accomplished under the Progressive label. State and federal laws were passed to regulate working conditions. Child-labor laws were adopted, and the cruel, inhuman convict-leasing system was abolished in many locations. More funds were provided for education and for health programs, roads were improved, and there was success in reducing hookworms and illiteracy. The statewide Democratic primary, with direct election of U.S. senators, was established in 1902. In 1907, the governor established a railroad commission in Alabama.

Progressivism, however, was for whites only,[7] and it didn't do a lot for the poor of any race. Industrial growth in Alabama had been large, percentage-wise, because the base was so tiny at the end of the Civil War, but it was small in absolute terms. The growth in business and industry profited relatively few, and it was financed in large part by northern investors who siphoned off most of the profits.

The economic difficulties of the rural population continued. More and more small landowners were forced into tenancy. Between 1880 and 1930, the proportion of Southern farms operated by tenants increased from 36 percent to 55 percent. Between 1900 and 1930, the number of white tenants increased by 400,000 while the number of blacks increased by just 147,000, so the system in its later years hurt more whites than blacks. All were poverty-stricken, always in debt, and unable to escape to an improved lifestyle.

Alabama Politics. In 1918, at the time of Richmond Flowers's birth, Alabama was still very rural. Interests were local, and county seats were important centers of power. A small group, the "courthouse ring" or "clique," dominated county politics and could usually deliver the vote.[8] The political relationships within counties were fundamental to political action across the state, and those seeking statewide office campaigned largely by meeting with and seeking the support of the courthouse ring. Elections were more or less fair, depending on the political stakes and the acceptability of candidates.

The possibilities in Dothan can best be summarized in Richmond Flowers's own words. With regard to buying votes and maintaining control in Dothan, he says, "I don't know that Dothan held any particular reputation that the other towns in the area didn't have. When I was very young, Dothan had an awful reputation for 'crooked elections.' Ballots would be bought in different ways. They would buy the officials that were running the box.

"After I'd finished law school and was in politics and associated with former political leaders of the town, they told me the main way they did it was through the County Democratic Executive Committee. The courthouse gang, which included the probate judge, the county commissioners, the sheriff, were all a clique. There were two or three very outstanding, very powerful men, usually lawyers, who were leaders in this group. If they stayed together, they'd deliver the county anyway they wanted to.

"When gubernatorial candidates came in, they'd go to about four or five fellows, and if they got the okay with them, well, they'd take on off. This was all they had to do because the Democratic nomination was tantamount to election. We didn't have any Republicans at all. They didn't care what the votes actually were, they didn't care whether they were counted or not, because when the County Democratic Committee met to certify, they'd certify it any way they wanted to. And that was the official vote.

"They'd buy ballots. I've seen a many one bought for a half-pint of whiskey. What they would do, they would keep people inside the polls. A person would walk in and draw their ballot and go to Mr. So-and-so who they knew and hand him the blank ballot, and he'd hand them one that had already been marked. Mr. So-and-so would watch them put it in the box, then as they went out he'd give a signal, and they'd get their whiskey. Then the blank ballot would be marked, and somebody else would come in. And they would just keep it going all day long. I think there was still a lot of chicanery going on with a lot of boxes even after the war. But that's when Dothan's politics began to clean up some."

Blacks Renew the Quest for Equality. Race relations continued to be defined in the most restrictive way. The radical period had passed, but blacks retained the place the radicals had assigned to them.[9] Hostility and prejudice were more intense than at any time since the Civil War.[10] To most whites, the subjugation and separation of blacks was complete. The issue was settled as far as they were concerned, and racial matters seemed quiet and under control. The repression of blacks was generating a reaction, however.

The prevailing view nationally was that of the "Atlanta Compromise,"[11] the author of which was Booker T. Washington, founder of Tuskegee Institute. Washington's position became widely known through a speech he gave in 1895 at the Atlanta Cotton States and International Exposition. He advised fellow blacks not to get involved in politics, and he urged honesty, hard work, thrift, and support of black business. Blacks first had to improve themselves intellectually, economically, and morally, and in time they would be accepted. This message of gradualism and accommodation was received with great enthusiasm by Southern whites, and it was accepted for a while by black leaders.

Things did not turn out as Washington predicted, however. The more accomplished blacks became, the more they were perceived by whites as "uppity" and threatening. This was especially true when they prospered and then did not act in the submissive, servile way that whites thought they should.[12] A black observer commented that, "The prejudice is not so much against the ignorant Negro, the riffraff, as it is against the intelligent, educated, taxpaying Negro, the Negro who is trying to be a man."[13]

Some of the people who had been strong supporters of Booker T. Washington now broke with him. The most famous was W. E. B. Du Bois, a Harvard Ph.D. who was a professor at Atlanta University and an accomplished writer. Early in the 1900s, Du Bois began to oppose accommodation in his writings, and he urged blacks to take a more militant stand. A harbinger of the future came in 1905 when Du Bois and some of his associates founded the Niagara Movement to pursue black rights. Du Bois by this time was demanding complete and immediate equality.[14]

Others took up the issue, and in 1908, in response to a call by Oswald Garrison Villard, grandson of William Lloyd Garrison, a National Negro Conference was held. This led to foundation of the National Association for the Advancement of Colored People. Its program stressed voting rights and was based largely in legal action. A goal from the start was to appeal to national public opinion and to the national conscience. By 1914, the NAACP had 6,000 members in fifty branches, and it achieved its first major victory when the Supreme Court declared Oklahoma's grandfather clause unconstitutional. At Richmond Flowers's birth, the issue of black civil rights was being slowly revitalized, though it was not perceived as a challenge by whites in Alabama and other Southern states.

3

Growing Up the Right Way— Through Good Times and Bad

Childhood

The period of Richmond Flowers's early childhood is known popularly as the Roaring Twenties, and it was marked by general prosperity and optimism. The automobile, the radio, widespread use of electricity in urban areas, and other technologies produced great changes in life style, and they gave the twentieth century its own character. It was a new era, full of hope.

One of the most memorable features of the Roaring Twenties was prohibition. Proponents believed that prohibition would mean the end of alcoholic beverages in the country. Instead, drinking became one of those forbidden, widely-indulged pleasures, and the period became known for speakeasies, bootleggers, and criminals of the likes of Al Capone. Without doubt, the reaction to prohibition contributed to the legacy of lawlessness and violence in the United States.

Dothan had grown to a population of 10,034 by the beginning of the 1920s, and the prosperous Flowers family was among its most prominent residents. Local citizens were caught up in the national optimism of the time, and all seemed well with the world.

Early Years. Richmond remembers his early childhood as a very pleasant time. "All of my brothers and me were born in the same house.

Then my father built a much bigger house across the street.

"It was big enough in our yard for us to play baseball and a little football, and we had a basketball goal. The kids came for four or five blocks around. One block away my grandfather built the first swimming pool in Dothan, and everybody came in. It was a big pool, ten feet wide and sixty feet long, and it had a covering on it. I learned to swim there when I was three years old. I started out dog-paddling and then watched the other boys. Swimming was the only sport I was truly outstanding in.

"I was everybody's kid on the block. Every other kid was everybody's kid on the block. Nobody thought anything about walking out and saying, 'Richmond, get out of my flower bed, you know better than that.' 'Yes'm.' Off I'd go to get into somebody else's flower bed. It was that kind of neighborhood, that kind of town.

"At meals, we all sat in the same places every time, all the boys, and Mother and Daddy. At dinner, the noon meal, it was a meat, four vegetables, soup, biscuit, cornbread, and at night, the same thing over again. We ate three big meals a day, and we were all required to be there. The table was a place where the family communed. I sat just to my father's left. When I got to be a teenage boy, he would shake his head and say, 'My little boy, I can't enjoy my meal because you eat so much.'

"I had a very, very warm relationship with my older brothers. They all just understood me. I was just their play-pretty, you see. I had some other warm experiences when I got big enough to whip them all, too."

The family could afford to travel. Richmond remembers, "My father would go to North Carolina every year because of his asthma. We went to Hendersonville and Waynesville, in the Asheville area. Every summer we would go up there and spend two weeks. Usually it was as close as he could get it to the harvest season so he could stay out of this area during cotton picking and peanut shaking time.

"We'd load up to go to North Carolina. We'd get up about daylight, and eat breakfast and take off and drive hard as we could. We'd get to Atlanta at 4:00 or 4:30 so we'd have time to get into a hotel. All of us would take a bath and eat something and go to a big picture show. The Fox Theater or something like that.

"Mother's sister went to Europe once after her husband died, and that was just a marvel to us. She went over on a ship and she came back on a ship and was gone about a month or six weeks. She was the only person I ever heard of traveling to Europe. My goodness, we didn't hear of many folks traveling to New York."

The family had pets as the boys grew up. "My father always allowed us to have dogs, and I was raised with big collies. We had collies, and when I was nine or ten years old, my older brother bought a beautiful German Shepherd puppy. I lived with that dog all through junior high and high school. He stayed in the car with me, and went everywhere that I went."

Richmond's experience with nicknames gives a clue as to the personality which later served his political career. "I had all sorts of nicknames as a kid. I grew up as 'Wimmy.' That's the name I had when I was the little redhead in the neighborhood who couldn't talk plain. That's as close as I could get—Wimmy Wowers. Wimmy stuck with me. Some of my oldest friends in Dothan still call me Wimmy. My mother in her late years got to where she called me 'Feller.'

"When I played high school football, I used to brag about being the greatest football player. Well, I knew I wasn't any good, but one of our neighbors worked for the *Dothan Eagle* in the sports department, and he called me 'Flash' Flowers. He was just doing me a favor with 'Flash Flowers, the snake-hipped halfback.' Then two or three weeks later, he says, 'Flash Flowers, the quivering quarterback,' and all that kind of stuff. Well, a lot of people kidded me, I think, because I could take kidding and I enjoyed kidding. I enjoyed being the center of anything, so if it was ridicule and kidding, I'd take that, too.

"I was a senior in high school during the Depression, and they sent all the colleges a list of graduating seniors so they could write them letters and encourage them to go to school. The lady who typed the list moved her left hand one key to the left, and my name came out Eixhmons Floqwea. Every piece of mail I got advertising a college was to Eixhmons Floqwea. I got a letter from everybody in the world except Auburn. My father, an Auburn man, says, 'Well, I don't much blame them.' He was a very good friend of the president at that time, Dr. Luther Duncan. He said, 'I don't blame ole Luther. I don't believe I'd want a student on my campus named Eixhmons Floqwea.' When Marion Military Institute retyped it on their letterhead, they changed Floqwea to Floqwedo, and that name stuck with me all through Auburn. A lot of folks today call me Flo, Floqwedo, Floup."

School Days. Richmond started school in September 1924, the year Silent Cal was elected president. He recalls with whimsy that his school career was marked by threes. "Every school I attended was for three years. I went to Howell Elementary School three years, Highland Elementary three years, junior high three years, high school three years, Auburn three years, and Alabama three years.

"My mother and father put me in school when I was five years old. I would have been six in November. In retrospect, I can see that was a mistake. But they felt that, because the crowd I was playing with was starting, I would feel I was falling behind if they held me back. I was always young the first of the year.

"I went first to the old Howell School. It was very historical. Claude Pepper, who was later the senator and Congressman from Florida, taught over there. He taught my oldest brother. Claude was one of those who went to school a couple of years, then taught, and then finished and went to law school. When I was in politics, I knew Claude real well, and I admired the man.

Richmond remembers being something of a mischievous little boy who was disciplined by his teachers. He started well. "My first teacher was very, very beloved, and I got along fine with her. I did extremely well the first two or three years in elementary school, and then after that, I got to where I laughed and talked a lot. I always talked, talked, talked, talked, talked. That kept me in trouble all the time. In the fourth, fifth, and sixth grades, I had a very enjoyable time, and yet, I stayed in trouble. I had to stay in, and I had to write on the board and wash the board about as much as anybody.

"My mother would talk to me, and I'd say, 'Aw, she just doesn't like me, Mother.' 'Doesn't like you? You just can't imagine the fine things she says about you to me.' Everyone of them would say, 'Oh Miss Ila, he's a good boy. He's just boy, that's all. I have to call him down. Don't worry about it.' I was just a little redheaded boy, that's all. I didn't do anything really bad. I had pretty good morals for a little ole redheaded boy." As for his performance as a student, Richmond recalls, "I was pretty good, but I was one of these typical students that made better grades than I deserved. I think it got me into some lazy habits that caused me problems later in college."

In 1928, when Richmond was in the fifth grade, the Democrats ran

Al Smith, Catholic governor of New York, for president. He opposed Herbert Hoover and was beaten soundly, in part because the country wanted to continue the Republican prosperity. Also, voters did not want to bother with the social issues Smith insisted on discussing. Smith's religion was a major issue in the election, and Richmond recalls an incident that illustrates some of the associated nonsense.

"I will never forget that one of my little friends said, 'My Daddy told me this morning that if Al Smith won this election, the Pope was in Mobile Bay on a submarine waiting to take Alabama.' I went home as distressed as anything, and told my father and asked, 'Daddy, is that so?' He said, 'Boy, let me ask you this, and you just think about it. What in the name of the Lord would the Pope want with Alabama?' He got tickled, and I got tickled, and I realized that it was something to laugh about. But it relieved me so much.

When asked, "Who were the great loves in your elementary years?" Richmond responded, "I had a very poor love life, 'cause I was so gawky and ugly, and I couldn't get a sweetheart to save my soul.

"I always fell in love just as soon as school started every year. Well, in the first grade I can very well remember I fell desperately in love with a pretty little brunette. I don't think I'd ever seen a little dark-eyed brunette. The next year, I don't know why, but I switched. Her name was Eloise Phillips, and nobody seems to know what happened to her. She was a beautiful girl, and she lived on the other side of the tracks. The next year I had a little blonde girl, and she was my sweetheart for about two years, but she got fat.

"Then I went to Highland. That's when, oh me, I fell in love with a pretty little blonde who danced. Her mother taught dancing and played piano for her to dance. In junior high school we got to be sweethearts, and we were sweethearts through freshmen in high school. Then I got replaced by the older boys, the juniors and seniors in high school. The next year I began to go with the freshmen, and she got replaced by the younger girls. But we remained friends."

Depression and New Deal

The Roaring Twenties came crashing down at the end of 1929 with the collapse of the stock market. In these latter years of the twentieth century, it is hard to fathom the seriousness of the Great Depression of the 1930s. By the 1932 presidential election, the country was literally on the verge of collapse. It was the greatest crisis since the Civil War.

William E. Leuchtenburg calls the Great Depression "one of the turning points of American history." Its effects cut impartially through the entire population, dashing the lives and hopes of rich and poor alike. "The six years from 1933 through 1938," Leuchtenburg says, "marked a greater upheaval in American institutions than any similar period in our history, save perhaps for the impact on the South of the Civil War."[1]

In the four years of Hoover's presidency, the bottom dropped out of the stock market and industrial production fell more than half. Industrial construction slumped during those four years from $949 million to $74 million. Fewer miles of railroad track were laid during 1932 than in any year since the Civil War, and that summer, steel plants, the great backbone of American industrial strength, were operating at 12 percent of capacity.[2]

By the end of Hoover's presidency in March 1933, fifteen million workers had lost their jobs, and national unemployment had reached about one-third of the total work force. Reporters told of Harvard graduates digging ditches in their business suits—and being thankful to have a job. National income had been cut more than half, and the crash of 5,000 banks had wiped out nine million savings accounts.[3] Farm income dipped sharply while taxes and mortgage obligations remained constant, and thousands of farmers lost their land.[4]

One writer noted that, by the election of 1932, the nation was characterized by panic, apprehension, utter hopelessness about the future, and inability to initiate or sustain any activity. Many believed that the long era of economic growth in the western world had come to an end. "In Hoover's last days in office, the old order tottered on the brink of disaster."[5]

In these desperate days, the Democrats selected New York governor Franklin Delano Roosevelt to oppose Herbert Hoover for the presidency. Roosevelt broke tradition by delivering his acceptance speech to the Democratic National Convention in person. In the speech, he gave his administration a name by saying, "I pledge you, I pledge myself to a new deal for the American people." Hoover was held responsible for the economic condition of the country, whether he deserved it or not, so Roosevelt won easily.

Immediately after his inauguration, Roosevelt initiated a profusion of new programs and new approaches, and the result was a great upheaval in national institutions. The New Deal tried a broad range of social and political initiatives, and if one approach did not work, something else was improvised. From the beginning, most Americans regained hope, and they were buoyed by Roosevelt's cheerful spirit and by the fact that the administration clearly was doing something to try to help the people. Roosevelt made believers of most and aroused bitter resentment in the rest.

There was some improvement in the economy as the New Deal progressed, but there were also periodic setbacks. Recovery was slow, and statistics show that the Depression did not really end until the beginning of World War II. Hard times continued through the 1930s, though there was no longer such a sense of crisis.

Roosevelt's ability to kindle hope was due in part to his own triumph over adversity. As a result of polio, he was paraplegic, totally paralyzed from the waist down. At Roosevelt's death, Winston Churchill gave a fitting tribute when he noted that not one man in ten million, so stricken and crippled, would have tried what Roosevelt did politically. "It was an extraordinary effort of the spirit over the flesh, of willpower over physical infirmity."[6]

Politics in the Early Thirties. An event, significant in its characterization of the politics of the day, occurred in Dothan during 1930, the year Richmond finished elementary school and entered junior high school. It involved a barn burning—a barn with ballots in it.

Richmond recalls that, "It was after Tom Heflin, who was Senator Howell Heflin's uncle, bolted the party because he was not going to support Al Smith for president. His father, Howell's grandfather, was a Baptist minister. Tom bolted the party, and the old Democrats said he's not going to do that. So in 1930, when Tom Heflin came up for reelection, the Democrats ran John Bankhead in the primary. Tom ran as an Independent that fall.

"Cotton Tom was a great orator and a colorful character. He was one of the old-time politicians who could point with pride and view with alarm. He could sell a dead horse to a mounted policeman, and they loved him. He got plenty of votes in Dothan.

"It was the biggest steal-out you ever saw. One of the men who was on the committee told me later, 'When we went to certify that election, the ballots were very one-sided for Heflin. So we certified the election [for Bankhead] and then said we'll report it the next day. We put all the ballots in Mr. Hugh Smith's barn and burned his barn down that night. But the committee had already certified the election, so the state committee accepted it.' That's the Democratic candidate; there ain't no Republican candidate. That's the election."

When asked if he thought that type of activity was prevalent all over Alabama in 1930, Richmond answered, "Oh, yes. The Democratic party just would not give up. You do what they say do, or you don't do. The U.S. senators controlled the party through the state committee, and the state committee in turn controlled through county committees. Later, the Democrat party was a Hill and Sparkman machine. They were powerful, powerful. Several governors tried to take the committee away from them and elect their own chairman. They couldn't do it. Jim Folsom tried it, and he couldn't do it."

According to Virginia Hamilton[7], the move to bar Heflin from running in the 1930 Democratic primary provoked a major fight which went all the way to the Alabama Supreme Court. Heflin lost. Senator Hugo Black, staying discreetly silent most of the time, urged voters just before the election to stay true to the regular Democrats. Bankhead received a 50,000-vote majority out of 164,000 cast and won 57 of the state's 67 counties.

Heflin claimed the election had been "one of the most fraudulent and corrupt ever held in Alabama,"[8] but, as Black commented, it would take a lot of fraud to produce a 50,000 vote margin.

Years in a Formative Period. The 1930s, the era of the Great Depression and the New Deal, were formative years for Richmond Flowers. During the decade, he attended junior high and high school, completed his undergraduate work in college, and began law school. Like others who grew to young adulthood in that period, he was greatly influenced by the work and social values associated with hard times and by that undisputed master of the scene, Franklin Roosevelt. The federal government accepted major new responsibility for the well-being of all elements of the population. It greatly centralized its power, at the expense of the states, and it showed itself prepared to use that power. No one of any serious political persuasion would thereafter question Social

Security, the regulation of banking and business, agricultural supports, public works, and the legitimacy of labor unions.

High School

Richmond started junior high school in the fall of 1930, early in Hoover's first year as president and just as the Depression was showing ugly signs of its true character. "I went to Young Junior High," he says. "It was the only junior high in town, and Minnie T. Heard was principal. I think she was one of the strongest character builders that this town was ever fortunate enough to have. Many a time, I've had her spank me while telling me what a good boy I was and what a leader I was and how she hated to do this so bad. I couldn't figure that out; if she hated it so bad, why did she do it? But I wouldn't say such as that. I wasn't that kind of a smart aleck.

"I went to Dothan High School where I participated in all sports. I can look back now and realize that entering school at five years of age really set me back athletically. I had speed that the average kid didn't have. I played high school football, but I got hurt a lot my senior year. I played high school basketball and baseball. I was athletic as I could be. I was pretty good at everything, and wasn't great at anything.

"The local swimming pools were the gathering places for the high school kids. We had Kelly Springs out on one side of town and Porter's Fairyland on the other, and we would all gather out there. At Porter's, they had a pavilion with a big juke box and dancing. The owners chaperoned, and the parents didn't mind their kids going out there, because they wouldn't put up with any foolishness. They'd tell your mother or your daddy in a minute if you're out there cutting up or if any of you dared try to sneak any beer in there.

"That was before air conditioning, and a lot of the parents would just ride out there to cool off at night. They wanted to watch us dance. The place was screened in, so it was free of insects, and if there was any breeze, it was cool. We'd do our courting going and coming; we didn't try to do it out there.

"That's the way we were. We'd talk to each other in a minute about drinking. We knew we had a good thing with the crowd. We were trusted, and the parents didn't mind us going places in groups like that. We knew once drinking started, it was going to break it up. I could take

Richmond Flowers as a high school student.

my high school annual and point out every boy that I knew who had ever taken a drink. Those that did, as Jim Folsom used to describe them, 'were the rough el-e-mint.' I was almost twenty-two years old when I took my first drink. My students can't believe it when I tell them that I have never seen marijuana, and I wouldn't know what a joint looked like if you put it on my desk. I never heard of anybody smoking marijuana when I was growing up."

Richmond remembers that a speaking contest in high school gave him his first incentive to consider law as a career. "One day the principal announced that the school was going to enter an oratorical contest sponsored by *The Birmingham News*. The valedictorian and salutatorian were going to have a contest to see who would represent us. I didn't fuss, but I said, 'Who picked them? Why can't some others get in?' 'Well, they can if they want to.' 'Well, I believe I'll get in it.' 'Well, but it's going to be serious. We're not going to have any of this joking. It's silly for you to debate against them.' That sort of offended me, and, with my nature, I decided I would try it.

"I got my brother Drury, who was as literate as he could be, to help me write a speech. It was on James Madison, and I worked and I worked. After everybody spoke at the contest, I knew darn well I'd won it. The A students got up and delivered theirs like twinkle, twinkle little star, and shucks, I had inflection in mine, and I had emphasis where it ought to be.

"My mother was very articulate, and she coached me on it. She said, 'If you're going to make a speech, make it right.' My father was past president of the Alabama Banker's Association. He had heard some speaking, and he sharpened me up. I won the school contest, and I went on and won the county and the district. Then they put me in the state contest. The Dothan folks thought I won the state, but the judges placed me second.

"The speech contest got me interested in law. I went against some first class competition, especially in the state meet with those from Birmingham, Montgomery, and Mobile schools, and I began to feel that I had a talent of expressing myself.

"I've forgotten most of the speech, but I did quote one line the other day. It was about the Civil War. Here I was a high school athlete and not a very good student. The line I remember was, 'Such sanguinary sacrifices and such odious bereavements have no redemption at the bar of mercy. They ruthlessly betray the insufficiencies of man.' My English teacher was in a crowd with Drury about a week later and said, 'By the way Drury, I meant to tell you, I thoroughly enjoyed your speech the other day.'

"I'm afraid I wasn't much of a student in high school and when I started college. I always said, 'Why, I could do well in school if I wanted to.' I'd been a good strong pass and a low B, and that's it. In high school, I always could make a B without even trying, so who wants an A, and I'm not worried about a C.

"I went to college with an 83 average. It took 85 to be recommended to Auburn, so I entered on probation. I was always a little afraid I might be kidding myself, that I might not be able to make good grades when I really tried. But before the war, I made most of my A's in college in sororities and football and campus and girls."

College in the Late Thirties

Pre-law at Auburn. "I started to Auburn in 1936 and went there three years for pre-law. I felt that my main talent was communication, and I took all the speech that was offered. I got to the place that I thought I could handle a crowd. I did a lot of speaking. I always felt it would be a big help in law.

"Well, you don't make it big in law practice through speaking. I realized it later, after I got into law school. Speaking is a talent, but law practice is not the place to make it pay off. You make your money in law in the stacks and the books, not up speaking. Most people think of Perry Mason and other big speakers, but it's not so.

"I don't know why I didn't see the inevitability of my getting into politics. When I was a small boy, and later in high school and college, people would say, 'You'll be in politics one of these days.' I said, 'You'll never catch me in it. If there's one thing I don't want to be, it's a politician.' But I think it was inevitable because my talents were in meeting people, campaigning, and trying to turn a situation into something else."

Richmond intended to start college at the University of Alabama, but his father had a different suggestion. "I always figured that I would go to Alabama because I knew at that time Alabama was the only law school in the state. But one day my father asked, 'Did you ever consider going to Auburn?' I said, 'Well, Daddy, not if I'm going to study law.' He said, 'You might go over there and study pre-law, and later you've got to go to Alabama anyhow. Then you will have made friends and know people at both schools.' Well, that excited me. I've always loved to meet and mix with people. It sounded great to me to be able to go to both schools, and I wouldn't take anything for having done it.

Richmond remembers Auburn as a beautiful experience. "It was so typical of what I had been used to. Auburn was a small, country college when I was there. We had an expression there that, 'the farmer had two daughters; one of 'em was pretty and the other went to Auburn.' When I was there, every female on campus lived in one dormitory. It had about 150 rooms, and there were 300 girls. All the pretty girls on campus were daughters of teachers and administrators. A lot of the girls commuted.

"It was a very small college. We had a custom that everybody spoke to everybody at Auburn. During freshmen convocation, they told you that was the custom; you speak to them whether you know them or not. It was very friendly. When I was there I didn't know but two boys who had automobiles on campus. That was in 1936, right in the middle of the Depression. Things were tough.

"You wouldn't believe it, but I was a cheerleader at Auburn. I pledged SAE, and the head cheerleader was an SAE. He kept encouraging me, 'Why don't you try for cheerleader?' I said, 'I don't want to be a cheerleader.' He said, 'Well, you can make a letter if you stay with it all the way.' I said, 'I can belong to the A-club here? Well, all right, I'll try out.' And I tried out and won. I was a cheerleader three years, and I had a good time.

"I had always hoped I could play college football, but I wasn't good enough. I had enough speed to go out for track, and I was used in dual meets. I wasn't the top sprinter, but I did all right. I ran in fraternity track meets, and I was a big star because I was fast just for inter-fraternity. I also played inter-fraternity football.

"At Auburn I had a housemother from Dothan, Mrs Hart. Every time we had a set of dances, the boys invited girls in from Birmingham, Montgomery, Dothan, and all over the state. Their mothers allowed them to come because the boys all moved out of the fraternity house, and the girls moved in. Mrs. Hart looked after them the whole time. With Mrs. Hart, it was just like sending them to one of your best friends. You know your daughter is going to be all right because your friend's going to look after her.

"I was skinny when I first went to college. Then I quit growing taller, and I put on some weight. I gained weight pretty steadily in college. I weighed 203 pounds and was six feet, one inch."

Law school at Alabama. "After three years, I transferred to the University of Alabama. That was the fall of 1939. Although Tuscaloosa was the biggest overgrown country town in the world, it was like moving from a small town to a big town to me. I lived there three years, and I hardly knew one street from the other in Tuscaloosa. All our activity was on campus. It was a big college, much bigger than Auburn, with a tremendous coed program. I loved both schools, but they were just as different as could be.

"I think my father was right. Just out of high school, I needed to be at Auburn. There was too much enticement at the University. By the time I got there I was in law school. I realized some work's got to be done, or you'll flunk out. They'll run you back home with nothing to do. The dean used to say that the law's a jealous mistress. They expected you to live like a hermit and work like a mule.

"I enjoyed some of the festive life at Alabama, but I didn't flunk out. I passed. But I was not a very good student. I was satisfied just to get by. Academics didn't mean anything to me. I was going to go back to Dothan to practice law, and nobody ever asked a lawyer in Dothan what he made in a subject. So I didn't care; I just wanted my degree.

"I met a girl from Birmingham that I was crazy about. She was an attractive little brunette and very, very cute. But I told her I couldn't talk marriage until I finished law school, and she said, 'well . . .' She flunked out. She just had so much fun at the university, she couldn't study. She told me she would wait forever, and she did wait about three months. Then she married someone else.

"Law students prior to the war were sorta the pick of the campus, and everybody sorta looked up to them. I had some prestige being a law student, and I was probably in the best physical shape I've ever been in in my life. I was tall, with big broad shoulders. I never will forget that one time I measured a 42-inch chest and a 31-inch waist."

Accident and War

The national and international climate was rapidly changing as the 1940-1941 school year began. This was to be Richmond's second year in law school. Germany conquered France in the summer of 1940 and was threatening to overwhelm all of Europe. Japan was mauling China in its attempt to build a "Greater East Asia Co-Prosperity Sphere." The increase in war preparation and the accompanying boost in production finally brought an end to the depression, and interest turned to Europe and to England's fight for survival. The populace hoped the United States would not get involved, but most feared otherwise as events unfolded. President Roosevelt was soon to change, in his own words, from "Dr. New Deal" to "Dr. Win the War."[11]

Almost as an omen of the new era, a single event ended Richmond's pre-war college days and catapulted him toward adulthood and responsibility. "I had a horrible automobile accident in February of '41," he recalls, "and it wound me up at the University before the war. I had been there a year and a half. I was visiting in Gadsden for the weekend, and my date had to go home. I took her home and started back to join my other friends. I took a wrong turn and hit a train. It threw me into a steel-top car, and it bashed my head all in. I was unconscious eight days, and semiconscious for almost three weeks. That's where I got these scars in my head.

"I was in a Catholic hospital in Gadsden. When I began to come out of it, I was a raving maniac. One morning I woke up. I turned over in bed and said, 'What in the hell happened to me?' Just like that. I would lapse occasionally and go almost into a sleep and say things I wouldn't ordinarily say.

"The second day after I woke up I felt good, and the sister said, 'Richmond we want you to have something good to eat, what would you like?' I said, 'I'd like a steak.' She said, 'Richmond, this is Friday. You know this is a Catholic hospital, and we don't serve steak on Friday.' I said, 'Sister, I tell you what you do. Go down there and tell that damn cook I'm an atheist and bring me a steak!' I wouldn't have said anything like that if I had not been nuts. My mother would say, 'FELLOW, don't say things like that.' Then I'd go to crying.

"The doctors finally told her, 'Mrs. Flowers, leave him alone. He's not responsible. Your boy's not going to say anything you don't want him to say when he's thinking. It will go away in a few days.' And it did. But I was a character for a few days.

"I broke my leg badly in the wreck. I had what they call a compound dislocation. They had to completely rebuild my ankle and tie it together, and it kept me out of the army for a while. I was very lucky with the ankle. One doctor in Gadsden was considered a good bone man. When the people I was visiting heard about the accident, they called and asked him to go over and check on me. He walked into the operating room, and they had me anesthetized from the hip down. He asked the doctor in charge, 'What are you going to do?' He answered, 'I'm fixing to take this foot off; there's no way to save it.' The bone doctor said, 'Let me look at it.' In a few minutes, he said, 'Let me work with it. We can always take it off later.' That's how close I came to losing that foot.

"They brought me home to recuperate, and I stayed in bed about six weeks, until the cast came off. Then I got up and around, limping. My father had a cottage at Panama City, and he took me down there in May. They told me, 'You're not gonna be able to stand the pain it will take to work that ankle out because some of it is fused. You'll never dance again because you'll never be able to stand on your tiptoes again.

"When I got down to the beach with my mother, I'd go out on the front and walk in the sand, and I'd walk and cry and walk and cry. I'd come in, and I heard her since then tell her friends, 'I never felt so sorry for a human being in my life. You could tell he'd been squalling like a baby.' And I did, every day.

"It took about three months to get where I could halfway move around. Then in July of '41, I had worked it out strong enough, and I went to work with the contractors building Napier Field. I was a junior labor foreman. I still had a pretty good limp, but I could get around good. I just kept on until I could walk as straight as anybody before I went into the service. But it was enlarged, and it would swell up badly if I exercised it. At Napier Field, I was making forty dollars a week, which was a lot of money in those days. We completed the construction in October, and I was laid off.

"Then I got a job as a cookie salesman. My brothers have always kidded me about it. I was working for the Southern Biscuit Company. I had a territory around here and didn't have to stay out overnight. I got a pretty good thing going because they had an outstanding cookie line. Then comes Pearl Harbor and the sugar shortage. They couldn't ship the cookies 'cause they couldn't get enough sugar. So I got laid off again.

"The army called me up for examination in January of 1942, right after Pearl Harbor, and that ankle was as big as my head. They told me I'd be pulled in in three months and sent me back home. So I didn't look for another full-time job.

"I went to help out at the bank for the three months because they were short of hands. My brother Drury didn't have any broken legs, and they drafted him quickly. Another man in the bank was in the National Guard and was pulled out. An older man got sick and had to retire. So they really had a shortage. They put me in a teller's cage. On November 7, I was called up and had to go."

Into the Army and Adulthood. "When I was called up, I was twenty-three years old and single. I was classified 1-B. This was limited service, which was for people who couldn't take basic training and combat training. But they could do desk jobs and quartermaster work, and they could go with the medics and relieve somebody else. They could do a lot of those jobs and release an able-bodied man to take combat training.

"They put me in the quartermaster. Then when I went to Officer's Candidate School, I went to Medical Administration. I ended up as a hospital administrator. My leg gradually got better and better, and before I left the service, I finally pulled what they call general service, and went overseas."

Civil Rights Between the Wars

The period between Richmond Flowers's birth and his entry into the army after three semesters of law school coincides exactly with one of the formative periods in American history—the time between World Wars I and II.

In the broadest sense, the 1920s can be seen as a period of adjustment to changes brought about by the First World War. The war wrought enormous change in Europe, and it thrust the United States into the position of major world power, even though a large portion of the population did not want the consequences and responsibilities of that status.

The 1930s were the era of the Great Depression, and were a time of readjustment to the excesses, miscalculations, misinterpretations, and failures of the twenties. The result was major change in the philosophy of government and in the definition of governmental responsibility, particularly in the area of social welfare. The country, almost begrudgingly, accepted a greater international role. The national government grew in size and strength relative to the states, and political power became more centralized.

It can be said, almost literally, that Richmond Flowers entered young adulthood in a different country from that into which he was born.

Slow, Steady Progress in Civil Rights. As the Twenties progressed, there was a subtle but basic turning point in the struggle for civil rights for blacks. The Supreme Court restated its role as the protector of constitutional rights, and it abandoned deference to decisions of state appellate tribunals on these issues. Justice Oliver Wendell Holmes voiced the emerging position. If the state courts failed to correct a wrong, he said, then intervention by the Supreme Court was demanded.[9]

As the situation evolved, the Fourteenth Amendment, with its due process and equal protection provisions, emerged as the most important of the three post-Civil War amendments in asserting constitutional rights. Eighteen cases which involved blacks and the Fourteenth Amendment were decided by American courts between 1920 and 1930, and most were decided under the equal protection clause.[10]

The white primary was under consistent attack during the period. In the South, black participation in the general election was of little consequence because the Democrats always won anyway. The real election was the primary, and whites tried various ploys to restrict black participation. In a series of cases, the Supreme Court gradually established the clear right for blacks to vote in primary elections.

The most famous incident involving civil rights in the 1930s occurred in Alabama. In the Scottsboro cases, nine black boys were tried on charges that they raped two white girls on a freight train in which all had been riding. One of the girls was an admitted prostitute and the other's claim to virtue was, at the very least, questionable. Eight defendants were found guilty and sentenced to death. The Supreme Court of Alabama set aside one of the convictions.

The case involving the other seven was heard by the U.S. Supreme Court in 1932. The Court overturned the convictions on the ground that the constitutional right to counsel had been denied, and this was a denial of due process. Two of the seven were retried and again were convicted and sentenced to death. In 1935, the high court set aside the latest convictions, this time on the ground that state practices had systematically and arbitrarily excluded blacks from jury lists and had in this way violated the equal protection clause of the Fourteenth Amendment.

The Scottsboro cases received enormous national and international publicity and played a role in changing the conscience of the nation. Furthermore, it was the first case in which the Supreme Court held that, under the Fourteenth Amendment, the right to have the assistance of counsel is guaranteed against state governments as well as the national government.[11]

Resurrection of the Klan. The Ku Klux Klan had died a natural death as Reconstruction faded. Grand Wizard Nathan Bedford Forrest ordered it disbanded in 1870,[12] and all remnants had disappeared by the end of 1871.[13] It remained strong in memory, however, and as time passed, it became greatly romanticized, like the "Lost Cause."

In 1915, D. W. Griffith released *The Birth of a Nation*, one of the first full-length motion pictures. Enormously popular, the movie portrayed the Reconstruction Klan as heroic protectors of Southern honor and of the purity of Southern womanhood. A new Klan was soon organized, and, according to its publicity, it was "a high class order for men of intelligence and character" who were interested in the protection of traditional American values.[14] After a slow start, membership began growing, and by 1921, almost 100,000 in several different states paid dues.[15]

The Klan was one of the largest issues in the 1924 Democratic National Convention. Southerners, assisted by William Jennings Bryan, successfully fought an attempt to denounce the Klan in a plank of the party platform.[16] A notable exception was Alabama Senator Oscar W. Underwood, who in effect sacrificed his political career by his stand against the Klan. The organization reached its height in the 1925-1927 period, when it was credited with a membership of between three and five million.[17]

As the Klan took on more of the vigilante character of its Reconstruction ancestor, it turned increasingly to violence. It assumed for itself the dictation of community morals and ethics, and, as an aspect of its self-proclaimed "pure Americanism," it professed an anti-Negro, anti-Catholic, anti-Semitic ideology. Beatings, public whippings, and murder were among its weapons.

The organization had a strong following in Alabama, and was especially active in Birmingham, with its large population of steel workers. It set up a statewide political machine which succeeded in dominating politics for about four years.[18] It flogged regularly, burned crosses, held parades, and performed mystic ceremonies in public. On July 4, 1923, more than a thousand Klansmen demonstrated in Tuskegee against President Harding's plan to place blacks in charge of a rehabilitation hospital.[19]

The increasing violence and lawlessness finally detracted from the Klan's appeal, particularly among the educated and affluent. As David

Chalmers puts it, "The godly came to realize the Klan was not. Terror went too far, the extremists ranted too loudly, and the leaders were too immoral."[20] As criticism mounted, respectable people pulled out.

By the beginning of the Great Depression, the Klan's power and glory were almost gone, and the Depression gave the majority of people more concrete concerns than "Americanism." Membership dropped to less than 100,000, mostly in the South. During the thirties, it tried to revive itself by denouncing first communism and then organized labor, but with very little success. It remained a small, ineffective organization on the edges of society until the *Brown* decision in 1954 provided a new spur to action.

Richmond's Feelings About Blacks. Richmond Flowers did not give much thought to civil rights for blacks when he grew up. The issue received very little press coverage and was not a prominent conversation topic. In this time of Amos 'n Andy and Step 'n Fetchit, he shared the feelings of the majority of white Americans—that blacks were inclined to buffoonery and should stay in their place. He did not develop the virulent anti-black feelings displayed by many other Alabamians, however, and he had a sense of fairness about the way all people should be treated. Undoubtedly, his attitudes were due in part to the fact that Dothan was not in the Black Belt and was not an Old South town. He gives major credit to his mother.

"I wasn't raised to be a racist. I believed in segregation, of course, because that's what everybody believed in those days, but in my mind there was a difference between a racist and a segregationist. Mother didn't believe in treating anyone wrong, and she stressed that on us. I've spoken before of the incident when I asked her why my father wouldn't let me use her nice car. 'No other young men have a nice car like that, and you don't need one. You be like the other boys.' That's good logic, and it impressed me 'cause now I understand why I can't use that nice car. That was her genuine philosophy, 'Don't pretend to be anything you're not, and don't do anyone wrong.'

"To watch us when we were children, my mother always kept a full-time servant, typical of what we used to call a 'mammy.' My favorite was a big, heavy-set woman with a heavy voice. We knew to do what Katie said. My older brothers would come home, and even if Mother wasn't there, Katie'd say, 'Mr. Drury, you're goin' have to speak to Richmond.'

He'd get on me pretty sharp. 'Now, you do what Katie says do. You're not going to have any company here, and we're not going anywhere else to play either. Don't mess a good thing up for the rest of us.' Paul, who was just three years older, would do the same thing.

"We always had black servants in the house, including a cook and the maid who did all the heavy cleaning. My mother just wouldn't treat them wrong, that's all. She didn't believe in treating any of them wrong. I think that's where I got my notions about race relations. I just couldn't go with the flow when it came to mistreating blacks."

4

Maturing to Serious Pursuits

World War II

The central event of the 1940s was World War II. It was the all-consuming morality play, the desperate worldwide struggle between good and evil, a time when there was no ambivalence and everybody stood as one. It aroused such supreme passion that there was no question of young men like Richmond Flowers serving their country.

World War II began in 1939 when Nazi Germany invaded Poland, and England and France, living up to a treaty obligation, declared war. The Germans struck westward in May 1940, and they overran the low countries and France with amazing speed. Fear and foreboding filled the air. An under-prepared England stood alone before the great colossus.

The majority of Americans during this period were sympathetic to England. As Leuchtenburg observes, the average American "wanted to help Britain, even at the risk of war, yet he wished too to remain at peace."[1] The national policy was to help England economically to the extent possible and, in President Roosevelt's words, to make the United States a "great arsenal of democracy," while staying out of the fighting.

The U.S. was thrust actively into the war by the Japanese attack on Pearl Harbor on December 7, 1941. This culminated several years of growing dispute between the two countries. U.S. leaders knew that war with Japan was probably inevitable, but at the time of Pearl Harbor, they wanted to give first priority to Europe.[2] Japan won a victory at Pearl

Harbor, but it also unified a previously divided and isolationist America.

World War II matched the "Axis" powers, primarily Germany, Italy, and Japan, against the "Allies," led by the United States, Great Britain, the Soviet Union, and China. The Axis were all totalitarian states, and propagandists told us the Allies were fighting to preserve democracy. Few doubted it, though more astute analysis would have challenged the dedication of the USSR and China to such a concept. No matter, it was a holy war.

Germany surrendered in May 1945, and Japan followed in August, after two atom bombs were dropped. Roosevelt died in April 1945, shortly after beginning his fourth term, and Harry S. Truman became president. Two great national heroes, Dwight D. Eisenhower and Douglas MacArthur, had emerged. The world geopolitical balance was changed forever. The United States and the Soviet Union were the new superpowers, and the postwar era was dominated by their bitter rivalry.

Army

Richmond went into the army in November 1942. He says that, like most other eligible men at the time, he wanted to go. "I probably could have faked my leg hard enough that they never would have taken me, but I have to admit I wanted in. Everybody was in, and the ones that were out were miserable because they were trying to get in. There wasn't any draft dodging in those days. It was too embarrassing."

Mustering In. "After I got drafted, I got a notice to report at 5:30 in the morning. The last thing it said was 'Breakfast will be served.' I walked down the street that morning, heading for the draft board. We were going for breakfast and then to the bus station to get on the bus and go. A great big, burly sergeant was standing on the corner by the Houston Hotel, and as I walked by he said, 'Hey, Red.'

"I turned around and said, 'Yeah, what is it, Sergeant?' He was a great big guy. He says, 'It isn't none of my business, I know, so don't tell me that. And I know you ain't gonna try to rough me up, but I'd like to know something from you.' I said, 'What is it Sergeant?' He said, 'Why in hell ain't you in the army? I see you walking around here all the time, all dressed up in a suit of clothes. Why in the hell ain't you in the army?' I looked down the street. I looked back up the street, and, in a very secretive manner as if I was trying to hide something, I eased over to him and said, 'It's politics.' As I walked off, the last word I heard him say was, 'Goddamn son of a bitch.'

"I was on my way to the draft board, and I don't know what made me do it—the devil, I guess. Here I am going to the army, and he's wanting know how come I ain't in the army. He was so mad, he could have killed me if he got his hands on me, I reckon."

Buck Privates and Sergeants. "We boarded the bus and left. We were examined in Fort McClellan, sworn in there, and sent home for one week. Then we went to Atlanta to Fort McPherson, which was a reception center where you got your uniforms and that sort of thing. From there I was sent across town to Lawson General Hospital and put in the quartermaster corps.

"I was a private and getting along pretty good. My brother Paul was interning at Grady Hospital in Atlanta. He and Grace had married, so about twice a week, I'd catch the streetcar and go down to Grady Hospital. We'd ride back out to his apartment and he'd feed me.

"I had trouble with Sergeant Shaddix, a three striper buck sergeant. He was regular army and had been in fourteen years. He was a shrimp of a little feller, but he was the cockiest shrimp you ever saw. I was assigned to a 68-man quartermaster detachment, and only four men in the entire detachment had finished high school. The first sergeant and I were the only ones that had been to college. The first sergeant was an Atlanta boy who went to Georgia Tech. He felt like he got an ole Auburn buddy in there—like he had a brother. We became very close, and Shaddix didn't like it much that a rookie was buddies with the first sergeant. I weighed 226 pounds, six-one, and Shaddix must have weighed 126, dripping wet, and was maybe about five-eight. We just didn't like each other.

"One afternoon, we were going to GI the barracks, and I had been to Paul's and was just a little bit late. When you GI the barracks, everybody joins in. You take everything on this side and move it across to that side, intermingle the beds with the other beds, and put the shoes up on the bed and scrub down. It's a real streamline operation. They really do scrub that barracks down, and they did it every week on Friday night. They do it in mighty quick time, so you don't mind. You take twenty-five or thirty minutes, and then you're ready to go.

"Just as he said, 'All right, let's get this place cleaned up,' I walked in. He picked up the shoes I had shined and lined up for inspection, and he threw them across the room and scuffed them all up. I said, 'You get your damn hands off my shoes you little shrimp!' He said, 'What'd you say?' I said, 'By God, if you ever do that again, we won't need those mops, I'll mop this damn barracks up with you, you little shrimp!'

"He says, 'Let me ask you something, Flowers. You see that?' He pointed to his stripes. I said, 'Of course.' He said, ' I'm a sergeant, DON'T YOU FORGET IT!!!' I said, 'Well, you keep your hands off . . . ' 'I'll do it if I . . . ' 'You better keep your hands off my stuff! I wasn't two minutes late.' The first sergeant was standing right by me, and I knew nothing was going to come of it. What Shaddix did wasn't right, and he knew it. But the old way in the army, the sergeant did whatever he wanted to with the private's stuff.

"The next day, the Captain called me in and says, 'Flowers, I understand you had some trouble with Shaddix last night.' I said, 'No sir, I didn't have any trouble. I got him straight pretty quick.' He said, 'Now, Flowers, you know better than that. You've had an education, you've had all the advantages of life. Sergeant Shaddix was a Jewish perfume salesman. He had some friends, and that's how he got into quartermaster. They sent him down here. You've had all the advantages, and Sergeant Shaddix hasn't. I want you to set an example for Sergeant Shaddix, or you and I are going to have trouble. And I have too much rank for you to have trouble with.'

"I said, 'Captain, let me get this straight. You are telling me, as a buck private, I've got to set a good example for the sergeant?' He said, 'That's right.' I said, 'Thank you, sir.' The next day I applied for Officers Candidate School. I knew that I'd never make it where a buck private has to set an example for his sergeant. The first sergeant just about kidded me to death. Every time I'd say anything, he'd say, 'You got to make a better example for me than that. You've got to make an impression on me.'"

Officer Candidate School. Richmond took the OCS test and made a passing grade. After a few weeks of nervous waiting, he got the word to report to school. "I was down at the office when my orders came, and the Captain came in and said, 'Flowers, you can report to the barracks and start getting your stuff together.' I said, 'Where'm I going Captain?' He says, 'You're going to OCS at Camp Barkley, Texas.' I said, 'Camp Barkley, Texas. What is that?' He said, 'You're going to medical administrator's school, to be a MAC.' I asked, 'What is a MAC,

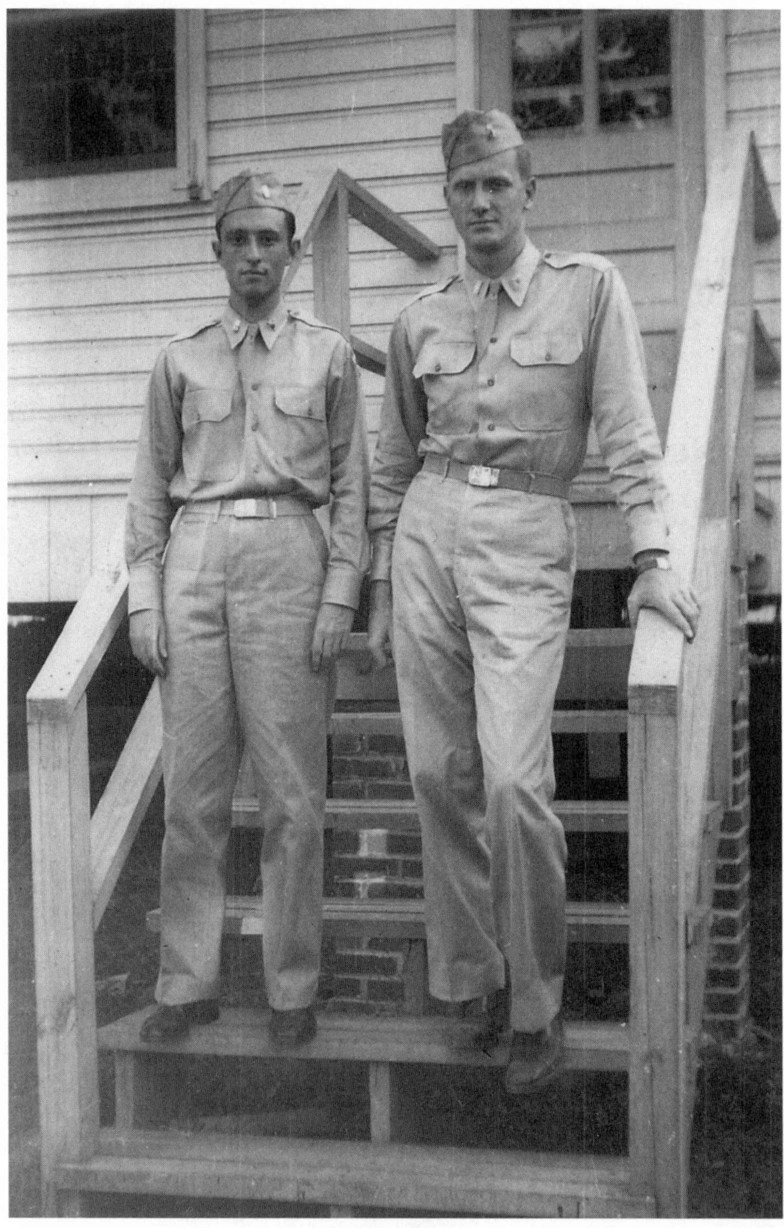

Richmond Flowers, right, as an Army lieutenant.

Captain?' He says, 'There's lots of them in the hospital. Go up there and ask Captain So-and-so. He got commissioned directly out of the ranks soon as the war cracked. He can tell you what it is.' I went highballing up there. I told the captain what my situation was and asked, 'Just what is a medical administrative commander? What do they do?' 'Well,' he says, 'uh, they are, uh, they have, uh, they're detachment commanders. And, uh, they, uh, they keep a lot of, uh, they're cadre commanders, and they keep a lot of records and do a lot of things like that.' 'Thank you very much, Captain.'

"I went back, and my buddy asked, 'Did you find out what a MAC is?' I said, 'No. But I found a captain up there who was a MAC, and he didn't know what it was. So I guess I'm in pretty good shape.' I didn't have any idea what I was getting into.

"Camp Barkley is right out of Abilene, deep in the heart of Texas. I had never been to Texas before. I got on a train, went to New Orleans, changed trains, and then rode straight to Abilene. They had a van for the candidates that were coming in. They picked us up and took us out and threw us in tarpaper shacks. They called it tent city, but it wasn't tents. It was just tarpaper shacks. It had a wooden floor for us to supposedly clean up, and it had cracks in it that wide. When they had one of those dust storms, it'd whip under that building and just come right up through the floor. We had to clean all that up. Keep it spit, polish, and shine, or else we weren't going to finish.

"The course lasted twelve weeks. We started out with a 68-man platoon, and eighteen graduated. This was in the middle of 1943, and they said, 'We are beginning to catch up on administrative officers. We don't need them nearly as bad. You, gentlemen, are caught in the middle. You're going to be weeded out. Many of you are just not going to make it, because we only have a certain number of requests, and that's all we're going to finish.'

"The competition got tough. The ones who didn't make it were shipped out to combat. They always shipped them to the combat engineers. So if you failed, not only did you know you weren't going to finish, you were going right overseas. I finished second in the entire class. I got to lead the rear guard in the graduation parade. The top man in the class led the entire parade. I was asked to speak at the graduation.

"About three days before we finished OCS, they called for volunteers for extra hazardous duty. They said, 'All we can tell you about the extra hazardous duty is, as soon as you get your commission, orders will immediately be cut promoting you to first lieutenant. And it is a dangerous extra hazardous duty.' They had about fifteen or eighteen to volunteer, and I was selected as one of the five to go. When they told me you're going to be a first lieutenant immediately, I said, 'I'll take my chances. That'll be the quickest promotion a fellow ever had.'

At the banquet the night before we were to be commissioned, they gave us a real nice recognition and send off. The next morning we were supposed to have a parade and be commissioned and get our bars. They got me up early, and told me to report to the battalion office. I rushed over there, and they said, 'Flowers there's been an awful mistake. You didn't tell us you were limited service.' I said, 'Well, Captain, I didn't think I had to. I thought my records showed it.' He said, 'This extra hazardous duty of yours absolutely cannot be with limited service. We're going to have to drop you off the list.' I said, 'Well, there goes my first lieutenancy. I wonder how long it will take me to get it?' He said, 'I'll tell you what, you pick any assignment you want, and we'll give it to you.' I said, 'Captain, I don't have any particular place. I was in Atlanta, and I liked the area. Get me as close as you can to Atlanta.' He said, 'You'll get the closest thing we've got.'"

One Single Officer and 6,000 WACS. "We went on into the parade, and they read out the assignments. 'Flowers, Richmond M. Fort Oglethorpe, Georgia.' Georgia? I'm close to Atlanta I guess. Fort Oglethorpe? I turned around to somebody and said, 'What is Fort Oglethorpe?' And one of the guys said, 'Oglethorpe is a cavalry post. The Sixth Cavalry is at Oglethorpe.' I said, 'Horses?' They said, 'Durn tootin. They've got some of the most beautiful animals you ever saw in your life.' I said, 'What the hell am I going to do with a horse? Reckon they got a horse hospital over there?'

"So we got our commissions, and we had this quick send off party before we departed the post. Everybody was asking everybody, and somebody says, 'Flowers, where you going?' I said, 'I'm going to a cavalry post.' He said, 'A cavalry post? There aren't any cavalry posts left in the army.' I said, 'There darn shore is one at Fort Oglethorpe, Georgia.' A guy over here just bent over laughing and almost fell to the floor. I said, 'What's so damn funny?' He said, 'Man, are you telling me you actually don't know what's at Fort Oglethorpe, Georgia?' I said, 'No, it was given to me as a choice assignment.' He said, 'Well, I suppose it is choice. That's where the Third WAC training center is.'

"He says, 'It's in Georgia, just over the Tennessee line. But you're really going to Chattanooga. The big town that's just four miles from it is Chattanooga.' And I said, 'A WAC training center?' 'Oh yeah, the WACs take their basic there. They got all sorts of tech schools there. They even got the WAC OCS there. There's not but three of them in the nation. I know, I came to OCS from over there.' 'Good Lord,' I says, 'why would a fellow put in for OCS when he's stationed out there.' He said, 'Males don't live very long over there. It's such a choice spot that everybody in the world wants it. Those that have a buddy in Full Service Command get sent over there. It's hard to stay.' I said, 'Well, good. I'll just go on over there for awhile' I went there and stayed two years in a WAC training center.

"I was hospital adjutant, but I got very close to the post personnel officer. Those of us in the hospital were the only ones on post on a garrison ration. The rest of them were on field rations, and they didn't have as much meat as we did. The personnel officer on the main post loved baseball, and so did I. We used to go to baseball games. Every now and then I'd take him a side of bacon or a ham or something that he couldn't get. So every time orders came in for somebody in my category to go, we'd put somebody else in. I ought to be ashamed, I guess. Everybody's coming and going, and for about six months, I was the only single officer on the post. There were fifty-three male officers on the post and six thousand women.

"I never got so tired of uniformed women in my life. That's why I liked Mary. I'd go downtown to get away from those durn uniforms. I tell you, it took a gorgeous animal to look good in the khaki uniforms they put on those WACs. They were too matronly looking. Before it was over, they changed and gave them some dress uniforms. They brought in some Powers models and sent them to Fort Oglethorpe for their training. They looked good in their uniforms cause they were a special design, a dress uniform, and they wanted to recruit WACs."

The Far East and MacArthur. Richmond went to Fort McPherson in July 1943, and left in August two years later to go overseas. The war ended early that August with the dropping of atom bombs on Hiroshima and Nagasaki. He eventually was assigned to general headquarters in the Far East and, as a hospital administrator in the theater surgeon's office, became part of General MacArthur's special staff.

"I went over on a navy ship. One of the navy men told me that if I'd go to my bunk and lay flat on my back and look straight at the ceiling, the costal swells wouldn't bother me, and sure enough, it worked like a charm. I'd lie there twenty or thirty minutes and say, 'Well, I got it made now,' and I'd get up about fifteen or twenty minutes. Then I'd go right back and hit that sack. After we got out of there, the Pacific lived up to its name and was just like a big ole lake. We went in sight of Honolulu and on to Anniwetok and refueled. At Anniwetok, you could go topside and see the water all the way across the island. They just bombed the thing flat. They knocked down all the sand dunes and the trees and everything else.

"When we arrived at the Philippines, they loaded us with full field equipment, helmets and everything, and we went ashore. We got on the personnel carriers and circled just like combat men did, and we hit the beaches with bayonets fixed. The war had been over for weeks, and the cameras were up there grinding. The only thing that disturbed them was the little Filipino saying, 'Piñas, Joe?' trying to sell us pineapples. They were taking some pictures for fear they wouldn't have another chance, and they picked us because we were handy.

"They loaded us on a train to Manila, and it was like the old War World I small-gauge trains they talk about—forty and eight. We had to stand up. They said they were taking us to a replacement depot. We started in the middle of the afternoon, and that night about 9:30 or 10:00, we were still riding. The further we went, the harder it rained. Then all of a sudden they stopped and said, 'Unload. You're going to have to walk sixteen miles to the depot; this is as close as the railroad gets.'

"I happened to be lucky and jumped on the back end of a truck. It was pitch dark, and we were told there were some Japanese holdouts in the hills just above us who didn't know the war was over. So be careful and don't light any lights. It was dark as pitch and raining like everything. Three or four of us found a little shack with a roof. It was locked, but no MP's or others were around, so we broke the lock and went in and went to sleep. By this time we were about dead. We woke up the next morning, and we were in the guard house. Thank goodness they didn't have any prisoners in there, or they would have escaped. We had broken into the guard house. But at least we had a dry night's sleep, and the sun came out bright the next morning.

"We found that the replacement depot had been used by the Japanese as a prisoner of war camp. They had 2600 prisoners of war in there, and it was overcrowded. We found out the next day there were six thousand junior officers in the thing. This is when we begin to realize that there was something different about our shipment. We were all junior officers. There were no enlisted men, and there were no senior officers. I mean, captains and lieutenants was all there were. We had bombardiers, infantry, artillery, engineers, every kind of officer in the world.

"This was an idea that MacArthur had for the invasion of Japan. He lost so many junior officers going into all those islands, he was going on the second wave. He was going to take in a complete replacement of junior officers. With the war over, they had no use for such a shipment, so we were just dead wood lying around there. They attempted to use us to let other personnel go home. We've got a bunch of junior officers. If you've got some people over here that have served, let them go home.

"We all thought, 'Suppose that bunch comes down out of those hills; they don't know the war's over.' Every now and then late in the afternoon they'd drop a knee-mortar on our camp. So they still had some ammo, and we knew it. Finally they came down because they were hungry. We were told one afternoon that we were going to have bacon and eggs the next morning. We had been on cornmeal mush for ten days. Twice a day it was cornmeal mush. We got up smelling it cooking. Those Japanese came down out of the hills, and they gave it to them. We still didn't get any bacon and eggs.

"Shortly after this, MacArthur's chief of staff visited the replacement depot, and he ordered it cleared out in twenty-four hours. 'I mean I want every man out of here in twenty-four hours. This is a shame and disgrace.' Within twenty-four hours we were all moved out. They sent us to the Twenty-fifth General Hospital Center, which had 2500 beds. There were five or ten of these hospitals in the hospital center, so you can see how many casualties they were preparing for. But at least this was a big, new military installation that was clean and hadn't been used. So it really was a very pleasant place to stay. The only thing that got you was boredom. We had absolutely nothing to do all day long. Look forward to a movie that night, maybe. Go to the movie, and that was it.

"Then I was assigned to the office of the theater surgeon, which was part of General MacArthur's special staff. The theater surgeon was Guy B. Dennett, a diminutive sort of a fellow. General Dennett was an old army buddy and close personal friend of General MacArthur, so he was the theater surgeon. At the end of the war, the only man in medicine who outranked him was the surgeon general.

"I was sitting there one day in Manila working on some records. And you know how you sense somebody standing there? Somebody just walked up. I sort of finished figuring and looked up, and there was His Majesty himself. General Douglas MacArthur!

"I stuttered about five or six times, 'Yes sir.' I did like they do in the comedy, knocked everything off my desk trying to stand. He said, 'Aw, sit down! Sit down, Captain. Where's Guy?' He didn't say, 'Where's the General?' 'Where's Guy?' About that time the administrative assistant, who was a full colonel, rushed out. 'Right this way, General. Yes sir, good to see you.' They opened the door, and General MacArthur walked in and said, 'Guy! You ole son-of-a-bitch, mumble, mumble.' He shut the door about that time. They came out just laughing. Old General Bennett says, 'Damn it, if your phone don't work, send a messenger over here and tell me you're coming. I'll get some of these fellows to stand around and salute for you!' I mean they were just old, old buddies. I just sat there with my mouth open.

"He was really impressive. Once after we were in Japan I got on an elevator. Just as the doors started to close, I heard, 'Hold it a minute, hold.' A big ole white stick came in, and they pushed the door back open. I recognized it because I had seen it around so much. It was General MacArthur's special guard—these six big soldiers he took with him. Everyone of them was about six-three or four, just physical specimens, the best looking guys you ever saw. They lined up, and he walked on the elevator. 'Morning, Captain.' 'Morning.' I couldn't speak. He got on the elevator and turned around. That's when I realized Douglas MacArthur was as big as he was. I'm standing there six-one, weighing 225, and he was taller and wider than me. He was a massive man. I bet you he was six-three or four. Broad shoulders. A great big guy."

When asked if he was sure he wasn't just in awe, Richmond

answered, "I hadn't thought about that. That may be it; he might have shrunk me up because he was a tremendously impressive man, tremendously impressive. I was just like the average GI, never had any use for Douglas MacArthur until I served close enough to him to observe him and have people explain to me what he was doing and why he was doing it. I was never so impressed with a man in all my life. He knew that Oriental mind, and he knew how to handle them. He knew they didn't respect a thing in the world but power, and he showed it in every move he made. He was a very, very impressive man. Certainly the man for that job. I was a great admirer of Douglas MacArthur after that.

"I was promoted to captain soon after I was assigned to general headquarters. I heard the general asked his colonel, 'How many of these first lieutenants that have been assigned to us are eligible for promotion?' He said, 'I don't know.' I was standing there, and I said, 'All but one, colonel. And he hasn't been a first lieutenant long enough for promotion.' The general said, 'Transfer him over to the laboratory headquarters there,' which was a plush assignment, 'and promote these others. It don't look good to have lieutenants sitting around general headquarters.' So that's how I got my very deserving promotion. I happened to be there when he didn't like to see lieutenants. All of the majors and lieutenant colonels that had served any length of time had been sent home. So it left them with a bunch of captains and lieutenants to do the clerical work."

To Japan by Ship. Richmond was in Manila from August to the end of December, when MacArthur began moving his special staff to Japan. Shortly after the move started, the group in Japan needed administrative help, and he got orders to fly up. It turned out to be an unusual trip.

"I went out that night and got on an airplane, and I got ranked off 'cause I was just a captain. Some colonel got on, and they told me to hit the ground. I went back the next night and got on the plane again. When I got on, I heard that the one that took off the night before had not been heard from since. So I felt a little bit nervous, but then a Brigadier General got on, and I got ranked off again. I walked off of that one with a smile. The next day, headquarters demanded to know where was the help they asked for. The answer was he kept getting ranked off of planes. So they sent some orders directly from MacArthur. When the colonel got them he said, 'They're going to think you're some kind of a big shot, when all they want is some clerical help. You're not going to get thrown off of any airplane with these orders.' Then I found out the second plane had not been heard from.

"So I went down to the port and got aboard a liberty ship. Only a small contingent of military was aboard because the hold of the ship was full of Japanese citizens going to be repatriated. When the ship's captain saw my orders, he says, 'Good Lord, Captain, you can take these orders and fly anything that's going out.' I said, 'Have you had any ships that didn't make it from here to Japan?' He said,' No, what are you talking about?' I told him about the two planes, and I asked, 'How about letting me ride up there on your boat?' He said, 'All right. Get aboard.' I got on Christmas Eve night.

"It was ordinarily a three- or four-day trip by ship. We sailed out and then got word that a big typhoon was coming into Okinawa. The ship's captain didn't seem worried. He just turned around and said, 'We're going with the blow.' We were speeding along, and I thought we were under a lot of power. But it was just the wind. They were riding it out at very low power. After about thirty hours it blew out.

"Then we had very pleasant, beautiful weather all the way up to Japan. I was at sea ten days, and when I got to Japan, they were hot. They had already sent some others up, and they thought I had deserted. They said, 'Where in the world have you been?' I told them that I got ranked off these two planes, and I caught a ship. I just figured I'd get on up here the best way I could. 'Well, you should have let us know.' I said, 'I didn't have any way to let you know.' It was close enough to the war that they were still under no-radio contact.

"I stayed in general headquarters in Tokyo, and that was the most pleasant part of my army service. The colonel was a flight surgeon, and he could draw airplanes. Occasionally he'd just draw us a plane, and say, 'Fellows I'm bored. Let's go somewhere.' We'd fly over to Korea, over to See-ule, as they called it then. We'd fly up in the northern part of Honshu, the big island of Japan, and they had fifteen feet of snow on the ground. That was most interesting. I went down to Yokohama and to Hiroshima and Nagasaki. I can tell you in a word what I saw at both places—nothing. Whew . . . it just turned big stone and steel buildings into an ash, a great ash you could blow away like that. Of course I didn't blow any of it, because I didn't know whether it was radioactive or not. It was some of the most horrible sights I ever saw in my life. It

A Flowers family photo taken near the end of World War II. From left, Richmond; Drury; Paul; Mrs. Flowers; John's daughter Ila; Mr. Flowers; John's wife Beryl; and John.

affected me greatly. I saw some of those faces for a long, long time after I got back.

"There was a very peculiar event after we got there. A request came through for penicillin for a member for the Japanese royal family. Any issue of penicillin outside the troops had to be approved by General MacArthur. Being a desk man, I saw the correspondence go through, and then it came back with an inquiry. The general would like to know what position the person was in, and was he cooperative. It came back through in a few days and said he was with the treasury department in a minor position. The report also said that it was the opinion of the surgeon general that if he didn't get it he would die. He added that, although the man did not cooperate and help us, he did not resist us. The answer came back, short and quick, 'Let him die.' I mean MacArthur was that way. He was just as tough as nails. Everybody in our command knew it, everybody in the Japanese command knew it, all the royal family knew it, and that's all they respected.

The Return Home. Richmond returned home after a short stay in Japan. "I was in Tokyo from early January to the end of March," he said, "and then I came home through Seattle. It took about ten or eleven days to make the crossing. We had a lot of Red Cross and nurse personnel, so it wasn't just a bunch of GIs looking at each other all that time.

We went into Seattle, and they processed us and loaded us aboard a troop train to go to Camp Shelby, Mississippi, to be discharged. I caught a ride with one of the boys to Laurel and then caught a bus from Laurel to Montgomery, and my mother and Drury and his brand new wife met me. Then we came on home." It was April of 1946.

Mary

Richmond met his wife, Mary, while he was stationed at Fort Oglethorpe. "It was in Chattanooga while I was with the Third WAC Training Center. Mary came to work out there. Her name then was Mary Catherine Russell. We had a requisition in for some clerical help, and when Mary applied for a job, they sent her up to the hospital to be interviewed by me. She was young but very impressive with a very mature attitude. So we hired her and sent her to the dental clinic as the chief clerk.

"In my rounds as adjutant, I visited every department at least once a week and sometimes twice. I'd go by and chat with her. She had all the figures I was asking about: how many people they'd seen and treated and all that. She was a very pleasant person. I asked her for a date, and she turned me down. She said, 'No, maybe later but not right now.' It was puzzling to me. You just don't know what it's like being a single male officer in a WAC training center. I couldn't understand anybody turning me down. I just kept kidding along with Mary, and we finally began to date.

"I had a date with her every Sunday afternoon and night. We went to a baseball game. Her stepfather was crazy about baseball, and I'd chat with him when I picked her up and again when I brought her back. We'd go to the game Sunday afternoon. Then we'd go to the Read House for dinner and to a movie in downtown Chattanooga. That was our routine for a long time. Then I began to have some dates with her on other nights, and just before I went overseas we were dating regularly. I told her that, if I got back, I wanted to marry her.

"She was a very mature person, and I found out why Mary went to work. She was a true Depression baby, and they had to watch their nickels and dimes. Her father died suddenly early in the Depression and left her mother absolutely strapped. Before I went overseas, I talked to her mother about the possibility of our marrying when I got back, and she said, 'Oh, that's fine.' She asked me if I would talk Mary into going to college for a year or two while I was gone.

"Her father had left a $5,000 educational policy for her, and it would be plenty to send her to the University of Chattanooga. So I talked to Mary about it, and she gave me the full story. 'Absolutely not,' she said. 'If I don't go to college, that will go to my mother, and she needs it to live on. All the king's horses and all the king's men can't send me to college.' Naturally I backed off. That was her way of doing for her mother.

"I realized right away that she was somebody different. She wasn't just a young, pretty face. She was a beauty, but that wasn't all. There was a lot to her; she had a great many very strong traits." In reminiscing about their meeting and romance, Mary remembered, "He had his choice of all the women in Chattanooga." And Richmond responded, "And I found the prettiest of them all."

After Richmond was overseas, Mary took steps to get better acquainted with his family. "While I was overseas," he recalls, "Mary visited my parents for a week. She came in on the Central of Georgia Railroad by herself, and in the last stretch, she got on a little train with a potbellied stove. She thought, 'Well, I'm going to the jumping off place.' But she always has said that she really did fall in love with the town. Dothan had a reputation for making new people feel right at home, and they did it for Mary."

Richmond wasted no time going to Chattanooga after returning home from the army. "I got back in mid-March, and in a couple of weeks, I went up to Chattanooga to get my marriage license. I always have a good laugh about it because I got it on April Fool's Day. And I had a good time kidding Mary about me marrying a child bride. The legal age in Tennessee was twenty-one. Mary was just twenty, and I had to take her mother along to give permission to buy the marriage license. She wasn't twenty-one until the following August."

Richmond and Mary were married on April 22, 1946, in the First Christian Church in Chattanooga. "It was late in the afternoon, he says.

Mary and Richmond Flowers on their wedding day.

"My brother Drury was my best man, and her sister was her matron of honor. Just her immediate family and my immediate family were there, so it was a small wedding.

"It was in a beautiful old church—one of the oldest in Chattanooga. The Reverend John Paul Pack married us. The last time we heard from him, he had the largest Christian church in America, in Seattle, Washington. I had been in three dozen weddings in Dothan and Chattanooga, and I had heard the vows over and over. But John Paul Pack, I shall never forget. I got so much more of hearing him say the vows; it just meant so much more to me than hearing it before. I guess, maybe, it was because it was my own. He was really good. He had a very fine appearance and manner. No wonder he went up in his church.

"We drove from Chattanooga to Atlanta and got there about dark. Then we went from Atlanta to Birmingham the next day. We drove from Birmingham down through Tuscaloosa and stopped at the old frat house and saw a lot of the bunch that were back after the war. Then we drove on to New Orleans, where we spent our honeymoon. On the way back to Dothan, we spent one day in Mobile seeing Bellingrath Gardens."

The newlyweds arrived in Dothan to start their new life together. Richmond remembers that Mary adjusted well. "She always felt that she would be happy in a small town. Chattanooga is pretty big, and early on, she missed the ways of the city. Even in those days, they would run up to Montgomery and Columbus to shop, so she got to be in a bigger place from time to time. But we were sorta poor folks, and we didn't shop too much anyhow. Mary has always, I think, thoroughly loved this town, and she was so amazed that so many people took to her immediately."

Back to Dothan and to Law School

Richmond Flowers and his new bride arrived in Dothan just about the time the 1946 governor's race was getting underway. Like many other returning veterans, he was searching for a direction for his life. He began by working in The Dothan Bank and Trust Company, which his family owned. "We got married in April of 1946, and I went to work in the bank in May. We were living with my parents, and I didn't know exactly what we were going to do. I worked at the bank and also got in a business venture with my brother Paul, who was practicing medicine in Dothan.

Searching for a Direction. "Paul and I started building houses. We'd build one house at a time. Paul would furnish the money, and I'd manage at the site. I would go by every morning and take orders for what they needed for the day, go buy it, and be sure it got there. Then, I'd go back by in the afternoon to check things and get anything they needed to start the next morning. In those days, right after the war, you'd start putting down a foundation and people would try to buy it. So we'd sell one at a time, as fast as we could build them, and we were making some money.

"I could work with the houses and do my job at the bank, too. The bank opened sorta late, so I could take care of the house we were building in the morning. Then the bank closed sorta early, and I'd get back there by 3:30 or 4:00 in the afternoon. I'd check with Paul about that time. He'd run his office all day and leave late in the afternoon to make house calls.

"Then, when the building business slowed down, I built us a house across the street from the bank. Mary was pregnant when we moved in, and we were living there in June 1947 when Richmond was born. That's where we took Richmond from the hospital. We only lived there six or seven months before I decided to go back to law school. I sold the house and went back and finished college.

"I worked at the bank about a year and realized that it wasn't for me. There were too many Flowers in one pot. My father was there. My uncle was there. My two older brothers were there, and my cousin was there. I was the sixth of six Flowers, and I was coming in on the bottom of the list. I was going to be an old man before I could be any kind of an officer. I realized I was heading up a very tough slow pathway to ever make any real money. It had pleasant surroundings, excellent hours and so forth. But I was a clerk, and I was still cocky enough to believe I had more sense and more ability than that. It wasn't just the bank. I had matured, and it sickened me to realize that I had three full semesters in law school, in a six-semester course, and had quit. So I went back to school in September of 1947."

The Return to Law School. Richmond remembers his second stay in law school as a happy time when he had little money but a great sense of accomplishment. "I didn't get any help from home. I didn't ask for any help, and I didn't want any help. I took the GI bill and what few little dollars I had, and the three of us went back to school. We were lucky enough to find this little two-bedroom apartment which was new. We put the baby in one bedroom, and we had the other one.

"We were as hard up as we could be, but we weren't suffering because I knew there would be better days. It's easy to live knowing that your family is not going to let you go down. We made it, and those were some of the happiest days we've spent in our marriage, with that little ole baby and just about to starve to death. It was one time I lived the hard life.

"I had the damnedest schedule. I got up very early every morning. The baby was going to have a 6:00 bottle, so I'd get up anywhere from 4:30 to 5:00 and continue my reading and studying and briefing of my cases that were assigned. I'd hear the baby wake up about 6:00. Then I'd give him his bottle, put on clean diapers, dry him out, and put him back to bed. A little later, you could hear him in there playing with his crib toys. That meant he was ready for his bath. By then, Mary was up and had fixed my breakfast. We had breakfast, and I'd go in and rinse and wring out all the diapers.

"I'd leave with the diapers on the way to school and stop at a launderette. I had a deal with the lady that ran it. I would go on to class, and as soon as the clothes were finished, she'd throw them in a basket and put them to the side for me. I'd come back by and pick 'em up, and while Mary was fixing lunch, I'd hang them out. Those were the old diaper days when you hung them out. I'd come in and study all afternoon, and late in the afternoon we'd go for a ride in the car. While Mary was getting the baby up to take the ride, I'd get the diapers in. They were dry by then, and I'd fold them and put them up.

"At first, we would ride up to an ice cream parlor, and get an ice cream cone. We did that for about a semester and finally had to cut it out. We couldn't afford it. That damn ice cream cone was costing fifteen cents a day and was cutting into our budget too bad. I stayed there three semesters, and we went out two nights. We went to see *Gone with the Wind* one night when it returned, and a couple invited us over one night to play bridge. Two nights in three semesters I left that house.

"It wasn't just money that kept us at home. I had to study hard. This time I came out with all guns blazing. When I first started to college, I made A's in campus, coeds, sororities, and football, but my school work didn't bother me much. After the war it was different. There was a seven-year gap in which I had worked, been in the army, gotten married, and had my first child. So when I went back, I was a different animal altogether. I went to the books and nothing but the books and tore them up. All I had was A's and B's during those three semesters.

"Studying took a long time because I'm a slow reader. Every test I've ever had showed my retention is high, but I read very slowly. I think I was taught to read words, and that worked a hardship on me in law school. The instructors each assigned roughly five cases a day, and I would read and brief every one of them. I never went to class without every case being briefed. Every week I'd fall a little bit behind, and every weekend I'd catch up. The only salvation I had was that Saturday and Sunday gave me time to catch up. I sat in my apartment one afternoon and could hear the cheers when Alabama was playing LSU. I had student tickets, but I couldn't go. The weekend was for catching up.

"One day we had a football game in town, and the professor asked for the first case to be recited. Someone answered 'unprepared.' It was a big game and a beautiful day, and there was frivolity all over the campus. Four or five fellows answered 'unprepared.' The instructor said, in very serious manner, 'Well, no sense in wasting each other's time any more. I'm just going to give everybody a zero and y'all can go.' He was kidding, no doubt, but it frightened me. I said, 'Now, professor, I can give you that case.' He said, 'Oh, Mr. Flowers, you got the first case?' I said, 'Yes, sir.' I stood up to give it, and he said, 'Well, I tell you what to do. Give us the fifth one.' I said, 'Yes sir,' and I flipped over and gave him the fifth one. He said, 'Have you got the third one?' I said, 'Yes sir, I've got every one.' I started with the third. He said, 'That'll be all, Mr. Flowers. Now, gentlemen, that's the way to make an A.' That was just his way of kidding, but I showed him I was prepared.

"I never will forget Thanksgiving that year. There wasn't any chance of us having a turkey and all that, so my mother sent me a canned hen. I found out that another young man from Dothan was up there in law school and would not be able to go home. Mary and I invited him over to our apartment for Thanksgiving dinner, and we ate this canned hen. It was an absolute delicacy. You know, those are the sorts of things that seem to strengthen you. We can look back and realize, probably, that was as happy as we ever were in our lives—two young people with a goal to achieve and struggling to do it."

In law school, Richmond first entertained serious thoughts about entering politics. Also, he found a cause worth fighting for. "We went up there in the fall of 1947, and I finished in November of '48. That's where I got a lot of ideas about living. Before then, when anybody would tell me I ought to be a politician, I'd say, 'That's the last damn thing you'll find me doing; I'll be dead before I'm a politician.' But after the war and the time back at the University of Alabama, I definitely got some ideas about wanting to do things. While I was in law school, I discussed the possibility of a public hospital in Dothan with some of my classmates and friends, and I came out with a burning desire to build it. That gave me a purpose. It keyed the whole thing and changed my whole life. There's no doubt about it."

In and Out of Law Practice

Richmond finished law school in November of 1948, shortly after his thirtieth birthday, and he returned to Dothan and began his practice. He continued five years, until he ran for the state senate in 1954.

Richmond recalls that his law practice was not very lucrative at the beginning. "I had a hard time. A new lawyer working by himself has a tough time, and my income was naturally very small. The bank referred me some work, but most of it was title work that you had to do pretty inexpensively. I did some business for a life insurance company which was formed in Dothan. They got into difficulties with their reserves, and they hired me to help with the negotiations to sell it. The company that bought it was Vulcan Life Insurance in Birmingham, and I went to work for them on a part-time basis. Just prior to running for the senate, I went with them full time for a little while. Then I went back to the practice of law to run for office. I really didn't have much of a practice; it wasn't highly lucrative at all.

"There really wasn't a lot of law work in Dothan at the time. A few of the larger firms had the retainers from the insurance companies, and the lawyers that were five to ten years older than I were handling all the criminal law and the civil law fights. Most of the older and more successful lawyers in town, you never saw them in court. They were retained because they were able to get settlements and stay out of court. Most of what I did was appointed law."

Long-Legged Lizzy. "I was appointed to the first murder case I ever tried. A woman was charged with murder. She was a black woman, tall and gangly, and extremely unattractive. She really looked undernourished. And she had no friends. She was one of these people, I found out in my investigation, who had never worked permanently for anybody. During the daytime, she would hang around the quarters, which we called Baptist Bottom in Dothan at that time, and hope that somebody would drive through and say, 'Do you want a day's work to do some cleaning?'

"She had killed a woman. It was on Saturday night, with frivolity everywhere. The beer joints and the night clubs and all the streets were full. That was what we called the quarters, where all the black people went and had a big time. There was always drinking and carousing, and it usually ended with a cutting or shooting. Anyway, she walked up to a woman and says, 'You're the woman that fought my Au-tee, aren't you?' And she answers, 'Yes, I am. I whipped her and I'll whip you if you don't get out of my way.' Lizzie said, 'Well, you stay right here, I'm going home and get my gun, and I'm coming back and kill you.'

"She went home, and when she came back, she asked, 'Where is she? I'm gonna kill her.' They said, 'Well, she's coming across the street right now.' She walked right out in the middle of the street with thirty or forty witnesses and said, 'I couldn't find no gun. This here knife will have to do the job.' She stabbed her in the chest, and it went right into her heart. The ambulance driver didn't even take her to the hospital. By the time they got there she was bled out. It was just awful, terrible. The autopsy showed the knife went right between two ribs and hit her in the heart.

"That Aunt, 'My Au-tee', as she called her, 'was the only friend I had in the world. She was the only person in the world to be nice to me.' And this woman 'whopped her'—that was the black expression—for no reason at all. She didn't injure her, she just 'whopped her', and for that Geraldine killed her.

"So there I was with my first murder case. The indictment read, 'Geraldine Lewis, alias Long-Legged Lizzy.' I began to work for some kind of compromise and some friends that would testify for her. I'd go talk to people, and they'd say, 'Aw, nah, Mr. Flowers. She's just trouble. She's bad news. She fights; she ain't worth nothing. You ain't gonna find nobody to testify for her.' I couldn't find one single soul to even be a character witness or say anything in the world. And I couldn't find anybody to doubt that story that the district attorney had. They said, 'that's just the way it happened.' Several witness heard it and saw it.

"The district attorney offered me forty years. He said, 'Rich, I'll let you plead her guilty for forty years to keep from having to try the thing.' So I went and told her. She said, 'Nawsir, I'd rather go to trial.' I said, 'Geraldine, they're gonna burn you. They're going to put you in the electric chair, I'm afraid. It was so intentional.' She said, 'That's all right. I'd rather be dead than live all my life in jail.'

"So we went to trial, and I had nothing in her behalf. I took the indictment and said to the jury, 'Now gentlemen of the jury . . . .' And it was strictly gentlemen; no ladies served on the jury at that time. I bragged on the District Attorney, because he was such a good one. And he was. He could cut you to pieces, and I was trying my first case. I told them what a capable prosecutor he was, and 'aren't we glad that the state hired such a capable man as this? But I want you to look at this indictment, gentlemen of the jury. Here is a woman on trial for her life. You haven't seen her before. Not one friend does she have that's willing to take the stand and ask you not to execute her. And yet, look at that indictment, gentlemen, on trial for her life. She's called Long-Legged Lizzy. She was never referred to in this trial as anything but Lizzy, Long-Legged Lizzy. Gentlemen of the jury, do you stand in trial for your life in ridicule in this great nation of ours? I don't think so. I think she's entitled to more than that.'

"Well, all the lawyers sitting around there waiting for their cases were sorta laughing and saying, 'What is he talking about? That's no defense.' Well, I didn't have a defense! I didn't know anything else to do. And, bless Pat, the jury came out and gave her twenty years. She went off. About a week later, I was playing golf with a good friend of mine who was on the jury. I said, 'Bill, not that I didn't appreciate it, good buddy, but where in the world did y'all come up with twenty years with that Geraldine Lewis case the other day?' He laughed and said, 'Oh, Rich, I told all those folks it was your first case. Let's give him a break. They were going to give her forty years like the district attorney suggested, and we cut it in half.'

Bucking the System. In another of his cases, Richmond showed his tendency to buck the system—and take his licks as a result. This happened several times in his career, and, in the end, it got him in really big trouble. He likens his disposition to go against the odds, whatever the outcome might be, to the behavior of a wildcat, and he thinks of himself as having the "heart of a wildcat."

He recalls the case: "It was sort of a technical situation. A list of people is furnished by the clerk, the sheriff, and the circuit judge to handle elections—the returns, the boxes, and all that. The list was tampered with one time. Some people were left off and others put on, and I was asked if I would try to help do something about it. I went against the County Democratic Executive Committee and against the County Commission. And of course, that's the most powerful politician in every beat and ward in the county. They went after me, and I went after them. The judge called me in before the trial and said, 'Richmond, you have prepared an unusually good case, and I think you deserve to win. But you're not going to win because I don't like to go against old timers. You're a young man and you've got plenty of time to be successful later, but you're going against some of the top lawyers in this county, and I'm not going to let you beat them.'

"That's not justice in my mind, but what am I going to say? I had to try every other case under that old man. I had no recourse because all the rulings were discretionary rulings of the judge. It is the rarest thing in the world that the supreme court or the court of appeals will reverse a discretionary decision because they say, 'He was there. He heard all the evidence. He observed all the witnesses. He's in better position to know than we are. Stay with him.' So it was all over. It stuck, and the election went the way they wanted it to go. That's one time I took on the odds and took my licks."

Ready for Politics. After a few years, Richmond realized that practicing law wasn't what he wanted in the long term. "I wasn't really crazy about the practice of law," he says. "I enjoyed studying law more than I did trying to practice law, because it is a challenge. Every case is a challenge, sorta like a puzzle. You figure on it and arrive at the answer. I enjoyed the associations and being a professional man, and I've never regretted going into law. Probably the smartest thing I ever did was go back and finish law school. But it was sorta like the banking business. I realized after I had been in it a while that it wasn't my cup of tea."

Politics was to be his thing. Richmond's original entry into politics was triggered by his interest in a charity hospital for Dothan. He had the idea when he returned from the army. What really got him going on the issue was an incident after he was practicing law.

"One of the local hospitals called me at two o'clock in the morning one time," he relates, "and told me that a woman who said she worked for us had been in an accident and was cut badly. I told them the woman worked for me, that she was helping Mary raise my children. They said, 'Now, it's not real serious, but it is a bad cut that needs stitching. I said, 'For goodness sake, sew her up.' They said, 'We have to have a fifty dollar deposit before we can touch her because she has no insurance. I said, 'I'll stand good for the fifty dollars; sew the woman up.' 'Well, you'll have to come on over here and give us the fifty dollars.' I said, 'I'm going to tell you one more time to sew that woman up, and if you don't do it, I'm going to call Dr. Moody and wake him up.' He owned the hospital. 'Dr. Moody's on my father's board down at Dothan Bank and Trust Company, and he's not going to like it atall about you telling me that I'm not good till eight o'clock in the morning for fifty dollars.' They said, 'Mr. Flowers, we didn't realize you were that close. We're going to do it, but it's against the rules.'

"I don't know that there was any particular fault in this. I don't blame them for trying to get the money; they ought to have their money. But we needed a place where people could pay according to what they made. If it was me, that's fine; charge me a hundred dollars. But if somebody comes in there and is cut and hasn't got any money, the Lord didn't mean for folks to get neglected because they were poor. I talked and talked about the thing and asked, 'How do you build a Hill-Burton hospital?' I found out you first had to petition for an election. I began to spread the word, and I sorta became chairman of a committee. They got enough petitions signed to call an election to see if the people would authorize a four-mill ad-valorem tax to raise matching money for Hill-Burton funds.

"By this time, my brother Paul had a little hospital in an old home. He had his office downstairs and thirteen beds upstairs. That was the third hospital in town. When we began, I needed money to buy sound systems to go around the county to tell them when the vote was, what they were voting on, how much four mills was, and what it meant. That was the first money we spent on that election, and you know who paid it? Paul Flowers.

"Paul always said, 'There's room.' When these other doctors called him and said, 'Paul have you lost your mind? Don't you know this thing will put you out of business?' He said, 'It won't put me out of business.' Paul was the first doctor in Dothan who had specialized training. He had a residency in OB/GYN. So he says, 'It's not gonna put me out, because I'm going to deliver enough babies over here to keep me going.' They said, 'But you're not going to grow any. You're just going to have that little clinic.' He said, 'That's all right with me. I still think there's room for a public hospital in Dothan.'

"Well, by this time, it's really picking up steam, and it had a whole lot of public sentiment. We won the election, and they began to collect the four-mill tax. Then they pulled every political trick in the book. I mean, some big powerful people got in on it then, helping the wealthy owners of the other hospitals. They turned me every way but loose because I was a neophyte. I didn't know it was going to be a fight. I thought, 'We won the election. Now the money will collect, and we'll build the hospital.' They had to appoint a hospital board, and they put me on it. They had me so outvoted, I couldn't do a thing.

"An administration friendly with the big folks here was elected in Montgomery in 1950. So I was dead. I even had a very outstanding attorney who was high up in the administration ask me, 'Rich, why don't you back off of this thing? Paul's got his hospital. He's gonna make all the money he ever needs. And buddy, I'm telling you, you ain't gonna ever get that money out of Montgomery. There's no way for you to get it. It has to be allocated by the state.'

"The next day, Guy Hardwick was in my office. I had helped him in the county when he ran for Lieutenant Governor. I said, 'Guy, the administration's got us locked out.' He said, 'That's right, and there's no way you can break through it. The word's gone out. Don't allocate that money to Dothan. Whatever they come up with, delay it, delay it.' I said, 'Guy, can a member of the state senate do anything about this?' He belly-laughed and said, 'Good gosh, I reckon he could! A member of the state senate has to do with all of those officers up there that are fighting you right now. They have to have an appropriation.' I said, 'Well, I'm running for the state senate.'

"He said, 'Oh come on, Rich, maybe run for the House and then step up.' 'No, I'm gonna run for the senate.' He said, 'Richmond, you don't just run for the senate first. You're liable to catch some opposition that's been in the House, and they'll make you look bad.' I said, 'I'm gonna run for the state senate, and if I'm elected, we're gonna build a hospital.' He said, 'You're as butt-headed as any man I ever saw. Go to it.'"

Equal Rights At Mid-Century, An Idea Whose Time Had Arrived

During World War II, A. Philip Randolph, founder and president of the Brotherhood of Sleeping Car Porters, made a strong demand for fair employment in defense industries and equal treatment in the armed services. In response, President Roosevelt issued an executive order which prohibited discrimination in defense industries and established a Fair Employment Practices Committee. It was the first time since Reconstruction that the federal government had intervened on behalf of black rights, and it established the precedent that the right to fair employment might be regarded as a civil right.[3]

During the war, the drift in public opinion toward more liberal racial attitudes which had begun during the New Deal, accelerated. Thoughtful whites became painfully aware of the contradiction in fighting the Nazis with their racist philosophy while permitting racial discrimination at home. After the war, the need for reform was further emphasized as the Communists blasted Western imperialism and held American democratic pretensions up to ridicule.

President Truman and Civil Rights. Harry Truman became president in 1945, and his administration opened a new era in the history of American race relations. Among precedent-setting steps, President Truman established the President's Committee on Civil Rights; appointed William H. Hastie to the Third U.S. Circuit Court, making him the highest black judicial appointee in American history; issued the directive that ended segregation in the armed services in 1948; ordered those doing business with the federal government to pursue a nondiscriminatory employment policy; and led the Democrats to adopt a strong civil rights plank in their 1948 party platform.

The report of the Committee on Civil Rights called for the full integration of blacks in all aspects of society. It recommended action by federal and state governments, and it cited moral, economic, and international political reasons. In his special message to Congress in February 1948, President Truman included Committee recommendations to:

1. Establish a permanent Commission on Civil Rights.
2. Strengthen existing civil rights statutes.
3. Provide federal protection against lynching.
4. Protect more adequately the right to vote.
5. Establish a permanent Fair Employment Practices Commission.
6. Prohibit discrimination in interstate transportation.[4]

While Congress refused to act, the report paved the way for new norms in American race relations. Further, it helped draw distinctly one of the major issues of the 1948 presidential election. For the first time since Reconstruction, civil rights was a major issue in a presidential race, and black political power was an important factor in the outcome.

Acting on the president's recommendation, the Democratic National Convention adopted a strong civil rights plank in 1948. This provoked a split, with several Democrats from Alabama and other Southern states walking out. One of the Alabamians who remained at the convention with the party regulars was a young politician named George C. Wallace. Later in Birmingham, a "Dixiecrat" slate of candidates was nominated to oppose Truman. The far left, led by former Vice President Henry Wallace, thought the platform did not go far enough on race matters. They formed the Progressive party, which took a vigorous stand in favor of civil rights and named still another set of candidates.[5]

With the Democratic vote split three ways, Republican candidate Thomas E. Dewey appeared a certain victor. Truman fought vigorously, however, and he emphasized labor rights and civil rights strongly in his campaign. To everyone's amazement, except apparently his own, he won the election. The outcome left no doubt that national attitudes on civil rights had shifted dramatically.

An Idea Whose Time Had Arrived. At mid-century, the stage was set for the most momentous changes in black-white relationships since the Civil War. From its nadir just after the turn of the century, the campaign for black rights had achieved a remarkable transformation. Led by the NAACP, the Urban League, and the Congress of Racial

Equality, those seeking change had prevailed through sound strategic moves and persistence.

Among contributing factors was the massive black migration which began early in the century and which was greatly augmented by the two world wars. Future racial adjustment would take place chiefly in an urban environment. The vote of the blacks in the North had reached such proportions that it could swing elections, and even Southern politicians respected black votes.

Some of the key civil rights principles the Supreme Court established were the right of an accused to have the assistance of counsel in state as well as federal judicial proceedings and the right of the federal government to act in federal courts against a state officer when a citizen has been deprived of life without due process. State practices which systematically and arbitrarily excluded blacks from jury lists were held to be a violation of the equal protection clause of the Fourteenth Amendment.

As Senator Everett Dirksen remarked, equal rights for blacks was an idea whose time had come.

5

A Political Career Begins As Civil Rights Takes Center Stage

Folsom and Flowers Win in '54

Richmond Flowers, in his enthusiasm for building a public hospital in Dothan, had decided to run for the state senate in 1954. The primary election, the only election which counted in Alabama in those days, was early in May, and Richmond started campaigning at the first of the year. Other candidates included James E. Folsom, running for his second term as a governor in the populist mold, and Richmond's Dothan friend Guy Hardwick, who was running for lieutenant governor. George Wallace, the young circuit judge in neighboring Barbour County, served as Folsom's south Alabama campaign manager.

There were no really large statewide issues that spring, just the usual debate over who could best continue the improvement of economic conditions in Alabama. Nationally, the Korean War had ended, Eisenhower with his calm demeanor was safely in charge in Washington, and the country was prosperous. Few among the majority population gave race relations much more than a second thought.

Folsom Wins Again. There were six candidates in addition to Folsom in the 1954 race for governor. The most prominent were James B. Allen and Jimmy Faulkner. Allen, later to become a U.S. senator, was the outgoing lieutenant governor and was conservative, openly concerned about the pending Supreme Court case on school segregation, and strongly anti-Folsom. Faulkner, a popular newspaper publisher from a small south-Alabama town, was classified as a moderate progressive. He traveled throughout the state staging "talkathons," at which unrehearsed questions could be asked, and he made extensive use of radio and television.[1]

The biggest issue in the election was Folsom himself. In his previous term as governor, he had strongly supported reform and had threatened the entrenched interests. For this, he was called a dangerous radical by his critics. Others felt that his outlandish behavior had embarrassed the state, and they wanted someone more educated and sophisticated.

Early in the campaign, the opposition tried to make an issue of corruption during the first Folsom administration. He laughed his way out of this, saying, "Sure, I'll admit I did some stealing while I was your governor. But the crowd I worked with, the only way you could get it was to steal it."[2] He generally refused to respond to attacks against him. "My mama always told me," he said, "that if you get mud on a clean white shirt, don't try to rub it off. That just smears it. Let it dry and it'll drop off."

To the shock of everyone, except perhaps Folsom himself, he won the largest primary victory in the state's history. He received 296,000 of a record 575,000 votes and carried sixty-one of the state's sixty-seven counties.

Richmond's Race for Senate. Richmond won his race for state senator in spite of the opposition of the political leaders in Dothan and Houston County. Given the stakes and accepted patterns in Southern politics, one might expect the election to have been rigged against him. Richmond feels that by the late 1940s people in Dothan and the Wiregrass were fed up with the worst abuses. "By the time I ran," he says, "there had been a lot of 'let's clean it up, boys.' The election where Cotton Tom Heflin ran for the U.S. Senate was so raw and so rotten it left a bad taste, and they finally put on the straw that broke the camel's back. The leaders around town said, 'Boys, we can't have any more of that.' The town began to grow a little, and people began to ask why the political power can't be spread around a little bit."

During the election, Richmond became identified as one of the Folsom group. He was not a natural in this role because he was born to privilege and came from a well-to-do family. He recalls how he became identified with Folsom. "Well, he didn't just pick me up; I was sold to him. You see, I had started the hospital fight, and powerful folks in Dothan_some of the Big Mules—had me stopped. Folsom's supporters knew about it. Some of them went to Jim and said, 'We need to take Flowers.' He said, 'Man, I can't use a banker's son.' Lewis Oppert, who was Jim Folsom's area campaign manager, says, 'You've got to trust me. We need to take him and help him build this hospital, and he'll be our man.' So I was sold to Jim Folsom."

The way the association of Flowers with Folsom was made in people's minds is a lesson in practical politics. "He came here for a big rally, and George Wallace was going to introduce him. But they arranged for me to 'introduce my old friend, George Wallace, who in turn will introduce the Governor.' George Wallace, who was from Barbour County, was Jim Folsom's south-Alabama campaign manager in the 1954 election. George was one of the top men in the state who was for Jim Folsom.

"The rally was in the stadium, and there must have been five or six thousand people. Folsom was on the platform before he spoke, and they arranged for me to come down out of the stand where everybody could see me, walk around there, kneel down by him, and have him put his hand on my shoulder like we're just chatting. Puttin' on a show is all we're doing, to show his crowd. Then I introduced George Wallace, and George Wallace introduced him. The crowd just went crazy over Jim, and they took me."

In reminiscing about some of the details of his senate race, Richmond comments on the seriousness with which people in small towns can take their group affiliations. Sometimes a naive candidate can get into trouble without trying, and the best strategy may be to stay silent and try to ride coat tails.

"I went down to Ashford and was going to go up one side of the street and down the other," he recalls. "There's only about two or three blocks downtown, you know. I was going up the street to hand out my cards and ask them to vote for me, and then I was going to go down the other side. A good friend of mine said, 'What in the world are you doing?' 'I was just going to pass out . . .' 'Get out of this town. This town is divided heavier than any town in south Alabama, and if they see you shaking hands on one side of the street, the other side of the street is going to be solidly against you. Now get out of here. We can tie you to the Folsom vote, and you'll get your share and come out a winner. But get out. Quit trying to campaign. Don't make any speeches. Don't hand out any cards. Don't shake hands.'

"I got out of town immediately, and it broke just like he said. I carried the town by a couple of hundred votes. Ashford had the second most votes of any place in the county at that time."

The *Brown* Decision is Announced. On May 17, 1954, only a few days after the primary in which Folsom and Flowers won their respective races, the U.S. Supreme Court announced its landmark decision in *Brown v. Board of Education*. The Court held that segregated schools were inherently unequal and therefore unconstitutional, and it ordered school systems across the country to desegregate "with all deliberate speed," though no means of enforcement was given. This decision reversed the separate-but-equal doctrine of the 1896 *Plessy* decision, at least as the doctrine applied to education.

Race and school desegregation did not become major issues in the 1954 state elections, however. People were not sure what the practical implications of *Brown* would be, and it did not matter anyway since the election that counted had already taken place.

Folsom's Republican opponent tried to make an issue of race in the fall. He stated that the true goal of black activists was not school desegregation, but "racial intermarriage, with a resultant mongrelized civilization."[3] He charged that the ex-governor was a pinko and "soft" on the issue. Folsom refused to be drawn into a debate on it. This rhetoric, from a candidate for the state's top office, helped fan the flames and pointed the way toward the low road which would be taken for a decade by Alabama and its leaders.

Richmond Flowers remembers how Folsom handled the race issue on one occasion. "He closed out his campaign one Saturday night here in Dothan, and someone asked him about the *Brown* decision and segregation. Folsom said, 'Well, you can put it in your platform, but you'll never see me make the good black children of this state go to school with the whites.' Everybody laughed, and he was such a colorful character that he got away with it."

Richmond was among those who did not give the matter much of a second thought. The farthest thing from this young, victorious candidate's mind was the possibility that the Supreme Court action and its aftermath would exert a powerful influence on his life and career. Yet the die was cast at this point. The primary election and the *Brown* announcement, two events which occurred within a few days of each other, merged in their effects in determining the future for Richmond Flowers.

A Young Senator Does Big Things

Richmond Flowers was thirty-six years old when he became a state senator. He developed quickly as an administration leader in the senate despite his freshman status. In the process of fighting for Folsom's legislative program in the senate, he began formulating the attitudes toward civil rights he displayed later as attorney general. As he says, he had never questioned the morality or desirability of segregation and was firmly for maintaining the prevailing system. But events moved him toward the moderate/liberal side of the issue.

Richmond compiled what can only be described as an amazing record for a first-term senator in helping his home town. Not only was the hospital completed, but under his leadership, the state made funds available for two other major projects. A traffic circle was constructed around Dothan, and because of the circle, a major highway was routed through. Also, a farm center with a large coliseum surrounded by an abundant exhibit and show area was constructed. The hospital, traffic circle, and farm center have been three of the major factors responsible for Dothan's growth and its emergence as leader in the Wiregrass region.

Dothan is now the major economic, retailing, and medical center of a large area which includes southeast Alabama, southwest Georgia, and part of the Florida panhandle. The 1990 census showed that Dothan itself had a population of 53,330, and the Dothan Metropolitan Statistical Area had a population of about 131,000.

How did a first-termer compile such a record? He did not do it by himself, of course. It all had to do with playing politics and with knowing the right people. "I was very fortunate that Guy Hardwick was my friend and was lieutenant governor," Richmond observes. "The lieutenant governor appoints all the committees in the senate. Guy appointed me to Finance and Taxation, which is the appropriations committee, to Judiciary, which handles all changes of laws, and he made me chairman of Public Health. These were very powerful appointments for a new senator.

"I was elected by the capital press group as the Outstanding Freshman Senator, but how could I help but be? Guy Hardwick put me on every powerful committee in the senate. And I tended to my business. I worked. Guy told me, 'Richmond, it doesn't make any difference whether you're a freshman or an old-timer. If you'll work, you'll become important right away, because about a third of them run the whole thing. Those are the boys that are working.' And I found it to be just exactly that. The other two-thirds just sit around. So if you're working and hustling, you become a leader right away.

"Another thing that helped was that I became an assistant floor leader for Governor Folsom and got to know him well. I had supported his re-election bid, and I was a strong supporter in the legislature. He returned the favor when he had a chance."

First, the Hospital is Built. The matter that got Richmond into the state senate at this particular time was, of course, the public hospital which he wanted to build, and he went to work on it immediately. The senators cleared the way for the hospital, by introducing what was called a "local bill." "This was a general bill with only local applications," Richmond explains. "It sounded like a general bill, but it was written so that it applied to only one county. We wrote it for counties with populations in a particular range. It was a very narrow range, from just below Houston County's population to just a little above it. Unbeknownst to us, we had caught Geneva County in our bill, but we didn't find out about it until later.

"What we did with the bill was to discharge the entire hospital board and have the governor appoint another one. Then we set up the mechanism to replace them later on. City commissioners would appoint some, and county commissioners would appoint some, but the main thing was to fire every member of the present board. The governor appointed a new board, plus a chairman. Within six months after I took office, the new board selected me as chairman, and we put the hospital under contract. It moved fast. The state had been collecting the tax since the first referendum was passed, so there was more than enough money.

"When it was dedicated, Lister Hill gave me a plaque. He was senior

U.S. senator from Alabama and co-author of the Hill-Burton Act. Jim Folsom was there, and he said, 'If there was any one man responsible for this hospital, you'd have to say it was ole Senator Flowers. Now he had some help. But he was the lead horse.' He loved to use those country expressions. 'He was the lead horse, and he was doing the most pulling.' That was very flattering. I was chairman of the board the first six or seven years the hospital was in existence."

The wording on the plaque given by Lister Hill is:

> To State Senator Richmond McDavid Flowers in whose steadfast vision of a great hospital his people found hope, in whose clear and courageous resolution to realize those hopes his people found leadership, in whose untiring labors for the common good of his people, their common good was achieved; this plaque is affectionately dedicated this 1st Day of September, 1957.
>
> Lister Hill
> United States Senate

"It's now the Southeast Alabama Medical Center," Richmond notes. "At first we called it Southeast Alabama General Hospital. We intended for it to be a regional hospital because we knew the state would never let funds go for us to build a small one. That's one place the opponents kept us at bay. 'We don't need any one hundred beds,' they'd say. 'Fifty beds is big enough.' They knew full well that the state wasn't going to support a small hospital in Dothan. They were going to delay forever. It was built with one hundred beds, and more were added quickly after that. A hundred was barely enough to begin.

"Well, Dothan, with the Medical Center and with Flowers Hospital, is now a regional hub for health care. We are so fortunate to have so many good medical men in here. We have become a leader in this area because we have the equipment and the hospitals. The Medical Center was set up to serve a large region under the original Hill-Burton plan. But it was some kind of a fight. I had enemies and may yet have some left in Dothan. Some of them hated me because of that thing.

"My brother always said there's room for a public and a private hospital in Dothan. There was, and there still is. Oh, they compete, sure.

But they compete about like banks. They don't get in knock-down, drag-outs. They just try to outdo each other from time to time. There's always going to be a little bit of competition when you've got professional staffs, whether they're lawyers, architects, engineers or what. Doctors are no different. They want to have a competitive edge."

Next, A Traffic Circle and a Major Highway. The main highway from Montgomery to Panama City and the Florida panhandle is U.S. 231. This is a major route from the Midwest into Florida and is heavily traveled. Travelers from the north can get to Montgomery by interstate, and they can pick up another interstate about 45 miles south of Dothan. But there is no way to connect these two points except by U.S. highway 231. Dothan gets a great deal of through traffic because of this. The fact that it is 100 miles south of Montgomery and about 100 miles from either Tallahassee or Panama City makes Dothan an ideal rest stop and, for many, a good place to spend the night. Along 231 in Dothan, there are many motels, restaurants, and service stations which contribute substantially to the local economy.

It was not always so. In the early 1950s there was much less traffic, but driving through Dothan was still a slow and irritating process. The state wanted to improve the route, and this posed a threat. As Richmond recalls, "There was a lot of talk about 231 bypassing Dothan, leaving Montgomery and splitting dead between Dothan and Enterprise, and going south from there. Enterprise wasn't happy about that and neither were we, because in those days, we felt that if you bypass a town, it'll shrivel up. So we were trying our best to work out something to keep from building the road in that location. We had the help of a senator from Coffee County at that time, because Enterprise didn't like the location they had picked. Geneva didn't like it, either. It just went into nowhere.

"We wanted the highway to come to Dothan, but what was obstructing us was the Bureau of Public Roads. The governor was willing to four-lane the road to Dothan from the north, and four-lane it on down to the Florida line. But the Bureau of Public Roads would not agree to building up to one side of a city with a four-lane and then picking it up on the other side. Unless you can go through it or around it with four lanes, they won't build the road. Well, 231 came over a two-lane overhead bridge and right through the middle of town. It would have cost a zillion dollars to put four lanes down there.

"So Quinn Flowers, a cousin of mine, came up with this idea for a circle. We used to ride around a lot on Sunday morning, drink coffee, and just mull about politics and what could be, etc., etc. Quinn said, 'If you'll build a circle around this town and move it out, it can be built for much less than trying to take the road through town. Because Dothan is flat, you don't have to have any big cuts, and there is a clay base. You can build roads here cheaper than you can anywhere else. It wouldn't cost half as much as that four lane that's around Montgomery.'

"Quinn told Lewis Oppert, and he told me. Oppert said, 'I believe the highway bureau will buy it. I know the highway director respects me enough that if I tell him it's valid, he'll buy it. I believe this will settle the thing.'

"So from that we jelled into building a circle around Dothan. All the while it was being built, the Bureau of Public Roads kept counting, counting, counting to see how many people drove that way, and of course, long before it was finished they realized it was going to be a huge success. There was opposition to it. The probate judge of this county refused to condemn some land to make a big intersection because he said it took too much property and the circle wasn't needed. What could he be thinking?

"Quinn Flowers had the idea, and Jim Folsom gave the project to me. I was one of his floor leaders in the senate, and I supported everything he promoted. So he gave me the circle. After they started building it, I'd go in his office, and he'd say, 'There's ole Flowers. Let's all stand and sing three verses of "Will the Circle Be Unbroken."' I'd say, 'Just keep 'em rolling, Governor, keep 'em rolling.'"

Governor Folsom used progress on the circle to make sure that Senator Flowers continued to support his programs. "The governor built it in three parts. He built from Headland Avenue to 231 North first, then Headland Avenue to 231 South, then 231 North to 231 South. He wanted to be sure that he didn't commit the whole thing and then have me change my mind and not support him. He knew I wouldn't change my mind after a while, but it took almost the whole administration to complete the thing.

"The circle was named for Ross Clark, Jim Folsom's brother-in-law who sort of raised him. Jim's father died very young. Ross Clark was the husband of his oldest sister, and he always looked after Jim, like a father. He was Jim's campaign manager and his financial advisor. In Jim's first administration, he handled Jim's money.

"After Jim's first term was over, Clark got indicted for tax evasion, and he killed himself. And it broke Jim up. He says, 'Damn 'em. They're after me. Why don't they fight me? Why do they fight my folks?' I was with him in Washington when he heard the news. It broke him all to pieces. Jim had very strong feelings for Ross Clark.

"The third part of the circle was in some doubt. Without a big hurry-up from the highway department, it might not get finished during Folsom's administration, and we were worried. We were up there one time, and Lewis Oppert, who was very close to Jim, says, 'Governor, I want to go ahead and finish that thing, because I want you down there to dedicate it. We want to name it after Ross Clark.' He hadn't mentioned that to me or Quinn or anybody. But, you know, I'm not that much of a dummy. I thought, 'Oh, Lordy! I guess Lewis knows what he's doing.'

"Jim blinked his eyes. He teared up, no doubt about it. He blinked his eyes and said, 'Ole Opery.' His name was Oppert, but Jim never called him anything but Opery. Says, 'Ole Opery really knows how to work a fellow, don't he?' He picked up the telephone and called the highway director and said, 'Finish that damn thing in Dothan, and I mean, as quick as you can!'

"That phone call was to the highway director, and he serves at the governor's pleasure. So we went to work and finished it, and that's why it's called the Ross Clark Circle. Without it, Dothan would have been bypassed so far that we wouldn't catch much traffic, and I'm sure we wouldn't have grown like we've grown."

Finally, a Farm Center with a Coliseum. The third major project which came to Dothan during Richmond's senate term was the Houston County Farm Center. This is the location of more than 100 events each year, including the National Peanut Festival. It occupies fifty acres of land and features a coliseum, exhibit halls, animal barns, and space for outdoor activities. The coliseum covers 40,000 square feet and will seat 5,000 people. It was completed in 1959.

The reason he first got interested in the project, Richmond remembers, was lack of a satisfactory meeting facility in Dothan. "Well, we had meeting after meeting here, and we didn't have any place that would seat a lot of people. We didn't even have the city auditorium then. All we had was that little ole thing down there, the Opera House.

"I wanted a big coliseum. Montgomery already had a coliseum. Well, I couldn't go in and introduce a bill that says Dothan wants a coliseum. So we did it under the guise of a farm center. I called it a Farm Center, a place to put on all of our farm exhibitions and our peanut festival, and so forth. And Emory Solomon, who was a house member from Henry County, joined me. He knocked the opposition off of me right and left, because he was big with the former administration and was almost considered anti-Folsom. He was not, but some of his buddies considered him that.

"He said, 'Boys, y'all got to help me with this thing.' 'Solomon, you gonna help Flowers?' He said, 'No, I'm helping ole Solomon. Henry County needs a place to meet, too. And we shore can't build it in Henry County; there ain't enough folks. If y'all will help me now, Henry County will derive a lot of good.' 'Oh, OK, if you want it, we'll go along with it.' We passed it. Only two have been built in the state. We passed that bill, appropriated that money, and away we went.

"Eustace Bishop, a businessman from Dothan, was up visiting with Guy right after the bill had passed. He was sitting in the big chair next to the lieutenant governor. Eustace laughed and turned around to Guy and said, 'Did you see that rascal? He stole a half-million dollars out of the state treasury for Houston County, didn't he?' Guy said, 'He sure did. That's just exactly what he did.'"

Keeping the Home Fires Burning. Richmond continued to maintain his residence in Dothan when he was in the senate, though his work in Montgomery caused him to spend a lot of time away from home. Mary and the children stayed in Dothan, and Richmond, Jr., began treatment for flat feet.

As things turned out, Richmond's senate work took most of his time. "At that time," he said, "the legislature of Alabama met biennially. We were supposed to have met only in '55 and '57, but we had five special sessions. So I was in and out of Montgomery almost constantly the whole four years I was in office. It was up and back. We had two regular sessions and five special sessions, and I spent very little time at home. I was one of the governor's floor leaders, and he'd call us up there on Monday. The senate would go into session on Tuesday and adjourn on Friday. I'd come home late Friday afternoon or Friday night and go back Monday. It was almost a full-time job.

"I'd go to the office in Dothan on Saturday morning, play golf Saturday afternoon, go to Sunday School and church Sunday morning, play golf Sunday afternoon, go back to Montgomery on Monday. Finally, I quit playing golf. I said, 'I've got a family growing up, and I don't even know them. I'm not spending any time with the children.' I quit playing golf so I could be with them on the weekends."

Richmond was still attempting to maintain a private law practice. "I was by myself in the law practice," he remembers, "and it went to nothing. I just had a Montgomery practice, representing a few people in Montgomery. If you're in the senate, most of the people expect you to represent them for nothing. So I did. And Mary kept the home fires burning."

Richmond is proud of his record as a senator. "I've made a difference in a lot of places," he says. "Had it not been for me and my service when I was in the legislature, we wouldn't have the hospital, the farm center, or the circle around Dothan, because they were strictly political gifts from Jim Folsom."

Reflections on Jim Folsom

James E. Folsom, the governor under whom Richmond served as a state senator, is one of those figures whose image improves with time. Most of the elite of Alabama and those who considered themselves "the nicer people" could not stand him during his successful political years. He acted like an ignorant country hick, they thought, and that was the image they were trying to escape. His behavior embarrassed them, and they feared that he reinforced the worst stereotypes about Alabama.

With the perspective of time, however, the focus can be on more substantive matters. Writers today examine what Big Jim accomplished as governor, they look at his racial attitudes, and they tend generally to be more favorable to him. Jack Bass, for example, states that, "For all his buffoonery, Kissin' Jim was a genuine populist and an advocate of racial tolerance and cooperation."[4] Several writers comment favorably on Big Jim's attempts to steer a moderate course and to fight segregationist hysteria in the legislature.[5] There is no doubt that he was full of compassion for the poor, white or black.

Richmond Flowers is one of his greatest admirers. "I think Jim Folsom was the greatest governor this state has had since I've been old enough to read about and notice politics. He had a program for the underprivileged, for the poor man, for the working man, for the downtrodden, and he passed a good part of it. Jim Folsom had a program, and you knew what it was. We haven't had a governor before or since who campaigned on a platform and then, as soon as he was elected, immediately went to work and tried to put it into law.

"He introduced and passed the first indigent care bill for hospitalization. He put on the first old-age pension. He passed a large bond issue, and he really built up and lengthened the farm-to-market road system. He said, 'Get those people out of the mud. Those people that live back off the main road, they're not going to come to town because if it rains they can't get to the main road. They need some farm-to-market roads.' He stepped up unemployment compensation. He had a welfare program he really believed in.

"It cost money, and he asked for increased taxation to do it, because Alabama has to have a balanced budget. He convinced the legislature and the 'big mules' in the state to go along with a lot of it. They increased the gasoline tax, and they increased cigarette and other luxury taxes. He put in the first hotel/motel tax. He was looking for revenue everywhere he could. He put the taxes before the public saying, 'This is what I campaigned on. This is what I'm going to ask the legislature to do.' Parts of it were killed, but significant parts of it passed."

Folsom as a Campaigner. "Jim Folsom had more natural political ability than any man I ever laid my eyes on," Richmond remembers. "He just had a knack of doing the right thing. He was such an attractive campaigner, a great big mass of a fellow and easy going. He was a big, good-looking guy, and when you put him in a blue suit, it looked like Man Mountain. He had wide shoulders and was very straight and erect, and he had a big beautiful smile.

"Now Jim didn't have any polish. Let's face it. It's hard to say that about a man whom you champion, but Jim had no polish. He was strictly a populist. He could make a nice talk. But in just mixing and mingling he was not polished, and in my opinion, he felt ill at ease among the elite. He sometimes used booze to help him over that."

The thing that irritated people the most about Folsom was his buffoonery in campaigning. He would pull such stunts as taking a nap in the gutter and kissing every female in sight. Richmond acknowledges this and says, "There's no doubt that he did these things, but he understood the 'common man' at the time. Jim could entertain a crowd, and that was all a part of his show. He did a lot of it for publicity. He used to tell the reporters, 'I don't care what you say, just spell the name right.' He could excite the lower class and part of the middle class. But he couldn't sway and charm the rest of the middle class and the upper class. He just wasn't acceptable to the social elite." As Folsom commented, the elite felt that the country folks ought to take their lead from the country club set and show appropriate servility. But the country folks had different ideas—and more votes.

Earning Support by Helping People. According to Richmond, Folsom deserved his second term as governor and would have helped the state had he been elected to a third term. "Jim earned the vote of the people that were supporting him. If he'd stayed away from whiskey, he'd have been governor the third time. But he didn't. It's too bad he wasn't elected one more time.

"Jim always had something extra in his program for old age. Few people realized at that time why the old age group is such a powerful vote. You say, 'Well, how many aged people are there?' But you don't take it all into consideration. A large proportion of those aged people who first got $18 a month under Folsom had to be supported by others. Many young couples who were just starting their families and trying to build a business and get established, they had Aunt Gussie or Uncle Bill or Grandpa or Grandma who had to be looked after. They couldn't just turn them out. So they lived with them.

"Now, if Grandpa can throw in $18 a month, say, by George, that's a help. Grandpa says, 'I'll put mine in. Y'all are supporting me. I'll do what I can to help.' So you're not just going to pick up that elderly voter, you're going to pick up that young couple and their brothers and sisters. Jim knew that, and that's one reason he went after the old age pension so hard."

Labor and the Big Mules. "He was always heavily supported by labor," Richmond recalls, "and I asked him about it once. I was in Washington with him, and we were riding out to Mt. Vernon. He had to go see Mt. Vernon every time he went up there. I said, 'Governor, where in the world did you get your ideas? You were born and raised in Elba, the same part of the country I was. There's no organized labor down there. Where did you get your strong connection with organized labor? '

"He said, 'Senator, you never heard me say organized labor in my life. I always said a working man.' And he slapped me on the leg and said, 'You work don't you?' I answered, 'You're darn right I do, Governor.' He said, 'Now, I'm just for the working man. Now those laborers, just 'cause a fellow belongs to a union don't mean he ain't a working man.' And he said, 'Those are the folks that have to be looked after, Senator.'

"'Don't worry about the big mules. Big mules are going to look after themselves. You can't take nothing away from them they don't want you to take.' He said, 'Big Mules.' He created that expression. He added, 'I don't mean anything derogatory about the power company and the telephone company and the steel company. They are the big mules. Their taxes pull the heavy load.'

Folsom and the Press. Folsom did not get much support from the newspapers in Alabama, particularly in the big cities where reporters considered themselves among the intellectual elite. Richmond remembers a personal experience where being known as one of the Folsom crowd rubbed off. "Grover Hall, of the *Montgomery Advertiser*, said to me, 'You're one of the most attractive faces to appear on Capitol Hill for years, but I don't like your attitude, and I'm going to give you hell every chance I get.' And he told me the truth. Now, isn't that a great attitude for a journalist? He was an editorial writer. I said, 'What are my politics, Grover?' And he said, 'You're just a Goddamned Folsom man.' He hated Jim Folsom so bad.

"To be attractive to those guys, you've got to be obstinate. You've got to be an 'aginner.' You've got to be 'No,' 'Whoa,' 'Hold on.' Don't spend, don't tax, don't do anything. Status quo, status quo.

"Jim Folsom said, 'You can't pay no attention to them lying dailies.' He told Fred Taylor one day, 'Fred, how is that old lying daily of yours getting along?' 'Well, Governor, you'd better pay some attention.' 'Ah, hell, you don't have any influence. I can walk your circulation before dark.' He was talking about the *Birmingham News*, the biggest newspaper in the state. Even Fred laughed at that. 'Governor, you've got to have longer legs than you've got to walk my circulation before dark.'

The Real Political Power. Folsom did a great deal for the common people of Alabama during the two terms he was governor, but according to Richmond, he had very little influence when he was out of office. "The real political power in this state at that time was the Hill-Sparkman machine. Senator Hill was the senior senator, and Senator Sparkman was junior senator. They took control of the state Democratic executive committee and made a Hill-Sparkman machine out of it. They ignored the governor's office because, to them, this was just local stuff. They never fooled with the governor's office, never entered into it, never got caught in it. They were more concerned with national politics and with things like the appointment of federal judges. There was a regular chain of command you would go through to talk to them and get action out of them.

"That was the day when a United States senator could go to Washington and then come home for election, and then go back and come home only for election. They stayed in Washington. They were the political machine, if there was one. Somebody might try to run against them, but they were just about unbeatable.

"At that time, Alabama had what was considered in Washington as one of the strongest delegations up there, because of the men who had served a long time in Congress. They were very, very close. They had their weekly meetings, and every time they could, they voted as a unit. They all voted the same way, and it made them a very formidable organization. They were the real political powers."

Folsom lost popular support during the segregation battles with the legislature during his second term, but he proved he was still a viable candidate in the 1962 gubernatorial campaign, which he lost to George Wallace. As Richmond notes, Big Jim had remarkable powers of recovery. "On both occasions, Jim went out of office very unpopular, and men who ran against him and his administration won. It was Gordon Persons the first time and John Patterson the second time. And both times, he came back very strong four years later."

Done In by Alcohol. Folsom began to indulge heavily in alcohol during his second term as governor, and in the end, it ruined his political career. "He became an alcoholic, in my opinion," says Richmond. "But even if he was not, he was drinking entirely too much. He was leaning on it for support. Every time he was going to make a speech, every time he was going to make an appearance, he felt like he had to have a big shot.

"Those who were around Jim knew in their hearts and minds that he was drinking a little too much, but there were so many people who loved him so much and so genuinely enjoyed being with him. Everybody that went by said, 'Jim, let's have a drink.' 'Okay, boy, get us a drink.' And, that was one of his downfalls.

"I use to see them sit with him and get him drunk or get drunk with him. They would be the very ones the next day you'd hear down at the hotel bragging about 'Me and the governor really hung one on last night.' His so-called beloved friends were the worst enemies he had.

"It'd just break your heart to see whiskey throw him, but it did. I think it was really a loss to the nation, because Jim not only was a populist but was genuinely a humanitarian. He might have helped this nation. He might have been the very one who could have carried us through this black/white situation rather than let it go to violence like it did. He was years ahead of the *Brown* decision on race relations. You know, when Truman got the nomination in '48, everybody thought he couldn't possibly win, but Jim Folsom supported him openly. Every time they'd try to dig with the Dixiecrat rather than a Democrat, he'd say, 'I'm for Harry Truman. Y'all can turn all that other stuff any way you want to, I'm for Harry Truman.'"

In the eight years after the 1962 election, Wallace was in full command. Folsom continued to try, but now his mystique failed him. Richmond remembers sadly, "After he got beat that second time, he ran every four years for something. But Jim wasn't well, and he couldn't campaign. He just simply wasn't well. Booze had gotten to him."

The Montgomery Bus Boycott

One of the most significant events of the era, the Montgomery Bus Boycott, began in December of 1955. The boycott removed any lingering doubts about the seriousness which most blacks felt about civil rights. It focused world attention on the issue, and it accelerated the impact on public opinion and on national resolve to seek a solution. The boycott also gave the movement, the United States, and the world a charismatic new leader in Martin Luther King, Jr.

The Stage is Set. The boycott began in December 1955 after Rosa Parks, an NAACP secretary, refused to vacate her seat on a Montgomery city bus and give it to a white. This was a violation of a city ordinance, and Mrs. Parks was arrested. The NAACP had been looking for a test case in Montgomery to try to relax transportation restrictions, and they asked Mrs. Parks to allow her case to serve this purpose. She agreed.

After the decision to pursue the case, blacks in Montgomery, under the guidance of church leaders, organized the Montgomery Improvement Association to handle details. As MIA president they elected Martin Luther King, Jr., a young minister who had come to Montgomery in 1954 as pastor of the Dexter Avenue Baptist Church and had completed his Ph.D. King and his followers were truly inspired. To provide transportation to boycotters, they set up a very complex organization which located personal automobiles which could be used, drew up schedules and routes, designated loading points, and distributed this information to the thousands of people who were involved. This complex operation was maintained successfully for almost a year despite harassment from the police and the city government.

The boycott was against the Montgomery City Lines, Inc., a subsidiary of a Chicago-based corporation. Before the boycott began, blacks comprised the overwhelming majority of the company's patrons in Montgomery.[6] By the time it was over, the bus company had lost a great deal of money and had a better idea of the importance of black riders to its operations.

King Emerges and Folsom Tries a Moderate Solution. Richmond Flowers had been a state senator for less than a year when the bus boycott started. He had become a floor leader for Governor Folsom during this time and was in close contact with the governor. This put him in position to be involved in steps the state government took to try to resolve the problem. It also gave him the opportunity to become acquainted with Martin Luther King. He remembers his first meeting.

"Well," Richmond recalls, "Martin Luther King's church is within a few hundred feet of the steps of the state capitol, and it was awfully convenient for him to step over to the capitol. Jim Folsom was never one to turn his back. He kept the conference table open. Any time a black wanted to consult with the governor, the governor would see him. Jim always called Reverend King 'Preacher.' He called him 'Preacher' but treated him with reverence.

"I remember the first time I met Martin Luther King, and it shows what customs were in the state. There was Jim Folsom who was supposedly ridiculously soft on the race issue, and yet King, who was waiting to see Folsom, was sitting out in the hall instead of the regular waiting room. They had a bench and a couple of chairs out there. From the hall you went into the governor's reception room, which was very large, and off of it was his executive secretary. Behind that was the governor's office.

"I went down there to see the governor about something, and I saw this black man sitting there. I walked on in, and the reception room was chock full of people. It always was. Jim Folsom always had the folks that just wanted to come shake his hand and see ole Big Jim. The legislature was in session, and he always opened the doors to his legislators, especially his supporters.

"So I walked in, and consulted with his secretary, and she took me right on in. He asked me, 'By the way, did you see Preacher King out there?' I said, 'No.' Then I thought, I said, 'Is he sitting out in the hall?' Jim said, 'Oh, I suppose so. You know how they segregate. They're not going to let him sit in here.' I said, 'Well, I saw a black man out there. I just didn't notice him or didn't recognize him. I'll stop to speak to him on my way back to the senate.' At the back entrance to the senate chamber there's a set of steps that comes out right by the governor's office.

"As I walked out, I introduced myself, and King gave me the great honor of saying, 'Oh yes, Senator, I recognized you.' I said, 'Well, Preacher, I'm sorry that I didn't recognize you. I would certainly have stopped then. I was so intent on what I was going to see the governor about, I walked . . .' 'Oh that's perfectly all right.' That's the first time I met him, and when he went in to talk to the governor, he told him he had met me.

"After that, every time King came over, the governor would just automatically say, 'Get Flowers down here.' Jim liked to pass particulars on to someone else, like all big executives do I suppose—but I wouldn't know, not ever having been one. Jim would make an agreement or he'd have an understanding, and then he'd say, 'All right, now Flowers, you take the Preacher, and you be sure that's carried out.' Then he wanted to put it out of his mind.

"While I didn't do any of the negotiation, I did sit in on the sessions, and Martin Luther King and I were well acquainted. He knew that if he stepped over there unannounced and saw me, I could get word to the governor. That's the way we came to know each other and talk. That's why I was down there the day that they apparently thought they had worked out a solution to the bus boycott.

"I walked back down the hall with him. We went out the front door and stopped on the top of the steps. And we weren't standing a foot from the star where Jeff Davis was sworn in as president of the Confederacy. We were standing there, and he said to me that he'd rather take a beating than go down there to that church and tell his people what he had to tell them that night."

Segregationists Refuse to Compromise—and Create a Cause and a Hero. What had happened was that Montgomery's police commissioner refused to accept the deal that Folsom and King had worked out. The initial demands of those leading the boycott were very limited. At first, all they asked for was 1) A more considerate, first-come, first-served seating arrangement (with whites seating from the front and blacks seating from the rear) so that blacks who were already seated would no longer have to stand up for whites, 2) guarantees that drivers would be more courteous, and 3) hiring of some black drivers. Concession by the establishment on these points would have ended the confrontation with very little change from prevailing practices.

Flowers remembers a session before the boycott began when the issue could have been settled. "Folsom and King were working it out," he remembers, "and King said, 'I'll tell you what we'll do, Governor. I don't believe we can settle it completely. But I'll take your terms and your suggestions if you'll agree with me to meet again in a year and see how it works out. And if we see it isn't working, then you'll agree to consider taking some more of our terms.' And the governor said, 'That's fair enough, what do you want right now?' King said, 'All right, for one year we will load from the rear. We will sit in the rear, but we want our percentage of the seats.'

"You see, the bus company had run surveys. They had qualified people run surveys to see what percentage of the bus population was black and what was white. They had no ax to grind. They wanted to protect their buses, and they were afraid that violence would tear them up. Some of the routes came right through the area where so many blacks lived. The people there had to come downtown to get to work. Even those that had domestic jobs had to come downtown and change buses and go out. And some of the buses that came from the black housing areas or residential areas would run all day long as much as 65 percent black. Governor Folsom was willing to accept the company's survey results, and so was Dr. King.

"King said, 'We'll accept your surveys on these buses, because that seems about right to us. We'll go along with you if you'll give us that percentage of the seats, so that if there's 10 percent of us standing, there'll be 10 percent of the whites standing.' You see, to mark seating areas, they had a little sign that fit into a slot on the seat back. Whites were in front of the sign and blacks were behind. When the whites filled their section up, the driver would just tell the blacks to get up and move to the back of the bus, and he'd move the sign back. And many times, there'd be blacks just crammed and jammed standing up in the back and empty seats up in the white section. That's what they were fussing about.

"King said, 'We will load from the back, and we will ride in the back if you'll give us the percent of the seats that the surveys show is black.' Jim Folsom said it was a deal, and he had his secretary get Montgomery police commissioner Clyde Sellers on the phone. Jim told him we had this thing worked out. The commissioner said, 'What do you mean worked out?' Jim told him the terms. He answered, 'Governor, you tell that damn King I ain't giving no nigger nothin'. There ain't no damn agreement. Make it perfectly clear there ain't goin' to be none. They'll ride the damn bus as we say ride them, or they can just stay off as far as I'm concerned.'"

The police commissioner of Montgomery was newly elected and he was an arch-segregationist who would later join the White Citizens Council at a big rally in front of 15,000 people at Montgomery's Garrett Coliseum. In spite of the very modest demands from the blacks, he and others in the white establishment refused to budge. Montgomery's leaders seemed intent on proving that integration and segregation could not coexist in any fashion. They seemed to fear that pulling one thread would unravel the entire fabric of white supremacy.[7] What they did by their intransigence was to force the struggle to a more intense and more substantive level.

The boycott lasted for a year. It ended in November 1956 when the U.S. Supreme Court held (in *Gayle v. Browder*) that Alabama and

Montgomery statutes which required segregation in intrastate buses were unconstitutional on the ground that they violated the Fourteenth Amendment. The city filed an appeal, but in December the Court specifically ordered bus segregation to end in Montgomery. Blacks voted to end the boycott, and the buses were desegregated peacefully. There were no major incidents, although there had been several bombings, cross-burnings, and beatings associated with the boycott, and a few random shots were fired at buses. At first, whites refused to get on the integrated buses but eventually relented. Black citizens and the civil rights movement had won a major, well-publicized victory.

The Senator is Affected. Richmond credits his experiences with King and with other aspects of the boycott with changing his own feelings. "I realized at the time," he said, "that this thing had to come to an end. Governor Folsom felt that way, and I thoroughly agreed with him."

"Martin Luther King asked me, 'Were you ever a segregationist?' And I said, 'Of course I was. All my life I was. I was raised in a segregated society, and would be less than honest if I didn't admit to you I enjoyed all the emoluments of a segregated society. But things have changed, the law has changed, cultures have changed, habits have changed, and I'm going to do what I can to see that my children are not segregationists, because it will just cause them unhappiness. The strict segregationist is not going to have anything but trouble from here on out.'"

Martin Luther King had no more contact with the Folsom administration after that, and he moved from Montgomery to Atlanta in 1959 and founded the Southern Christian Leadership Conference. Richmond saw him very little after the end of the boycott. "Most of my later conversations with him were at meetings or demonstrations and that sort of thing. I had all sorts of messages indirectly, but he never came to my office again, even after I was attorney general. Stokely Carmichael came to my office and Rap Brown came once, but King never did after he moved. He didn't come back to Alabama a whole lot.

The bus boycott was extremely important in the boost it gave the civil rights movement. It proved to both whites and blacks that blacks could organize and run a very complex organization. It showed that they were serious, dedicated, and disciplined. This greatly raised the level of self-respect among blacks, increased their confidence and reduced their fear, and it motivated them to continue the struggle at a more intense level. The boycott provided for the emergence of Martin Luther King. It made a national figure of him and helped set the course of nonviolent protest which generally held for the next decade.

The boycott broke stereotypes and challenged the notion that the acquiescence of blacks in segregation and racial etiquette meant approval or preference.[8] It shattered the myth among Southern whites that the civil rights movement resulted entirely from outside agitators and that blacks in the South were contented and happy.[9]

Failure of the Moderates. The bus boycott also went a long way toward hardening white opinion in 1956. Several things, such as militant rhetoric on the part of blacks plus the attempts to enroll students in schools caused increased concern. But the bus boycott took it to a new level. Alienation and fear increased during the year, and membership in the White Citizens Councils grew very quickly.

A basic Citizens Council message was that whites must not tolerate liberal (or even moderate) dissent from within, but must stand united against the swelling black tide. Many whites were not convinced of this but were confused as to which course should be taken. Only a tiny fraction were for integration and equal rights, of course, but the majority were law-abiding and wanted things settled peacefully. They wavered for a time, and during this "window of opportunity," strong leadership might have carried the day for moderation. Unfortunately, such leadership was not provided. The moderates hesitated in indecision. They let the radicals take the initiative, and by the time they realized the destructive turn events were taking, it was too late.

Dexter Avenue Baptist Church. Dexter Avenue Baptist Church, where Martin Luther King was pastor and from which the bus boycott was managed, is only one block from the front entrance of the historic state capitol building in Montgomery. The Confederate government was formed in the capitol building in 1861, and Jefferson Davis took the oath of office on its portico. Directly in front of the church, in the middle of the avenue, is a stone monument on which is inscribed, "On this spot, Dixie was played for the first time by a military band." Dexter Avenue Baptist Church, now named the Dexter Avenue King Memorial Baptist Church and still in active service, is now a national historic monument. On looking at it and at the capitol, one is awed by the realization that two events which contributed so significantly to shaping the character of the American people and their government could have occurred in such close proximity in a small Southern town.

Reaction Rules the Day

Historian C. Vann Woodward refers to the civil rights movement after World War II as the "Second Reconstruction," and he divides it into two periods. The first and milder period, from roughly the end of the war until the *Brown* decision, was led by the judicial branch of the federal government and to a lesser extent by the executive branch. There was a good deal of rhetoric, primarily by politicians, about preserving Southern ways and customs, but the race issue did not dominate the political scene.[10] *Brown* moved the Second Reconstruction into its radical period.

Southerners claimed, with some validity, that there had been progress in providing more opportunity for black citizens. The pace was glacial and totally unsatisfactory to blacks and their leaders, however. They were forcing the issue, with increasing prospects of success.

The Forces of Reaction Prepare. The forces of reaction were watching and mobilizing. A special legislative committee, charged with finding ways to preserve segregation in the schools, was set up in 1953 during the Persons administration. Chaired by Albert Boutwell of Birmingham, it was known as the Boutwell Committee, and it continued to operate during the Folsom administration. Boutwell, who was later a leader of the anti-Folsom bloc in the legislature and still later a mayor of Birmingham, was a thorough segregationist.[11]

The committee's report, delivered in the autumn of 1954, outlined the basic legislative approach which would later be followed. The strategy was to delay in every conceivable way and to win by outlasting the opposition. The report encouraged every type of complicated law and regulation to try to tie up the legal system. A new law was to be passed every time an old one was overcome. Group-action lawsuits were to be avoided so that each complaint would have to be tried separately and would prolong actions endlessly. Great care was taken in writing legislation to achieve this result. The belief was that delays would be very expensive to the NAACP and other civil rights organizations and would finally deplete their treasuries. Also, it was felt that the federal government would tire of it and finally give up, as it had in the past.

Members of the legislature urged Governor Persons to call a special session to implement as many of the Committee's recommendations as possible. He was in the final months of his administration, however, and he refused, feeling that there wasn't time and that the matter should be left to his successor, who had already been elected.

In February 1954, the Alabama States Rights Association was formed in Birmingham as a hedge against a possible adverse court decision. It pledged itself to the protection of segregation and states rights and to war against those who would try "to indoctrinate school children with socialism, communism, and race integration."[12]

Marking Time Nervously. After the *Brown* decision was announced in May 1954, there was a year of marking-time until the Supreme Court handed down its decree on implementation. In the Deep South, white responses to *Brown* were overwhelmingly negative. Since Alabama was not a direct party to the suit, however, there was no immediate desegregation of schools, and the segregationists were not yet able to rouse the people to all-out resistance.[13]

Whites had kept saying to themselves and to anyone who would listen, "Just keep outsiders out of it and give us more time. We'll solve the problem in our own way." They convinced themselves that only a few agitators were causing trouble. This was self-delusion, of course, as events were beginning to show. At the state NAACP convention in Selma in November 1954, speeches by local leaders and by civil rights activists from other parts of the country tended to be very militant.[14] Blacks tried to integrate a school in Montgomery in September 1954, and a large number of school boards were petitioned for admission of black students in 1955. The press played these events up, making it more apparent to all that the drive for change was serious.

Second *Brown* Ends the Waiting. The year 1955 turned out to be critical in Alabama. It began with the population nervous but still waiting to see what would happen and hesitant in its actions. It was, of course, the year of the Montgomery Bus Boycott. By year's end, attitudes had hardened, bitter reaction was well on its way toward controlling events in the state, and race had become the overriding political issue. Folsom attempted to steer the state to a moderate course, but, tragically, he proved inadequate to the task.

One of the critical events of the year was announcement of the second *Brown* decision by the Supreme Court on May 31. It dealt with the way in which the original decision was to be enforced. The second *Brown* order was far weaker than the proponents of change had hoped. It referred sympathetically to the "solution of varied local school problems" and noted that this would require time. It placed the responsibility for solving problems on local school authorities, and it charged the federal district courts with the duty of passing upon "good faith implementation."[15] The local school board would bring its desegregation plan and schedules to the district court for approval. If the court considered them unacceptable, it could devise its own desegregation plans.

The decision stated that desegregation should proceed "with all deliberate speed," suggesting to those opposed to change that it could be a very drawn-out process. The South thought it had won a victory, since enforcement of the *Brown* rulings was to be by local judges who could proceed with all deliberate speed. The *Montgomery Advertiser* stated that "there may be as many cases as there are schools in the South." This would mean "generations of litigation."[16] The Supreme Court had tried to do local communities a favor by letting them take responsibility for change. In doing so, it had misjudged the depths of feelings and the intensity with which its ruling would be opposed.

In a move which, as it turned out, had special significance because of the powers given district judges, the Eisenhower administration in October 1955 appointed Frank M. Johnson to be judge of the Middle District of Alabama, which included Montgomery. Johnson was thirty-seven at the time and was the nation's youngest federal judge. He and George Wallace, later to be arch enemies, were in law school together at the University of Alabama in 1941 and 1942 and were friends. Richmond Flowers was in law school at the same time and knew both men.

The Legislature Reacts. The state legislature took its cue from the tone of the Supreme Court's words. Second *Brown* gave the distinct impression that the strategy of delay recommended by the Boutwell Committee would work, and legislation crafted around this idea soon flooded in. Everything else, including the legislative program which was the basis of the governor's landslide victory only a year before, was either shoved to the background or was judged by its relationship to desegregation.

These white Alabama students protesting school desegregation illustrate the racial feelings of the era.

A whole group of segregation bills were presented to the legislature during 1955. One granted broad new powers to local school boards in assigning students. Another empowered the government to do away with public education and to subsidize private schools. Still another allowed school boards to fire any teacher, regardless of status under the tenure law. Others were outrageously unfair and clearly unconstitutional, but this did not seem to deter the politicians. They were playing to a powerful issue, and intentional or not, their actions were contributing to a climate of chaos and defiance of the law. Folsom vetoed or stopped as many of the bills as he could.

The developing temper of the times is illustrated by an incident at the University of Alabama. In May 1955, psychology professor Vernon Sims was accused by parents of a female student of teaching that integration was not harmful and that segregation was unconstitutional. The coed's father wrote to *Alabama Magazine*, then a white supremacy-leaning publication, and for a time the magazine raised a tempest about the matter. Sims had been on the faculty for 27 years and was widely respected. The trustees stood by him, and the matter quickly died.

By 1956, the lights of reason, toleration and moderation were all but out. According to C. Vann Woodward, "Negrophobia" had taken hold.[17] A moderate by then was one who opposed violence, and an extremist was one who favored compliance with the law.

In January 1956, the Alabama House, in a resort to an ancient and discredited precept, passed a resolution stating that the *Brown* decision was null and void and of no effect in Alabama. The pre-Civil War doctrines of interposition and nullification had been resurrected in the struggle to fight desegregation.

These doctrines held that a state could interpose itself between its own legal apparatus and that of the federal government when it decided the federal government had exceeded its authority. In this way, the theory held, a state could nullify any federal action it chose. This could only be true, of course, if individual states were superior to the federal government, and that question was settled forever by the Civil War. Educated people knew that the doctrines had no legal standing and could have no lasting effect. Laws based on them made good emotional propaganda, however, and might succeed in causing delay because of the necessity of court action to refute them.

Folsom reacted strongly and refused to sign the resolution. He dismissed it as "hogwash." "It reminds me of an old hound dog hollering at the moon," he said.[18]

Wallace Breaks with Folsom. Early in 1956, George Wallace decided it was time to break with Folsom, who had been his mentor. Wallace had a burning desire from an early time to be governor, and he put enormous time and energy into achieving this aim.[19] Wallace was first elected to the legislature in 1946, and during his early years there, he was a leading liberal. A member of the Persons administration says that Wallace was regarded as a dangerous left-winger.

Richmond remembers that "George was a screaming liberal when we were in law school. I sat with him in a good many classes. I'd ask him, 'George, where in the world did you get all of those ideas?' He'd say, 'Rich, you've got to keep up. That's what the folks want, man.' I said, 'But George, you were born and raised right down there in Barbour County.' He just said what the people wanted to hear."

In the 1954 election, when he was Folsom's south Alabama campaign manager, Wallace was circuit judge in his home district, which included Barbour, Bullock, and Dale counties. He had won the post in 1951 when, at age thirty-two, he had become the state's youngest trial judge. The term ended in 1958, and he planned to run for governor. He had been a strong Folsom admirer and supporter and had patterned his campaigns after those of the governor.

As Folsom's fortunes fell, Wallace became more and more uncomfortable with his close association. He began to feel he had to break with Folsom to protect his own political fortunes. This decision became final after an uproar which resulted when Folsom invited black Congressman Adam Clayton Powell of New York into the governor's mansion for a drink. Wallace looked for an excuse to break.

Richmond remembers well the incident which provided the excuse. "When George was elected circuit judge, he ran against Judge Clayton, who was from one of the oldest families in Barbour County, and they drew knives. It was a rough, ugly election, and George won. Well, they had a county commissioner to die, and George asked Folsom to appoint one of his supporters.

"Now, the son of the county commissioner wanted to be appointed, and he brought a letter to Montgomery that Jim had written his father thanking him for his help in the campaign. 'You come to Montgomery any time you want to,' the letter said. 'I am indebted to you, and I will be glad to show you any preference I possibly can.' This young man asked to be appointed.

"I was working on some legislation for one of Jim's programs and was talking to House members from Henry and Barbour counties, trying to get them to vote for the bill. They were sort of pro and con. Finally one of them said, 'Rich, I believe I'll go with him, and I believe that Sim will vote for the governor's bill if he'll appoint Joel Robinson to that County Commission post over there.' And he showed me a copy of the letter. "I said, 'Well, I'll go see him right now. I won't wait until morning.' I called the mansion, and said, 'How about me bringing these two fellows out there?' Jim said, 'Yes, sir. You bring them right on out.'

"So the three of us rode out to the mansion, and we shook hands and had a drink, of course, and Jim said, 'Well, it's his, especially if you boys will go along with my bill tomorrow.' They said, 'Governor, will you announce it first thing in the morning?' He said, 'Sure I will. I know both of you. If you say you'll do something, you'll do it.' They said, 'Yes, sir.

There's no doubt. But we'd like for it to be announced in the morning.'

"They knew George Wallace was coming up there to raise sand about it. This boy had opposed George in his race for circuit judge, and his family had generally opposed the Wallaces in the county. The two legislators knew that George was coming, and they were afraid that, as powerful as he was with Folsom, he might block the nomination they wanted. When George got to Montgomery the next morning, it was in the paper. Jim had announced it.

"Well, George was walking the floor down at the Jeff Davis Hotel before the legislature went into session that day. Foots Clement (a close political ally of Lister Hill) was sitting on one of the couches. And George was in the lobby just raising sand, just cussing Jim Folsom for everything in the world. Foots called him over and asked, 'George, what's your trouble?' He said, 'Foots, that no-good, big footed, you know what (just profaned him to beat the band) that double-dealing double-crossing . . . '

"Foots said, 'Wait a minute, George, sit down.' I was talking to Foots when he called George over, and I heard it all. He said, 'Sit down, George. Cool off. Now, what's the matter?' And George said, 'I'm through with him. That man fought me like a tiger in my own county, and now Jim's appointed him to a position. I'll never have anything else to do with him.'

"Foots said, 'Now wait a minute, George. You're too good a politician for that. Don't split with him over an appointment because you'll be just another disappointed small-town politician. If you really want to split with him, pick an issue. Fight him on an issue, George. Can you think of anything that you differ with Jim politically on?' George says, 'Well, he's weak as hell on the nigger proposition.' Foot said, 'Well, that's it. Take him on. If you're gonna denounce him, denounce him on an issue.'

"It was about three days later that the fighting little judge made that statement that he was going to lock up any FBI man that came in his county. And just a few weeks after that he got in a confrontation with Judge Johnson and said he wasn't going to give him any of the voting records of Bullock County.

"George split with Jim right there. And George was the 'great segregator' after that, because Jim never was. Jim, as George said, was 'soft' on the race issue. When I think back about how they worshiped George for being such a segregationist, it was all a political game. He was mad because he had been whipped in a little contest. George never talked to Folsom about it and was never friendly with him again. He split with him and began to really bad-mouth him after that. He said Jim was soft on the niggers. George never called a black anything but a 'nigger.'"

Autherine Lucy and the University of Alabama. The first court test of second *Brown* decision ruling, that district judges should preside over the desegregation process, involved the attempt to enroll Autherine Lucy at the University of Alabama. The original suit was filed in 1953. A district court ruled that Miss Lucy should be admitted, and the case went all the way to the U.S. Supreme Court, which upheld the district court. The university was ordered to admit Miss Lucy in February 1956, at the beginning of the spring semester.

Violence erupted quickly after Miss Lucy enrolled and tried to attend class. Those trying to obey the ruling were caught by surprise and were unprepared. The first violence was by students, but they were soon replaced by outsiders. Within two days, the crowds on campus had grown to more than two thousand, most of whom were blue-collar workers at factories around Tuscaloosa. This mob threatened Miss Lucy's life and caused major disorder on the campus. Lucy was suspended at this point for her own protection, and then she was permanently expelled after her attorneys entered and lost a suit in which they alleged that university officials conspired to prevent her from attending class.

Mob violence carried the day, and it was a dark day indeed for Alabama. After more than a thousand cases of admission of black students to formerly all-white colleges in the South, this was the first instance of violence.[20] The hard-liners were encouraged because they had taken a violent stand, had disobeyed the law with impunity, and had won. This suggested that they could get by with the worst kinds of disorder.

The Lucy case drew considerable national publicity, and it led to a reassessment by federal officials and civil rights leaders of the difficulties which lay ahead. Expectations that the South would quietly accept desegregation were reexamined. The federal government, which had based its approach on the assumption that change would come slowly and peacefully, was taken by surprise. Many people began to realize that stronger action was needed if the *Brown* decision was to be enforced.

One by-product of the Lucy incident was an increasing attempt at thought control in higher education. News reports had indicated that certain faculty members favored integration, and with the Sims incident cited earlier still in mind, the right wingers figured that college teachers could not be trusted. Every college had a Citizens Council chapter on campus or in a town nearby, and there was a constant watch on the way that such topics as "integration" and "socialism" were handled. Within eighteen months of the Lucy affair, more than thirty faculty members had left the University of Alabama. More generally, it was a time when the Citizens Councils and their fellow travelers attempted "intellectual strait-jacketing" among all citizens and when many responsible citizens were "terrorized into silence."[21]

White Citizens Councils: The Decent Man's Alternative to the Klan. An early white response to the *Brown* decision was the Citizens Councils, which were first organized as an alternative to the Ku Klux Klan for the "respectable," law-abiding citizen. Their stated purpose was to organize resistance to desegregation efforts and to protect the "Southern Way of Life." The first chapter was founded late in 1954 in Indianola, Mississippi.

The Councils claimed that desegregation was part of a huge international conspiracy to promote communism, and that Communists wanted racial amalgamation to weaken the American people. The Councils proclaimed themselves against violence. Rather, they advocated intense economic pressure against blacks and social ostracism to influence behavior in desired directions,[22] and they were particularly concerned with preventing black registration and voting.

Citizens Councils did not attract many members in Alabama in 1954. During the next year, however, as events unfolded and attitudes hardened, the Citizens Councils made great inroads among working men. Perceptive politicians took their cues quickly. In February 1956, an Association of Citizens Councils of Alabama was formed, and a massive Council rally attended by 15,000 was staged in the state auditorium in Montgomery. Some of the leading members of the state legislature attended. Senator James Eastland of Mississippi was the major speaker, and he railed against communism, integration, and the civil rights movement. The Citizens Councils grew very fast in Alabama after that, and most observers credit them with helping to incite the population.

Richmond Flowers says that, in the beginning at least, there was a big difference between the Councils and the Klan. "The Council was not violent at first," he says. "They just wanted to do whatever they could to maintain segregation. Sam Engelhardt, one of our leading senators, was a member. He was the one who introduced a hotel segregation bill. He came around here one day and said, 'I just found out that we haven't got a law on our books to keep niggers from registering in hotels. Sign this.' Sam and his friends never called them blacks, they never called them colored, they called them 'niggers.'

"I said, 'Wait a minute, Sam. How many of them have tried to register?' 'Well, none yet, but as soon as they find out.' I said, 'Sam, soon as you drop that bill, they're going to try to register in every city in this state.' And shore enough, they did. I didn't sign it. But he didn't fall out with me about that. He just felt I was a little more liberal than he was."

Engelhardt was a wealthy landowner from Macon County who had been in the state legislature since 1950. He was a leader in fashioning Alabama's response to federal desegregation efforts. Engelhardt became executive secretary of the Association of Citizens Councils when it was formed in 1956. By late 1957, however, he cut his ties with the organization as it became more violent and Klan-like.

The New Face of Politics. An election for delegates to the 1956 Democratic National Convention was held in the spring, and Folsom ran for the post of Democratic National Committeeman. As governor and a staunch Democratic loyalist, he would normally have been a committeeman and one of the leaders of the delegation. During the election, the Citizen's Councils conducted a survey of the racial views of candidates. Folsom said, "I answer only to the people and not to haters and baiters."[23]

In the election which followed, he suffered the worst defeat of his political career. Segregationist Charles McKay beat him by a margin of 232,751 to 79,644. McKay won majorities in sixty-four of the sixty-seven counties in the state. This indicated clearly the low estate in public opinion which Folsom's stand on the race issue, broadcast widely by the Councils, had taken him. George Wallace, who as a loyalist Democrat refused to walk out of the 1948 convention, had modified his public image sufficiently to be elected. These results demonstrated to Alabama politicians that support for segregation was becoming a prerequisite for political success.[24] The rhetoric became stronger and the sides polarized further.

In March, the Alabama House passed a resolution to encourage and finance the emigration of blacks to Northern and Western states. Folsom fought this bit of silliness and managed to get the resolution repealed. In April, the Interracial Committee of the Jefferson County Coordinating Council, which had been organized to try to lead the state's largest county in a progressive direction, dissolved itself under pressure from the Citizens Councils.

In July 1956, a "Declaration of Constitutional Principles" was introduced to Congress by Georgia Senator Richard Russell. Coauthors included Strom Thurmond of South Carolina, John Stennis of Mississippi, and Sam Ervin of North Carolina. Later known as the "Southern Manifesto," the document criticized *Brown* as a usurpation of power by the judicial branch of government. It said that public education in some states could be destroyed as a result, claimed that the action was taken without regard to the consent of the governed, and urged reversal of *Brown*. The Manifesto was signed by 101 of the 128 members of Congress from the eleven former Confederate States, including Senators Hill and Sparkman of Alabama and all Alabama Congressmen. In a speech from the Senate floor, Virginia Senator Harry F. Byrd called for massive resistance.

These actions gave comfort and encouragement to the radicals because they suggested that court decisions following from *Brown* were not legally binding and that the law related to civil rights could be flouted. As Woodward notes, such signals from the upper ranks of society were interpreted in the lower ranks as authorizing revivals of "Ku Kluxery," violence against black people, and various acts of terror.[25]

The race issue had clearly gained great political power. Both Alabama senators had previously been known as liberals,[26] and Lister Hill had been a friend of Franklin Roosevelt and a staunch supporter of the New Deal. Hill recognized the shift in the political winds. Not only did he sign the Southern Manifesto, he fought against extending the life of the Civil Rights Commission and participated in filibusters against other civil rights legislation.

Violence Increases. One of the disturbing trends in 1956 was the increase in violence. The KKK was riding again and was growing in membership and popularity. Bombs were going off and dissenters were being beaten. In January 1957, there were six bomb explosions in Birmingham, four at black churches and two at the homes of prominent black civil rights leaders.

One of the most despicable acts of the whole era occurred in September 1957. Five members of the Klan drove to a black section of Birmingham. They randomly picked Edward "Judge" Aaron, a 34-year-old black veteran. They seized him, drove back to their meeting hall, and castrated him with razor blades they had bought at a nearby store. They poured gasoline on the wounds and drove to a remote location where they threw him out. He survived, but the incident disturbed even the conservatives, who were afraid that "the good fight" was being compromised by such actions.

In August, Congress reacted to the worsening situation by passing the Civil Rights Act of 1957, the first civil rights legislation of the twentieth century. The act was greatly weakened by Southern congressmen and by the fact that the Eisenhower administration did not support it very forcefully. It was significant because it indicated that the legislative branch of the federal government was finally becoming involved with the issue. The act set up a Civil Rights Commission, and it provided that a black who thought he was denied the right to vote could apply in writing to the attorney general, who would then move on the case.

Little Rock—Eisenhower Finally Acts. In September 1957, the executive branch of the federal government was finally moved to action. Central High School in Little Rock, Arkansas, had been ordered integrated at the beginning of the fall term, and little trouble was anticipated. However, Governor Orval Faubus of Arkansas, who had earlier been a moderate, stationed Arkansas National Guardsmen around Central High to prevent integration. Spurred on by his action, mobs gathered at the school on the day the black students were to try to register. Major violence was clearly a possibility.

President Eisenhower surprised everyone by taking strong action. The National Guard, already on the scene, was nationalized, and additional federal troops were brought in. The school was integrated, and order was maintained. This event was traumatic for the segregationists, for it showed that the federal government would act with regard to the issue, and with force. It demonstrated (again) that the federal will and power could not be successfully opposed by state or local officers, if it were applied with sufficient vigor and supported by federal court decisions.

The Radicals Prevail. The year 1958 was the last year of Folsom's second term as governor and of Richmond's term as senator. An incident in Birmingham illustrates the prevailing climate. Physician James Butler was selected as Birmingham's "Citizen of the Year" in 1958. He wrote to a newspaper stating that as a healer and citizen, he felt an equal obligation to all people regardless of race. He received hundreds of letters and telephone calls, most calling him a Communist and traitor. He was threatened with death, and someone shot into his living room.[27]

By this time, the die was cast. Scores of court decisions involving school segregation cases had been rendered, and in every one the lower courts upheld the Supreme Court ruling that enforced segregation was unconstitutional. Segregationists watched this with growing dismay and realized that they were in for a long, determined fight.[28] The radical period of the Second Reconstruction, which was marked by massive Southern resistance and by violence and lawlessness, was under way. Moderation died and race became an obsession in Alabama and other Deep South states.

It is clear, with the benefit of hindsight, that the federal government made a big mistake early by not stating and demonstrating in clear, unmistakable terms that the law *was* going to be enforced. Nobody in authority, North or South, anticipated the intensity of the response. But the course that was taken at first, sympathetic to local communities in its intentions, had the unfortunate effect of encouraging resistance and lawlessness.

Richmond Tries for Attorney General And George Learns a Lesson

The 1958 Gubernatorial Race. The gubernatorial race in 1958 began with fourteen candidates, all promising to maintain segregation. Alabama now had 55,000 black voters registered. This was substantial growth, but it was still too small to affect the outcome of a statewide election or to influence seriously the campaigning of candidates.

The two who emerged as strongest and who met in a runoff election were Attorney General John Patterson and Circuit Judge George Wallace. Patterson had shown himself a hard-line segregationist the previous four years, and he made strong statements on race during the campaign. While generally maintaining a low-profile during the runoff, he portrayed Wallace as soft on segregation, and he refused to disavow Klan support.[29] Patterson spoke successfully to the passions and prejudices of the average voter.

Wallace had switched from his moderate position only two years before, and he was still learning how to play the hard segregationist game. In the 1958 race, Wallace openly refused Klan support, and he made a big issue of Patterson's presumed association with the KKK, a topic raised repeatedly by the *Montgomery Advertiser*.[30] Wallace tried to maintain decorum and to use language befitting a graduate of the state's top law school.[31]

During his last year as circuit judge, Wallace had made every bold pronouncement he could in anticipation of the governor's race. He tried to paint himself as a staunch segregationist and to get publicity on this count. He claimed to defy the Civil Rights Commission by denying it access to voter registration records in Barbour and Bullock counties. Judge Johnson issued a show-cause criminal contempt order against Wallace but later dropped it because Wallace, in fact, made the records available. He gave them to a grand jury and then told the Commission where to find them. Wallace wanted the contempt hearing to proceed so that he could be seen as a martyr and could gain publicity. Johnson, however, figured out his game and outmaneuvered him. Wallace was furious.

Patterson played the hard-line game more effectively and won the election. Wallace was second, and he took the defeat with bitterness. Richmond recalls that this experience led to one of Wallace's more famous statements. "George had got beat because John Patterson came across as even a bigger segregationist during the campaign. That's when George said, 'I'll never be out-niggered again.' At that point, George became the champion race-baiter of them all. He said, 'I'll never be out-niggered again.' And he wasn't."

Richmond Tries and Develops. Richmond Flowers made his first race for attorney general in the 1958 election, and he lost. "At that time, you could not succeed yourself in the senate," he explains, "so I ran for attorney general. I set up these speeches and began to visit here and visit there, and be pleasant here and be seen there. I just wanted to be seen where crowds were and to speak when I could. I was a good storyteller and very much in demand for speeches, in club meetings and churches and even in bars and lounges.

"MacDonald Gallion was my opponent. He'd worked in the attorney general's office for years and years, and he was an assistant attorney general at the time of the election. He had run once before, so I was pretty much in a no-win situation and knew it. But in those days most everybody that ran statewide would run one time to run again. They'd run for identification. That's what I did. I said, 'I'm going to get out there and get seen as best I can, then for four years I'm gonna campaign right. Campaign, shake hands and smile and be attractive this first time and just meet folks.' I was just getting them to know me. And it worked because I was elected four years later.

"I lost by about 40,000 votes. I didn't make a bad showing at all. I wasn't the least bit disappointed in my showing because I was unheard of, totally and completely. I'd been in the senate, but there are so many people that serve in the legislature. They live there in Montgomery for a summer and see their names in the *Montgomery Advertiser*, and they don't realize that those folks up in Albertville and Marshall County and Madison County and Florence, Sheffield, Tuscumbia, and all those, they never heard of them. I thought everybody in the world knew the senator from Houston County, and I got up there and found out during the campaign they didn't even know who their own senator was, let alone the senator from Houston County."

Richmond learned some important things about statewide campaigning during the 1958 race. One was to spend as little time as possible traveling. "Alabama is set up peculiarly in the fact that a big part of its vote is in the north," he says. "The first time I ran, I would go up to north Alabama, and then I would come home. One lesson I learned was that I was spending half my time driving to north Alabama and driving home. Dothan's just too far away.

"I didn't know any better. I'd leave here on Monday morning, and it'd be Monday afternoon before I got anywhere in north Alabama. We'd meet and try to campaign. And then late Friday afternoon or early

Saturday morning, I'd take off for Dothan. Then Monday morning I'd go back. I realized that was a mistake. So the next time, I centered in north Alabama."

He also learned again the importance of visiting rural locations, talking to people, and asking directly for their vote. "They didn't care whether or not a person had been in the senate. What mattered was to impress on them that 'I shore would like to have this job, and if you don't have any special choice, how about please voting for me?' You put it on that basis, and get to enough of them, they will vote for you because they don't care who the attorney general is. If they haven't got some friend running, they'll say, 'I'm going to vote for ole Flowers. He asked me to. He was up here to the Rotary Club. He was up here to the Lions Club. He spoke to our Chamber of Commerce.'

"I spoke to a Chamber of Commerce meeting one night when there were fifteen people there. It was over in a little settlement between Troy and Eufaula. Their Chamber of Commerce invited me up there, and the members and their wives made about fifteen people. But I got all the votes in that area. Nobody else would go in there.

"In north Alabama, we stayed out of the cities and went to those small towns, where nobody would go. The first set-up they threw for me was just south of Gadsden. They set up on a crossroads. There was nobody there, and I asked, 'Boys, who are we talking to?' They said, 'That's all right. You just get on up there and make a talk.' So one of my helpers sang his songs. One or two cars came by, and they sorta stopped curiously to see what was going on. They heard some music. By the time I spoke there may have been twelve or fifteen people that stopped to hear me, and they passed pleasantries. 'I'll shore keep ya in mind, Flowers. Appreciate your coming up.'

"My helpers told me, 'Now go in that store and leave some literature.' I said, 'Boys, you know this literature costs money.' 'Do what we say; go ahead.' So I went in there. A fellow said, 'Set some down over there. By George, we appreciate folks coming to see us out here.' And one of the boys from Gadsden said, 'Ask him how many people vote out here.' I said, 'Is this a polling place here?' 'Oh, yes sir, we've got a nice box here.' 'How many people vote here?' He says, '450.' I hadn't seen a soul.

"That's the way rural north Alabama is. You don't see the people, but they are there. And that was one box I checked. I just about got them all. It was purely and simply, 'Hey, y'all look after this fellow. He come by here the other day and put on a little show and shook all the hands. Look after this here fellow. He's our friend.' And they went in there and voted. I bet you I got over 350 votes, and my opponent got practically nothing in that box. There's another thing; everybody in north Alabama votes."

Richmond stayed away from the race issue during the campaign. He was still for segregation, though compared to Patterson and other candidates, he was "soft" on the issue. When it came up, he would say something like, "We have to try to preserve our way of life," and then move into the humorous vein in which he excelled. He soon discovered that he could get campaign mileage out of his old-time oratory, and he worked on making this approach more effective.

Richmond lost the election, but he had developed his style and an effective way of campaigning. He had met a lot of people and made a good impression, and with the size of his vote, he was confident that he could win the next time. He set his sights on the 1962 election.

6

FOUR YEARS OF CAMPAIGNING WHILE CIVIL RIGHTS ACTION INCREASES

Between Campaigns

Richmond Flowers had liked being a state senator and holding a position of power and influence in the Folsom administration. He enjoyed politics and knew he was good at it. Politics was now his profession, and he was intent on going as far in it as he possibly could.

After his defeat in the 1958 race for attorney general, he found himself in the awkward position of being out of office. He did not intend to stay that way long. He knew that a first defeat wasn't particularly harmful to his re-election chances. The '58 race produced a considerable benefit, in fact, by increasing his name recognition throughout the state. A second defeat would be much more serious, and he started to work immediately to be sure it didn't happen.

The civil rights movement had reached new levels of organization and determination by the beginning of 1959 when Richmond left the state senate, and the stage was set for some of the most dramatic events of that era. The next four years saw the sit-ins and the Freedom Rides. Martin Luther King and the Southern Christian Leadership Conference honed and demonstrated their ability to highlight injustices and to sway the nation's conscience. Kennedy's election in 1960 left no doubt that life had changed and there was no going back to separate but equal.

The majority in most of the Southern states realized during the 1958-1962 period that at least some of the black demands for equality had to be met. Most realized that defiance and violence of the Little Rock variety were harmful to everyone, so steps were taken by those in authority to bring about the necessary social change. Alabama, however, choose to continue the hard line. Governor Patterson never softened his rhetoric nor his approach, even though business leaders in the state began to pressure him to do so.

Richmond Flowers wanted to run again for attorney general, but meanwhile, he had no income and he had to make a living for his family. "Those were some pretty hard times finance-wise," he remembers, "because my income was down, and to get myself better known, I was covering the state out of Dothan. Now that's hard to do. I practiced a little law, just enough to make expenses.

"The year I began to run for attorney general, the local bar association elected me vice-president, which is the incoming president. They did that for me so I could say I was the president-elect of the Houston County Bar Association.

"Earlier, I started an insurance agency with Buck Flowers, a cousin of mine. It's still going as Flowers Insurance Agency. I sold life insurance for a while before I ran for the senate, and then Buck and I opened up the agency. We had a full line casualty and life agency, and we ran it about four years. The whole time I was in the senate we were starting that agency up. When I was off and gone, of course, he was running it. Later, I gave him my half of it."

Running for Office. Unofficially. Richmond believed that his primary need with regard to his political career was to gain greater recognition in Alabama and to make a good impression. He started immediately to make public appearances all over the state. He stayed in touch with old friends. "Governor Folsom went back to Cullman," he says, "and we'd hear from him from time to time. He'd come by on his way to the mineral springs at Cottonwood. He was planning to run for governor again. Another thing I did during the four years was to lobby in the legislature. When the legislature was in session, I spent a lot of time in Montgomery.

He was not officially a candidate. Formal filing would come much closer to the election. He was campaigning, nevertheless, "just as hard as

I could campaign. I hit the ground running after I got beat. I was considered an outstanding story teller, and I capitalized on it. Those four years were a very integral part of my becoming attorney general.

"I made these very humorous speeches with little substance to them. I spoke everywhere, every time I could get a Lion's Club or Rotary Club or Kiwanis Club and especially at ladies night. That's when I would put on what I called my twenty-five and five. I would just thoroughly entertain the ladies, after they came expecting to be bored to death. I would send my topic, and it would be some of the dullest stuff you ever heard, like 'How the Common Market Will Affect the Prosperity and Progress of Your Community' and so on.

"The women would say, 'O Lord, how boring is this fellow going to be?' and then I'd tell twenty or twenty-five minutes of stories. They were 90 percent dialect stories because I could handle the black dialect. Then I would end up saying, 'Now having covered my subject, I appreciate the opportunity of being here with you', and then make a nice bow-out and everybody loved it. They had been thoroughly entertained for the evening.

"They were just tickled to death to have a successful program, because getting programs for civic clubs is hard work. I always prided myself that I dressed immaculately, and I wasn't too unattractive and could speak. I could handle the King's English, and I used my jokes. I always ended on a serious note with a very dramatic ending, and, oh, they just ate it up. Just ate it alive."

The Campaigning Technique Evolves. This may seem an unusual way to conduct a political campaign, but it was no accident. The technique had been carefully evolved and was based on Richmond's experiences in attending banquets and on his observations of the ways of voters.

It all began early on in Dothan. "The first annual meeting of the bar association I attended," he remembers, "everybody brought their wives. I took Mary. Some dummy asked the chief justice to speak, and the chief justice not only bored hell out of the lawyers on some technical subject all night, but Mary doesn't even know what he said, what he looked like, or anything else. The women were just bored to death. And I took a lesson from that. I said I can beat that; I'm going to entertain the ladies. I'm going to give them something to remember. I made up my mind that

I was going to be just as attractive as I could possibly be and entertain them. They'll remember it when I come back through asking for votes.

"I would always say that I was a candidate before, and chances are I'll be a candidate again. They'd all come up to congratulate me, and say, 'I don't see how in the world you lost.' I'd say, 'I can give you the secret if you won't let it go any further. It wasn't really publicized, but the main reason I didn't get elected, I didn't get enough votes.' And they'd say, 'Oh, you're just a mess. I'm gonna vote for you next time.' And they did.

"That four years I was out of office, I really did work. I specialized in the smaller towns in the highly populated areas, and I covered this state. Of course, you have to get an invitation. But when the word gets out that you're available and that you're entertaining and you don't charge, the invitations will come. I let it be known that I was available, especially for ladies' nights. And I got phone calls and letters. That's another thing about north Alabama. You speak in one town, and they're going to hear about it for fifty miles around, and they'll invite you. I'd take them all, especially if I could line one up one night and another the next night. I'd just go up there and stay. You have to stay away from Wednesdays in some of those communities because of prayer meeting and church. But Mondays, Tuesdays, Thursdays, and Fridays, they were big.

"Most of those clubs would want to pay me an honorarium or my expenses, but I didn't take any money for expenses. If they offered me an honorarium, I'd usually tell them, 'I appreciate it, but if you want to give me anything, just send it to the Methodist orphanage in Selma.' That went over big. Then I would ask them, 'Do you know of any other meetings close to you where I could make another speech?' 'Yeah,' they'd say, 'twenty or thirty miles over there I got a friend, and I know they're looking for a speaker.' 'Well, how about calling them and suggesting me.'

"I had a great big map in my office. And I tacked it out to see that I had geographically covered this state. I would call some of these people that were going to campaign with me. If there was an area there where I had not been, I'd call them. I had one man helping me who had gone to Auburn. He was a big worker in the Auburn Alumni Association, and he knew folks all over this state. I had another helping who was the same way with the University of Alabama. So I'll call them and say I need some speeches in a certain area. 'Oh yeah, I know ole so-and-so up there at so-

and-so, and I know so-and-so.' They'd know a half a dozen folks and they'd call them.

"I was putting my image out there as a fine contender and a new face on the political horizon. You speak to the elite when you go into these civic clubs or chambers of commerce. You're going to get some radio coverage, and if you wanted to, you could go by the local newspaper in the afternoon, and they'd be tickled to death to interview you because you're speaking here tonight. Just about everybody had a weekly, and you'd get a little coverage."

Carl Goggins, Chief Assistant. Richmond's chief assistant during this period was a Dothan friend who got little more than companionship for his efforts. "I had this friend who traveled with me," Richmond recalls. "Carl Goggins was his name, and he ran the weekly newspaper, the *Houston Herald*. Carl was just as hard up as I was. I had a credit card, and that's about all.

"We'd leave here some time on Monday or Tuesday, and his paper would go out on Thursday. It had to go to press on Wednesday night. He would stay on the phone a good bit with his helpers, and they'd put it out for him. Then we'd usually come back in here on Thursday or Friday.

"We'd get back and he'd come by the office and say, 'Rich, let me have ten dollars. I want to go to Panama City this weekend.' I'd say, 'Carl, I haven't got ten dollars, buddy. Besides we got to go next week to so-and-so, and I've got to pay a motel bill there. I can let you have five.' 'All right, give me five.' He'd go to Panama City with five dollars. A friend of ours had a cottage down there, a big, typical summer cottage with a big porch on it and swings. He'd let Carl sleep on his porch. So Carl would go down there and drink a little beer. Beer didn't cost too much then—twenty-five or thirty cents, you know. He'd drink a little beer, sleep on the porch, and come back. Monday, we'd strike out again. Go somewhere, make another speech. He stayed with me most of the time."

Big Jim and Joking Your Way into Office. Richmond remembers with fondness an incident involving Big Jim Folsom. "About halfway through those four off-years, Jim Folsom came through Dothan. He was going to run for governor again. Jim came through town and said, 'Rich, I got to go down to Panama City and I'm tired. Will you drive me down there?' Well, I knew there was something in Jim. There's a method in his madness somewhere. But I said, 'Why sure, Governor. Be glad to.' 'I've got to go down there and see somebody,' he said. 'At the outside I'll be there an hour. Then if you'll bring me back, I'll just drive on over to Cottonwood.' He used to take those hot baths over there and loved them.

"Going down there he chatted aimlessly, and then all of a sudden he said, 'Let me ask you something. You were up in Cullman the other night?' I said, 'Yeah, sorry I missed you.' I expect Jim eased out of town. I mean, he's running a governor's race, and he didn't have to get mixed up with me. Maybe not. He might have been campaigning somewhere like I was. 'You were in there on Thursday night,' he said. 'I came back in Friday afternoon.'

"He says, 'Everybody in town, especially the women folk, are talking about how funny you were, what a great speech you made, and how much they enjoyed it.' I said, 'Well, I've been at it a good while.' He said, 'Tell me something, boy, are you gonna joke your way into that office? That's a pretty responsible position.' I said, 'I sure am. But let me tell you why.' I said, 'Governor, I'm not running for your spot. Nobody cares who the attorney general is or the lieutenant governor. It's nothing but a popularity contest.' He just laughed. He said, 'A what?' I said, 'It's just a popularity contest. The best-known man is going to win. And this is my way of getting known.' 'A popularity contest. I never have thought about it like that.' I said, 'Now the governor's race is different. You've got to have a program, and you've got to talk about what you did before and what your opponents are not able to do. But me, I just get out there and make a few speeches. And the best-known man is going to win lieutenant governor and right on down the line.' 'Well, that's a new one on me. Well, boy, I hope it works.' I said, 'It will. You'll see.'"

A Manner of Speaking. Today, Richmond's way of campaigning would be considered highly racist and highly sexist by a lot of people, and he would not get by with it. But it was a different time, with different norms and values, and he was not intentionally insulting anybody. In fact, he says, this possibility never entered his mind. He was a typical white Southerner displaying the thought and speech patterns which were typical of Southern politicians. Later, when he proved to be moderate on race, people thought he had changed. He doesn't see it that way. To Richmond, entertaining was one thing; fulfilling the responsibilities of high state office was an entirely different matter. When he was trying to obey the law as attorney general, he became the screaming liberal to the national press, and that wasn't true either.

In his campaigns, he was like the others. "Let the redhead fight the Yankees," he said. "We'll fight it out just as long as we've got a fighting chance." What he was promising to fight about was protection of the "Southern Way of Life." This meant segregation to the audience. "I never used the word 'segregation,'" Richmond says. "Protect our Southern customs, the Southern way of life, the malarkey that they all used, knowing full well that they couldn't do it. I never used the word 'segregation,' because I had a pretty heavy black vote then. And I was a Big Jim man. The blacks trusted me.

"The thing really popped when John Patterson was governor. Patterson was a strong segregationist, and he did nothing to help matters. Everybody had to be a 'seg,' and people were trying to 'out-seg' each other. Of course, I was out for four years, and I was determined to be re-elected. I did it with Negro dialect stories, a lot of which were hilarious. That's why a lot of people say I changed so. I didn't. I just told those stories the same that everybody else did at that time.

"One speech I made about it was called, 'Where Have They Gone?' In other words, the type of black fellow we used to know, where has he gone? Now we've got the arrogant, the demanders, the demonstrators, the destroyers. Where has the old-timer gone? Then I would tell a great, as we used to say, a great 'nigger' story. But you can't say that anymore. I was born and raised with them, and I know their dialect."

The Patterson Administration

John Malcolm Patterson, who served as governor of Alabama from 1959 to 1963, was born on September 27, 1921. He was in the army during World War II and rose to the rank of major. He was on active duty again during the Korean War. Patterson attended the University of Alabama and received a law degree in 1949. He returned to Phenix City, Alabama, his home town, and entered law practice with his father, Albert Patterson.

According to a law school classmate, John Patterson showed no particular animosity toward blacks. In fact, the race issue was discussed very little in law school. Students were concerned with passing their courses and with how they were going to make a living after they graduated.[1] Patterson apparently did not have political aspirations at that time in his life. He later stated that when he first started practice, he was content to be a small-town lawyer.[2]

Phenix City at the time was known as "sin city," a center of immoral and illegal activity which thrived by serving soldiers at Fort Benning, across the Chattahoochee River in Columbus, Georgia. Gambling, prostitution, and other such vices were rampant. Albert Patterson, John's father, ran for attorney general of Alabama in 1954, and one of his major campaign promises was to clean up Phenix City.

Albert Patterson won the Democratic primary, but less than two weeks after the election, he was brazenly gunned down while walking along the street in Phenix City. The state Democratic executive committee appointed his son, John, to be the Democratic candidate. John Patterson was thirty-two years old and had only been out of law school for five years.

He is described as "tall, intelligent, charming, and extraordinarily ambitious."[3] There was very strong feeling across the state about the events in Phenix City, and because of what had happened, John Patterson enjoyed widespread sympathy and popularity. He had only token opposition in the general election and won easily. This was the election in which Folsom was elected governor for the second time and Flowers was elected to the senate.

Patterson was a bitter foe of Governor Folsom during his term as attorney general. His father had formerly been a friend of Big Jim, but Folsom supported Albert Patterson's opponent for attorney general in the Democratic primary. John, showing his youth and other traits which would characterize him as governor, was vindictive and tried to extract revenge.

Patterson Finds His Issue. John Patterson soon realized that he had a chance to be elected governor in 1958, but he knew he could not win solely because of his father's assassination, as he had in 1954. He had to find a strong issue. Observing the developing climate and the mood of the populace, he settled on race, and thereafter, he took a hard line and became an uncompromising segregationist.[4] According to an acquaintance, he was not unusually racist; he was just facing up to what he perceived as political reality.

In 1956, Patterson decided to boost his image as a segregationist with an attack on the NAACP. He found an old Alabama law which required out-of-state corporations to register with the Secretary of State and pay a $10 fee. In June, he asked a judge of the Circuit Court of Montgomery to find the NAACP in violation of this law and to issue a temporary injunction so that the organization could not conduct business activities of any kind. Patterson charged the NAACP with encouraging the Montgomery Bus Boycott and with supporting the attempt by Autherine Lucy to desegregate the University of Alabama, activities which he said were illegal, and he asked for a full list of members and copies of all branch chapters.

Circuit Judge Walter B. Jones issued the injunction and ordered the NAACP to hand over the requested records. When it refused, he held it in contempt and imposed a fine of $100,000. The U.S. Supreme Court struck down the fine in 1958, but it let the injunction stand. This meant that the NAACP had to remain inactive in the state.

The case was not settled until 1964, and through all of the legal wrangling, the injunction stood. So John Patterson in effect put the NAACP out of business in Alabama for eight years. This raised him to the front ranks of white supremacy, gained him much fame, and greatly improved his political prospects for the immediate future.

Patterson boasted during the 1958 gubernatorial race that he had run the NAACP out of the state. According to William Nunnelley, the 1958 race signaled the beginning of a period in Alabama politics during which the candidate who was the most militant segregationist had the best chance of becoming governor.[5] This was possible because very few blacks voted.

In his inaugural speech in January 1959, Patterson took a very hard line and pledged to preserve segregation in the state even if it meant closing the public schools.[6] After the soft-spoken and moderate Folsom, this was a clear signal that defiance was to be the order of the day and that disobeying certain laws was acceptable.

The politicos in Montgomery heard the message, and so did groups such as the Ku Klux Klan who were ready to commit violence given the slightest hint that the law would not be enforced. Undoubtedly, John Patterson was doing what he thought was politically expedient. It worked for a time, but inadvertently, he was also preparing the way for a political master who would completely overshadow him.

Legal action relative to civil rights continued on a broad front. Federal District Court Judge Frank Johnson ruled in September 1959 that blacks must be allowed to use municipal parks in Montgomery, and suits continued to be filed to allow blacks into previously all-white schools.[7] Governor Patterson threatened to call the National Guard if the federal government attempted to force integration.[8]

During this period, the state Legislature continued to pass what observers refer to as a lot of "childish" bills which the members knew were certain to be declared unconstitutional.[9] The bills, it was claimed, would defy the federal government, support state's rights, and strengthen segregation. A few legislators may have believed such things could be achieved, but for most, it was a political show.

Staying Loyal in 1960. Ever since the Dixiecrat revolution of 1948, there had been bickering among leaders of the Democratic Party in Alabama as to whether all candidates of the party should be supported. The struggle was between "loyalists" and "states righters;" that is, between those who wanted to remain loyal to the national party and those who did not. One of the primary issues was whether electors would pledge themselves to vote for the party's candidate for president.

The states righters claimed that they could influence presidential elections by keeping the option to vote for whomever they pleased. They argued that no one could win the presidency without the South and that they could deny a majority in the electoral college, throwing the election into the House of Representatives. Here they could bargain and deal. They were not deterred in their ardor by the fact that the last time an election was thrown into the House was in 1824 and that, given the electoral college mechanism, their chances varied from extremely slim to zero. Loyalists pointed to the obvious danger that, if the Democrats won at the national level, disloyal members would be shut out of patronage and influence. Congressmen and senators with longevity had much at stake and tended to be strong loyalists.

Patterson remained a loyalist in this struggle. As governor, his activities relative to civil rights were sharply at odds with the philosophy expressed by national leaders. Nevertheless, he strongly opposed a break with the national Democratic party, and in 1960, he was an ardent supporter of John Kennedy.

The South had been solidly Democratic for almost a century because of the Civil War and Reconstruction and the Jim Crow system. Franklin Roosevelt had included blacks and labor in his New Deal coalition, however, and had sent the party decidedly leftward. Now, at the national level, it was clearly more committed than the Republicans to civil rights, and it was the more liberal on social issues. This was the basis for the rebellion of the states righters, and it was also the basis for increased Republican strength in the Deep South.

A *Birmingham News* editorial expressed the feeling of many Alabamians: "We can vote against a Democratic party which has been stolen from us by a coterie of left-wing liberals. . . . This is not the party of our fathers, but of self-proclaimed intellectuals who are out to provide America with a new blueprint for bigger government, more spending, and still more 'go-to-Washington.'"[10]

It was respectable, in other words, to vote Republican. This choice was galling to "true" Southerners, but it was the only way many knew of protesting, short of outright violence. So the Republican party grew in the South, and within a quarter of a century, it had in Alabama elected a governor and members of both houses of Congress.

The Republicans were still organizing themselves and building self-confidence in 1960. They fielded a full slate of candidates in the general election and attempted to challenge Senator John Sparkman, who had been the Democratic vice-presidential nominee in 1952. In the May Democratic primary, Senator Sparkman faced and easily defeated the arch segregationist and far-right-winger, retired Admiral John G. Crommelin. The Republicans named Julian Elgin, a successful businessman, to oppose him.

The general election was a Democratic sweep. Alabama gave Kennedy some 57 percent of its vote, Sparkman was re-elected with more than 70 percent, and all Democratic congressmen were re-elected. The populace demonstrated that old habits die hard.

The Struggle to Vote Continues. Registration and voting continued to be a central issue of the civil rights movement during the Patterson administration. In February 1959, the Justice Department sought an injunction against the denial of voting rights to Macon County blacks.[11] Governor Patterson strongly criticized this action, and a committee of the Alabama Senate approved a bill to let registrars destroy registration

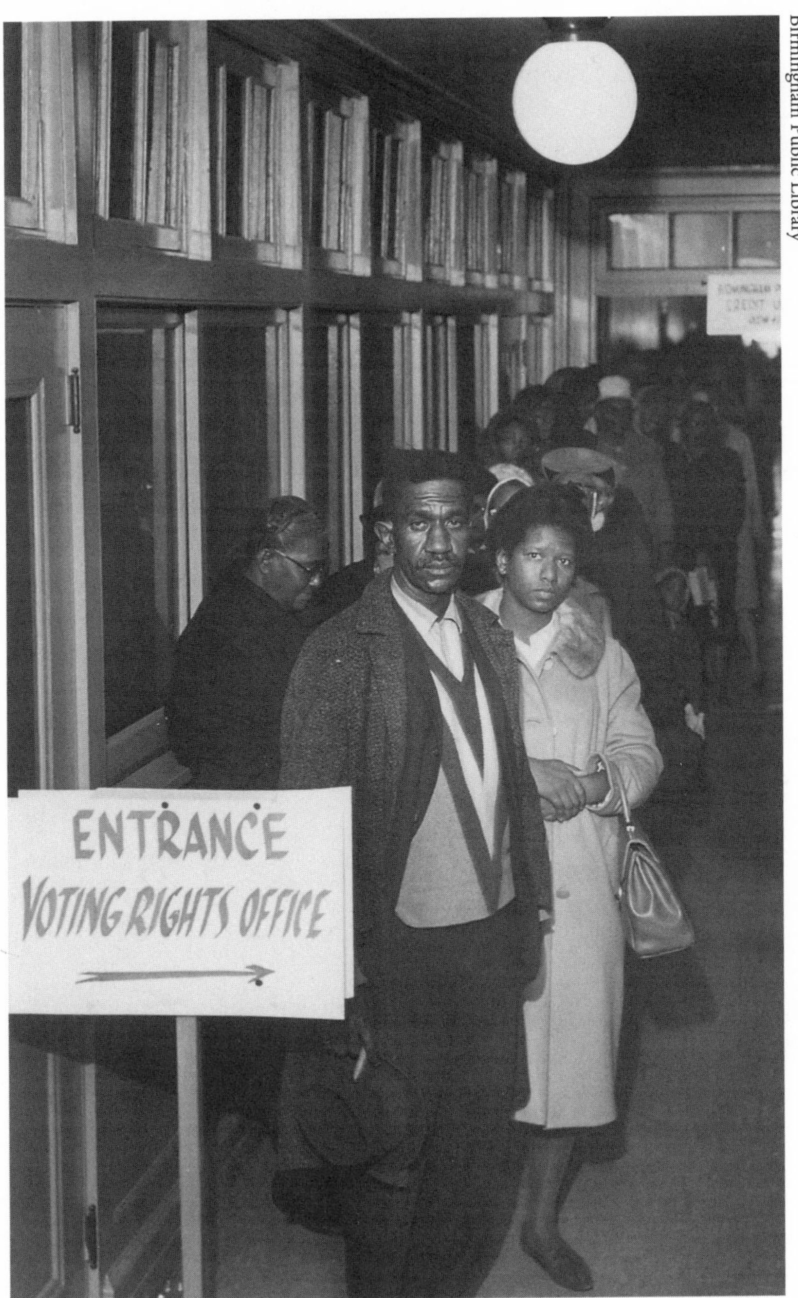

Birmingham Public Library

Black efforts toward voter registration steadily increased from World War II to the passage of the voting rights act in 1965.

applications. The Justice Department then sought and won a court order barring Macon County from destroying the records.

The federal Civil Rights Commission reported in May 1959 that there had been 119 voting complaints filed in Alabama, the highest number of any state.[12] The Commission stepped up its investigation of complaints in Alabama, and Governor Patterson ordered state officials not to cooperate.[13]

In June, the governor reported that he was having difficulty getting registrars. He said that people would not serve for fear of being "hounded" by the Civil Rights Commission.[14] The lack of registrars meant that no one could be registered, and on the surface, this affected everyone the same. But most whites were already registered, so the effect was to continue the *status quo*.

Action on voting rights continued on a broad front. Local blacks, encouraged and supported by national organizations, conducted a number of registration drives, and the state government continued to resist. In March 1959, a Dallas County grand jury limited the Civil Rights Commission's examination of voter records[15] and this provoked additional activity. There were federal actions in 1960 in Macon, Montgomery, Sumter and Wilcox counties. Action was later extended to Bullock, Choctaw, and Perry counties.

The U.S. sued the state and three Bullock County registrars in 1961 for discriminating against blacks through a "vouching" system, in which voting registration applicants had to be backed by persons who were already registered. At the time, the county had twenty-two hundred whites registered to vote and five blacks.[16]

This suit against the state was possible because of an important principle established in recent court actions. In March 1959, Judge Johnson had dismissed a Justice Department suit against the state on the grounds that the 1957 Civil Rights Act did not authorize the United States to sue states to enforce the rights of blacks. Jurisdiction was limited, he said, to commencing civil proceedings against individuals.[17] The Supreme Court overturned Johnson's decision in May 1960. The ability to sue states gave much broader sweep to court decisions and undermined the obstructionist strategy of tying the courts up with interminable suits.

In every case, the federal agents finally got to see the voting records they wanted, and the voting drives eventually succeeded. An article in the *New York Times* in July 1962 commented on the increase of black voters in Macon County. It was called the most spectacular voting rights success in the Deep South.[18] In 1958, there were 1,004 blacks registered in the Black Belt counties of Barbour, Bullock, Pike, and Russell. By 1968, this number had grown to 14,792. In Bullock County, the number of registered blacks increased from four to 3,203 during this period.

In a related matter, the Supreme Court ruled in November 1960 (in *Gomillion v. Lightfoot*, argued by Montgomery black attorney Fred D. Gray) that the 1957 state law which allowed Tuskegee's boundaries to be redrawn was unconstitutional. The Court held that a state may not change boundaries of a city if the effect is to exclude virtually all black voters.[19] This was, the Court said, a violation of the Fifteenth Amendment.

The Supreme Court held for the first time in the Tuskegee decision that the federal courts could rule on a case involving political districting, and this opened the way for federal court intervention in reapportionment. The traditional view had been that political abuses should be corrected at the polls, but a judge noted that there is no relief at the polls for those who cannot register and vote.[20]

The Governor on Sit-ins and Freedom Rides. Two key events in the civil rights struggle, the sit-ins and the Freedom Rides, occurred during Patterson's term as governor. His reaction to them reveals something of the character of his governorship.

The sit-ins began as an entirely local affair by college students in North Carolina in February 1960, and in less than a month, they spread to Alabama. On February 25, thirty-five young blacks staged a brief demonstration in the grill of the new Montgomery County Courthouse. The incident did not amount to much. The grill was closed immediately, and no arrests were made. Patterson, however, demonstrated one of the weaknesses of Alabama politicians by over-reacting. He suspected that the students were from Alabama State University, a local black college, and, in an action clearly outside of his sphere of authority, he ordered the school's president to expel any students who were involved.[21] The university finally dismissed 11 faculty members and 100 student demonstrators, leading to a protest which was joined by the NAACP.[25]

The Freedom Rides in 1961 were a much more serious matter

which involved terrifying brutality and a serious breakdown in law and order. In the midst of the crisis, Patterson showed that he missed the larger point with his comment, "When you go somewhere seeking trouble, you usually find it. I lay full blame on the agitators who come in here for the express purpose of stirring just such a thing. We can't act as nursemaids to agitators. They'll stay at home when they learn nobody is there to protect them. The State of Alabama can't guarantee the safety of fools, and that's what they are."[23]

Patterson's Legacy as Governor. John Patterson was Alabama's governor at a very critical period, and decades later, it seems clear that he was the wrong man at the wrong time. According to Marshall Frady, Patterson changed the "tacit and sometimes modestly charitable" preoccupation with blacks in Alabama politics to a "volatile, unabashed, brutal irascibility."[24] Frady quotes an Alabama political observer as saying, "We'd always prided ourselves on being at least a little more polite and civil on these matters than our neighbors. Patterson was a new departure for us."[25]

William Nunnelley says that Patterson, "fanned the flame of defiance with his attacks on the NAACP in 1956 and his racist campaign for governor in 1958."[26] And John Craig Stewart observes that, while Patterson's uncompromising stand on integration was an effective political strategy in the short run, ultimately it hurt both the man and the state of Alabama. "The holding action only complicated and made more difficult the inevitable", he notes.[27]

In many other respects, Patterson was a typical governor of Alabama, and he had some outstanding accomplishments to his credit. In 1957, the National Chamber of Commerce had named him one of the ten outstanding young men in the United States. The education bill passed under his leadership in 1959 provided the largest school appropriation in the state's history. He continued the previous administration's commitment to better roads in the state, and with his support, a $60 million highway bond issue was passed. He served as chairman of the Tennessee-Tombigbee Waterway Development Authority. He strongly supported the Tenn-Tom project and testified before a House subcommittee on public works in its favor.[28] He worked hard for economic expansion in Alabama and did his best to get the state legislature reapportioned more fairly.

Patterson was not alone among the state's educated and elite in harboring strong resentments about what was happening in the civil rights struggle. The feeling was near unanimous, in fact, that local rights were being trampled and that outsiders were trying to dictate to the state's citizens how they should behave and what they should think.

What Alabama needed at this critical time was not a typical reaction, however; it needed a gifted, insightful leader. What it got, instead, was a man too young and inexperienced to understand the long-range implications of the situation. An associate describes Patterson as "arrogant as hell when he was governor."[29] James S. Taylor comments that he was "Long on ambition but short on political experience."[30]

What difference would it have made if he had acted with more insight and restraint as governor? Perhaps none. But a strong argument can be made that it would have prevented the extreme polarization which occurred. Most people in the state did not want violence. A very small proportion was actually involved in such acts, and most were more restrained and prudent than events made them appear. As a local politician observed, the situation forced people to take sides and forced them into more extreme positions than they wanted. There was no middle ground.[31]

Patterson's hard line had an effect he did not intend. George Wallace, ever the artful judge of political winds, believed he lost in 1958 and Patterson won because of Wallace's relatively soft stand on race. Thereafter, Wallace made the issue his own.

Civil Rights During the Patterson Years

The four years from January 1959 to the end of 1962 were a period of rapid maturing in the civil rights movement and of rapid change in the treatment of black citizens in most parts of the South. The year 1960 has been called pivotal in two respects. First, it marked a change in tactics and leadership in the civil rights struggle. A critical mass had been reached, in effect, and the black community came together on a broad basis with new determination to achieve full citizenship.[32]

Second, it marked the period when resistance to desegregation and to fuller black participation in education, politics, and other aspects of national life began to crumble rapidly in all but the Deep South.[33] Political, business, and religious leaders realized that change was inevitable, and in many cases they recognized injustices of the past and became converts to the cause. Moderates in the population attempted to support change peacefully, and others were brought along because they had no choice. Trouble was prevented in most cases through clear statements of purpose by those in authority and unambiguous demonstrations that law and order would be upheld.

Also during this period, an important shift was occurring nationally in the attitudes of whites. Before the *Brown* decision, most people did not have strong feelings about the issue, but events caused a marked shift in the direction of racial equality and fair treatment. The Montgomery Bus Boycott caught the attention of the nation, and the obvious injustices which occurred in the next few years could not be easily ignored. Civil rights leaders realized the importance of sensitizing the nation's conscience to the issue, and they were successful in appealing to it. The time to do something really significant about civil rights in the United States was approaching.

New Leaders, New Methods in the Civil Rights Struggle. The civil rights movement had previously been led almost entirely by the NAACP, with its somewhat cautious approach of seeking constitutional rights for blacks through legislation and litigation. Emphasis was on voting rights, educational equality, and access to public services and jobs. By the late 1950s, successes had raised expectations, and the NAACP's pace was too slow for many. This resulted in a challenge for leadership of the movement and for a change in its methods.

The first challenge came from CORE, the Congress of Racial Equality, which had been founded in 1942 by members of the Christian-pacifist Fellowship of Reconciliation. It was dedicated to the dual principles of nonviolence and interracial cooperation. Its members pioneered the use of direct action techniques of protest, such as picketing and sit-ins at public facilities.[34] Part of the leadership challenge was to Martin Luther King, Jr., who had moved from Montgomery to Atlanta in 1959 so that he could direct the Southern Christian Leadership Conference more effectively. King found himself challenged by younger people and harsher methods, and he had to produce results to maintain the initiative. In King's view, civil rights demonstrators who were beaten and jailed by hostile whites educated and transformed their oppressors through the redemptive character of their unmerited suffering.[35]

Young blacks were not so sure this was true. Most were for nonviolence, but experience led them to doubt that their own suffering would change the more defiant whites. They formed other groups, with younger leaders and a more direct action agenda. Among these was the Student Nonviolent Coordinating Committee (SNCC), which was organized at Raleigh, North Carolina, in April 1960, shortly after sit-ins had begun that February. The fast tempo of change took the NAACP and even CORE by surprise, and they found themselves driven to more aggressive actions.

The Sit-Ins. The sit-ins, which swept the South in the spring of 1960, were a master stroke in promoting sympathy and favorable sentiments toward the cause, and among civil rights activists, they helped decrease the popularity of legalistic techniques. The Montgomery boycott was of unquestioned importance in moving King to national leadership, mobilizing black feeling, and projecting nonviolent action. The sit-ins, however, broadened the movement, took it to a new level of massive involvement, and increased the determination of blacks to achieve rights. They also forced whites to face some of the moral dilemmas which they had been adept at avoiding.

Southern whites had argued long and hard that the trouble related to civil rights was caused by "outside agitators," who for various reasons wanted to disrupt things.[36] Central to this argument was the myth that the great majority of blacks liked things as they were and were happy with the Southern Way of Life. If outsiders would just leave them alone, they would be content to continue living as they had, guided and helped by paternalistic, magnanimous whites. The Montgomery Bus Boycott dealt this myth a sharp blow, and the sit-ins finished it for all practical purposes.

On February 1, 1960, four black students from the Agricultural and Technical College in Greensboro, North Carolina, entered the lunch counter of the local Woolworth's department store. They politely asked for coffee, and when service was refused, they continued to sit in silent protest. The poignancy of this event was unmistakable, and it got immediate nationwide publicity. These were not outside troublemakers at all but were local young people making what was surely a reasonable request in a peaceful way.

The activity caught the imagination of college students, who were looking for a more effective way to express themselves on an issue about which they felt deeply. In a week, the sit-ins spread to six other cities in North Carolina, and by the end of February, they had spread to seven other southern states. By April, demonstrations were occurring in fifty-four cities in nine southern states. Before the end of the year, some 70,000 blacks had participated in sit-ins in over a hundred southern cities. Over 3,600 arrests occurred.[37] It was an amazing demonstration of spontaneous mass action.

The sit-ins made it to Montgomery, Alabama, in February, and produced the noted response from Governor Patterson. On March 31, ten students from Miles College and Daniel Payne College in Birmingham staged sit-ins at five downtown department stores. They had to plan very carefully even to make it into the stores, for the police, under commissioner Bull Connor, were alert to the possibilities and were trying to prevent such activities. The ten were arrested immediately for "trespass after warning."[38]

The sit-ins had a jarring effect on whites, many of whom were churchgoers who claimed to believe in brotherly love. It became more clear that they must either reconcile their deep religious faith to social change or try to explain away the contradiction between faith and reality. Woodward says that, "The self-discipline and fortitude of the youths, who silently bore abuse and insult, touched the white South's respect for courage."[39] A practical result was a softening of attitudes in all but the Deep South states and a rapid increase in the desegregation of public facilities. In the largest sense, the sit-ins were a gigantic moral victory which captured the imagination of the nation.[40]

The 1960 Civil Rights Act. Nationally there was an increasing demand for fair treatment of blacks and for progress in assuring rights. The 1957 Civil Rights Act had been significant because it was the first national legislation since Reconstruction, but it was weak and gave the government little enforcement authority. Pressure was building on the national government to do more.

Congress began work on a new civil rights bill, and immediately it got into a typical sectional fight. The majority wanted a strong bill, but Southerners in the Senate weakened it with a successful filibuster. Congress passed the 1960 Civil Rights Act on April 21, after months of struggle, and President Eisenhower signed it on May 5.

The 1960 bill was designed to advance rights without eroding the power and authority of local and state officials. Like the 1957 Act, it addressed the key area of voting, and it extended the power of the Justice Department in this area.[41] It gave broad authority for the attorney general to seek injunctions in civil rights cases, and it set up a permanent commission to fight race discrimination in employment on federal contracts.

Of great importance, it granted the federal government authority to bring voting rights suits against states as well as individuals. This set the stage for federal involvement in reapportionment and for cutting through the strategy of delaying matters by forcing the government to act separately on each individual complaint.[42]

The 1960 Election. The 1960 elections pitted Democrat John F. Kennedy against Republican Richard M. Nixon, and whatever the outcome, there would be a shift to younger leadership. Kennedy boldly proclaimed that it was time for major change in the country, and he was the one to lead it. Nixon, the incumbent vice-president, was necessarily more restrained since he was part of the old regime, but he tried to emphasize his youth and vigor. The actions of candidates and parties indicated just how far the civil rights issue had come since the previous election. The national conventions of both parties in 1960 adopted outspoken anti-segregation planks for their platforms and expressed approval of the sit-in demonstrations.

Kennedy was Catholic, and, despite his great charisma, he faced a difficult fight on this account. No Catholic had ever been elected president. In addition, Republicans were making serious inroads in the previously "Solid South." Kennedy needed all of the help he could get, and he was the first presidential candidate to campaign vigorously for the black vote.

The fight between loyalists and states righters was going strong in Alabama, and Republicans, who had won the state for Eisenhower in the previous election, believed they had a good chance in 1960. The major newspapers in the state supported Nixon, but in spite of it, the loyalists carried the state for Kennedy.

Kennedy won by the narrowest of margins in November. He received a large majority of the black vote, without which he would not have been elected. He was therefore deeply indebted to his black constituency. At the same time, he was heavily indebted to some segregationists who kept their states in the Democratic column, and he did not wish to jeopardize other parts of his legislative program by overtly pushing civil rights too hard.[43]

He had a political tightrope to walk. He attempted to placate Southerners by following their recommendations in appointments to the federal district courts. On the other hand, he ordered the federal housing authority to cease discrimination in the financing of private homes. The presidential committee for securing fair-employment policies was charged with putting pressure on offending firms. And for the first time, blacks were given a significant number of positions in the middle and higher levels in departments of the federal government.

The fact that Kennedy was president during this period was significant for the civil rights movement, both on its own merit and by the fact that the Democrats, the more socially liberal of the two major parties, controlled both the White House and the Congress. The president and his brother Robert, whom he appointed attorney general, had openly proclaimed their views, and there was never any question about their own feelings, only about the extent to which they would go, given political realities. They showed restraint, but when local leaders proved that they would not preserve order and protect individual citizens, they stepped in and made clear the commitment of the federal government.

Resistance Hardens in New Orleans. A school desegregation battle in New Orleans which climaxed in late 1960 and early 1961 demonstrated that, despite the progress being made elsewhere, defiance was still very strong in the Deep South. The case had been underway for several years and had gone through a tangled legal maze as the state tried to defy federal court orders. Bass states that, "No Southern state matched the vigor, imagination, and frenzy displayed by Louisiana in battling to maintain segregated public schools."[44]

The case began in 1952 with a class-action suit, but proceedings were delayed pending the decision of the Supreme Court in the *Brown* case. In 1956, the school board appealed, and during the next few years, the case produced forty-one separate judicial decisions.[45] Finally, on November 14, 1960, four black first-graders entered two previously all-white schools, and the New Orleans public schools became the first in the Deep South to desegregate. The next day, a mob of 3,000 poured through the downtown area of the city and threw bottles and stones at passing blacks, and that night, black teenagers retaliated by shooting at and beating whites.[46] The event was widely publicized, and as Woodward notes, "it exhibited to the world American racism in some of its more revolting aspects."[47]

Resistance in New Orleans came to an end in February 1961 after the Justice Department entered the case. New attorney general Robert Kennedy was watched closely as he faced the decision of how to proceed in a politically sensitive situation. He stood firm and declared that the authority of the federal government and its courts must prevail. The Justice Department made clear that state officials who defied court orders faced possible jail sentences. The resistance of the state superintendent and other high-ranking individuals quickly crumbled.

New Extremes at Ole Miss. New Orleans was ugly, but perhaps the ugliest incident of all prior to the Wallace-inspired antics in Alabama was the attempt to integrate the University of Mississippi. This happened during the last year of Patterson's term as governor. The event demonstrated graphically just how far Mississippi was from accepting the law of the land, and in the end it provoked a serious constitutional crisis involving state versus federal authority and the right to due process and a jury trial.

Mississippi native James Howard Meredith had decided when he was in the Air Force that he wanted to attend his home state university, and he applied for admission on January 21, 1961. Medgar Evers, NAACP field secretary in Mississippi who was assassinated in 1964, assured Meredith that his organization would provide legal assistance.

As Meredith's application proceeded through the courts, the university employed a variety of delaying tactics. The federal district court, which had the first level of jurisdiction, was headed by a judge in sympathy with state and university officials, and he did everything he could to delay. This caused matters to be shifted to the Fifth Circuit Court of Appeals and created a cumbersome situation in which different levels of the federal court system were fighting each other.

After much legal maneuvering, the Fifth Circuit Court ordered that Meredith be registered in July 1962. This was too late for him to attend any part of the summer term, so the actual enrollment would have to be delayed until September. In the meantime, the case had received extensive publicity, locally and nationally, and Mississippi's major newspapers strongly supported defiance.

In August, the Justice Department entered the case as the confrontation between the state and the national government grew to crisis proportions. Mississippi Governor Ross Barnett went on statewide television and said he was interposing the sovereignty of the state of Mississippi to nullify the federal court order for Meredith's admission. In this action, the governor directly challenged the authority of the United States to enforce the orders of its courts.[48]

The university's board of trustees gave Barnett control of admissions, and on four occasions, either he or the lieutenant governor personally blocked efforts to register Meredith. The Fifth Circuit Court declared the board's action void and in a special session in New Orleans, it prepared to hold all members of the board in contempt if they did not obey the enrollment order. After being informed by their lawyers that the court could do this and could impose both jail sentences and fines, the board members agreed to cooperate. Governor Barnett continued to physically block Meredith's admission and to issue proclamations based on his interposition action.

Meredith was finally registered early in October 1962 with the help of a large group of federal marshals. A mob of 2,500 which included a large number of university students gathered on campus. The crowd became more restless as the day progressed, and that night, violence broke out. In the riot which ensued, two persons were killed, twenty-eight federal marshals suffered gunshot wounds, and 132 people received other injuries. The Mississippi National Guard had been federalized by President Kennedy, but its units did not arrive on the scene until the next morning. It took the federal troops to restore order. Meredith attended classes, but he had to be protected for some time from the jeering and jibes of Ole Miss students.

The case became a great constitutional crisis because it involved once more the question of whether a state official could successfully defy the authority of the federal government and whether federal law took precedent over state law.

Governor John Patterson of Alabama made a point several times during the Ole Miss affair of publicly supporting Ross Barnett.

King Fails and Learns in Albany. Publicity had been a primary goal of civil rights leaders since the early days of the NAACP, and now, the need was more critical. Martin Luther King realized this, and a major part of his strategy was to dramatize situations, gain favorable publicity, and in the process affect public opinion. To succeed, he needed assistance from local whites, from the very ones who considered themselves his enemy. Hateful rhetoric, unruly crowds, and police brutality all played into his hands.

King and the Southern Christian Leadership Conference were looking for a new target of opportunity, and they decided to accept an invitation to lead a desegregation drive in Albany, Georgia, in 1961. Albany was a city of 56,000 which had developed in the last few years into an important commercial center in southern Georgia.

King hoped to bring Albany's white leaders to the bargaining table by filling the jails with demonstrators and overextending the city's capacity to deal with the protests, and he hoped for extensive coverage by the media. The SCLC group arrived in Albany in November 1961, and it began the campaign in December with a speech by King and a parade which he led through the downtown area. The Albany campaign lasted until the summer of 1963, and it resulted in thousands of arrests.

However, it turned out to be one of King's biggest failures, in the sense of effecting change and gaining publicity. The campaign was unfocused. King went to Albany with little preparation and scant knowledge of the situation. While there, he failed to set up a clear chain of command and to assert himself. He did not focus on specific goals, such as transportation or education, but attempted rather to attack all vestiges of segregation on a broad front. The result was an incohesive, uncoordinated effort.[49]

Albany also stymied King because the local white leadership was prepared. The police chief researched King prior to his arrival, and he decided to use the same nonviolent approach that King advocated. The chief arranged to place demonstrators in jails in neighboring cities and counties, and a buildup in Albany which would have generated publicity and pressure never occurred. This strategy was coupled with a policy of protecting demonstrators who were arrested and assuring that they were treated courteously. Those arrested were charged with breach of the peace and unlawful assembly rather than violation of the city's segregation ordinances.[50] The confrontation which the SCLC hoped to use to dramatize its movement failed to materialize.[51]

King's movement suffered a major failure in Albany, but it learned and profited from the mistakes it had made. The experience taught King the necessity of prior planning and preparation, and he learned that strong leadership and organization were essential as a campaign progressed. In addition to everything else, King had been outsmarted in Albany, and from that he learned the importance of choosing a target location where the reaction needed to produce maximum publicity was likely. He knew that the perfect foil was waiting in Birmingham in the person of police commissioner Eugene "Bull" Connor.

The Freedom Rides: Major Violence Shakes Alabama

While the education battle flamed in New Orleans and Mississippi, Alabama proved that it belonged among the ranks of the most defiant and most lawless with an outlandish performance in the widely publicized Freedom Rides.

James Farmer was elected national director of CORE in January of 1961, and he acted immediately to push the organization's direct-action agenda. In late April, CORE announced that a group of college students was going to attempt a "freedom ride" through the South, beginning in Washington and ending in New Orleans.[52] This was shortly after the Supreme Court had outlawed segregation in interstate transportation terminals,[53] and it was designed to dramatize the lack of desegregation in such facilities in the South.[54] The Freedom Rides made CORE one of the most popular of the civil rights organizations.

The Freedom Rides began on May 4, 1961, with two chartered buses, and they made their way through Virginia without incident. There was some minor harassment and a few arrests in North Carolina, but nothing of greater consequence occurred there. The first violence was in Rock Hill, South Carolina, where John Lewis, a twenty-one-year-old black from Pike County, Alabama, was beaten by several whites as he attempted to enter a restroom marked "white only."[55] Lewis later became chairman of the Student Nonviolent Coordinating Committee, then headed the Voter Education Project, and still later was a member of Congress from Atlanta.

The riders went through Georgia with no problems. On May 14,

Mother's Day, they left Atlanta in two buses, a Greyhound and a Trailways, and headed toward Birmingham. The buses arrived at noon in Anniston, Alabama, an industrial city of 38,000 about thirty miles from the Georgia line. Crowds waited at both bus stations. They threw rocks through some of the windows of the Trailways and trapped riders inside the bus for more than twenty minutes. Police finally appeared and cleared a lane through the mob, and the bus headed for Birmingham, which was about sixty miles away.[56]

The same thing happened to the Greyhound when it arrived at its station in Anniston with fourteen passengers. An unruly crowd was waiting, and a lot of rocks were thrown. E. L. Cowling, an Alabama state police investigator, was aboard the Greyhound, and he ordered the driver to move out. The police cleared a path, and the bus began its trip to Birmingham.

On the two-lane road between Anniston to Birmingham, the bus driver found himself between a car and a pickup truck, which would not let the bus pass. A tire was shot out on the bus, and it pulled into the parking area by a country store. An angry crowd gathered and shouted for the riders to get off. Rocks were thrown, and someone threw a molotov cocktail (a bottle of gasoline with a burning cloth stuffed in the neck), through a back window. The bus started burning. The riders got out, after a near panic, and the bus burned completely. Members of the mob attacked some of the riders. State troopers finally arrived at the scene. They pulled their revolvers and ordered the crowd to disperse. One fired a shot into the air.

About the time that order was restored, a convoy of cars led by the Reverend Fred Shuttlesworth, a black civil rights leader from Birmingham, showed up. Twelve riders had to be taken to the hospital in Anniston for emergency treatment.[57] All were then transported by Shuttlesworth to his home.

Meanwhile the Trailways arrived in Birmingham. A crowd, which included Robert Shelton, imperial wizard of the United Klans of America, waited at the Greyhound station. When they learned that the Trailways had arrived, they headed for that station, which was several blocks away. The mob attacked the riders, and one was injured so badly that he required fifty stitches.[58] A local radio reporter was on the scene, describing events from his car. Three men smashed his windows and dragged him into the street. He managed to escape, understandably shaken by what had happened.[59]

The reporter said later that there were no police at the station when the Trailways bus arrived. This was despite the fact that serious trouble had already occurred, and they had been alerted and knew of the danger. Police Commissioner Eugene "Bull" Connor explained that, "Many (of the policemen) were taking the day off because it was Mother's Day."[60] Connor claimed in the days that followed that there were a few officers in plainclothes at the Greyhound station.

Montgomery was the next destination of the riders, and it was now clear that maintaining law and order was going to be difficult. Attorney General Robert Kennedy called Governor Patterson, who had been a strong Kennedy supporter in 1960, and asked that the state provide protection. Patterson turned him down. The governor said that he could assure no more than the normal security afforded to any interstate traveler.

Attorney General Kennedy dispatched John Seigenthaler, a special assistant, to Montgomery. He was accompanied by John Doar of the Justice Department. They talked with Patterson and made it clear that, if the state wouldn't provide protection, the federal government would.[61] Patterson backed down a little. He assured his visitors there was no need to send in U.S. marshals, so they reported back to Washington that they had his commitment to preserve law and order.

The Greyhound terminal in Montgomery was next door to the federal building where Frank Johnson, among others, had offices. When the bus arrived, no special security arrangements were in evidence, and a group of about two hundred whites quickly gathered. Trouble started when a Klansman began cursing and slapping at a newsman who was taking pictures. The crowd turned violent, and it quickly swelled to nearly one thousand. Seigenthaler, Kennedy's representative, was knocked unconscious while attempting to aid a young girl. Four out-of-town reporters were beaten, along with riders from the bus. While all of this occurred, Montgomery police officers were several blocks away, attending to other duties such as directing traffic. Some of the blacks who were beaten had no connection with the Freedom Riders but just happened to be in the vicinity.[62]

A young black, William Barbee, was knocked to the pavement and struck repeatedly with a heavy club while the mob shouted, "Kill him! Kill him!."[63] At this point, Colonel Floyd Mann, the Alabama Public Safety Director, drew his pistol and ordered the attackers back. Mann then called for state troopers, whom he had placed on alert several blocks away, and order was restored after they arrived.

John Doar, who had seen all of this, called Robert Kennedy from inside the federal building. "It's a crowd gone mad," he said. "They're beating the students. It's the worst thing I've ever seen!"[64] The decision was made to send 450 U.S. marshals to Montgomery. Doar drew up a petition for a federal injunction against the KKK and the Montgomery police, but he had to get it signed before it would be valid. Judge Frank Johnson had deliberately gone fishing that day because he felt that prevention was an executive function and judicial remedies should come later. It took Doar several hours to locate the judge.

On Saturday night after the bus terminal disturbance, a group including the riders gathered at the black First Baptist Church in Montgomery, and a mob began to congregate outside. Colonel Mann deployed about two hundred Alabama highway patrolmen to try to control things. Someone threw a rock through a church window, and while those inside sang freedom songs, the mob grew more boisterous. Four hundred U.S. marshals arrived about this time. The mob had grown to about two thousand and was threatening to overwhelm the marshals and rush the church. Several cars were set afire, and it was clearly touch-and-go as to whether the highway patrolmen and marshals could maintain control.[65]

Faced with the potential for a major riot, Patterson finally called the National Guard and declared martial law. Guardsman with fixed bayonets marched into the area, and at this, the mob backed down and started drifting away. At dawn, the people inside were escorted from the church.

Twenty-seven riders went on to Jackson, Mississippi, with heavy protection from a military escort. When the bus arrived in Jackson, the riders were arrested on charges of breach of peace and refusing to obey an officer. Each was fined $200 and given a suspended jail sentence of sixty days.[66] Mississippi Senator James Eastland charged that the Freedom Riders were "Communist inspired" and that the trip was devised to embarrass the president before an upcoming visit to Europe.[67]

The Freedom Rides did great harm to the reputation of Alabama. A sufficient show of force at the beginning would have prevented all of the trouble later, but state leaders either did not understand or did not care about this point. Alabama Congressmen George Huddleston, Jr., commented that the Freedom Riders "got what they asked for in trespassing upon the South and its well-established customs."[68]

This incident had one positive effect in that it shook the state's business community and many others in leadership and power positions. The audacity and violence of the mobs caught them by surprise, and they were shocked that political leaders and police let matters get out of control. Many finally realized the extent of the damage being done to the image of the state, and they began to understand more clearly the likelihood of serious long-term economic consequences.

The Second Campaign for Attorney General

Richmond's Big Plan. Flowers's second campaign for attorney general was part of a larger plan for his political career. "When I was in the senate," he remembers, "I had considered running for lieutenant governor. A lot of senators do. And frankly I thought I would like to have a full-time job. I would like to have a political job that paid me.

"I had an overall plan, and I've said I might have been better off had I stuck by it. I hoped to run for and serve as attorney general and at the end of my term, let out the rumors that I was going to run for governor. Keep the leaks going right up to the last minute, and then run for lieutenant governor.

"Then after my term as lieutenant governor, I was going to run for governor and, had that worked out, I would have been in position to run against Sparkman for the United States Senate. I figured if I was elected attorney general, I could be elected lieutenant governor and then governor. 'When I jump into the Senate race,' I figured, 'I can run against Sparkman once, and if I don't beat him the first time, I'll beat him the second time just as sure as I'm sitting here because he is getting old.' And had I stuck by that . . . . But I got in all that ruckus with Wallace, and it changed everything."

Richmond had been giving speeches and working hard to become known since he lost in the 1958 election, but this was all on an informal basis. He did not become a declared candidate until a few months before the 1962 primary.

The 'Little Red Wagon' of the Flowers campaign.

"The way it's set up in Alabama," he says. "You can't campaign officially before you have qualified. All you can do is be visible and say, 'I am considering qualifying when the time comes to qualify.' Everybody knew you were just getting around the formality.

"The qualifying time was then in January. You didn't need more time because there was very little or no Republican opposition. I didn't expect to have Republican opposition. So I qualified in January. The primary was in May and the runoff was in June. It was over after the runoff because the general election did not matter.

"All the work we had done to get known was very important. Every man who was elected that time had run a previous statewide race. Every single man, the lieutenant governor, the attorney general, commissioner of agriculture, president of the public service commission, everybody."

The Campaign Staff. Three men played key roles in Richmond's second campaign for attorney general. They were Dennis "Sawdust" Lassiter, the campaign manager; A. F. Casey, a heavy machinery salesman who entertained; and Carl Goggins, Richmond's Dothan friend. Richmond remembers each fondly.

"Sawdust Lassiter from Gadsden was my campaign manager. He

worked for one of the city commissioners in Gadsden, and he had contacts with a lot of people. I met him when I ran for attorney general the first time. He was the campaign manager for George Hawkins who was running for governor out of Gadsden. Those running for governor would have rallies, and all of us step-down candidates would always go because they would draw a good crowd. We could pass out our literature and occasionally get to speak. I met Sawdust at one of these rallies, and he told me that he was attracted to my campaigning.

"Sawdust was a very attractive young man and was as gregarious as he could be. He saw me during my first campaign, and he told George Hawkins, a friend of mine, 'that big redheaded son-of-a-gun, he's got something to sell.' George and I had been in law school together. George answered, 'Well, he's smart as a whip,' and he said a lot of nice things about me to Sawdust. As soon as the campaign was over, Sawdust contacted me and got me a couple of speaking engagements in Gadsden. He said, 'Come on up here. I want you to stay with me. We'll line up some more speeches. If you're going to run again, I want to help you. You're my kind of candidate.'

"That's the way we got together. He really helped me in lining up those speeches all across north Alabama. He was born and raised there and he had some tremendous contacts and friends in the fire departments and the police departments. He'd always fooled with local politics, and he knew all the deputy sheriffs real well. He played high school football, and had a scholarship to the University of Tennessee. So he was outstanding, and up in that area, he was dynamite.

"When I started my second campaign for attorney general, I moved to Gadsden. Sawdust let me just move into his house. I didn't come home but three times during the campaign, and when I came home, it was on a full campaign swing going through Dothan over to Geneva County and right on to Covington County, Escambia County, and Baldwin County.

"I campaigned out of Gadsden because it was so much easier. My campaign was still pretty poorly financed. I couldn't take my crew into motels because that cost so much money. It was me, and Sawdust Lassiter was along. We had a piano player, and there were always about two other people to hand out literature and do things that needed to be done. We kept at least five people with us all the time, so you can see what that meant for a motel. That's pretty expensive. Gadsden's pretty centrally located, and no matter where we were in north Alabama, we'd go back to Gadsden. I quit the campaign trail many a time at ten-thirty or eleven o'clock at night after a shift change up there, run back over to Gadsden, spend the night, and get back out there the next morning at seven o'clock when it changed again. It was maybe forty or fifty miles over from Gadsden, but it helped us. It saved so much money, it helped us tremendously.

"My entertainer was a heavy machinery salesman, a young man named A. F. Casey. Casey was one of these guys who could sit down at a piano and just thoroughly entertain a huge crowd with cute songs that they had never heard before. He had worked with me in the first campaign. north Alabama was his territory, and he knew every county commissioner.

"He used to come down to the highway lettings in Montgomery, and he would always go into the lounge and play. He was an outstanding piano player. He had a lot of little novelty tunes he would sing. And while we were singing and cutting up and having a good time in the lounge at night, we got the idea of his helping me to campaign. "He had one that everybody used to love. They'd say, 'Casey, play "My Little Red Wagon."' It was a very novel little tune. We used to say that when we ran again, we were going to have us a red wagon we pulled around.

"Casey helped in another way during the second campaign. He had a helicopter that he would use to go out to jobs. He'd go out to a contractor and put down right on the job, especially with the road builders because they were building these new roads at the time. He had my signs all over it. He'd fly it around. It was novel as it could be. That second time we really ran a campaign.

"Carl Goggins traveled with me as much as he could. He was a single man, and he could leave sometimes because he had a little help at the newspaper in Dothan. Carl wrote a political column for weeklies in the state, and he got a lot of attention. It was a needed thing. He started out by just giving it away, then just asking for expenses, and so on. He made a little money out of it. Then he sold the little newspaper and went into mutual funds. The last time I saw Carl, he was in mutual funds, and I think he was doing real well.

"Carl's paper was a member of the Alabama Press Association, so he took me to one of their meetings. If you as a candidate were invited, you could go. Otherwise, you couldn't. But, old Goggins invited me. 'You're welcome, and we appreciate your coming,' they all said. I made a lot of friends at that meeting telling stories.

People like a good story teller. Goggins and I made a good pair. He'd cue me just right. 'Rich, tell them that story about . . . Y'all ought to hear this. That's one of the best . . .' He'd build it all up, and I wasn't afraid of him overbuilding it. I had the black dialect down. I could do as well as any professional you ever saw with it. I look back now, and I'd probably made a whole lot more money if I'd gone into the entertainment field rather than politics. I could have been a stand-up comic."

Pitching the Campaign to the Folks. Richmond and his friends had developed a technique for the campaign. "When it came time to qualify, we had everything all set up. We had speakers on all the trucks. We qualified the first day it opened up and then hit the road.

"We got us a little buckboard and painted it red to make it look like a little red wagon. It was just a trailer, hooked behind a red station wagon with signs all over it. We put a piano on that little buckboard and wired it for sound, and we put four big speakers on it. We would pull into one of these little towns in north Alabama, run the speakers up, and Casey would start pumping that piano. He'd sing 'Little Red Wagon' and 'Ole Parson Brown', 'Sweet Georgia Brown' and numbers like that. He'd draw them for a mile around. 'What is that going on downtown?' They'd go down there, and he'd entertain them a little while. Then they would introduce me, and I'd make a little speech.

"We put words to Casey's Little Red Wagon tune, and that was our theme song. He sang, "Won't you ride in my little red wagon? I'd love to ride you down the street." We changed the words to, "Won't you ride in our little red wagon? We'd love to ride you down the street. Won't you ride in my little red wagon? Ole Rich has got them other candidates beat. Hold tight till we get to the capitol; we'll all be together, you and me. Won't you ride in my little red wagon? Just you and Rich and me." And he'd sing that thing, and it was catchy. The little red wagon got to be sort of notable around the state.

"We'd run what we called a little pitch. We'd move a sound truck in and tell them the little red wagon was on its way. You don't have to stop. Just listen right where you are in your stores, and we're going to talk to you. You don't have to come out. We don't want to interfere with you, just want to introduce you to Richmond Flowers who is running for attorney general. Folks would listen. The whole thing didn't take fifteen or twenty minutes. I'd say, 'I'm not going to hold you up and make any long speech and bore you to death. I'm just running for attorney general. I want your vote and support.' And bingo, we'd go on out of town.

"We'd catch a shift change early in the morning. We'd get through with it and would run and get us some breakfast. Then we'd start again and campaign all day long. Then we'd either start a rally or make one if it was anywhere within fifty or sixty miles. Then we'd catch a late shift change. The last two weeks, I had it organized so there wasn't any way in the world a man could cover the territory I was covering. I was just combing north Alabama. That's where the votes are."

Learning to Use the Old Red Head. "When I started campaigning the second time, I always wore a hat. Most men in those days wore a hat. Well, I had some cards in my left pocket, and I got in good practice grabbing one out with my left hand and shoving it off. Shake your hand and give you a card. Then I realized when I'd been campaigning two or three weeks, every now and then I'd get in a crowded place and have both hands busy. You hand someone a card, you shake their hand, and here's a lady. You speak to her, and you've got your hat on. It was Southern tradition for men to wear hats. But it was also Southern tradition that, anytime you speak to a lady, you tip your hat. And if I'm shaking hands with one hand and passing out cards with the other, I can't tip it. I could speak to Miss Smith or Miss Jones without a hat on my head, but she wouldn't forgive me if I had a hat and didn't tip it. All I needed to do was just touch it, but I couldn't because of shaking hands and passing out cards. So I threw that hat away, and I haven't worn one since.

"Within the next few days, I was out shaking hands and one or two people said, 'Give 'em hell, Red. Stay with 'em, Red.' And I begin to figure, 'Hey, I may have something that will spring me out of the others.' So after that, every time I made a speech, I would say, 'If you'll make me your attorney general, I'm gonna look across that Mason-Dixon Line and say, 'Yankee, you better send the best you've got 'cause this ole redhead is ready and I'm gonna stay ready. And I'm gonna fight with all the fire there is in that ole red head.' And it caught fire. 'Give 'em hell, Red. Stay with 'em, Red.'

"I wrote my own speeches. I knew what I wanted to say, and I thought I knew how I wanted to say it. I had some good critics. My mother would listen to me. As for enunciation or pronunciation, she had no equal. She would hear it, and she would correct any little mistakes that I had. For instance, she was the one that taught me, 'every body in this race except you is running for attorney ginral; you run for attorney general. I said, 'Run that by again, Mother.' 'Gen-er-al, not ginral.' I don't know whether it made any difference or not, but I developed a pride in that sort of thing when I was speaking. That's the sort of thing she picked up, and she was a wizard. There's a difference, too, especially on radio and TV. She was good at that. She helped me."

It's Best to Rest on the Sabbath. With the strenuous style of campaigning Richmond and his friends had set, he soon found himself exhausted. Sunday was the traditional day of rest, but he thought he should be seen going to church. A friend straightened him out on that. He explains how he got the complete day to rest. "In those days the Bible Belt had enough effect that you didn't campaign on Sundays. You just didn't do it. I was in Huntsville one Sunday, and I got up and went to Sunday School and later went to church. I had a good friend tell me, 'Rich, once is enough. Don't do that. It'd be different if you were at home, but you didn't know one soul in there. People are so suspicious. They'll say you got up and went to Sunday School and church, and you're not all that religious.' Well, I always went to church at home, but I didn't know whether they knew that or not, and I had to admit to him that I expected to meet some people there. So I took his word and quit that. I did not go to Sunday School and church anymore. Sunday, I just dropped out of sight. I'd rest up in Gadsden. I never got out of the house.

"Campaigning is the hardest work I ever did. It will wear you out. I was tired, and I would sleep late on Sunday morning. Sawdust and his family gave me a room by myself. They closed it off and even had the children so they wouldn't run up and down the hall. I'd get up and eat a big breakfast, never put on my clothes, sit around in my pajamas and robe, and about the middle of the afternoon, Sawdust would give me a list of names. He'd say, 'I want you to call this one, and this one, and this one. Just tell him you're in town, ask for his support.' Sawdust would tell me exactly who it was, and make it perfectly all right for me to call. I'd spend a couple of hours on the phone. Other than that, all I did on

Sunday was sit around on big over-stuffed couches and rest. I'd take a little nap, call these people, go to bed early Sunday night, and then hit that road early Monday morning.

"I lost a lot of weight in the campaign, and I couldn't have held out much longer. The last three or four weeks, I went day and night, day and night. You get three or four hours sleep, and by the time the weekend comes, you are a goon. You are worn out; you just have to rest."

The Rock and Other Things on the Way. Richmond remembers with fondness some of the amusing things that happened during the campaign. "We always laughed about one lady up in Gadsden," he recalls. "She was an older lady. She said she didn't have much to do with politics but said, 'these folks over here want me to vote for Richmond Flowers. I'm gonna listen to him on TV, and if he impresses me, I might vote for him.' In closing my speech on statewide TV, I said, 'So, it's on this rock I build my house. I now rest my case with the sovereign judgment of the people of Alabama, with fervent prayers that they will endorse my candidacy for attorney general.' And I looked that camera right in the eye and was very sincere about it.

"One of the Gadsden workers told me, 'When you closed that speech, she jumped up out of her chair and says, "He's put it on the rock! I'm really gonna vote for him now! He's put it on the rock, and I'm gonna vote for him!"' He said that she jumped out of her chair, and she got on the telephone right then and began to call her old busybody friends. She told them, 'He's all right. I just seen him on the TV and he's great.' He said she called right up till the time she went to bed.

"One real funny incident that happened during that campaign was in Mobile. We had about five or six people in our entourage, and Sawdust was over in Baldwin County and had to come across the causeway. We'd told him we'd meet him in the Admiral Semmes Hotel. Well, we waited and we waited, and finally he came up about thirty or forty minutes late. I jumped all over him. I said, 'Why in the dickens, where in the world have you been?' He says, 'I didn't have a quarter to come through that damn tunnel.' I said, 'Aw, for Lord's sake, why didn't you just call us?' He said, 'And I didn't have a dime to make a damn telephone call either!' I said, 'Boys, if we don't win this election, we all will have to take bankruptcy.' He had to go all the way around to the bridge, and it took it about twenty-five or thirty minutes. He didn't have a quarter to come through the tunnel. I said, 'Well, my goodness, the hotel is right at the end of the tunnel.' He said, 'Yeah, but that ticket taker is on the other end.'

"I said, 'Now boys, we're going to have to do something about this. If we haven't got but a dollar between us, we're going to have to divide it up so folks can make phone calls.' I ran a pretty inexpensive campaign because I simply didn't have the money to spend."

Willard Livingston, Reluctant Opposition. In his second campaign for attorney general, Richmond's most serious opponent was Willard Livingston, son of the chief justice of the Alabama Supreme Court. Livingston had worked a number of years in the attorney general's office and was chief assistant attorney general before the campaign started.

Richmond had thought it was going to be an easy race. "I was considered a shoo-in until I drew the son of the chief justice," he said. "His father put him in the race. He didn't want to run. He had been working in the attorney general's office ever since he got out of law school. Willard Livingston was his name, and his father was old Judge Ed Livingston, the chief justice. Had Willard had any campaigning ability or had he gone out and worked at it, I don't think I could have handled him. The chief justice had banks of telephones, and he called just about every lawyer and every judge in the state. He would call the bar associations and get all the officers and say, 'I want you to run an ad down there and in the ad get every lawyer in the county to endorse Willard for attorney general.'

"What were these judges and lawyers going to tell the chief justice, especially the good ones that had appeals going up there? I had them to call me boiling mad, and they'd say, 'Rich, I'm locked. I can't do a thing in the world.' I had one judge call me and say, 'Now I'm going to do what I told him I would do. I'm gonna vote for Willard. But I called you to tell you my wife has agreed to kill my vote. She's going to vote for you. I told the judge I would vote for Willard because he just put me right on the spot. As I hung up the phone, I told my wife I have never been so humiliated in my life, treated so unprofessional.'

"Willard didn't have any political ability. I never expected to have any trouble with him. He didn't want to run to begin with. His father was one of the old school, an old blunderbuss. He taught law at the

University, and then, after ten or twelve years, he wrote all his ex-students and asked them to elect him to the supreme court. And they did. He was a very colorful old character. I knew Willard wouldn't be any political trouble. I didn't run against him; I ran against his father.

"Willard's father was born and raised in the Sylacauga/Talladega area, but he had practiced law in Tuscaloosa. So Willard was raised in Tuscaloosa. He married into a very prominent Troy [Alabama] family. Willard was a highly respected, well-regarded man, but he was bashful. Willard was not a politician. I don't think he left his office a dozen times. He didn't want to run. After the campaign had been going for some time, I realized my opponent couldn't possibly cover the ground I was going to cover. We were organized and were going from early to late. I figured that he couldn't go to a half a dozen places and that I was going to kill him before he realized what was happening.

"So late in the campaign, I would say in my speeches, 'Now, I don't have anything against my opponent, but I want you to remember I came here to see you. I came here to ask you for your vote because I want to be your attorney general. I'll tell you what I'll do. I'll be just as fair as I can be. If Willard Livingston shows up in your home town and asks you for your vote, vote for him. Forget about me. He's a good man and he'll make a good attorney general. But he's not going to do it, friends. He doesn't want the job as bad as I do. He's been on a state payroll for fifteen years. His daddy has been on a state payroll, and they're going to stay down there and draw their money. They're not coming up here and fool with you.'

"That's pretty hard politics but that's what it got down to those last few weeks. It worked, and I ate him alive. I led him more than 30,000 votes in the first primary and increased it in the runoff. So, I beat him, and I beat his daddy, too."

The Alabama General Affair. In May of 1962, a few days after the primary and before the runoff election, an ad appeared in the Birmingham newspapers accusing Richmond Flowers of wrongdoing in connection with Alabama General Insurance Company, which had gone bankrupt in 1957.[69] Hard-hitting in tone, the ad asked, "Is this the man [Flowers] that you want to fill the high state office of attorney general for the next four years?" Richmond says that the ad was the work of Willard Livingston's father.

The thing that set it off was a cartoon which Richmond had published. "His father got awful mad at me," he recalls, "because during the last few days of the race, I ran an ad of Willard and a big high chair. There was a baby on the floor and an old man standing behind, and it was a good caricature of Judge Ed. Everybody could tell who it was. The high chair was the attorney general's office. Willard was squalling and saying, 'Papa, I want that chair.' It made the judge so mad, he cursed me and said, 'By God, you've got to run against me.' I said, 'I've not only had to run against you, you're the one I'll beat because you're the only one I've had to contend with. If you'd let him alone, I wouldn't even have had to campaign.' Well that just made him madder and madder. The ad they put in the paper was a mean one, but I knew Willard hadn't placed it. I knew Willard, and he was not malicious. It was done by his daddy."

The scandal referred to in the ad involved the Alabama General Insurance Company, of which Richmond had been president. Organized in 1955, Alabama General specialized in the sale of surety bonds to public officials, state contractors, and the state government. Members of the Folsom administration posted their bonds through Alabama General, and so did construction companies who sought to win state contracts. Also, Alabama General sold a large number of surety bonds to the state government to cover cases where private citizens had claims against the state which involved litigation.

While the company was perfectly legal, the fact that people might try to curry favor with the administration by buying its policies suggested a possible conflict of interest. Eventually, the company failed. Alabama General was in trouble by late 1957 because it did not have the reserves to meet its obligations. There was an investigation, and several people were indicted. Since no one actually lost any money, however, trials were never held.

Richmond acknowledges that his involvement in Alabama General was a mistake. "Several members of the legislature formed an insurance company, and after they had been in existence a while, they asked me to be president because I had some insurance experience. Well, my ego worked on me a little too hard. President of an insurance company, you know. Also, I needed income because I didn't have any law practice after I got into the legislature. It was headed up by several very prominent politicians and other people with big names, and a lot of people were willing to be involved. So I took the job of president. There was a lot of potential."

Richmond blames "outside manipulators" for the weak financial position of Alabama General. "At first, when I was trying to save the company and get some assets into it, I did not know it was being manipulated. I didn't realize that some of the people involved were international scoundrels," he says, "until they took a few of us to New York and said that we had a chance to take over a holding company. It was a very large company that had several corporations in it. I realized things weren't right when I was introduced to Ben Jack Cage, an internationally known philanderer and scoundrel. He had raised money for insurance companies in all sorts of ways, and then had bled them out. I resigned from that and came on back home.

"I realized at that time that this company had been scuttled. I did what I thought was the honorable thing and put it in receivership. I got a whole lot of criticism for running it into the ground. Well, it was into the ground when I took it over. And the people who were advisors to the organizers were not serving in any official capacity in the company. They were just a bunch of international manipulators. Everybody immediately pounced in and wanted to know where all the money went. Then they realized there wasn't any money in there."

Expectations for Civil Rights Action. A great deal had happened on the civil rights front between 1958 and 1962. The likelihood for more activity in Alabama was great, and Richmond says he knew there would be some cases, but he had no inkling of the extent to which it would go. He thought Wallace, who was leading in the race for governor, was just engaging in the usual political rhetoric. Like many others in the South, he thought the worst of the disruption was over.

"I had known George Wallace since we were in high school," he remembers, "and I knew he was one hell of a campaigner. During his '62 campaign he said, 'I'll stand in the school house door. I'll do everything I can to preserve the Southern way of life,' and I said the same thing. I would always say, especially when I was out in the boondocks, that this ole redhead was ready to fight the Yankees. 'I'll be right here, and I'm gonna preserve the Southern way of life.' That was the way everybody campaigned, so I didn't think a great deal about it.

"The blacks didn't pay any attention to that. They knew good and well you had to say that to get elected. George never used the word segregation and neither did I. Southern way of life. That was the old cliche to get you by. George and I were not at odds at that time. We had been friends in law school and were friends politically through the 1962 election.

"I thought just about the worst of it had blown over. We'd had eight years of it. The year before I went in as attorney general, an article in the paper said that it was the first year since *Brown v. Board of Education* that there had been no violence in the schools."

The 1962 Election

The 1962 election was critical for Alabama. Massive resistance had collapsed in much of the South, and most of the states of the old Confederacy were progressing in relative peace and harmony toward more equitable treatment of black citizens. The civil rights movement had gained momentum and strength, with growing support from the federal government, and significant change was inevitable. The question was whether the people who realized this could gain control of state government and could steer things in a more constructive direction.

Most important was the race for governor, for the chief executive sets the moral climate and has at his disposal all of the power and authority of the state. Also, he is the legislative leader. The race for attorney general was also important since it determined who would be Alabama's top legal officer. In a local election of great significance, voters in Birmingham would decide whether to change the form of their city government and in the process remove Bull Connor and the other segregationist commissioners from office.

The Race for Governor. Seven candidates entered the race for governor. This group included James E. Folsom, George Wallace, Bull Connor, and an attractive newcomer from Tuscaloosa, Ryan deGraffenried. By law, John Patterson could not succeed himself. In a necessary ritual, all of the candidates declared their support for segregation, so this was not an issue. Still, one of the keys to the race was convincing the voters, still white by a wide margin, of the depth of one's commitment to the cause and of workable ideas of how to fight for it. Folsom was trying for a third term in 1962 and was still a major political force. The other candidates directed much of their energy to attacks on

Big Jim, and the primary on May 1 shaped up as Folsom against the field. Many voters at this stage indicated that they were more against Folsom than particularly for any of the others.

George Wallace knew that the 1962 campaign was critical to his own future. The fact that he had run four years before and lost was not particularly harmful since, as Richmond stated it, candidates ran once to run again. They had to get themselves known and get voters to pay attention to them. A second defeat would be much more serious, however, for it would mark him as a loser.

Wallace tried to create the image of a scrapper who would not give in to outside pressures in preserving segregation. He called himself "the fighting little judge" during the campaign, referring to the fact that he was a former Golden Gloves champion in Alabama and to his claim that, as circuit judge, he had defied the federal courts in their demand for voting records.[70]

Wallace had learned in 1958 not to use high-toned language but to appeal directly to the rural and the blue-collar voters. Before the May 1 primary, he referred to Federal Judge Frank Johnson as a "scalawagging, carpetbagging, race-mixing, baldfaced liar" and said there "wouldn't be room enough in this state" for him and Johnson if he were elected governor.[71] The "liar" part was in reference to voting lists in Barbour County in 1958. Johnson first cited Wallace for contempt but later withdrew the citation because, he said, Wallace aided federal agents in getting the voting records and in effect obeyed the court order. Wallace claimed that the judge backed down in failing to carry through with the contempt citation.[72] The facts are, as has been proven by historians, that Wallace obeyed, but he tried a subterfuge to make himself appear to be a martyr.

Wallace said during the campaign that he didn't like federal judges "making the law. If they're going to make the law, they ought to be elected. There are some mighty good federal judges, but most of them are tending to destroy our personal freedom." He said he would refuse to obey any order to mix the races in schools "to test the validity of the federal courts." He claimed he could make the government in Washington back down because, if federal authorities "ever put their hands on the governor of a state, this would swing public opinion toward the direction of the Southern attitudes." He assured voters there would not be any violence if he were elected. He specifically stated that, as governor, he would follow Mississippi to total segregation rather than take the moderate course of Georgia.[73] As the campaign progressed and Wallace gained support, those close to him reported that he was convinced his "hard fight-to-the-last-ditch" stand on segregation was the reason for his success.[74]

On other matters, Wallace tried to appeal to the rural conservative religious values of the state's population. Discussing economy in government, he said he would wipe out the liquor agent system, reduce expenses of the governor's mansion, and cut back the costs of legislative sessions. He promised that no whisky would be served in the governor's mansion under his administration because it would set a bad example for the rest of the state, particularly the young people, and he said he would eliminate the "free riding" on state yachts.[75]

Folsom Ruins his Chances and his Career. At the beginning of the 1962 race, the big question was whether Big Jim Folsom could win a third term as governor. His popularity had reached a low at the end of his previous term because of his stand on racial issues and because of alleged corruption among members of his administration. The question now was whether he could re-establish the old magic with the common people of the state. All of the other candidates ran hard against him in the primary. They believed he could win, and so did many of the leading political writers.[76]

Folsom's fortunes in 1962 are important because they weigh on the question of leadership and on the direction the state was to take at this critical juncture. He was a known moderate on race. A central issue in interpreting the period is whether any moderate could have been elected. A lot of people believe Folsom could have won, and the embarrassments of the next four years could have been avoided. He stayed away from strong statements during the campaign and soft-pedaled civil rights. He said that he favored maintaining segregated schools, but he also made a point of emphasizing that he would maintain law and order. As it turned out, it was not the race issue that defeated Big Jim but one of the most bizaare incidents in Alabama political history. He made a fool of himself on statewide television.

Richmond Flowers is one of those who believes that Folsom would have won the 1962 election if he had not appeared drunk on television the night before the election. Richmond was asked how it would have been possible for Big Jim to be elected since he was known to be moderate on race. He answered that, while it was true that most people could not have been elected without taking a hard line, there was a wide range in attitudes on the issue. "There were liberals elected from north Alabama," he said. "Those from the Black Belt, where there were very few black voters, were making the greatest effort to keep people separate." Given this diversity, Flowers argues, Folsom had enough charisma and could focus enough on his populist themes to overcome feelings about race.

The incident which finished Big Jim in the 1962 race—and for all practical purposes ended his political career—occurred the night before the primary election. A statewide telecast was scheduled, and a tape, which had recently been made, was supposed to be shown. Folsom thought everything was in order, and he hit the bottle a couple of times as he relaxed. The tape, however, could not be found.

As Richmond recalls, "He went on television obviously drunk. His wife begged him not to go on live. They had a good film they could have put on. She was begging him not to do it, but it did no good. He walked around behind a couch and was introducing his family. He stopped behind his wife and said, 'Of course, this is Jamelle.' He put his hand right at the base of her head and just turned her hair over in her face. 'Everybody knows and loves Jamelle.' Remember this was on statewide television. You know what the women thought when he took his wife's hair and just messed it up. He didn't think a thing about it at the time. But he just didn't realize. You know good and well he would not have done it if he hadn't been drinking. I thought, 'I'm not believing what I'm seeing.' But he did. He just stuck it right up under the back of her neck and turned it over in a flash. 'Everybody knows and loves Jamelle.' And the poor thing was embarassed and trying to straighten her hair up. He forgot one of the kid's names. Of course, he had a lot of them. He says, 'Uhhhhhhh, this is uhhhhhh, what is your name boy? Oh sure, that's ole Jim. I know Jim.'"

"That's the reason he lost. I believe he had become an alcoholic. He was not when I first met him, but the third time around, he was leaning on it. He thought, 'Well, I feel good and I look good.' But in truth, he couldn't handle it. He got just as drunk on two or three drinks as he'd get on two or three bottles. He was one of those that it nailed quickly. He'd slur his words. But that was late in his political career."

The primary election was held on May 1, 1962. Wallace led all candidates with a little over 200,000 votes, and deGraffenried was second with about 160,000. The first returns showed Folsom far behind, but as the rural vote came in he began to catch up. In the final count, deGraffenried led Folsom by just a little over 1,000 votes and made the runoff against Wallace. There is no question that Folsom would have been in the runoff had it not been for the TV episode. Whether he could have defeated Wallace in a two-man race will remain a matter of speculation. Attorney General MacDonald Gallion was fourth in the balloting with 79,000, and Birmingham Public Safety Commissioner Bull Connor was far back in fifth place with a little over 23,000 votes.

Ryan deGraffenried, whose second place finish put him into the runoff against Wallace, was a state senator from Tuscaloosa. He had been in the legislature eight years and had served in both houses. He was an attractive man, thirty-six years old at the time and very bright. He campaigned on a promise of "good government," and urged voters throughout the state to help him carry his message of "good government and leadership."

DeGraffenried was known to his closest friends to be relatively liberal.[77] In the runoff campaign, he contrasted his approach to that of Wallace by saying, "I am for segregation, but threats and dares get us nowhere." He maintained, correctly as it turned out, that Wallace's "threats, dares and loud-mouth rabble-rousing" would invite integration suits and invite federal court action.[78]

The *Birmingham News* endorsed Ryan deGraffenried in the runoff election. In explaining why, it reflected the growing rift in the old alliance between Jefferson County and the Black Belt in the state legislature. The paper said that Alabama did not need a governor from the Black Belt region. It commented editorially that, "The state has plainly suffered through failure to grow industrially," and it explicitly made the connection between economic growth and racial tension. It still could not bring itself to say that Alabama's defiant stand was wrong but stated instead that, "the image of Alabama outside this state has been hurt by too many losing court cases."[79]

Reporters speculated on what would happen to Folsom's followers in the runoff. The former governor said nothing for a time. He was reported to be deeply hurt by his loss, and he sulked around his Cullman home feeling sorry for himself. Finally, a few days before the election, he endorsed deGraffenried.

George Wallace won the general election by a margin of 335,144 to 266,699 and was set to assume the position he had always dreamed of. He intended to keep building his political fortunes, but one choice which was not open to him, unless the law was changed, was to win a second term as governor four years later. By law, an Alabama governor could not succeed himself.

Ryan deGraffenried had run a good race and had won respect. After the election, the *Birmingham News* commented in an editorial that deGraffenried had emerged as a "potent figure in Alabama politics."[80] It had been his first statewide election, and according to Richmond Flower's adage—you run once to run again—he was in a good position for the next race.

The Race for Attorney General. Four candidates entered the race for attorney general, but Richmond Flowers had a great advantage over the rest because of the energy he had put into getting himself known across the state. In the primary, Flowers received 203,981 votes to 169,133 for Livingston. This difference was not a majority because of a small number of votes the other candidates received, so a runoff was necessary.

Very little attention was paid in the press to the race for attorney general, supporting Richmond's claim that it was popularity and name recognition that counted. The purported insurance company scandal was hardly mentioned. An ad endorsing Willard Livingston appeared in the *Post-Herald* on May 22 and listed the names of 256 lawyers, many of them quite well known. The *Birmingham News* endorsed Livingston on May 24, less than a week before the runoff, commenting only that he had a lot of experience in state government and had a good record as assistant attorney general.

Livingston tried to play the race issue. He claimed that printed ballots were distributed among blacks listing Richmond as the statewide choice of the black political bosses. "When thousands of Negro voters back a candidate, it can only mean that the candidate is the choice of NAACP Negro radicals and trouble makers," he charged. Livingston boasted that, as assistant attorney general, he participated in suits against the NAACP, CORE, the Freedom Riders, radicals, and other "trouble makers." "As attorney general, I will continue to defend our segregated institutions," he said, "because I believe segregation is the best policy for both races."[81]

In the runoff election, Flowers received 297,725 votes to Livingston's 252,590, so Richmond had increased his lead since the primary by about 10,000 votes.

After the election was over, Richmond felt some regret because Willard Livingston had been dragged into the race, and his career was about to be ruined. Richmond saw a way out. "Willard had been in the attorney general's office over fifteen years, and the men who were still working there liked him," Richmond remembers. "Before I was sworn in, I talked to him. I said, 'Willard, you can have any job you want in the office except the chief assistant. I'm going to select my own chief.' He says, 'Well, Richmond, that's so kind of you,' because he thought I was going to kick him out. He said, 'You know, my first love is the tax department.' I said, 'They've got to have an attorney, and they can't beat you.' The only thing about the tax department is you have to be appointed by the attorney general and approved by the governor.

"So before John Patterson went out of office, I went over to see him as the attorney general-elect. Patterson had been attorney general, and he congratulated me. He said, 'You know if you'll recommend him, I'll certainly approve him, and he can go on to work over there now.' I said, 'That's even better.' And I went back and told Willard. Then I talked to MacDonald Gallion, the outgoing attorney general, and Mac said, 'You know in a minute I will.' So Gallion recommended him, the governor appointed him, and he went to work for the revenue department before I was ever sworn in. Willard was tickled to death. He was out of all of it, and he still drew his same salary."

Reflections on the 1962 Election. The 1962 election marked an increase of Republican strength in the state. At first, Republican voting among the masses had been mostly protest, an attempt to deliver a message to the national Democrats. But now, as the reality of the civil rights struggle and the pressure to change sank in, a substantial number of voters did what was unthinkable only a few years before. They decided that they were conservatives and made the mental switch. For the first time since the Civil War, it became acceptable to be a Republican in Alabama.

At the same time, the desire to be done with disruption caused by racial matters was growing in some quarters. At a rally for Lister Hill in Montgomery, Lieutenant Governor James B. Allen, who was later a U.S. senator, stated that he was trying to bring public opinion to a policy of opposing violence, mob rule, and inciting to violence. "We cannot have happen here what happened [at Ole Miss]," he said. He was interrupted by loud applause from the audience.[82] The results in Birmingham gave hope that moderate control was possible, but it remained to be seen what the practical outcome would be.

7

Strange Bedfellows: Governor and Attorney General on a Collision Course

Attorney General at Last —And Life Takes an Unexpected Turn

The runoff had been in May 1962, and since the Republicans did not field a candidate for attorney general that fall, Richmond was in effect attorney general-elect for several months prior to taking office. He had plenty of time to prepare his family and get set for an important step in his career.

"The state constitution says that all constitutional law officers should live in Montgomery," he says. "Some good friends in the real estate business got me an apartment, and I went up there in August. I started building a new house immediately, and we moved into it in November, before I took office.

"Mary and I put the children into public school in Montgomery. One child was in the second grade, one was in the fifth grade, and one in the tenth grade. My oldest son played football for Sidney Lanier, which at that time was the largest school in the state." This was Richmond, Jr., who had been born with unusually flat feet. He was an outstanding athlete when the Flowers moved to Montgomery. He became a star halfback at Lanier High School and was later an All-American end at the University of Tennessee.

Richmond gave an early indication that he was not a diehard segregationist. "Between my election and inauguration, Ross Barnett was causing all kind of trouble in Mississippi. He ended up getting fined $10,000 a day until he quit defying the federal court order. Around Christmas I was invited over to Greenville to make a speech, and when it was over, someone asked, 'Are you going to be willing to stand in the schoolhouse door with the governor?' I said, 'Let me make it perfectly clear so there won't be any misunderstanding. The day that I'm convinced a stand in the schoolhouse door will maintain our Southern way of life, you will find me in the schoolhouse door. But if they start charging me $10,000 a day, I want you to know I can't stand that ten minutes, and I don't intend to.' I didn't get any applause when I sat down."

Inauguration Day. The first inclination Richmond had that things were not going to be as he expected came on inauguration day in January 1963. He and George Wallace, the new governor with whom he was on friendly terms, both made speeches. "Our inaugural speeches were just as far apart as they could possibly be," Richmond recalls. "Wallace made his strong plea for segregation, and I made a plea for moderation. George threw the gauntlet in the dirt and said, 'Segregation today, segregation tomorrow, segregation forever.'

In his speech, Richmond predicted with what proved to be keen foresight that "Alabama's soul will soon be laid bare before the world." He commented on the need for good leadership.

"Never before have we seen the time when one hasty, ill-timed or unplanned move could set us back so that our children would be denied equal opportunities in life."

"We in the Deep South have become a militant minority through no fault of our own," Richmond continued. "The socialistic changes occurring around us are revolting to us, and to accept any part of most of them asks us to abandon a way of life that has been precious to us for many generations." He assured his audience, "I stand ready to do battle for our Southern traditions and, as of this day—the day of my inauguration—my every thought and effort will be spent toward preserving segregation and protecting the rights of the State of Alabama and its

Top: Flowers takes the oath of office as Attorney General from Judge Virgil Pittman. Bottom: On inauguration day, from left, Flowers with his brothers Drury, John, and Paul.

officers from any encroachment from the federal government."

This had been standard rhetoric, more or less, but then Richmond sounded a note of caution. "The officers of this state must stand up for their people," he said. "But the people of this state must discern and distinguish between a fighting chance and a chance to fight. A fighting chance, no matter how small, will be held forever. . . . But to defy the same federal arm that speaks for America to Castro, Khrushchev, and Mao Tse-tung; to pre-announce that any decision concerning us that is contrary to our likes will not be heeded can bring nothing but disgrace to our state, military law upon our people, and political demagoguery to the leaders responsible."

George Wallace did not care for the last sentence. "George boiled over when he heard me," Richmond recalls. "He said to some people sitting close by, 'He's called me a demagogue. If it's the last thing I do, I'll nail him.' And that's where the split began. His own people told me, 'You used the wrong word with him. I don't believe he'll ever have any more use for you.' I said, 'So what? The word, I think, was well selected. He is a demagogue if he says he's gonna segregate the state of Alabama. He's not going to do it. The quicker he begins to impress Washington that he's trying to cooperate, the easier the life of the citizens of Alabama is gonna be. And as long as he keeps up this resistance, there's going to be bloodshed.' After that, I was *persona non grata* in the governor's office. I would go over there and try to work with him, but he didn't want anything to do with me. He just separated himself from me."

Running the Office. Richmond figured he needed to smooth some ruffled feathers when he first went into office because many of the staffers were close friends of Willard Livingston. "I always had the attitude that it's all right for a new broom to sweep clean," he says, "but you have to seat yourself. The first thing I needed to do was talk with the personnel in the office who had supported Willard. Willard was a very likeable fellow, and I wouldn't expect them to feel any other way about him.

"Every attorney general has to have a chief assistant. He runs the office while the attorney general is off making speeches, traveling around, etc. Seymore Trammel, who was Wallace's finance director, came to me and told me that George didn't want any Jews in his administration. I said, 'What do you mean? Who are you talking about, Seymore?' He said, 'He doesn't want Randolph Lurie.' Now, that put me in a fix because I liked Randolph, and I tried to think of something.

"I made Randolph, who had been a part of the attorney general's office, my chief assistant. It worked out beautifully for him, and it worked out beautifully for me because I had a trusted friend as the chief assistant. He's the guy that keeps the new man out of trouble, and he probably had as much knowledge, know-how, and experience in state government as any man in Montgomery. And this secretary who had been with him for twenty years was as bright as she could be. I told him, 'You just keep steady.'

"I called in the men one at a time, and I spoke to them as a body. With all the kindness I could exude, I said, 'Gentlemen, I want you to keep doing what you were doing, doing as good a job as you were doing. The only change will be, gentlemen, I want you to realize, and I want you to help me convince this capitol, that I am the attorney general. I ran for it and worked for it. It's mine.' They were just as understanding. They said, 'It should be yours. And if you want to be a good one, we'll certainly help you.' I said, 'That's all I ask.' I also said, 'I don't want any political decisions going out of here.'

"I told the same thing to my opinion committee. When the attorney general gets requests for an opinion, he doesn't just write it or get some individual to do it. He organizes an opinion committee, and they sit on it just like a court of appeals. And they split sometimes. I had seven men on the committee, and they'd split 4-3. I told them, 'When opinions come over here, and we've got some friend who has asked for them, don't put out an opinion that I'll be criticized for. It's got to be good solid law, or I'm not gonna put it out. Now, if you split 4-3 or 3-3, then gentlemen, we will look after our friends. If the thing can go either way, it's going to our friends.' They said, 'That makes sense, and if that's the way you want it, that's the way it's going to be.' I knew it was going to be because I had Randolph riding herd on them. They all knew him and respected him. They knew he was loyal to me, and he wasn't going to let me get any wool pulled over my eyes. So we took off, and they were perfectly easy from the very first. They were sound, and they were secure that I wasn't after them. They were satisfied and pleased with what I'd done with Willard.

"Sawdust was my executive assistant. He arranged my conferences and speeches and politicking and moving around. Randolph was running the office. I had a private secretary, Katherine Haponski, who kept my appointments and so forth. It was her business and my business and nobody else's where I was going or what I was doing. She handled everything very confidentially. I really organized the office quickly and had very capable, very competent help. I had old timers in there. We had well over 100 years of experience in that office, and I let them use it. I had no bones to pick. I was happy, and they were happy. That's the way I organized it, and I never got a criticism or a complaint from any of them."

The Business of the State. Richmond recalls that most of his work as attorney general was actually pretty dull. "You don't generate very much of it. You sit there waiting for something to happen," he says. "A tremendous amount of it is very routine, and the part that's not routine, you don't ever know when its coming.

"The attorney general is chief legal officer of the state and takes care of all of the state's legal business. He is also the chief law enforcement officer. He is the chief prosecutor and is over all of the city and county prosecutors. In this capacity, he deals daily with policemen, sheriffs, and others concerned with law enforcement. The attorney general defends state officials charged with misfeasance in their duty, and he defends state laws. The attorney general at that time was also the state's securities commissioner who regulated the sale of stocks and other securities.

"Every department in state government has to have legal advisors, and those are all assistant attorneys general. The Department of Conservation, the Highway Department, and the Revenue Department all have a sizeable group. The assistant attorneys general are all lawyers. There were 19 working directly in my office. But in all the state government, there were about 120. These were all under the control and at the call of the attorney general.

"If there is an appeal from any local criminal court, then the attorney general picks it up and handles it for the state. Locally, the district attorney prosecutes, but if there is an appeal, the district attorney is through with it. The attorney general takes the case to the criminal court of appeals or the supreme court, whichever it is.

"All public officials have the right to ask for an opinion from the attorney general. Suppose you are a county official, and you want to spend some county money, but you are not sure whether you are allowed to spend it for the purpose you have in mind. You just write the attorney general and ask, 'Can I spend county money for this purpose?' And the attorney general writes back 'yes' or 'no.' That doesn't make it legal, but it covers your skirts. The court can still reverse it, but you won't be in trouble. All the cities and counties have access to the attorney general. So you see, there is a right smart of administrative work in writing those opinions. This was handled by the opinion committees, which I mentioned.

"We also had a trial section, and there was a criminal section where all criminal appeals came. We had a civil section for any civil appeals. It was my decision as to who would try what cases. Usually, they would show me an agenda, and I would approve it. I had to add a federal section soon after I got in because we had so many suits in the federal courts. All of the education suits wound up in the attorney general's office. The civil rights groups would bring their suits in federal court. They would sue a school board, and the state would be in it immediately because a school board is an arm of the state. The attorney general knew they would keep appealing, so he would usually take over right from the start. That way, there was no chance of it getting messed up at a lower level.

"When the Justice Department was trying to knock down a state statute, they always brought the suit in federal court, and the attorney general defended it. We also came into it any time a desegregation suit threatened to bring down an Alabama law. Most people think segregation was just custom we had always practiced, but it wasn't. It was law, and it was easy to attack. Anybody could see that there was unequal protection under the law. The attorney general found himself on soft ground. How in the world could you defend it?

"The main ones I worked on in federal court, however, were school cases. In these, we would appoint a biracial committee and see if it couldn't be worked out. Gordon Madison, an experienced, brilliant lawyer, was the head of the federal section, and he was constantly negotiating. He trusted me, and I trusted him. Gordon had some friends over in Wallace's office, people who had worked in the attorney general's office before, and he even had the respect of Wallace. If he could work it out quietly, they would go along. But if my name was going to be mentioned, or if the agreement was going to say, 'The governor has consented to this,' they wouldn't do it. Gordon worked out a lot of things like that.

"I tried a world of law suits before Frank Johnson," he says, "because we had a lot of civil rights suits. I lost them all, but I tried them. You couldn't defend what I was obligated by my position to defend. One of the things I got so unpopular about was trying to work out compromises. They just wanted you to fight. George Wallace said, 'You've quit the fight.' I'd say, 'The fight's over. We've lost the fight. Now we've got to live with the beast.'"

In a January 1966 speech to the Committee of General Counsel of the Federal Bar Association, Richmond spoke about the jury system and his recommendations for changes. A major point was that a fair trial is impossible if a jury is not truly representative of the population. "It is my duty," he stated, "to make absolutely certain that criminal laws are enforced, that criminal trials are prosecuted vigorously, and that the rights of the weakest man or woman . . . not be impaired by killers in the day or night. This is what I stand for in the State of Alabama. This is what I'm hated for by some. But I must do my duty as I see it."

Confrontation With George. Central to Richmond's experiences as attorney general and to the aftermath is the dispute which developed with George Wallace. It was neither planned nor expected. "I did not start out being opposed to George Wallace," Richmond says. "We had been friends in law school and friends politically in the Folsom era. In fact, I boasted of the fact that I knew every candidate in the race because I had served in the state senate. I can work with anybody, and I tried my best to work with George.

"George didn't have any Republican opponent and neither did I, so between the primary election in May and inauguration the next January, we rode to some meetings together. I'd call him and ask him if he was going to fly down to so-and-so meeting. 'Yeah, come on and go with me.' We were really on a very friendly basis. My inaugural address is what started it. He totally disliked my attitude and wouldn't tolerate me. The split just developed. We never had any direct confrontations. It was all through the media and through our staffs. After we were inaugurated, I showed him full respect. I always went over to his office when I needed to see him."

Richmond recalls a specific instance that left no doubt that his behavior did not suit the governor. "During my first year in office, I needed some help on an appropriation. Prisoners had started filing special writs in federal court claiming that they were falsely imprisoned. Very few of them were actually getting out, but they had filed in federal court and were entitled to a hearing. We had to keep sending lawyers from the staff down there, and it was straining our budget. I went over to see George about a small special appropriation to defend the suits and tide us over. I got there about 2:30 in the afternoon and waited till 5:30 to see him. When I arrived, the outer office was full, and his secretary said, 'Sure, General, I'll get you in there.' (You're addressed as 'general,' which I hadn't known before.) She said, 'I'll tell him right away that you're here.' She went in there and then said, 'He'll be right with you.' He emptied that office before he saw me. Most of them were political hang-arounders who just wanted to say, 'Hello there governor, I shore voted for you.' He made me sit there because he wanted to show me I wasn't welcome in his office.

"That is just not done. The attorney general goes to see the governor. The governor doesn't have any engagement so important he can't see him briefly about state business and then go on with his regular business. When I finally went in his office, he cussed me out and said, 'Where the hell did you get hooked up with these niggers? I ain't giving you a damn dime to help no niggers with.' I made up my mind then, 'The next time I come in this office, you'll call me and tell me when to come.' So I didn't ever go in that office again because he never called me. The only times I ever saw him were on the floor of the senate, in the halls of the capitol, and other places.

"He called me a couple of times, and we did communicate. We had a lot of mutual friends we talked through. We talked through the Speaker of the House. We talked through Rankin Fite who was the former Speaker and was his speaker pro tem and his floor leader, and we talked through the lieutenant governor who was a friend of both of us. And a couple of the senators would help. We had a lot of friends that got along with both of us and didn't get into our differences. We'd send each other messages. I was as close to him as I needed to be.

"Early on we got into a fight which was purely political. He introduced House Bill 9 to the House of Representatives. This bill set up for the highway department a legal office which was separate and apart from the attorney general's office. Well, all the highway lawyers are assistant attorneys general. Whether they are full-time or specially appointed for one condemnation proceeding, they are still assistant attorneys general. We fought it out in the legislature, and I knew my way around there better than he did.

"So I laid back and tripped him two or three places in the senate and finally defeated his bill. He wanted to send over a list of the lawyers who would be appointed to condemn the land for the highway department. I said, 'No, I'm going to appoint those lawyers myself. That's what the constitution says; that's the law.' The fight went on the best part of the first session, and I whipped him. Two or three people in the legislature told me, 'I'm not supporting you in general, Richmond, and I want you to know it. But you just happen to be on the right side of this, which is legal and moral. The governor's got no business taking that department over, so I'm gonna vote for you.'" Marshall Frady refers to this incident as an attempted "punitive maneuver" by the governor against Richmond.[1]

"As the dispute between us developed, I got to be fair game. His senators and his house members and his cabinet members, to get in good with George they'd take a lick at me, even when they didn't have to. There would be no excuse in it. Several of the people in office at that time would take a cheap shot at me. They were just trying to improve their standing with George, trying to be a hero because they jumped on me, and that made my life pretty miserable."

George Stands in the Schoolhouse Door. When George Wallace ran for governor, he promised he would prevent school integration by personally standing in the schoolhouse door if necessary. Nothing so characterized his first term in office nor added to his obstructionist image as this symbolic act. It was futile, of course, as experiences of Ross Barnett and others had amply demonstrated, but the hard liners did not care. As Richmond observed, they just wanted you to fight to the bitter end.

Two blacks, Vivian Malone and Jimmy Hood, had applied for admission to the University of Alabama in 1962 and were denied. District Judge Hobart Grooms upheld his ruling in the 1956 Lucy case that applications to the university could not be rejected on the basis of race. The judge directed the school to admit the two students to the 1963 summer term.[2] They were to be enrolled on June 11, 1963.

Wallace went to Tuscaloosa to keep his campaign pledge. At first there was a standoff with U.S. Deputy Attorney General Nicholas

Katzenbach as Wallace refused to back down and let the students through. The governor had a portable podium set up in front of the entrance to the auditorium, and he read a five-page statement to the large gathering of reporters.

"I proclaim and forbid this illegal act," he said.[3] Wallace had a large contingent of the Alabama National Guard present, ostensibly to back up his stand. Using a previously prepared order, President Kennedy federalized the Guard, and the large contingent at the university was conveniently under federal command. Wallace stood aside, and the students registered.

That evening, President Kennedy addressed the nation about the situation. "This is not a sectional issue," he said. "Difficulties over segregation and discrimination exist in every city, in every state of the Union, producing a rising tide of discontent that threatens the public safety. . . . We are confronted primarily with a moral issue. It is as clear as the American Constitution. The heart of the question is whether all Americans are to be afforded equal rights and equal opportunities." He informed the nation and Congress that he was about to ask for extensive federal legislation to redress the multiple injustices suffered by blacks. Thus began a campaign which culminated in the Civil Rights Act of 1964.[4]

Later, it was revealed that Wallace had discussed with federal authorities the best way to handle the situation so that order could be maintained and everyone could save face. His defiant stand was in effect a charade.[5] Years later he said "We were mistaken" and claimed he was actually trying to prevent violence while carrying out a pledge to maintain the state government's authority over education.[6]

Richmond refused to become involved, further separating him from the governor. "I wouldn't have any part of it," he says. "I spoke against it and intimated again it was nothing but demagoguery. It wouldn't do any good. He knew it wouldn't do any good; he was doing it to popularize himself. I was not in Tuscaloosa, and took no part in it whatsoever. When I made speeches, people would ask, 'What do you think about George's stand?' I'd say, 'It was a stand all right, a grand-stand! That's all in the world it was, a grandstand. It didn't do one bit of good in the world.'"

In 1965, Miss Malone became the University's first black graduate.

Her success led the way to an integrated student body which is now more than 10 percent black.

Wallace's stand in Tuscaloosa was an example of what Richmond calls "fanning the flames of discord." School systems would work hard to prepare a desegregation plan which could be implemented without disorder, and just as they were ready to set it in motion, Wallace would interfere. Violence often resulted. Instead of helping the state move through this very difficult period, the governor keep stirring up trouble.

Staying the Course as Pressures Increase. Why did he continue to follow the same course when he found himself increasingly separated from the governor and other state officials? Richmond explains, "In my mind, I had no alternative but to obey the law. Anything else was like telling the chief of police to pick out the laws he liked, crack the whip on them, and forget the others. I couldn't do that.

"First it was Supreme Court decisions. Then we got executive orders and then legislation. So I said, 'When you get the legislative, the executive, and the judicial all agreed, it's all over.' I always said that the states' rights issue was settled at Appomattox in 1865. It was settled by the Supreme Court in *McCulloch v. Maryland**when Congress was given implied powers to carry out its responsibilities. You haven't got a branch to hang on. You're going to fight the executive, the legislative, and the judicial, and then you're back to revolution or rebellion again.

"I always took the greatest pleasure when people told me I was ahead of my time. They would say, 'Rich, man, I know you're right, but you're ahead of your time.' I'd say, 'How sweet it is to be ahead and not behind.' My crowd used to get so mad at me when I'd pull that on them. They would say, 'Rich, we don't want to get too far ahead of this thing.' 'How sweet . . .' 'Oh, shut up! I don't want to hear that!' How sweet it is to be ahead and not behind.

"I had good friends who told me, 'You're right. I know you're right, and I ought to be ashamed but I'm not. And I'm not going with you either. You'll be lucky if you live through it.' 'Aw, they won't kill me.'

---

*An 1819 case which held that the states had no power to threaten the supremacy of the federal government in matters committed to its jurisdiction.

And I'd stop and think that it wasn't many years ago when they killed an attorney general in this state. 'If you get behind me and help me, we'll get through this,' I'd say. 'All you have to do is go according to the book, boys, and it'll work.' But they weren't willing. 'Well, Rich, you're my friend, but you understand I have to make a living. I have to live with these folks.' That's all you could hear. 'Everything in the world I have is right here in this county. I've got to live with these folks, and I'm going to live with them next year and the year after that, after you're gone.'"

The Liberal Image Develops. Richmond Flowers was politically ambitious, and he had his plan worked out for becoming at least a United States senator. Part of his scheme was to get the right kinds of publicity and to be well known. What happened to his image while he was attorney general was the last thing he ever expected—or intended.

George Wallace quickly achieved national fame with his strong statements and his stand in the schoolhouse door. He proved to be an expert at getting and keeping attention. He was soundly disliked by the national press, loathed by the liberal establishment, and offensive generally to moderates and people of good will outside of the Deep South. Richmond was kind of an innocent bystander to all of this. He had his own agenda, and as he said, he did not intend for his inaugural remarks to be taken personally by the governor.

At first Richmond was ignored by the press, but soon the contrast between his efforts and those of Wallace began to get attention. Certain writers began picturing Richmond as a kind of hero, a liberal who was fighting desperately for the rights of man in darkest Wallace country. Receiving adulation is pleasant to most, and Richmond began to warm up to the attention he was getting. He made speeches all over the country and wrote articles. By the last year of his term as attorney general, he, too, was well-known nationally. He and Wallace became symbols of the two sides of the struggle. Unfortunately for Richmond, this imagery developed in Alabama as well as in other states. To many of the locals, he came to be seen as an ogre fighting against their great hero, one of those despised liberals who somehow got into high state office. The label persists. In a book published in Birmingham in 1991, his racial views are referred to as "ultra liberal."[7]

As his fame spread and he received more and more invitations to speak, he tried to make the point that in his own mind, he had not really changed. He would deliver the speech he made as law school orator in 1948 and follow it with his inaugural address made fifteen years later. Then he would say, "I ask you, when did I turn around? You can see that I've been a progressive all along. I never considered myself a liberal. But I always said, I am a very aggressive progressive. I believe in moving out. I believe in mushing on. Try something new to make things better. Back off if it's wrong. Let's try to make things better, always."

He received many invitations to speak at universities. "I spoke all up and down the east coast," he remembers, "and I got many invitations into the Ivy League. When you speak in the Ivy League, it's understood that you give a prepared talk, but then you're going to submit to questions and answers. It happened at such places as Amherst, Columbia, Dartmouth, and Duke. It also happened at Birmingham-Southern, which would rival any of the eastern colleges in pouring the straight-line, hard-line questions to me after I made a prepared address.

"I was amused and highly entertained, but I mean they came after me up there. And it was on a liberal line, too. Invariably, they said, 'General Flowers, you're not a liberal.' I answered, 'Well, now that's all according to where I'm being judged. I'm not a liberal by a far sight as far as your philosophies are concerned, but in the Deep South, in Wallace country, I'm a pink ole screaming Commie!' 'Why you're not a liberal at all,' they'd say. 'You're barely over the line of moderation.' I said, 'That's where I'm trying to stay. That's where I'm doing my best to stay. I hope to be a man of moderation and be willing to give up some of the conservative attitudes and ideas that I was born and raised with. The old days are gone, and we don't want them back. Even though our leaders are promising them back, we don't want them.'

"Not too long after Malcolm X was killed in 1965, I was speaking in Tuskegee, and the president of the university told me, 'Mr. Flowers, we appreciate what you're doing.' I says, 'Well, Doctor, I'm not doing anything. I'm just doing my job.' He said, 'Yeah, you're doing your job. But you be careful.' He said, 'You look at Malcolm X. These transitory leaders are always cut down. You ought to know your history that well. If you don't, go back and read it. When new ideas come, sensible, reasonable ideas, those who lead the fight must go, politically or otherwise. Then new leaders will temper their ideas, and they'll take it up and go.'

"I think things have improved ever since then, but he was right. Those that get caught in transition, they get trampled every time. You can't live through transition to save your soul. I was one of those that came in with the old and went out with the new."

Reaction to a Different Attorney General. The reaction predicted by the Tuskegee president began soon after Richmond was inaugurated. "I went in office in January, and by March and April it had already gotten so bad that I hired a bodyguard," he says. "I skimped here and there, and I hired a former deputy sheriff. He was a great big strong guy who used a gun well and wasn't afraid of the devil himself. When I was on the job, he stayed right with me all the time."

A lot of threatening telephone calls came to Richmond's office. "I finally put in a private line that only my wife knew about. Later, I gave the number to the Speaker of the House and the senate floor leader because I was real close to them. Any time that phone rang, I knew it was a very important call because so few people had the number. Every afternoon when I started to leave the office, I'd pick up the phone and say, 'You can quit listening now, you SOB, I'm going home.' They could tap those lines but they couldn't get the numbers on them."

Late in February 1965, after Richmond had been attorney general for a little over two years, the newspapers reported that a wire tap had been found in his office telephone.[8] "It would transmit any conversation on my private phone about five to six hundred yards," he reports. "That distance would just about extend to the governor's office. I gave the transmitter to the FBI and asked them to check it out. They told me, 'All you have to do is turn this radio on to a particular frequency. This little light will come on when the telephone is in use, and any time you want to listen to the attorney general's private telephone, just flip it on and you'll hear.'"

A more frightening incident concerned the Ku Klux Klan. Richmond recalls, "One time when I was in New York, I got a call from the FBI, and they said they understood I was going to make a speech in Mississippi. I said, 'No, that speech has been canceled.' They said, 'Well, we've called to tell you to be very careful about going to Mississippi. When it was announced you were going to speak, the Klan over there informed the Klan of Alabama that as a courtesy to them, they would have you killed. You be careful about going to Mississippi. We don't believe they will leave their state and go to Alabama, but don't go to Mississippi unless you notify us or the Justice Department.'

"Just as a courtesy to the Alabama Klan, we'll get him while he's in Mississippi. That's what the caller told me. I thought, 'Yeah, and I'm the queen of the May.' I called back immediately and got the Justice Department and the civil rights division. I got Mr. Doar, who tried 90 percent of the lawsuits down here, and he said, 'Yes sir. I told them to call you.' That call was just as genuine as it could be. Luumpp—I swallowed heavily. 'Thank you, John.'"

Actual physical violence against Richmond occurred in October 1965, after he had been involved in several well-publicized suits involving the Klan. It happened at a football game. "Dothan High School played Lee High School in Montgomery," Richmond recalls. "My brother Paul and his family and a good many of my friends came up, and I met them at the game. I didn't care much about seeing Dothan and Lee play because my boy was in Lanier, but I wanted to see my brother and friends. Dothan defeated Lee, and of course, I cheered for Dothan. We were all cheering for Dothan. When the game was over, we got up leisurely and started walking down the stadium steps.

"Two young white men came up to me. One of them said, 'Hello, Mr. Flowers,' and he stuck his hand up to shake hands. I said, 'Hi, young man.' When I put my hand out, he caught it with both of his and snatched me forward just as hard as he could. I didn't go forward down those steps because a big fist put my head flat against those steps and my feet shot out from under me. He hit me in the mouth, and I spit blood everywhere. I've still got a lump in my chin from that thing. I don't know how long I was out, just a few seconds I expect. My brother Paul chased them and shouted, 'Stop those men! Stop those men!' I said, 'For God's sake, stop *him*! Don't let him get hold of those fellows. They'll beat him to death. He's older than I am.' They got away in the crowd, but it didn't take until about noon the next day to find out who they were. Both of them had records. One was for child molestation, and the other was for drugs.

"That night they were out at their local beer joints bragging about knocking hell out of the attorney general. The police knew who they were. I wouldn't give them the satisfaction of going after them because no jury in Montgomery would have convicted them for getting me. A columnist for the local paper wrote, 'A lot of folks think maybe he got what he deserved.'"

A Nice Side of Things—Meeting Interesting People. Richmond's position in state government and his growing reputation as a fighter for justice paved the way for him to meet a range of interesting people. He remembers fondly his interaction with Robert Kennedy. "I was a great admirer of John Kennedy and still am today," he says. "I never became socially associated with the Kennedys, but as a state attorney general, I was always welcome in the attorney general's office in Washington. Robert was U.S. attorney general when I went in, and we established a friendship.

"I admired him and liked him. Occasionally, I'd get down in the dumps, and I'd say to myself, 'Well, I'm just going to take a trip to Washington.' He'd always laugh with that little clipped speech of his and say, 'Buck up, General, this too will pass. We'll whip it; we'll put it behind us.' Once when I was in Washington, the papers carried a notice that he had been five days in Alabama, incognito. He was just moving around, observing, not letting anybody know he was there. When I went in that morning, I said, 'I understand you've been down in my state for four or five days.' He said, 'I have. I found out that Alabama right now is in a football/Negro syndrome, and if you're not prepared to discuss those two subjects, you'll be left out of 90 percent of the conversation. Between Bear Bryant and Martin Luther King, that's all they talk about in Alabama.' Now that was the truth, the whole truth, and nothing but the truth.

"I was standing in the capitol hall one day after Robert got into the United States Senate. You could hear the Kennedys everywhere they went because there was always a big entourage following them. Down the hall was coming Bobby Kennedy with all of these people around him, and I realized I was right in front of his Senate office door. So I just backed up against the wall. He started in the office and caught sight of me out of the corner of his eye. He said, 'Wait just a minute. General! You didn't tell me you were in town.' I said, 'Well, sir, I don't have any business. I just wanted to pay my respects.' 'Come on in!' He walked in his office and told his secretary, 'Tell everyone just hold off for a little while. Come on in, General.' He and I walked in his office and left the outer room full of reporters, photographers, and TV cameramen.

"He said, 'I've been wanting to see you. I knew you'd be up here sooner or later. I want to give you something.' He said that his brother Jack, a few months before he was killed, bought some mementos that he gave to very special friends. 'I found the last three of them the other day, and I know for a fact that he wanted you to have one. After these three are gone, General, there won't be any more because Jack bought these himself.' He gave me a PT-109 tie clasp which I still have. It was the most absorbing thing I ever had happen to me. I've had a lot of people laugh at me and say, 'I bet he didn't have more than 10,000 of those things.' He may not have, but he convinced me that I got one of the last three, and that John Kennedy himself wanted me to have it, and he gave it to me for him. That's the way it's going to be, buddy, no matter what you think. I'll always keep it and cherish it."

"I argued two cases before the Supreme Court, and I got on a chatty basis with Archibald Cox. He introduced me to the Supreme Court when I argued a case one time, and then we had our pictures made together. When I finished the argument and sat down, he pushed a little note across the table that said, 'In all of my experience, I have never seen this entire court as attentive as they were to your arguments. Congratulations!' I saved that note for years. I showed it to somebody one time, and I said, 'Here's a note Archibald Cox wrote.' They looked at it and said, 'Sure, and I'm George Washington.'"

Richmond also interacted with a number of top civil rights activists. "I ran into Roy Wilkins at the 1964 Democratic Convention," he remembers. "He was standing by a rail looking over at the floor. I walked up and said, 'Aren't you Roy Wilkins?' He turned around and said, 'I wouldn't let any of my people know I didn't know who you were, Mr. Flowers, and I'm mighty happy and proud to meet you.' That's the first time I'd ever laid eyes on him. We had quite a nice chat. He just smiled and shook my hand, 'What can I do for you?' I said, 'Nothing. I've opposed you in a lot of lawsuits,' and he said, 'Yes, you have. Sorry we couldn't be together.' I said, 'Well, we must have been 'cause you've beat me in every one so far.' Roy Wilkins was a very polished individual, I thought. He was very sensible, very reasonable."

Stokely Carmichael was younger and more militant than the older leaders and less likely to try to accommodate the feelings of whites. He came into Richmond's office one day with a confrontational demeanor.

"He said he was in Lowndes County helping people to vote," Richmond remembers. "He said, 'I feel I have a constitutional right to do that.' I answered, 'Anybody who ever read the Constitution would tell you, Stokely, you've got every right to do that.' He said, 'I'm over there aiding my brothers and sisters to vote, and they're riding the highways and byways over there with flashlights and shotguns and every thing else looking for me.' I said, 'I know that, too, and you'd better be careful because there's nothing I can do to protect you. Every bit of the protection is under the governor.' He told me of a few instances where he had close calls, and it scared him pretty bad. I said, 'You won't have any action from this office prohibiting you from aiding people who are registering under the voting rights bill because it's your constitutional right and it's their constitutional right.'

"The newspapers knew he was there, and as soon as he left they came in. I told them exactly what I had told him, that Stokely Carmichael had a constitutional right to do what he is was doing and those molesting him were the ones breaking the law, not him.' The next day the paper came out with an article on Carmichael visiting Flowers, but the headline was 'Flowers Agrees with Carmichael.' You read it and it was harmless, but the redneck doesn't read. They're certainly not going to read five or six or eight or ten inches of column because that's an all-night assignment for the crowd that was out chasing him. All I said was that I agreed he had a constitutional right to do what he was doing. I don't believe there's a lawyer in Montgomery who wouldn't have agreed with me."

On a trip to the west coast, Richmond learned something about the insensitivity of top business people to black thinking and black aspirations. The person who provided this experience was Louis Lomax, a black writer, reporter, and TV newsman. "Louis was a bright guy with a lot of good college degrees," Richmond says. "He told me a story of when they burned Watts. He said, 'When that thing broke, I got a call from the chairman of the board of the biggest bank in Los Angeles. He wanted me to meet with a biracial group as quickly as possible. He knew that something had to happen. We met in the office of the publisher of the *Los Angeles Times*. Now you talk about going to the ivory tower, there I was. I was the only black in there, but there were four or five bankers and the publisher of the *Los Angeles Times*. After we passed our greetings and sat down, the publisher of the *Los Angeles Times* said, 'Before we start, will someone please tell me just where Watts is. The man didn't even know where Watts was. Now wasn't he interested in race relations?' Louis was as articulate a man as you ever saw. He told me, 'Damn it. I'm not suppose to like you, but I do.'

"He was very much of an activist and a leader, too. He used to say, 'All I want is to make enough money to buy me one of these big houses over in the hills of Hollywood and have me a little white man, a little white jockey with a brass hoop, as you come into my place.'"

Of all of the civil rights leaders he met, Richmond feels that Martin Luther King, Jr., was the most outstanding. As attorney general, he had very little direct interaction with King, though one memorable conversation stands out in his mind. "It was the time Martin Luther King asked me if I was a segregationist. I acknowledged that I was, that I was born and raised that way. 'But,' I said, 'I'm enforcing the law. The law's changed now. It's no longer segregationist.' He said he appreciated my position, and 'God bless you. I hope you're able to hold out, and I hope nothing happens to you. If there's anything we can do to prevent anything happening to you, we will.' But he never asked me for any help, and he never suggested that I call him for help. He just let me know that he was aware of my position.

"There's no telling how many thousands of lives Martin Luther King saved in this state with his nonviolent approach. Look at the riots in such places as Los Angeles, Chicago, and Detroit. Martin Luther King maintained control here in the South. Other blacks were meeting and preaching 'kill and get killed. Let blood flow in the gutters.' King fought hard for his leadership among his own people, and, as long as he was living, he was always able to keep most of the black general public committed to nonviolence. Had the other bunch ever gotten the leadership, I believe there would have been some type of death toll in this nation."

Birmingham and Bull: A Boost For National Legislation

National opinion toward civil rights had been slowly changing, and the nation was about ready to give the federal government the power to end legal civil rights abuses. The tactics of King and the others had worked, with the help of the George Wallaces and Ross Barnetts.

Congress was not yet fully persuaded, however. Another dramatic episode was needed to give the decisive thrust.

The Freedom Rides marked Birmingham as a prime target for such an event. By 1961, the city had earned a reputation as one of the South's toughest and most segregated cities.[9] It was known to many as the "Johannesburg of America."[10] Harrison Salisbury's *New York Times* articles in 1960 had placed Birmingham on center stage, and the treatment of Freedom Riders in the city in May 1961 proved that many of Salisbury's criticisms and characterizations were accurate.

The Most Segregated City. The racial climate was never very good in Birmingham. In the years after World War II, some fifty bombings had occurred, with black churches and synagogues among the targets. One part of the city was attacked so often that people called it "Dynamite Hill."[11]

By 1950, as the nation entered the postwar period of prosperity, a few leading citizens tried to take progressive steps on the racial front. They formed the Birmingham Interracial Committee in 1950, and in March 1955 the Birmingham Community Chest sponsored an Educational Institute on Race Relations at a local college. It was the first unsegregated meeting of its kind in the city's history and was attended by eight hundred delegates.[12]

Attitudes hardened quickly after the *Brown* decision, however. As the civil rights battle heated up, the Ku Klux Klan increased its membership and its activities in Birmingham. City politicians began to take stronger pro-segregation positions. In the face of political pressure and increasing racial tension, the Birmingham Interracial Committee disbanded in 1956.

The major civil rights leader in Birmingham was Reverend Fred Shuttlesworth. In 1956, after Governor Patterson had the NAACP enjoined from activities in the state, Shuttlesworth and some of his associates organized ACMHR, the Alabama Christian Movement for Human Rights. The ACMHR began its activities by filing a suit that demanded that the city hire more black policemen. A bomb exploded at Shuttlesworth's home on Christmas Day, 1956.

Shuttlesworth and his group were active in a number of areas. They went after transportation and got a favorable ruling from federal Judge H. Hobart Grooms. In April 1961, just a few days before the Freedom

Rides, the Fifth District Court of Appeals ordered that bus terminals in Birmingham be desegregated and separate waiting rooms abolished. There was also an attack on segregated education as blacks sought admission to white schools.

The Ku Klux Klan instigated a number of impudent, repulsive acts as tensions increased. Klan members attacked singer Nat King Cole, an Alabama native, on stage during an April 1957 performance for a white audience in Birmingham. The Klan conducted parades through the city's black neighborhoods, and in a single night in August 1958 it burned crosses at eighteen public schools to protest possible school desegregation.

The Freedom Rides Shake Local Complacency. Given all that had happened the past five years, it seems that race issues might be an overriding concern in Birmingham by 1960, but they were not, at least among the city's white leadership. Race and civil rights were mentioned very little in Birmingham newspapers prior to the Freedom Rides. Going through the papers, one gets the sense of business as usual. Smoldering resentment was expressed periodically in editorials, a lot of it directed toward "outsiders interfering in local affairs." Voters in Birmingham passed a large bond issue for a variety of improvements in 1960, and the *News* exulted, "We're off to a flying start for the Soaring Sixties."[13] Clearly, the potential for upheaval the civil rights movement held for Birmingham was not yet grasped.

The Freedom Rides in 1961 changed the complexion of everything. This incident surprised city leaders and gave their self-confidence a jolt. In embarrassment and consternation, they realized that they were not off to a flying start in the new decade. In an event symbolic of the general plight, the city's professional baseball team, the Barons, left in November 1961 because the owner was afraid of what would happen if other teams brought black players into town. The Barons had been in Birmingham since the early part of the century, and Bull Connor had gained his first fame as their play-by-play announcer.

The city's well-being and reputation quickly became a central concern. A front-page editorial in the *Birmingham News* on May 16, 1961, two days after the incidents at the Trailways bus station, stated, "Thugs must not take over our city. Many blunders marked the eruption of violence Sunday. The biggest was that of Governor Patterson in announcing he could not guarantee protection." The following day, another front-page editorial stated, "It is essential that our city government and our state government not only have the cooperation of rank and file as well as city leaders, but that we—the people—demand that they preserve law and order." An editorial cartoon showed a large figure titled "The People" surrounded by disorder caused by "Fear and hatred in Birmingham's streets." The caption said, "Stopping it is OUR job." In an insight the politicians had apparently failed to grasp, the *News* stated that one of the greatest dangers of the racial crisis was letting the extremists take control.

The newspaper did not change its position on fundamental civil rights issues, however. It was irritated by the actions of the Freedom Riders and Shuttlesworth, claiming that they came "with a chip on the shoulder," trying to incite trouble. "All of us resent those who were deliberately sent or came through misguided zeal to test our mettle and our tempers," it stated. "When we permit that temper to explode, when we permit violence to run amok, that is when they win their point."[14] It quoted an *Atlanta Journal* editorial, that "Those who beat the riders played right into their hands."[15]

As the pressure built, local writers and leaders kept saying, "Wait, let us handle things in more orderly fashion." But the other side kept increasing pressure. The locals felt that they were not being given a fair chance. Their irritation and frustration is understandable. It is also true, alas, that their prior actions proved that little would have been done if pressure had not been brought.

Birmingham Business Leaders React. Birmingham's leadership finally realized that the negative publicity was doing great harm. James Free, a respected local columnist, quoted an Atlanta newsman on the publicity connected with the Freedom Rides. "It is just this kind of racial bias stories out of Birmingham and Alabama that have been helping the industrial growth of Atlanta for years," he said. "Everyone knows the cities have been bitter rivals for new industry, for new government offices, and for national attention and prestige generally. It's only in recent years that Atlanta has spurted well ahead." The newsman said that Atlanta Mayor William B. Hartsfield could name several industries which came to Atlanta because of the racial image of Birmingham and Alabama.[16] There was no question that Birmingham's economy was

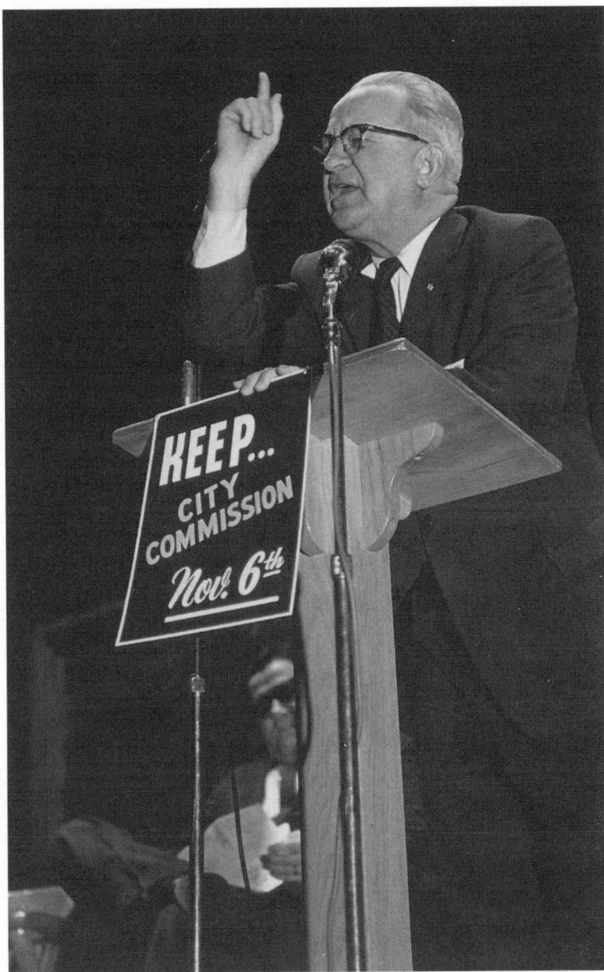

Bull Connor on the campaign trail in Birmingham.

Birmingham Public Library

lagging. The city lost 10 percent of its jobs during the 1958-1961 period.[17]

The Birmingham Young Men's Business Club, which had publicly criticized Connor for his actions during the Freedom Rides,[18] was convinced that something had to be done. A biracial Senior Citizens Committee was organized in August 1962 to try to ease racial tensions and prevent further disorders.[19] The board of Directors of the Birmingham Chamber of Commerce passed a resolution calling for enlargement of an already-existing study committee which it had formed in April 1961 by the Chamber. The committee now included members from the

Chamber, the Committee of 100, and the Birmingham Downtown Improvement Association.

Members of the Business Club decided that the only hope for resolving matters lay in removing Bull Connor and the other city commissioners. This was only a year after the victory of Connor and the other hard segregationists in city elections. Citizens for Progress was formed with the purpose of trying to change Birmingham's form of government.

To force an election on the issue, it was necessary to collect 7,000 signatures on a referendum petition. Citizens for Progress actually collected more than 11,000, and the referendum was held in November 1962. More than 36,000 people voted in the election, and 52.1 percent choose to change the government to a mayor-council form. This was, in effect, a vote to kick Connor and the other commissioners out and pursue a more moderate approach.

Connor, Albert Boutwell, and two others were candidates in the race for Mayor in the new government. The first election for new officials was held in March. Boutwell led but did not receive a majority of the votes cast, and a runoff was necessary with Connor, who finished second. Meanwhile, in February, the commissioners sued to have the change in government postponed. They claimed that, because of a conflict in Alabama laws, they should be allowed to complete their terms.

A runoff election was held on April 2, and a record of 51,278, some three fourths of the electorate, voted. Boutwell won with more than 57 percent of the vote. The new mayor and the nine new council members were inaugurated on April 15, 1963. The city commission refused to give up its quarters, however, until the state supreme court resolved the issue of timing. At this critical point, the city had two governments, each claiming authority. On May 23, the Supreme Court handed down its decision, saying the commissioners must vacate their offices immediately. Connor and the other commissioners left.

The timing was critical. The SCLC had been working on plans for a campaign in Birmingham since the first of the year and had originally planned to begin it in March. The group's leadership agreed to postpone demonstrations until after the runoff election for mayor so as not to help Connor. It turned out to be a race between those trying to bring about change in the city and those trying to exploit its dark side.

Project C. Martin Luther King had failed in Albany, and the SCLC now faced a period of critical decision. King and his followers knew a success was needed, and, wiser for their experiences, they looked to Birmingham. They knew that, if they could get their campaign started in time, Bull Connor would be in charge of Birmingham's police and fire departments.[20]

Fred Shuttlesworth later recalled that he told the SCLC leadership, "Birmingham is where it's at, gentlemen. I assure you, if you come to Birmingham, we will not only gain prestige but really shake the country."[21] King observed that Birmingham had been "the country's chief symbol of racial intolerance," and he reasoned that, if a campaign were successful, it could "break the back of segregation all over the nation."[22] The SCLC leadership decided on "Project C" ("C" for confrontation) in Birmingham.

Wyatt Tee Walker, an aide to King and executive director of SCLC, began visiting the city in January 1963 and laying groundwork with local leaders. He did a much more thorough job of planning than in Albany. Walker was enthusiastic about the opportunity. "My theory was," he said, "that if we mounted a strong nonviolent movement, the opposition would surely do something to attract the media and in turn induce national sympathy."[23]

By March 1, 1963, the SCLC had the names of 250 people who had volunteered to participate and who had pledged to stay in jail at least five days.[24] Preparations were such that the campaign could begin at the end of the month, but, at the urging of local black leaders, the SCLC leadership agreed to wait until after the April 2 elections.

Demonstrations began on April 3. The marches were peaceful the first few days, and the police remained restrained in their response. Police dogs and patrolmen armed with clubs appeared briefly during a demonstration on Palm Sunday, April 7, but they were not used. More and more demonstrators appeared each day, however, and a few arrests were made. Meanwhile, members of the business community were still attempting without success to negotiate a settlement.[25]

On April 10, it became clear why Connor and his force had kept a low profile. A circuit judge that evening issued an injunction against marching without a permit, giving Connor a stronger pretense for action. The injunction was served on King, Shuttlesworth, Ralph

Abernathy, and other campaign leaders the next day. King had made the mistake of obeying such an order in Albany and had weakened the campaign there. The SCLC leaders decided to violate the injunction and to take the line of civil disobedience. Against the advice of the others in the movement, King decided to lead the demonstration on the streets.

King, with local leaders Fred Shuttlesworth and Ralph Abernathy, headed a demonstration on Good Friday, April 12, 1963, and all three were arrested. Shuttlesworth made bail so that he could continue to lead the protest. Funds were available for King and Abernathy to make bail, but they remained in jail to dramatize the campaign.

While King was in jail, Boutwell and the new council members were sworn in, but the old commissioners refused to vacate their offices. David Vann, one of the Senior Citizens Committee negotiators and a future mayor of Birmingham, recalls, "The day we swore in the new mayor and council, the headline said, 'A New Day in Birmingham,' and before the day was over, we discovered we had two mayors, two city governments, and Dr. Martin Luther King and the SCLC marching up and down the street."[26]

About this time, eight leading white clergymen in Birmingham signed a document in which they criticized King for the timing of the demonstrations and asked for a pause until the new Boutwell government could have a chance to improve matters. The ministers were well-meaning, and their position was backed by a good deal of logic since the city had already set in action the mechanisms of change. King answered with his famous "Letter from the Birmingham Jail." He wrote it by hand over several days and passed sheets from his cell to individual visitors. It was typed and returned to him for final editing.

King explained in the letter why the blacks felt they could not wait. They had waited for more than 340 years "for our constitutional and God-given rights," he said. "When you are humiliated day in and day out by nagging signs reading 'White' and 'Colored;' when your first name becomes 'nigger,' your middle name becomes 'boy' (however old you are) and your last name becomes 'John;' when you are . . . plagued with inner fears and outer resentments; when you are forever fighting a degenerating sense of 'nobodiness'—then you will understand why we find it difficult to wait."

The letter was very eloquent and was a master propaganda document. It made the Birmingham ministers look like crass hypocrites and helped paint an unflattering image of the city and its people. King explained in beautiful broad terms why the time had come to change and why the injustices of the past could no longer be tolerated. He pointed out the conflict between America's stated ideals and its actions. He neglected to mention the more immediate reason why a few more days could not be spared. The reason was, of course, that Bull Connor would no longer be in office.

Project C began to falter without its top leaders, and King and Abernathy decided to come out of jail on April 20. The local and national media were virtually ignoring the protests, and the police were acting with unexpected restraint. Then, in a master stroke, King called on black students to join the demonstrations and help "fill up the jails."[27] A number of black leaders were reluctant to have children take part, but the decision stood, and hundreds of students began participating in the marches.

At the beginning of May, the police became less restrained. Connor, in the limelight and in his glory, stayed on the street directing his troops and making himself available to the press. On May 2, after a meeting at the Sixteenth Street Baptist Church, hundreds of blacks headed toward the center of town a few blocks away. More than 1,000 people, including 319 school-age children, were arrested for parading without a permit and refusing to move along when requested to do so by police. Birmingham firemen, also under control of Connor, readied their hoses, and the police brought out German shepherds in an attempt to frighten people.

The scare tactics did not work, and if anything, they backfired. The demonstrations grew more intense the next day, and Connor ordered the use of the fire hoses and the dogs. Several blacks were bitten.[28] On May 4, hundreds of black children and adults left Sixteenth Street Baptist Church and headed downtown. Firemen immediately began smashing them with powerful streams of water. Two fire hoses were equipped with monitor guns capable of blasting bark off of a tree.[29] Clothing was torn off of some marchers in full view of the national press. David Vann commented that, "Once the hoses and the dogs were brought in, the ball game was over. They created very dramatic pictures. There was no way Dr. King could have bought that kind of thing."[30]

The demonstrations culminated on May 7 when some fifteen

The nation watched as police dogs attacked marchers in Birmingham, 1963.

hundred blacks, including a large group of school-age children, overflowed into the city center and caused a massive traffic jam. The marchers sang freedom songs and chanted, "We want Bull Connor."[31] The crowds at the nightly meetings grew, and media coverage, which had been mixed in its sentiment at first, became much more sympathetic to the SCLC cause.

An International Media Event. By the second week in May, the demonstrations in Birmingham had become an international media event. Newspapers around the world ran dramatic pictures of German shepherds confronting young black children. Other pictures showed marchers staggering under the pressure of water from the hoses and having their clothes stripped from them. Birmingham dominated the national TV news programs.

On May 7, a day when more than 2,000 persons were arrested, an agreement was worked out between the full Senior Citizens Committee and the SCLC. Among points in the agreement were desegregation of lunch counters, restrooms, fitting rooms, and drinking fountains within ninety days, and better employment opportunities for blacks. That night the SCLC leadership decided to end the demonstrations.

The Ku Klux Klan had been quiet throughout the demonstrations, presumably to keep from stealing Connor's thunder. It disagreed with the settlement, however, and proceeded to try to undermine it. Klan members set off several bombs, including one at the motel where King had been staying. A riot by blacks ensued, and the agreement seemed in danger. President Kennedy ordered 3,000 federal troops into position near Birmingham and made preparations to federalize the Alabama National Guard. Violence ended after one day, however, and the truce held. On May 13, the Young Men's Business Club voted to endorse the agreement reached by the negotiators.

The Alabama Supreme Court handed down its decision clarifying the election results on May 23, and the old commissioners, including Bull Connor, moved out of city hall. Within a few days, the new city council authorized Mayor Boutwell to appoint a committee to help carry through the agreement reached by the SCLC and the Senior Citizens Committee. On July 23, the city council repealed the segregation ordinances that Bull Connor had upheld so vigorously.[32]

However, the worst was yet to come. On September 15, as Youth Day was being celebrated in the Sixteenth Street Baptist Church, a Klan-planted bomb exploded. Four black girls were caught in a stairway by the blast and died instantly. Later that day a white 16-year-old Eagle Scout shot and killed a 13-year-old black youth. And that evening, an Alabama state trooper shot and killed a black man.

The national impact of the events in Birmingham was enormous. "The movement was really about getting publicity for injustice," Andrew Young said,[33] and it achieved this purpose brilliantly. Wyatt Tee Walker, the SCLC planner, stated that "There was never any more skillful manipulation of the news media than there was in Birmingham." It was all possible because of the actions of Birmingham's police commissioner, of course, and President Kennedy commented that "The civil rights movement should thank God for Bull Connor."

There is no question that Project C was one of the pivotal moments in the civil rights revolution. Historian Arthur Schlesinger, Jr., wrote that the events in Birmingham "abruptly transformed the mood of the nation," and Martin Luther King later remarked that, "the moral conscience of the nation was deeply stirred and, all over the country, our fight became the fight of decent Americans of all races."[34] Meier and Rudwick note that Birmingham "precipitated an enormous outpouring of direct action and fiscal support in the North."[35]

While a brilliant success for King and the SCLC, Project C was an unmitigated disaster for Birmingham. The image of the city and of the state plunged to new lows. King and his followers succeeded in portraying the struggle as a battle between good and evil, with the blacks on the side of righteousness. Connor, the very image of hate and cruelty, represented malevolence in this scenario, and, as the situation progressed, he came to typify all of white Birmingham to the world.

Bull Connor, Perfect Dupe. More than any other single individual, Bull Connor made the civil rights triumph in Birmingham possible. He was poorly educated and unsophisticated, an official who used his power ruthlessly, and one accustomed to having his way without question. William Nunnelley, Connor's biographer, calls him the "quintessential segregationist."[36] Ed Hughes, a columnist for the *Atlanta Constitution* who was a Birmingham native, wrote that Connor typified "the ultimate in conservative and racial bitterness."[37] He was the perfect dupe for the civil rights leaders.

"Bull Connor was the best-named politician Alabama ever produced," Richmond says, "because he was so much bull, and that's all he was. He was coarse. He was crude, and he was just an out-and-out racist. He was just as ignorant as he could be, but he had quite a following.

"During the King demonstrations in Birmingham, I was listening when the reporters approached Bull Connor as his men washed women and children along the street with the powerful fire hoses. They asked him, 'Why did you use the dogs after you had brushed those people back with the fire hose?' He answered, 'I had to wash them niggers off before them dogs would bite them.' Now, he said that on the national hookup, as a city official of Birmingham. He was on the city commission and was police commissioner. I was attorney general then, and that's what I was up against. It just made me sick."

The Civil Rights Bill of 1964. Birmingham gave new strength to the civil rights movement, and it greatly increased support among the national electorate for strong legislation. President Kennedy started his staff working on a bill. Southerners still held positions of strength in

Congress, however, and a long, hard fight to get the legislation enacted loomed ahead. There is a real question as to whether President Kennedy could have gotten the bill passed, at least before the 1964 election. He was very charismatic and had grown in office, but he still lacked skill in moving controversial legislation through Congress.

In June, only a month after the truce in Birmingham, George Wallace helped the cause along—and further besmirched the image of the state—with his stand in the schoolhouse door at the University of Alabama.

More support was gained in August 1963 with the March on Washington "For Jobs and Freedom." More than 250,000 people walked down Constitution Avenue from the Washington Monument and gathered at the Lincoln Memorial. Speeches were given by a number of leaders, and the climax was an address by King. All three networks covered King's speech, giving him an audience of several million in addition to those assembled in front of the Memorial.

Before this vast audience, King gave what was probably his greatest oration. His "I Have a Dream" speech was a magnificent performance, a resounding call to national conscience. Summing up the issue in one sentence, he said, "I have a dream that my four little children will one day live in a nation where they will not be judged by the color of their skin, but by the content of their character."

The event which probably assured that the new civil rights bill would pass was the assassination of President John F. Kennedy in November 1963. New president Lyndon Johnson, in his first address to Congress after the assassination, stated, "No memorial oration or eulogy could more eloquently honor President Kennedy's memory than the earliest possible passage of the civil rights bill for which he fought so long."[39]

Johnson made passage of the bill a top priority. He had the skills in political manipulation that Kennedy lacked, and he played to the emotional state of the nation, sympathetic and distressed after the slaying of its young leader. Johnson used all of the deftness, personal persuasion, and political know-how he had developed in his years in Congress and as minority leader of the Senate.

The bill passed the House of Representatives on February 10, 1964, by a vote of 390-130. In the Senate it faced greater difficulties. There were seven months of debate. Hundreds of obstructionists amendments were introduced, and Southern senators staged a long filibuster. Finally, on June 10, the Senate shut off debate by evoking cloture, the first time it had taken this action on a civil rights measure. The bill passed the Senate by a vote of 73-27, and President Johnson signed it on July 2.

It was the most comprehensive civil rights bill ever passed by Congress, and it significantly increased the means of enforcement over past measures. Among its provisions, the Civil Rights Bill of 1964:

- Prohibited discrimination in public accommodations
- Required equal access to public facilities.
- Authorized the attorney general to institute suits to desegregate schools or other public facilities
- Outlawed discrimination in employment on the basis of race, color, religion, sex, or national origin and established a permanent Equal Employment Opportunity Commission
- Gave added protection for voting rights
- Authorized the federal government to withhold funds from public institutions, such as schools and hospitals, that showed evidence of discrimination.

The obstructionists and right wingers still had one hope. President Johnson was challenged by conservative Barry Goldwater in the 1964 presidential election, and opponents of the civil rights bill thought the results might deliver a blow to the activists and weaken federal resolve to enforce the bill's provisions. Johnson, however, won by one of the largest margins in U.S. history.

Selma Becomes a National Crusade

The Civil Rights Act of 1964 was a great triumph for the civil rights movement. Martin Luther King, Jr., was receiving international recognition for his work by this time and had become a great hero.[40] He was presented the Nobel Peace Prize in Oslo, Norway, in December 1964.

The 1964 bill soon proved to be weaker than desired in the key area of voting rights. Progress was being made in adding blacks to the voter rolls, but it wasn't as rapid as civil rights leaders wanted. Intransigent local officials could still delay and impose ludicrous tests on blacks trying to register. While most localities realized by now that they must register all qualified voters, a few pockets still held out.

Charles Morgan, head of the Atlanta regional office of the American Civil Liberties Union who had grown up and gone to college in Alabama, expressed the essence of the matter. "How easy is it to cast a ballot," he asked, "when you're afraid someone, from the sheriff on down, might shoot you and nobody will do anything about it?"[41]

Selma is Chosen as the Target. Black leaders wanted national legislation addressed specifically to voting rights, and they needed a suitable location to run a campaign and dramatize the need. It was almost too much to hope for another Bull Connor, but the state of Alabama was able to supply a second gullible police officer who was almost as good. After careful observation, King and his group chose Selma, where hard-nosed Jim Clark was sheriff. Slightly more than half the population of Selma was black, but this population group accounted for only one per cent of the registered voters. There was no question that blacks had been systematically excluded from the voting process.

Selma, some fifty miles west of Montgomery on the Alabama River, is the county seat of Dallas County. It was incorporated in 1820, only a year after Alabama joined the union, and it became an important agricultural center and cotton shipping port in the antebellum period. Selma was the site of one of the last battles of the Civil War, and it had a proud Southern heritage. With a population of about 22,000 in 1965, it was the largest city in the Black Belt.

Selma's business leaders had tried to avoid trouble. In 1960 they helped elect mayor Joseph T. Smitherman, a moderate who saw accommodation as the best policy in dealing with racial change. Smitherman appointed moderate Wilson Baker as the city's commissioner of public safety. Baker supervised law enforcement within the city, and he worked with the black leadership to try to find solutions acceptable to all.[42] Sheriff Clark, however, had authority throughout the whole county, and he and Baker were soon in jurisdictional disputes.

Civil rights strategists could defend the choice of Selma and Dallas County because of blatant past discrimination in voting, and they believed that Sheriff Clark would respond violently to demonstrations. Clark was more subtle than Bull Connor. He was known to have a short temper, however, and to lash out when sufficiently provoked. Early in

January 1965, King announced he would launch an Alabama Negro voter registration drive in Selma.[43] He began the drive with a rally on January 3. The campaign was an immediate media event, with national and international coverage.

Selma turned into much more than a media event, however; it soon became a national crusade. Thousands of people all over the country reached the conclusion that they should be personally involved, and they descended on the city. Ralph Abernathy says that, for many Americans, "Selma would be more synonymous with hard-core resistance than any other city in America."[44] There finally seemed to be a national consensus that it was time for the struggle for equal rights under the law to end.

Violence Erupts. On January 18, King was attacked by a white man while he was registering at the Albert Hotel in Selma. He was the hotel's first black guest in more than 100 years. He led marches to the court house daily trying to register voters. Sheriff Clark was much in evidence during all of this. He and his men treated marchers roughly and made arrests, and his militancy was played up by the national press. The Selma Chamber of Commerce meanwhile was trying desperately to get a solution and preserve the peace.[45]

Late in January, the NAACP Legal Defense and Education Fund sued in federal court for an injunction against Clark and other officials, and it asked that cases of 223 persons arrested in Selma be transferred to federal court.[46] Frank Johnson was the federal judge before whom most of these cases were heard. On February 1, King and 770 other blacks were arrested during a voter registration march for parading without a permit. King decided to stay in jail to dramatize the situation. The next day, 520 marchers were arrested, and a day later, more than 1,000 black students were arrested during demonstrations at the courthouse in Selma and in nearby Marion. During this series of incidents, Clark personally struck two black women in full view of news cameras.[47]

Richmond Flowers was about half way through his term as attorney general when the Selma campaign began. He believes that the governor had to have been in agreement with the moves police made in Selma, and when asked if Wallace was involved in the decision to confront the demonstrators, Richmond exclaimed, "Surely! None of the rest of them would dare do anything on their on. George had a flat order, 'Don't let them do anything. Stop anything they try to start.' Of course, Jim Clark was one of his close personal buddies. Clark rode around on horses all the time, pushing them back with horses and then hitting them with cattle prods."

The campaign was having its intended effect in bringing voting rights to the forefront. Senator Jacob Javits of New York, a leading Republican liberal, commented that the arrests showed the "limits to effectiveness" of federal law in protecting voting rights and that additional legislation to create federal registrars was needed.[48] Fourteen Democratic members of the House went to Alabama, against the wishes of their Southern colleagues, to determine whether new federal legislation to guarantee voting rights was needed.[49]

Marching to Montgomery. Late in February, King announced that the voter registration campaign would be stepped up. In a very dramatic gesture, he called for a march of fifty miles from Selma to Montgomery, where a petition would be presented to the governor. Wallace issued orders forbidding the march, saying that it would disrupt traffic on U.S. Highway 80, then a two-lane road between the two cities, and would endanger public safety. King announced that the governor's order would be defied.

The first attempt at the Selma to Montgomery march was on Sunday, March 7. Large numbers of reporters and network television cameras were on hand. On their way out of Selma, the demonstrators crossed the Edmund Pettus Bridge over the Alabama River, and violence erupted. In full view of the press and television cameras, state troopers and a sheriff's posse used clubs, bullwhips, tear gas, and electric cattle prods in a brutal attack. At least seventeen blacks were sent to the hospital and another forty were injured as the marchers were turned back. Civil rights leader John Lewis suffered a skull fracture.[50]

The national reaction was spontaneous and furious. Demonstrators took to the streets in cities all over the country, and thousands more, including 400 clergymen, poured into Selma to join the march to Montgomery.[51] It was now Jim Clark and his little band of deputies against an aroused nation, with little question as to who would win. Clark, like Bull Connor ten months earlier, found himself with a much larger problem than he had anticipated.

Judge Johnson, seeking more time to study the situation, issued an injunction against further marches on the highway, but King was under heavy pressure to do something quickly. President Johnson and the Justice Department had by this time sent former Florida governor Leroy Collins, head of the government's new Community Relations Service, to negotiate and try to keep peace. Collins worked out a face-saving agreement with King and state officials. A march was to begin on Sunday, March 14, and cross the Pettus bridge, but it would end peacefully on the other side when state troopers confronted the marchers. This came off as planned except, when King and the marches reached the stopping point, the troopers fell back instead of blocking the highway. This made it appear that King and his group could have gone ahead but quit.[52] A Unitarian minister, Reverend James Reeb, was severely beaten during related demonstrations, and he died two days later. A black man, Jimmie Lee Jackson, was also killed during the Selma protests.

Further action was delayed by the civil rights leaders pending the decision of the federal court. Court orders had been defied on other occasions, but the judge in this case was Frank Johnson, who was known to be fair and courageous. Judge Johnson refused to enjoin Alabama officials from interfering with further marches until he could hear the case and rule on the competing claims. There was a very serious question as to which should prevail, the rights to public assembly and free speech or the rights to safety and unimpeded passage on a public highway.

Governor Wallace flew to Washington during the pause and met with President Johnson at the White House. The president told Wallace that police brutality in Selma must not recur, and he asked the governor's cooperation in seeking a peaceful end to the demonstrations. President Johnson indicated that a federal court order to permit the Selma-to-Montgomery march, if issued, must be obeyed. He stated that maintaining security was the state's responsibility, and he asked Wallace to assure that the marchers would be protected. The president said that federal troops would be used to protect blacks if necessary.[53]

After Wallace returned to Alabama, he answered the president in a rather defiant mood. Wallace stated that he would allow the Selma-to-Montgomery march only if directed to do so by a federal court and only after appeal. Judge Johnson issued a ruling on March 17 that the march could proceed. He based his ruling on the novel principle that the magnitude of a demonstration which was permissible depended on the size of the injustice suffered. He enjoined Wallace, Clark, and other Alabama officials from harassing or threatening demonstrators and ordered them to provide full police protection.

Wallace in a press conference estimated that over 6,000 troopers would be required to assure safety, and he said that Alabama could not afford the cost of mobilizing the National Guard, as suggested by the president. President Johnson then federalized almost 2,000 Alabama National Guard troops, and he moved another 2,000 army troops into the area. He also made available 100 FBI agents and 100 federal marshals.

On Sunday, March 21, the march began when King, Under-Secretary of State Ralph Bunche, and Reverend Ralph Abernathy led 3,200 across the Pettus bridge. Hundreds of army and national guard troops were posted along the route. The court order had limited the number of marchers to 300 along the two-lane section of the highway, and when they reached the place where the two-lane started, 2,900 returned to Selma by a special train. The group of 300 camped at night in fields along the road.

The marchers reached the Montgomery city limits the evening of March 24 and camped at the edge of town, three and a half miles from the capitol building. The next day, the group of 300 was joined by more than 20,000 sympathizers from all parts of the country and was led by King to a rally in front of the Alabama state capitol, the building in which the Confederacy was organized in 1861. Dr. King addressed the crowd and asked then to continue the civil rights struggle by nonviolent means. Downtown was relatively empty since Governor Wallace had declared a holiday for all female state employees. The governor agreed that he would see a delegation from the group on March 30.

Some law enforcement officers and other state officials tried to discredit the marchers by claiming they were guilty of widespread misconduct. The thought of intercourse between blacks and whites, particularly black men and white women, was and is a white supremacy obsession. Sheriff Clark, in a little book he was credited with writing, stated that "sex and civil rights go together," the ultimate defense to his followers for his crude behavior.[54] In a speech on the floor of the U.S. House of Representatives, Representative Bill Dickinson of Alabama accused the Selma to Montgomery marchers of "sex orgies and drunkenness."[55] This charge was widely repeated, along with the claim that Communists were behind it all.

Richmond Flowers was in perfect position to know what really happened. He reports, "My people who had infiltrated reported that the behavior of the marchers was normal. There was some drinking, but it was not excessive. We heard these wild tales of wide open sexual encounters, but it just wasn't so. I can't say for certain that there were no sexual activities, but if there were, they were hidden. We were getting the reports that there were wild orgies out there every night, that they were drinking and smoking marijuana. That couldn't be so, because not only the sheriff and his folks patrolled up and down that road, but so did the FBI. The folks I had were dressed up like sympathizers, marching along with them."

Murder and Renewed Determination. Viola Gregg Liuzzo was a Detroit housewife who had come to Alabama to participate in the campaign. The night of March 25 she was murdered while ferrying marchers between Montgomery and Selma. This brutal and senseless killing, committed on an open highway by members of the Ku Klux Klan, furthered the national resolve to do something about the situation. It removed any last doubts on the part of decent citizens in Alabama that they must reestablish law and order.

An ad in the *Birmingham Post-Herald* on April 14, signed by twenty-two major Alabama business groups, urged Alabamians to back equality in employment and voting.

Reverend Andrew Young, a King aide who was later mayor of Atlanta, Congressman, and U.S. Ambassador to the United Nations, stated that the voting rights drive would be extended to Lowndes County as a result of the Liuzzo murder.[56]

In the midst of the crisis, President Johnson called a joint session of Congress. He asked for a new law which would eliminate illegal barriers to voting rights and would provide for registration by federal officials if necessary.[57] In April, when it became apparent that a new voting rights bill would pass, the Alabama House of Representatives in a preemptive move approved two bills to ease voter registration requirements.

To Richmond Flowers, an interesting aspect of such events as Selma was that he knew most of the actors personally. Jim Clark was like Connor in that he was a politician from an era which had passed.

Richmond remembers that in earlier times, Clark had been a big supporter of Jim Folsom. "He supported Jim because 'Jim was our kind of folk.' I mean, Clark was that type, and, of course, George Wallace had supported Folsom, too. George Wallace at that time was not a racist, and I don't guess Jim was either, because Jim Clark was a heavy legman for Jim Folsom. When Folsom was campaigning, Jim would be out there running supplies to this place and that and getting bumper stickers out. He was that sort of man. He didn't have any money to give them, but he would work. He would take his pickup truck, fill it up with Folsom material, and ride anywhere sticking it all over.

"Then Jim Clark showed up as sheriff in Dallas County, and some other aspects of his personality came out. As sheriff, he would hurt you if you crossed him. I never had a confrontation with Jim Clark because I knew what would happen. Of course, I didn't have confrontations with any of them. It just wasn't my place as attorney general to ride horses and that sort of thing. I would express strong differences of opinion with them and condemn what they were doing. They used all kind of raw language in sending their messages back to me."

The 1965 Voting Rights Bill. Congress would pass voting rights legislation with little delay. It had been ten years since the *Brown* decision, and finally the judicial, executive, and legislative branches of government were in full harmony on the issue.

The 1965 Act greatly extended the government's power to end voting abuses. The Justice Department was authorized to send federal examiners to register voters in states in which less than 50 percent of the voting-age population had participated in the last election.[58] Another section required that voting qualifications or prerequisites in a jurisdiction covered by the act had to be cleared by the U.S. attorney general. This short-circuited one of the most effective strategies of the obstructionists, which was to string out litigation by passing new laws to frustrate judges' decrees. The Voting Rights Act shifted the burden of proof on claims of voting abuse from the federal government to the state, and it drastically cut down the amount of litigation.[59]

The impact was immediate. Within two months, more than 56,000 blacks were registered in twenty counties to which federal examiners were sent. The next year, black voters in Dallas County helped to defeat Sheriff Jim Clark. Blacks began exercising their voting rights all over the

South, and the number of black officeholders soon increased dramatically.

The 1965 Voting Rights Act and the 1964 Civil Rights Act together spelled the end of legal discrimination because of race. As C. Vann Woodward puts it, "Jim Crow as a legal entity was dead."[60] The acts gave legitimacy to the decrees of the federal courts, beginning with *Brown*. Southerners had complained with some justification that the courts were making laws instead of just enforcing them, and Congressional action on the two acts gave proper constitutional authority to federal civil rights actions.

A great victory had been won by the civil rights movement, and many, in great exultation, thought it was the ultimate human rights triumph in the United States. That idea was short-lived. Very soon, events showed that at most a major battle had been won, and that the fight ahead was still long and treacherous. In August 1965, only three months after the Voting Rights Bill was signed, major rioting broke out in Watts, a section of Los Angeles. White America was stunned to discover that the century-old promise of full equality for black citizens was still unfulfilled.

The Hard Fight for Justice

A very difficult problem for law enforcement officials during the most bitter phase of the civil rights struggle was to get juries to convict persons who were guilty of assault and even murder. A report of the Southern Regional Council and the American Civil Liberties Union in October 1965 noted that twenty-six civil rights workers had been killed since 1960, and there had been only one conviction.[61]

The jury system, normally a great strength in the fight for justice in the United States, was a hindrance in this situation because the jury of peers was often in deep sympathy with the accused. Charles Morgan noted that there were two major instruments of power in maintaining segregation in the South—the mostly white electorate and the all-white jury.[62] Jim Crow depended on the ability to terrorize with impunity.

Another aspect of the problem was that law enforcement officers in many locations were members or supporters of the Ku Klux Klan and were themselves involved in the violence. The very people responsible for enforcing the law were undermining it, and when they committed some outrageous act, they could depend on being acquitted.

The near impossibility of bringing the guilty to justice created a serious crisis in maintaining the rule of law. As the state's chief legal officer, Richmond Flowers was responsible for dealing with this problem. On several occasions, when it seemed that the most heinous crimes might go unpunished, he stepped in and prosecuted the case himself. When he did, he was seen by many as the enemy, part of the outside group attempting to interfere in long-established customs.

Two of the most difficult cases occurred in Hayneville, the county seat of Lowndes County in the Black Belt. "It was predominantly black down there," Richmond observes, "but not a single black had ever voted. None had ever sat on a jury, and not one had ever been to a decent school. They were just as ignorant as they could be. If one of them ever learned to read and write, he got out of Lowndes County as fast as he could." Richmond later said that trying the Klansmen in Hayneville was his worst experience as attorney general.

Richmond's first case in Hayneville involved the murder of Episcopal seminarian Jonathan Daniels. The second Hayneville case was the retrial of a Klansman accused of murdering civil rights worker Viola Liuzzo during the Selma to Montgomery march in 1965. Richmond had to be escorted into and out of the courthouse for his own safety during the Liuzzo trial.

The Daniels/Morrisroe Case. In August 1965, Episcopal seminarian Jonathan M. Daniels, of Cambridge, Massachusetts, and Catholic priest Richard F. Morrisroe of Chicago were in Ft. Deposit, a small town in Lowndes County, helping blacks in a drive for voter registration. They had come south a week earlier to attend a meeting of the SCLC. Both were white. They were part of a group arrested on charges of disturbing the peace and taken to jail in Hayneville, the county seat.

One day the whole group was released from jail and told to go home. When they came out, they noticed that the streets were deserted and the town was very quiet. The group asked Daniels and Morrisroe to go to a store across the street and buy some soft drinks. They were accompanied by two young black women with whom they had been working. Part-time Deputy Sheriff T. L. Coleman shot both men with a shotgun. Daniels died instantly, and Morrisroe was critically injured.[63] The incident drew immediate attention from the national press.

In September, a Lowndes County grand jury indicted Coleman for manslaughter. Attorney General Flowers was quoted as being shocked that a first degree murder indictment was not returned.[64] Fearing that the county would not prosecute the case properly, the attorney general personally took over.

Richmond recalls the details. "Allegedly, Daniels and Morrisroe were protecting a girl," he says. "They had all been released at the same time. Street talk was it was a setup job. They had been in jail several days and were the talk of the area. That morning everything got real quiet in town. There was a big gathering at the sheriff's office, where a group was playing dominoes. Someone came in and whispered something to Coleman, who was in the game. He said, 'Excuse me, I gotta go. I'll be back in a minute.' Everybody looked at everybody as if this was the signal. He got up and walked across to the store with an automatic shotgun. He moved into the store, and stood halfway back out of sight so that when they came out of the sunlight and opened the door, they couldn't see him. As soon as they opened the door, he said, 'You're trespassing.' They said, 'We wanted to get a soft drink.' Coleman said something like, 'Don't take one more step,' and bluoee. He blasted with the shotgun.

"Jonathan Daniels, the Episcopal student, was hit in the midriff. It blew him across the porch out into the street, and it killed him instantly. Morrisroe turned to run, and when he had gone three or four steps, Coleman shot him in the back. The force of it blew him out in the middle of the street. He lay there a little over an hour before they could get anybody to move him. He almost died and had to stay in intensive care for months.

"They weren't going to try Coleman for anything but manslaughter. They claimed they didn't think it was murder because he pled self-defense. When I first went down there and it was manslaughter, I refused to try it. I dismissed it and told them to reconsider. When I came back, it was manslaughter again. I told the judge I wasn't ready for a manslaughter trial and asked for a postponement. He refused to delay and made me go to trial immediately. He knew I was within my rights in refusing to go to trial if I wasn't ready. But you can't blame him. He had to live down there. He had property down there. Everything in the world he had was down there.

"I didn't want to try the case without Father Morrisroe. He hung at death's door for a while; then he was a long time recuperating. He was way up East, and I didn't know whether he would testify or not. I pled with him to come back, and he turned me down twice. Finally he agreed to come. I also asked him if he would remove his habit in a public place and show the jury the horrible scar in the middle of his back. He did not have a single mark in the front, but there was this awful scar where he was shot in the back. Coleman was pleading self-defense, and yet he shot Morrisroe in the back.

"At the trial, we turned him to the jury and said, 'There, gentlemen of the jury, is that proof enough?' As he was putting his habit back on, one of the jurors says, 'Preacher, let me ask you something.' He said, 'Sure.' A juryman's got a right to do that, though it doesn't happen very often. This man said, 'Preacher, did you kiss that little nigger girl in the mouth?' The priest said, 'I have never embraced a woman in my life.' The juryman said, 'That ain't what we heered down here. Heheheheheh.' All of them laughed and just stomped and spit. There were no blacks on this particular jury.

"Two or three defense witnesses said that they saw Daniels and Morrisroe pull something out of their pockets that looked like pistols. Now, they had just got out of the jail fifteen or twenty minutes before. Nobody found a pistol, and there was no hard evidence of one. We had witnesses who were in the ambulance with Morrisroe. We had the people who treated him in the hospital. None of them saw a pistol. But two or three of the local fellows said, 'It looked to me like he had pistol.' Defense witnesses testified that blacks had removed weapons from both men after they were shot.[65]

"The trial lasted just a couple of days, and it only took the jury about twenty minutes to reach a verdict. They didn't stay out any time. They cleared him on self-defense." At the time, Richmond called the verdict a terrible miscarriage of justice, and one of his aides said that work on the case would continue.[66] The Justice Department considered trying Coleman on charges of denying the civil rights of Daniels and Morrisroe, but no other legal action was taken.

There is no question in Richmond's mind that the shootings were intentional. "It was a premeditated thing," he says. "There wasn't any doubt that the whole thing was planned. They let those people out of jail in order to kill them, and the executioner of the county was the one who did the killing. Coleman had already killed two other people down there.

"In the minds of those Lowndes County people, it wasn't against the law to kill a civil rights worker. I tried the case under guard. As attorney general I wouldn't go down there unless I had my own bodyguard standing immediately behind me and troopers on each side. And I wasn't just being fancy. The troopers would tell you, 'You better have protection down here in Lowndes County, especially Hayneville. There's no hate like the hate down here.'"

The Liuzzo Case. Viola Liuzzo, wife of a Teamster official in Detroit, was murdered while driving on the Selma-Montgomery highway. She was returning to Montgomery after transporting marchers to Selma, and was near Lowndesboro, a small town in Lowndes County. Leroy Moton, a young black man, was with her. A large contingent of newsmen was in the area to cover the march, and the blatant murder received immediate worldwide attention.

Within two days, President Johnson announced the arrest of four members of the Ku Klux Klan in connection with the slaying. Alabama Klan Wizard Robert Shelton denied that any of his members were involved. He claimed the Liuzzo killing was part of a Communist plot to denigrate the KKK and 'destroy the right wing in America.'[67] Governor George Wallace denounced the slaying and said he had ordered state officials to cooperate with federal agencies investigating it. He offered a $1,000 reward for apprehension of the killers.

"The events in the Viola Gregg Liuzzo case were brutal, absolutely brutal," Richmond says. "Three of the Klansmen were from Bessemer, a suburb of Birmingham. The fourth, Gary Thomas Rowe, was from Birmingham. He turned out to be an FBI informant. Those Klansmen came down there looking for trouble. The investigators traced their steps the day of the killing and found they had been there all day riding around, but they hadn't done much. Moving in the daytime was not their thing.

"Late in the afternoon, they stopped at a service station and made some calls. Then they drove on down the highway. About twenty minutes before the shooting, they were stopped for speeding by a highway patrolman. He gave them a ticket and let them go. They were not specifically looking for Liuzzo. They would take anybody. They just wanted to do something now. One of them testified later that the Grand Wizard of their Klan had ordered them to go down there and get someone. They spotted Mrs. Liuzzo's car and pulled up close to her. She saw them and tried to get away. Soon the two cars were running side by side at ninety miles an hour. One of the men testified that they were very close to her. Every man in the car except the driver leveled his pistol right at her, and they emptied their guns into her car. She was a perfect target. She couldn't dodge or anything at ninety miles an hour. She was just a sitting duck, and they killed her.

"The Liuzzo car slowed down and the Klansmen passed. As they watched in a rear view mirror, her car gradually lost speed, eased off the road, and sort of nudged into a fence. The driver testified he turned to Gary Thomas Rowe and said, 'Hell, you missed her.' Rowe answered, 'Missed her, hell. That bitch is dead and in hell, I guarantee you.' Moton, who was in the car with Mrs. Liuzzo, testified that he got out, jumped over the fence, and ran into the adjoining field.

"To show you the attitude we were facing," Richmond continued, "when the state found Mrs. Liuzzo's vehicle, they took her body to the state laboratory in Montgomery. The first thing they asked the laboratory to do was see 'if she's had intercourse.' She had just been shot all to pieces, and that's the first thing they asked. When you've got your state officials in that kind of shape, it's scary, and I don't mind telling you I was scared. I stayed scared a lot of the time."

The Trial. The trial began in Hayneville early in May. It was there, Richmond explains, because "a section of Lowndes County sticks up between Montgomery and Selma, and the highway cuts across it. As fate would have it, Mrs. Liuzzo was killed in that section, and it was necessary to try the Klansmen in Hayneville."

Joe Breck Gantt, chief trial attorney in the attorney general's office, worked on the case. "He went down there and tried it, supposedly with the help of the district attorney," Richmond recalls. "The district attorney didn't do one thing in the world, so Joe had to try the entire case. The jurors voted against first or second degree murder, but they deadlocked 10-2 on a first degree manslaughter charge. A mistrial was declared. We decided right away that the state would seek a retrial." The defendants marched in a Klan parade after the first verdict and were given a rousing ovation.[68]

Richmond came into the trial a little later. "The district attorney said he wasn't going to try it again," he says, "because he couldn't get a verdict. That's when I came in. He'll tell you now that he was going to prosecute, and I was just grandstanding and pushed him out of the way. He wouldn't prosecute that suit any more than the judge would give me any kind of a break." The second trial, of Klansman Collie Wilkins, got under way in October.

Richmond knew from his experience in the Daniels case that he faced a near-impossible task trying to get a conviction in Lowndes County, and he tried to get the trial moved. "In Alabama the state cannot change jurisdictions without cause," he says. "They took the jury from the voting list, so I didn't expect to have any blacks. There were not enough white males who didn't belong to or sympathize with the Ku Klux Klan. I wanted to prove it was impossible under their setup to pick a fair jury. When this happens, they must give the state a change of venue and move it to another county.

"In a voir dire examination, you put all the jurors outside and you bring them back in and question them one at a time to see if you can disqualify them for cause. I would bring them in, and after getting their name, I would ask, 'Are you a member of the Klan? Do you sympathize with the Klan?' Then I would ask, 'What do you think of a person who will come into this county from another state or another part of this state and aide and abet the black people of this county in integrating your schools, your churches, and your restaurants? What is your opinion of them; is it good or bad?' Well, every one of them said, 'It's bad. I wouldn't have anything to do with 'em.'

"After this, I moved for a change of venue. The trial judge refused the motion, and I asked for and got a recess. I went over to Montgomery to the state supreme court, and there I ran into Ed Livingston. He was still souring from the election, and he threw it out of court. So I went back and took the jury they gave me. The FBI informed me before the trial was over that three active members of the jury were under surveillance as Klan members. And of course the rest of them were sympathizers."

Before the trial started, the Lowndes County Jury Committee placed six blacks on the list of prospective jurors. Three were disqualified, but three actually served. Richmond recalls, "Right at the last minute, they selected a few Uncle Toms and put them on. They were the first that ever served on a jury there, and they sat the whole time with their heads down. They were told, 'You get on that jury and you vote not guilty.' There was no way out for them down there. I knew they'd come back not guilty. It was the biggest farce you ever saw.

"You just can't believe the things that happened. As I got out of the car every morning and walked towards the courthouse, all sorts of obscenities were thrown at me. One time, just as I walked out, somebody spit all over me from above, and there was the biggest howl and laugh you ever saw. They would say, 'Stand clear, officer, and let me get a shot at him.' I had to put up with that all day long.

"I knew if I exposed myself in Lowndes County, they'd kill me in a minute. Nothing would been done about it either. Things were rough over there, and I admit I was scared to death. When the attorney general of the state walks to the courtroom and gets spit on, you know it's a bad scene."

"Leroy Moton, who was in the car with Mrs. Liuzzo, came over from Georgia and testified. He was so scared and so ignorant that he made a terrible witness. He stuttered and stammered, and 'I'se forget' and that sort of thing. But he did verify that they were just riding along, and all of a sudden bullets were flying everywhere. It's a wonder he wasn't killed except they pointed their guns straight at her, and they were so close.

"When I gave my closing argument to the jury, I said, 'I won't be attorney general much longer; in a few short months you'll have a new one.' The courtroom applauded and shouted. The point I was trying to make was that acquittal would set an awful precedent. 'If you let these people go with the evidence we have against them, if you allow these men to kill this woman because she disagreed with us politically, you have declared open season on your own governor. Your governor is speaking all over this country, and a lot of places he is going, they don't believe in his political philosophies either.'

"The case lasted a week. Then it took the jury one hour and twenty minutes to reach a verdict of 'not guilty.' They said they would have taken a little longer, but they wanted to go to a ballgame in another town. That's what you're up against in Hayneville." Courtroom spectators applauded when the verdict was announced.[69]

"I polled the jury when they returned the verdict," Richmond continued. "I asked one of the leading blacks in that area to be just outside of the rail. I told him, 'When I poll this jury, I want you to ease up, so the blacks on the jury can see you looking them right in the eye.' I asked each juror, 'Was not guilty your decision?' 'Yes sir.' He was just beyond me, and they wouldn't look him in the eye. They wouldn't look toward me, and they wouldn't anymore look him in the eye than anything. They just hung their heads, and you could just barely hear them, 'Yes sir.'

Federal Trial Gets Convictions. A few months later, two of the Klansmen were tried in a federal suit in Montgomery for violating Mrs. Liuzzo's civil rights, and they were given ten-year sentences. They were not tried for murder because the federal government has no murder statute. The Justice Department prosecuted the trial in Montgomery.

It sounds like a light sentence, but Richmond explains, "Violating her civil rights was about a tough a thing as the feds could get them for. She had a perfect right to drive that public highway unmolested, and they shot and killed her. So they violated her civil rights." Wilkins and Eugene Thomas served the full ten years in prison.

In looking back, Richmond remembers, "I had trouble during the Liuzzo case identifying Klan members in Hayneville, and I asked Katzenbach for help. He told me he couldn't give it to me because he had undercover men there, and if he delivered those names to me, the Klan would know where they came from. 'The life of my informer will be in danger,' he said. That's what they call protecting their informers, and I guess I can see why they do it. But they didn't help."

Reflections on George Wallace

The confrontation with George Wallace was a dominant aspect of Richmond's experience as attorney general. It was responsible for his national reputation, and ultimately, it influenced profoundly the course of his life. Richmond remembers meeting George Wallace while they were still in high school.

"I knew George very slightly in those days," he recalls. "We were from the same part of the state. When I went to law school at the University, I had already known him for a long while. As a youth, he was very, very personable and was gregarious as he could be. He was an attractive individual and very lively. He was always a friend to the downtrodden."

Richmond had some interesting classmates when he started to law school. "Both George Wallace and Frank Johnson were in my original law class," he remembers. "In fact, I sat with George in a couple of courses. In law school we sat two to a seat. George and I sat together sometimes because we knew each other and were friends." Richmond did not graduate from law school with George Wallace and Frank Johnson because of the automobile accident in Gadsden.

Wallace received his law degree and entered the Air Corps in January 1943. An illness forced him to drop out of pilot training, and he later became a flight engineer, an enlisted rank. He flew a number of missions in the Pacific on B-29s. After he got out of the service, he came back to Clayton, the county seat of Barbour County, where he went into law practice.

An Alabama Liberal at the 1948 Convention. The 1948 Democratic Convention was the first since Reconstruction in which civil rights played a big role. The party was considering a civil rights plank for its platform, and many Alabamians were perturbed. A slate of "walk-outers," who were pledged to leave the convention if the plank was adopted, ran as delegates. Voters split the twenty-six-person delegation evenly, with thirteen regulars and thirteen walk-outers. The principal delegate from Wallace's district, a walk-outer, was sick and could not attend. In a parliamentary maneuver, the temporary chairman would not let Wallace vote until the convention officially started. The delegates elected walk-outer Handy Ellis, a former lieutenant governor, as their chairman. Senator Lister Hill was the choice of the regulars but lost.[70]

"I paid close attention to the 1948 convention," Richmond says. "I was in law school with a wife and a baby three months old. And law students are so political, you know. This was the convention where the term 'Dixiecrat' was coined. The Alabama delegation was upset because of Truman's doings and because of the civil rights plank. I was listening when the walkout happened. After a lot of back-room maneuvering, the convention adopted a stronger civil rights plan than the Southerners expected, so Handy Ellis stood up and said, 'We bid you good-bye.' He led the way out and was joined by some very prominent Alabamians, including Bull Connor, then police commissioner of Birmingham.

"George stayed in the hall, and when the roll calls came, he cast votes. The chairman challenged him, and he said, 'I am an alternate delegate now taking my position as a full delegate, and I support the Democratic Party and all it stands for. My name is George Corley Wallace.' That didn't surprise me the least bit. I had known George as pretty much a liberal.

"Bull Connor got mad at Hubert Humphrey, the mayor of Minneapolis who made a big stir at the convention. In his speech, Humphrey said we had been dodging this issue for years and years, and we're not gonna dodge it any longer. He told the South, either you go along with us or as far as we're concerned you can walk out. And out they walked. The reporters caught Bull Connor right outside and asked him, 'Mr. Connor, what did you think when Mayor Hubert Humphrey made that statement in his speech?' I heard Connor say, 'It made me so al-fared mad, if arn airplane could have lit, I'd a flew right out of there.' The reporters and everyone else laughed, and I felt very humiliated and embarrassed."

Half of the Alabama delegation had left. Lister Hill and former governor Chauncey Sparks were among those who remained. Later in the convention, Wallace nominated Georgia Senator Richard Russell for president in a symbolic gesture.[71]

During his legislative service, Wallace was considered a liberal by the establishment in Montgomery.[72] In 1953, he was elected judge of the third judicial circuit, which included Barbour County, and he spent a lot of time in Montgomery, tending to political matters. Most of his term was uneventful, but toward the end, when he had decided to run for governor, he knew he had to do something to get publicity. At his own instigation, he became known as the 'fighting little judge,' and he started taking a segregationist stand.

Governor. Richmond remembers that Wallace made the biggest change after the first gubernatorial race. In Richmond's mind, the change was both surprising and extensive. "He had been a humanitarian as a youngster. There was no doubt about it. And he had believed in the Folsom philosophy. He went on principle when he was a young man. He went on his personal beliefs, and he went up well. People respected him. But you certainly couldn't say he was a humanitarian with 'segregation today, segregation forever' when he went in as governor. I felt that he had changed his principles. He would probably argue with me that he always stuck by his principles.

"When I saw George turn from segregationist to racist, that's when I departed. He literally despised that race of people. It got to be the talk of Capitol Hill. You could walk in his office, and he was so torn up over this thing you couldn't even talk to him. If you went in and tried to talk about anything, he would rant and rave about these damn niggers. These niggers this and these niggers that!

"He really became a racist. He'd tell you, 'Some of my best friends are. . . .' But that's bull, that's baloney! He had the meanest folks around him. He had some of the worst racists around him you ever saw. I know of two men very closely associated with him who said, 'I don't believe in segregation. I believe in slavery.' And then they'd laugh. That was big funny to them. Those were his chief advisors, people like Ace Carter.* If they didn't feel that way they couldn't work around him.

"Something I didn't know was that he was the type individual you could not differ with. If you differed with him, he wanted nothing to do with you, on anything. I just thought I was going to go my way, and he would go his. There was no sense in us having differences, because the governor's work and the attorney general's work were so different. He didn't want anything to do with me, because, he said, I had quit the fight."

Fanning the Flames of Discord. Richmond feels that the most destructive thing Wallace did was to constantly create trouble. "After we were in," he says, "those incidents seemed to flow one right after another. I was out of one into another, out of one into another. There were no long restful times when all I had to do was give a few city or county opinions. It was always trouble. Every time anybody might bring George to accountability, he'd stir up something else so he could take another stand. If you don't want to STAND UP FOR ALABAMA, as he said it,

---

*Asa E. Carter, a Wallace speechwriter in the early 1960s, was a rabid segregationist who was known to be a member of the Ku Klux Klan. Later, Carter wrote several successful books, including *The Outlaw Josey Wales* and *The Education of Little Tree*, a sensitive book about the treatment of American Indians.

he'd shake 'em again, and his followers went right behind him.

"Things would start going along pretty smooth. It would look like everything was working out, and then he'd stir something else up. Deliberately! George would fan the flames of discord, as I used to say. I know a lot of people were sick of it, but Alabama didn't have a chance. Every time things would begin to cool, he'd fan it up again and get it just as hot or hotter.

"I don't believe he did anything out of conviction after he got beat the first time he ran for governor. Everything he said was to help George. He would appear to have convictions, as when he threw the gauntlet in the dirt and said, 'Segregation today, segregation tomorrow, segregation forever.' That didn't work six months, and he was backing off saying what he meant was he was for state's rights. Well, that doesn't make any sense at all. But he was an artist. George's greatest talent was he always knew what the people wanted to hear. Whatever it was, he was always willing to say it, and he did say it.

"I believe that George Wallace had absolutely no regard for the people of Alabama or the state of Alabama. He put on this red-neck attitude that he knew the red-necks would just eat up and make him unbeatable politically. He just whipped it. He fanned the fires of discord just as hard as he could. He didn't care what happened to the people of Alabama. He was looking after George.

"He always made the same speech. It didn't make any difference what you asked him, he'd give you that same little set speech about the pointy-headed liberals. I asked a group in Washington one time, 'When are you all going sit down with that fellow and make him answer your questions?' A man answered, 'You can't get him to answer your questions. All he'll do is give that same little speech over and over.' George would deliver those little speeches and let the Kluckers cheer, and then he'd walk off. He didn't answer any questions.

"It's hard to realize now just how tremendously strong the feelings were at that time. The people wanted you to fight! I'd say, 'We've lost the fight. Now we've got to live with the beast.' George was telling them all we could win this thing. We're going to break up all this busing, and there's not going to be any integration of our schools. He knew he was appealing to the red-neck, appealing to the ignorant, appealing to the uninformed.

"What disappointed me was I thought surely there was a large block of sensible people who would say, 'Well, okay George, but that's not very practical.' If you gave them a choice, I thought, they would go the other way. But I was just mistaken. He was right, politically, and I was wrong. But I have no regrets. I couldn't live with myself if I had taken the other stance. The majority of people were glad he was doing it. The smart ones knew he wasn't going to be successful, but they wanted somebody to do it. They knew the Ku Klux Klan was a despicable body, but they were glad the Kluckers were there doing the dirty work."

When asked if he thought Wallace was actively involved in the Klan, Richmond answered, "No, I don't believe he was. I never picked his tracks up. Some of his people were. His director of public safety used to speak to them. We recorded one speech that he made to the Klan. He encouraged them and said, 'We'll support you. We'll win this together. We'll win this fight.' But George was way too smart to get mixed up with the Klan. He knew sooner or later the Klan was going to do something like they did in Selma, and he was not going to get mixed up in that. Sooner or later, they were going to kill somebody. Some of their leaders that were so despicable he wouldn't associate with them anyhow.

"When I was speaking and talking about the Klan, they loved to slip me that question about the blacks, 'Would you like for them to come in your house and sit down and eat?' I said, 'There are lots and lots of people I don't want to come into my house and eat. But it's not because they're black, and it's not because they're white that they are not going to be asked in there. I don't expose my family to anything but ladies and gentlemen, and that doesn't depend on the color of their skin.'"

The Cost to Alabama. Richmond joins a lot of other people in believing that Wallace ultimately hurt the state tremendously. "He knew full well he couldn't do what he said he would," Richmond believes. "He was a good student. George Wallace was not anybody's dummy. He was the strongest political figure this state ever produced. But what did he do to the state? Every month or so, George would announce this big industry that was coming in. There was no industry that ever came in this state; it wouldn't develop, not while he was prancing around like little Mussolini.

"As for George, I have as compassionate a feeling as a man can possibly have for George C. Wallace. It's so sad. It's so sad for a man to end up lonely, in pain, incontinent. He's just here, that's all. I wouldn't swap places with him for all the money in the world."

Is Richmond too harsh in his criticism of George Wallace? Opinion is still strongly divided, of course, and only history can answer. A comment by Wayne Greenhaw, a Montgomery newspaper writer who followed Wallace during most of his political career, is worth noting. Greenhaw concludes:

"While Governor Wallace did not hold the gun himself, he created the atmosphere of hate in order to become a nationally recognized spokesman for ultra-right-wing conservatives. Most of his life he had yearned to become a national figure. Within five months of his taking office, he led the racist pack."[73]

Four Turbulent Years End

Richmond Flowers had gone into office as an avowed segregationist, promising to protect the state from federal encroachment and to continue the struggle for segregation as long as there was a fighting chance. His experiences in office led him to take increasingly strong stands against defiance, however, and he strongly believes that it changed him. A question as he headed into the latter months of his term was what the consequences would be.

The Klan Investigation. The Ku Klux Klan operated outside of the law, and, as the two Hayneville cases showed, it was difficult to get convictions against Klan members, especially in rural areas. The fight against the Klan in a real sense symbolized the larger struggle to restore the rule of law.

Richmond realized this, and he and his advisors made the decision early in 1965 to investigate the Klan formally. On April 22, the attorney general's office sent a letter to Governor Wallace explaining that a full scale investigation of the KKK in Alabama was proposed and asking for his support. The request was ignored. Richmond decided to continue anyway. His office did not receive any help or support in the investigation from the governor or any other state official or agency.[74]

The formal investigation began in May, and a news release in June quoted Richmond's rationale. "I am thoroughly convinced that the Klan is not simply a secret conservative society," he said, "but more closely resembles a sort of terrorist shadow government in some parts of

Alabama, making and enforcing its own laws, channeling the direction of some local and state politics and virtually controlling some local law enforcement agencies."

An interim report on the investigation was published in October 1965 and received considerable publicity. The report held that the Klan exercised strong political influence in the state in spite of its small numbers, and it said that many policemen and state troopers were members. The report pointed out that Klansmen had been implicated in twelve of the seventeen racial murders in the South since 1963, and in none of the twelve had there been a felony conviction.[75]

Much of the Klan's success in Alabama was attributed to Governor Wallace, who the report said refused to do anything to curb the organization. Asa E. Carter, a special assistant to Governor Wallace and an outspoken white supremacist, was listed as head of an organization called the Original Ku Klux Klan of the Confederacy.[76]

Richmond wrote an article about the Klan which was published in the May 3, 1966, issue of *Look* magazine. In the article, Richmond noted that the average Klan member was "a fifth-grade school dropout, with a background of social and economic failure. The Klan gives these rejects a channel for their frustrations." The average citizen was reluctant to speak up because "his home may be bombed by a self-appointed, self-anointed social misfit." Even so, the article pointed out, the Klan's membership in Alabama was only two thousand, about 0.1 percent of the state's population.[77]

Richmond believes that part of the reason the Klan was difficult to control was support for their anti-black activities by some of the "better" people. "I spoke to the brotherhood over at the Synagogue one night about some of my Klan findings," he remembers. "After it was over a man I knew said, 'Rich, I hope you don't mess with those fellows. I'm glad they're out there.' I said, 'You want them to clean up all these blacks, don't you?' 'Damn right!' I said, 'You know who they're going to start on when they get them cleaned up, don't you?' 'What are you talking about?' I said, 'Jews! They hate them about like they do the others.' 'Aw, no. Not this bunch. This bunch is helping us.'

"I thought the elite of Alabama didn't want to get into that stuff. I thought they were tired of it and wanted some integrity and some decency. But I found that they'd say, 'I'm glad they're out there to tell you the truth. Maybe that's the only way we can handle them. Get some folks like that to help. They'll handle them.' I realized that I was just wrong; there were not enough who wanted it another way."

The Publicity and the Stakes Grow. Richmond insisted in his last months as attorney general that the majority of Alabamians were ready for change. In June 1965 he flew to Los Angeles to appear on NBC's regionally televised "Press Conference" show. Before leaving Montgomery on this trip, he said to reporters, "Alabama is now at the threshold of an economic, educational, and social breakthrough. I feel that the story of Alabama's new image should be told."[78]

Throughout 1965, he carried his belief and his fight to Democratic clubs all over the state. Speeches were delivered in such locations as Montgomery, Tuscaloosa, Anniston, Huntsville, Dothan, and Tuskegee. In these speeches, he said, "I gladly speak in behalf of my party, the national Democratic party. I am a Democrat. No prefix, no suffix, and no apologies."

He promised to give "plain and honest talk. This kind of talk today is not popular," he said. "Today, the most popular talk is loaded with demagoguery, bigotry and hate, based upon false hope and promises." Party members faced the challenge "as to whether a man under the Constitution is a citizen if he be of a different race than ourselves. . . . We must appear as a mockery before God if with one hand we tended to these people (in other countries) the bread of life, while with the other we brush aside the petitions of our own people.

"Many of our so-called state Democratic leaders of today have abandoned the party," he continued. "They have preached bigotry, racism, and demagoguery." He had no choice, he said, but to support the party that has been so good "to me, my family and state, and if such decision should damage or even end my political future, so be it."

In November 1965, Richmond said in a speech to Harvard Law School, "The South's greatest need at this moment is the tough-minded man or woman who is capable of making rational judgments involving choices that may be both unpalatable and unpopular but which nevertheless must be made if we are to emerge from the economic and political shadows. . . . We do our state no service when we counsel defiance of the laws of this nation."

"The basic foundation of a democratic system of government is built on respect for the law. No matter how distasteful it may be, if it is the law, it must be recognized and respected. We must insist that men use their minds not their biceps. The emphasis must be on the three 'R's' of Reason, Responsibility, and Respect!"

Also in November, a *Look* magazine article about Richmond was entitled "New Politician from the Old South." "Flowers whacks out with bone-jarring candor against the status quo," it reported. "He has declared war on the Ku Klux Klan. He ridicules Governor George Wallace's defiance of federal authority." The article noted that, "Richmond Flowers is gambling that Alabama voters can take the truth. 'Using race as an issue is coming to a screeching halt,' he insists. 'I want to tell the nation, Alabama's not all head-bustin'. There's a group here—not as small as people think—sick of all this.'"[79]

Wallace Fights to Succeed Himself. In all of this, Richmond was positioning himself for future political activity. The Alabama Constitution prevented Wallace from succeeding himself, and Richmond believed that, with Wallace out of the limelight, a more reasonable position could prevail.

George Wallace was himself pondering the possible loss of the limelight. He had entered a number of presidential primaries in 1964 and had done quite well. He was a national figure by now, with backing for his defiant approach throughout the country. He wanted to consolidate his power in Alabama and continue building support on the national scene. He claimed that he had a chance to be elected president. At the very least, he now believed that he could become a major power broker at the national level.

He needed a political base from which to operate, however, and unless something was done, he would be a private citizen with meager financial resources and little power when he left office in January 1967. Wallace considered a number of options, including a race for the U.S. Senate against John Sparkman. Finally, he decided to ask the electorate in Alabama to amend the state constitution so that a governor could serve successive terms. He was certain a large majority of voters would support this move, but first he had to get the legislature to pass a bill calling for a statewide referendum.

In September 1965, Wallace called a special session of the legislature to push his plan. Before the session began, he appealed to the people in a statewide radio and television address. Rules committees in both the House of Representatives and the senate were dominated by Wallace supporters, and they cleared the bill without discussion. It went to the House floor and was quickly approved by a substantial margin.

When the bill got to the senate floor, however, there was an unexpected development. Opposition senators started a filibuster and were able to keep it going. According to Marshall Frady, Wallace had gone beyond the pale in his audacity.[80] Members of the legislature would go along with almost anything, but they would not sacrifice their own careers by becoming known as complete lackeys.

Wallace tried every maneuver to win the fight, and in the process, he showed a darker aspect of his nature. He met individually with the offending senators and tried to bully and intimidate them. One reported later that "He threatened to destroy you completely—morally, physically, financially."[81] He stopped road projects and said the state would withhold a large appropriation to a junior college. He went to the state supreme court in an effort to reduce the number of votes needed to override a filibuster. In the end his tactics backfired, and he failed. On October 22, after three weeks of filibustering, the senate voted on the bill and defeated it.

This defeat stymied Wallace momentarily. He thought again of running for the U.S. Senate, and then he hit upon a strategy that was to have a major effect on Alabama politics and on the life and career of Richmond Flowers. Wallace decided that he would have his wife, Lurleen, run for governor.

Richmond Continues to Clarify. In his public statements, Richmond made his opinions and intended actions clear. Increasingly, he took a stand which was different from that of Alabama politicians of the past. Public figures will often be deliberately obscure on sensitive issues, particularly when they think their own position might offend large groups, but, for better or worse, Richmond did not choose to do this. Friends warned that he was endangering his political career, but he believed his was the voice of the future and that his time would come.

In a February 1966 political speech in Huntsville, Richmond said,

> "We have in our generation, you and I and our children, to determine whether or not we are going to live in a manner

befitting the latter half of the twentieth century. You have got to heighten responsibility at the local level if we are to fulfill the American dream in Alabama. And that responsibility means to stand up and tell the truth—paint it just like it is—and try to figure out some way to develop and grow in step with our times and the fantastic opportunities that they offer.

"Too long has political demagoguery, which refuses to recognize progress and change, forced us unnecessarily into federal court," he continued.

"Too long have we held our independent self-reliant attitude about states' rights while at the same time continuing to practice states' wrongs.

"Too long have we ignored the real formula to progress, prosperity and prominence—wasting our substance in belaboring issues that even our sister Southern states such as Tennessee, Georgia, Louisiana and North Carolina have put behind them."

Richmond's fame continued to grow, and he received more and more invitations to speak around the country. In March, the Tennessee College Young Democrats honored Richmond as their man of the year for "helping to bring the South new respect and dignity."[82] This was personally gratifying, no doubt, but it helped to mark him at home as a threat to the old order.

Richmond spoke to the attorney generals' seminar in Springfield, Illinois, that same June. His topic was the law and the necessity of respecting and obeying it in a democratic society. "Let there be no question of where we stand on human rights and our rejection of discrimination," he said. "Surely the continuing social task for the morally sensitive citizen is to impart reality to the yet unachieved ideal of full and equal participation by all in all our values and opportunities"

"Civil disobedience is an *ad hoc* device at best, and *ad hoc* measures in a law-centered society are dangerous," he continued. "Civil disobedience under these circumstances is at best deplorable and at worst destructive. Whatever the causes for the recent mob actions in American communities or for brutal slayings by nightriders, it is an obvious fact that there has been a violent breach of two cardinal principles of our American society—the respect for law and order, and the recourse to orderly process of law to see redress of any wrongs."

Richmond made one of his most moving statements in an address to the Southwide Lawyers and Physicians Conference in Lake Junaluska, North Carolina, in July 1966. This speech proved that he had changed a great deal in the four years he had been attorney general.

Commenting on the difficulties of his term, he said,

> "What sustained me throughout all of this, and through subsequent abuse which has come my way for having changed my attitudes toward segregation, is the sure conviction in my own heart that my determination to do what was 'right' has not changed. What had changed was my own understanding and comprehension of what was right.
>
> "I admit that I have looked at segregation through the eyes of a man who was raised from a boy on the privileged side of a racially segregated social system. In the past I have even rationalized that Negroes actually preferred it that way. And I have embraced other comforting justifications which the segregated society has held out to salve the conscience of its worried white participants.
>
> "What is being asked of all of us as Americans these days concerning civil rights is to be faithful to our obligation continually to renew our assessment of what is 'right,' to look about us and ask, in quiet and personal candor, is it really 'right' that some people in our land should be treated as belonging to a separate caste, and relegated to second-class status, because of their appearance, or who their parents were, or where they came from? Can the denial to millions of our citizens of their right to be judged on merit alone be reconciled with our American ideals?
>
> "To be relegated to a second-class school, to find only second-rate jobs available, to be restricted to a slum or a second-class neighborhood, to be excluded from so very much of the main current of the life of your community and nation, to be reminded in countless big and little ways every waking hour that one is considered 'inferior'—in short, to be a Negro in such a society—must really be like being lynched a little bit over and over again every day of a lifetime.

"Wherever poverty is at its worst, there you find that both the greater percentage of the poor and the poorest of the poor are Negroes. And this, friends, is no accident. No heartless God so willed it. We did it, we white Americans. It was we who installed the institution of slavery on this continent. It was we who perpetuated it as long as we could. It was we who found more subtle substitutions for slavery when it was ended. It was we who set up the society of forced segregation and tried to make it function to our material benefit, even though in the process it contributed to our spiritual impoverishment."

The Personal Price. Richmond and his family paid a heavy price for the stand he was taking and the liberal image that developed. Personal threats started when it first became evident that he would try to uphold the law and not stand with Wallace. Many of the incidents were quite frightening. "The civil rights movement affected me either way it went," he recalls. "Every time anything happened, I got another piece picked off of me. My immediate family was aware of the danger, but they supported me 100 percent. Mary would say, 'Honey, are you safe? Do you think you're safe? Is it worth it?' And I'd just say, 'Well, there's no turning back now, honey.' 'No, I guess not.' But we tried not to talk about it much.

"They called the house all the time," he remembers, "and that frightened me. I had good reason to believe they were watching my house, because they never called when I was at home. My wife sometimes got a call when I wasn't there. But you let us both leave, and they'd get my little girl on the phone and tell her, 'Your daddy's going to be killed. He's going to be dead if you don't tell him to stop messing around with our business. You're going to see him right over there in the corner in a casket.' That little girl was in the second and third grade. You know she was scared to death. Here I'm responsible for this child, and they're calling up and giving all kinds of messages like that.

"It got to be common for us to have crosses burned in our yard. I'd get up early every morning and do my walking. I had a big German shepherd I had trained to heel. He was a big one; I wouldn't have wanted to fool with him myself. He would walk around with me. I was never afraid to be out walking by myself, not with that dog, and not in the daytime. The Klan didn't move much in the daytime.

"Rarely a week rolled by that there would not be some cross out there, wrapped up in some rags and as crude as it could be. Some of them could have been done by kids because they would rarely burn completely up. We had several that the Klan put up. When you get one of those you can tell because it's wrapped good with wire. The material on it is soaked, and the whole thing flames up. I'd clean them up and throw them in the trash so the neighbors wouldn't see it. I had an old pitchfork that I kept back in the back, and I'd pull the cross out of the ground with it and either pour water on it or stomp it out. I'd pick it up, throw it in the trash, put the lid back on, and go on around the block, me and my big dog. It was just enough to keep you irritated and to keep you wondering.

"My minister at the time was Dr. Joel McDavid, a man who was distantly related to me. I asked him, 'How can you possibly espouse so totally the fatherhood of God and completely ignore the brotherhood of man. How can you satisfy your stand?' He said, 'If I did anything else, it would split my church. My church is more important than my opinion or my thoughts or ideas. I'll do anything to hold my church together.' And that's the way he explained it, defying the brotherhood of man while he embraced the fatherhood of God.

"I would say the Methodist church was not as bad as a lot of them, though I lost my job ushering there once. I belonged to the First Church of Montgomery, and I had been ushering for some time. One day the papers said that there might be kneel-ins in several of the bigger churches. When I went to get my boutonniere, which all the ushers wore, they were out. I asked, 'Who got my boutonniere?' 'Must have run short. You can take up the collection.' I laughed and said, 'The ushers always take up the collection. What's the matter?' 'I don't know.' I walked outside, and somebody told me they had read about the kneel-ins in the paper that morning. All of a sudden I realized I'd been fired from ushering. They were afraid I would seat them in the congregation. I walked to the back of the church, and they had the two back rows with ribbons on them, just like they were reserved for a wedding. If any of them came, they were going to put them in those two back rows."

The price that Richmond finally paid for his stand was his career. "Its a good thing we can't see into the future," he says. "Nobody would have taken that job if they could have seen the future, unless it was someone who would take it in the same vein that George did. I have no doubt that, if I had gone with the flow, I would have been in the United States Senate. I would have been governor, and then I'd run for the Senate and I'd have won. But I wasn't raised that way. I just couldn't go with the flow. I just couldn't go with the way George said, 'Segregation today, segregation forever.' I knew that couldn't be."

"I've had these so-called political pundits who figure why you do this and why you do that. They think it was all for some kind of selfish gain. It was not. I talked to my people. I told them that it might do me in. But if it does, so be it. I used that expression many a time in speeches. So be it. I'm not that important. My ideas are, and when I go down somebody will pick up my ideas. My ideas are not going to die with me because I talked to too many people that believe in those ideas.

"Our hope lies in the future. At my age I can just change my ways a little, but my children are not segregationists at all. And they're certainly not racists. They accept every individual as a lady or a gentleman, as long as they're acting as ladies and gentlemen. Can you imagine that we used to fill up Legion Field [the football stadium in Birmingham] with white football fans? Today our stadiums are full of blacks on the field, off the field, everywhere. We've come a long way, but we've still got a long way to go. That's what we have to remember."

8

Vengeance Wreaked

Beaten by a Dime Store Clerk

The 1966 political season opened in turmoil and uncertainty. The Voting Rights Act had passed only a few months earlier, and the Alabama Democratic primary would be the first significant election in the South in which blacks could participate. Would blacks vote as a block and create upheaval, as the segregationists had predicted?

The future of George Wallace was also uncertain. Observers knew he was popular, but they thought he had been weakened when he lost his bid to get the state constitution changed to allow him to succeed himself as governor. There was speculation that he might have his wife Lurleen run, but she had major surgery early in January.[1] Wallace was considered more likely to run against John Sparkman for the U.S. Senate nomination. A win would keep him in a position of power and meet his needs for an operational base. A question was whether his brand of racism would still pay political capital.

The leading candidate for governor in the early stages was Ryan deGraffenried, the state senator who lost to Wallace in a runoff in 1962. Attractive and popular, deGraffenried had kept his statewide organization intact. He announced formally on January 20, classifying himself as a progressive, neither conservative nor liberal.[2] The Democratic nomination was not conceded to him, however. With Wallace apparently out of the picture and the attitudes of the electorate uncertain, it seemed to many to be a time of opportunity.

Former U.S. Representative Carl Elliott qualified and opened his campaign for governor on January 21. He promised to "bring racial peace to Alabama"[3] and pledged to have close relations with the national administration. "Alabama must get back in the mainstream of American culture and economy," he said.[4]

Former governor John Patterson entered the race on January 30 and announced that he still held strongly his segregationist views.[5] James E. Folsom, the ex-governor who had barely missed the runoff in 1962 after a disastrous TV performance, entered and was considered a strong candidate. At the end of January, the field of Democratic candidates for governor seemed solid, and it represented a wide range of political opinion.

A New Race. Everything changed on February 10. After campaigning all day in northeast Alabama, deGraffenried took off in bad weather for a short flight to Gadsden, where he was scheduled the next day. He was warned that flying the small plane in such conditions was dangerous, but he expressed confidence in his pilot. The plane crashed on a mountain side shortly after takeoff, and both the pilot and deGraffenried were killed.

George Wallace, like a number of other politicians, did a quick reassessment, and he decided to risk his political future on a bold move and have his wife Lurleen run for governor. A member of Wallace's family later said that if deGraffenried had lived, George would not have run Lurleen.[6] She qualified on February 24. This move sharply altered the race for governor, and it removed Wallace as an opponent of Senator Sparkman.

In the press conference which followed Lurleen's qualification, George stated, "If my wife is elected, we are frank and honest to say that I shall be by her side and shall make the policies and decisions affecting the next administration." He would be her number one assistant and would receive one dollar a year. Lurleen commented that her election would enable George to carry on his programs, including presumably his presidential race. George got in a sharp jab at Richmond Flowers during his speech.[7]

Observers wondered what Richmond would do. The *Birmingham Post-Herald* on February 19 quoted an insider as saying that Richmond, "an arch political foe of outgoing Governor George Wallace," would enter the race.[8] Richmond announced his candidacy on February 25. In his remarks to the press, he took gibes at Wallace and at the governor's segregationist backers, and he defined himself as the most anti-Wallace of all the candidates.[9] He promised to move the state "from the idea of defiance to that of reason and progress."

There is no question that Richmond had greatly irritated Wallace. On January 9, at a meeting of a joint legislative council, Wallace surprised those present by departing from his agenda and urging impeachment of the attorney general. Wallace said that Richmond was not properly discharging the duties of his office. A *Birmingham News* reporter noted that this little outburst let the attorney general know for sure he had got under Wallace's skin.[10]

On March 1, state senator Robert Gilchrist, who had led the fight against the gubernatorial succession bill, entered the race. Gilchrist was a popular moderate who had been close to deGraffenried, and he was considered by many to be deGraffenried's "replacement." Five other candidates eventually entered, each believing that a woman could not possibly win. There were now a total of eleven in the race, Lurleen and ten men. The *Birmingham News* commented editorially on March 3 that the people of Alabama were served poorly by a party in such disarray that it allowed almost a dozen candidates in its primary.[11]

The Black Vote. Everyone was concerned about the black vote. Black registration had reached about 112,000 by the summer of 1965. Then, after passage of the Voting Rights Act, it grew in less than nine months to 250,000, about a fourth the number of registered whites.

The Democratic State Committee recognized the new reality by removing the "white supremacy" slogan from the party's ballot emblem. Black leaders had threatened to form a third party if this step were not taken. Wallace supporters tried to stop the action, and Richmond was the only Democrat in a statewide office to advocate it.[12] The committee also rejected a plan to help white office holders retain posts in counties where black voters were in the majority. These actions were seen as a rebuke to Wallace and a spur to Richmond.[13]

For the first time since Reconstruction, a large number of blacks entered races. Black candidates were named in every county in which blacks were in a majority, and some qualified in other counties.[14] Black leaders indicated their intention to wrest Black Belt dominance from whites, and black registration caught up with whites in Bullock County and Lowndes County. In March, black leaders formed the Confederacy of Alabama Political Organizations to support statewide candidates.[15]

This upsurge in black political activity, the result of the Voting Rights Act, was striking. It changed the political equation, and the threat of blacks creating a third party or voting Republican worried leaders of the national Democratic party.

Richmond's Decision to Run. Richmond says that he had not planned to run for governor in 1966. "I had my plan all worked out," he recalls. "I was going to let the rumors go out I would run for governor so that I could get a lot of publicity, and then I was going to run for lieutenant governor. From the lieutenant governor's office, I was going to let it go out that I wanted to run for governor later. It was pretty apparent they would pass the two-term bill, and I'd be able to run twice in one position.

"Our senators were getting old, and I knew that within eight years, one or maybe both of them would have to retire. Rather than run for governor, I was going to wait them out and then run for the U.S. Senate. Sure enough, one of them dropped out right away, and the other stayed on awhile and then had to quit.

"I was going to support Ryan deGraffenried for governor. Ryan was a good man. He wasn't ultra-radical, and he wasn't ultra-liberal. He would support and vote for any good legislation no matter whose program it was. Legislation he didn't like he would fight like a tiger. I called him one day after looking at my polls and said, 'I'll ease into Tuscaloosa this afternoon and go to a hotel. How about easing around to see me. I've got some figures you'll be interested in concerning the governor's race.' He met me, and I showed him my poll. He said, 'Well, let me show you something.' He showed me his poll, and they were within a half percent of each other. They were two complete and separate polls, and they showed that Ryan deGraffenried was going to be elected governor without a run-off. "I wanted to plan some strategy with him. I told him, 'I'm gonna talk and talk about running for governor to get all the publicity, but then I'm gonna run for lieutenant governor. My close-ins know it, and if your close-ins know it, it won't be any surprise, and we can realign quickly.' I ask him if he had any objection to my serving as his lieutenant governor, and he said he'd be happy to have me. We had a lot of mutual friends, and I could have gotten a lot of support from him.

"Within two weeks he was dead, and it was a brand new race. The lead horse was gone. Things were changing fast, and I had to make a quick decision. I decided I would try to do the same thing with Carl Elliott that I had planned with Ryan. Carl was a good friend, and we thought alike in many ways. He had been a damn good congressman. I kept trying to get word to Carl that I wanted to talk to him. I planned to say, 'Look, you want to run for governor, you run for governor. Don't pay any attention to my publicity. I'm going to be rumored as a candidate. But then I'll run for lieutenant governor. We can help each other.' I wanted him to go ahead and run for governor with the full support of Washington and the State Committee and the money that they could raise. Carl was afraid I was going to ask him not to run, and he avoided me.

"So I qualified and ran for governor, and I went after and solidified the black vote. I thought a lot of the deGraffenried people would come over to me since Ryan was a progressive. I thought there was a substantial group of whites who were sick and tired of standing in the schoolhouse door and all that, and they would quietly vote for me because I gave them a choice. My polls showed that, with the black vote I was going to get, if I received only a fourth of the white vote I was a winner. I didn't think the people of Alabama would elect a woman under any conditions. I didn't think George Wallace could do it."

Lurleen, the Unlikely Candidate. Richmond wasn't the only one who thought Alabama would never elect a woman. In January 1966, before the campaign really kicked off, the possibility of Lurleen running was treated in the newspapers almost as a joke. Sure, George was desperate after his defeat in the senate, but he couldn't be serious about running his wife. As Anita Smith wrote, the expectation was that, if George ran Lurleen, "the Wallaces were doomed to take their places as laughingstocks in the annals of Alabama politics."[16]

Alabama voters were conservative, and giving a woman what was seen as a man's job was the last thing they were likely to do. Furthermore, she was considered to be totally unqualified. She was referred to as a nice,

Flowers, center, with aides on the way to file qualifying papers for the 1966 race for the governor's office. At left is Sawdust Lassister. The man in the dark suit in the background is Jimmy Evans, later to be attorney general himself. The man at right is Joe Breck Gantt, who would later be convicted along with Flowers.

charming lady who was a good hostess in the executive mansion and who took good care of her children. She had not been to college and had never held any kind of job except as a clerk in a five and ten-cent store right after she finished high school. She was considered shy, with no political aptitude nor ambition.

Also, she had undergone a serious operation in January, and there was a real question of her physical fitness. The *Birmingham News* carried a front-page story about the operation on January 10. It was for "a tumor of the uterus," a cancer which had been found the previous summer, and the operation involved a "hysterectomy, appendectomy, and thorough abdominal exploration."[17] After the surgery, the physicians said that, so far as they knew, Lurleen's long-term health outlook was "good."[18] A confident long-range prognosis after such a serious episode would not normally be made for at least a year.

Insiders knew that Lurleen and George had experienced marital difficulties for several years.[19] George was openly rude to her and basically wanted her to keep house, smile when told to, and otherwise stay out of his way. When George got a telephone call from her, Marshall Frady reports, he was prone to say something like, "Don't you know I'm busy? What the hell do you want?" Lurleen had seriously considered divorcing him,[20] a fact which she later acknowledged.[21]

Richmond thinks that the cancer issue was deliberately ignored by the medical community. "The doctors knew it," he says. "My own brother, who was a physician, told me. We were out on his boat, just the two of us. I told him I was thinking about running for governor, and I said, 'Of course, I'll probably have to run against Lurleen.' He said, 'You might. You might not.' I asked, 'What do you mean?' He said, 'Oh, I expect she will be able to run, but she could be sick before then. If she's got what the newspapers say she has, I've seen them drop like flies in a few months.' She lived nineteen months and two days from that moment. Just when she needed tender love and care, she got stress and abuse."

The health question came up from time to time during the campaign, but it was never made an issue by the other candidates. The newspapers wrote of Lurleen's operation, and the Wallaces did not try to dodge it when asked. Their answer was that she had been given a clean bill of health.

The Campaign. Richmond kicked off his campaign on March 22 with a TV broadcast from Mobile. He was helped by his son, Richmond, Jr., who was a well-known track star and football player. Richmond called for moderation. He said, "We must assume local responsibility to prevent a federal takeover. The state has to decide between the present attitude of defiance and discord that invites more federal court orders, or one of reason and progress that can realize Alabama's true potential. The people of this state have already been through too much following the Pied Piper of defiance."[22]

This made good sense to a lot of people, but Richmond was not the only one saying it. So were Carl Elliott and Bob Gilchrist and, to a lesser extent, several of the others. The fact that there were so many candidates made it difficult for any of them to stand out. At rallies across the state, all ten male candidates would sometimes speak. Remarks had to be brief, and listeners were more likely to be confused than enlightened. The *Birmingham News* commented that, with ten men and one woman running, it was hard to tell who was where.[23]

As the campaign progressed, it became clear that Lurleen was a stronger candidate than anyone had imagined, and the others found themselves attacking Wallace and his record. *Birmingham News* Washington correspondent James Free observed in early April that "It's Lurleen against the field. Lurleen is the one to beat. She's drawing the largest crowds." Free noted that no unkind words are being said about Lurleen.[24] The ten men, who were losing, didn't know how to campaign against her. George was the culprit, but he wasn't the one running.

Moderates and liberals in Alabama thought that Carl Elliott would be their man, and in the early days, he was considered a strong candidate. The *Alabama Journal* speculated in February that Elliott rather than John Patterson was likely to inherit most of the deGraffenried vote.[25] A few days later, when Richmond showed signs of entering, the *New York Times* said that a Flowers candidacy was likely to cut sharply into Elliott's support. "If Mr. Flowers and Mrs. Wallace were not in the race," the *Times* noted, "the contest for the Democratic nomination would be mainly between Mr. Elliott and former Gov. John Patterson, a strong segregationist."[26]

There is no question that Elliott was the candidate preferred by the national Democratic party. In March, in a move engineered from Washington, the Alabama Labor Council, AFL/CIO, endorsed Elliott.[27] James Free wrote that Elliott was regarded as the only Democratic candidate who could restore a really effective relationship between Alabama and the Democratic administration. Regarding Richmond, Free reported that "The answer from Democrats in Congress, the Justice Department, and the White House is that Flowers is a loyal Democrat all right, but he is too much of a 'loner' to be counted on as a team player."[28]

Evans and Novak claimed in their "Inside Report" column that Washington was testing to see if Elliott could win. "The problem with Flowers is that, even if he makes the runoff and wins the vote of every single registered Negro, he probably would lose in a landslide to Lurleen Wallace. Out of an estimated 600,000 white voters, Flowers would be lucky to get 75,000." They commented on Richmond's unpopularity with white voters. "The question," they said, "is whether the Negro leaders, disorganized as they are, will have the foresight not to waste the Negro vote on Flowers."[29]

Richmond had created a dilemma for moderates and liberals. They doubted he could win, but he had taken away a substantial amount of support from Elliott, their favorite. Unquestionably, he irritated national Democratic leaders by sabotaging their strategy. Elliott himself thought that Richmond cut into his chances and expressed bitterness about it in later years.[30]

Aware of the 250,000 black voters, none of the candidates talked about segregation or integration or used racial slurs. George Wallace, who did most of the talking in Lurleen's campaign appearances, attacked his favorite targets, the federal government and the liberal press. He promised to focus on improvements in education and to continue to fight against the encroachment of federal power in state affairs.[31]

In general, Wallace ignored the other candidates, though he did take regular swipes at Richmond. His stock comment was that Richmond had been searching the Wallace record with a fine-tooth comb, trying to find corruption and stealing, and "If anybody would recognize stealing when he saw it, it would be Richmond Flowers." The *Birmingham News* commented on the insinuation of this remark and said that Wallace should either produce evidence of wrongdoing or stop saying it.[32]

On April 10, the *Birmingham News* endorsed Bob Gilchrist. "No candidate can be elected governor who cannot win the support of substantial numbers of conservatives," it said, and Gilchrist was the most promising. The writer commented on the peculiar stance of Wallace, the "Law and Order" man who undermined his own state constitution and advocated defiance of federal law.[33]

Richmond needed a way to distinguish himself from the pack running against Lurleen, and he decided to take a calculated risk and openly seek the black vote. "I strengthened the civil rights aspects in my campaign," he recalls. "When I'd speak to black groups I'd tell them, 'When I'm governor and you come to Montgomery, you're gonna get jobs, and I don't mean with mops and brooms. You're gonna get good jobs behind desks and typewriters. Not because you're black. You won't get a job in my administration simply because you're black, but you'll never be turned down for a job just because you're black.' That was what they wanted to hear, and they'd all cheer and shout."

The *New York Times* noted that Richmond was "the first major white candidate in modern times to campaign directly among Negroes in the Deep South." This shocked whites and startled blacks, the article observed. The *Times* also stated that Richmond believed the Johnson administration was trying to persuade black leaders to back Elliott. "Mr. Flowers constantly quotes President Kennedy and avoids mentioning President Johnson by name." He said to the blacks, "If you turn your back on Richmond Flowers, on orders from Washington, then no other Southern politician will have any reason to come to you. They'll know that the place to go for the Negro vote is Washington."[34] On April 18, Richmond was formally endorsed by the Alabama Democratic Conference, the state's oldest black political organization, and he was later backed by the Confederation of Alabama Political Organizations.

As the campaign neared its end, The *Birmingham News* considered the leaders to be Lurleen, Carl Elliott, John Patterson, and Bob Gilchrist. On May 1, two days before the election, the *News* conceded that Lurleen was ahead. It noted that, for the first time, no major candidate had run as a hard-line segregationist.[35]

Lurleen in a Landslide. The primary election was held on May 3, 1966, and as predicted, more than 800,000 voted. This was by far the largest number in the state's history. In a startling outcome, Lurleen Wallace had a clear majority against her ten male opponents and did not have to face a runoff.

Lurleen received about 52 percent of the votes. Richmond was second, but it was a poor second with only 18 percent. Carl Elliott was an even poorer third with about 8 percent, and Bob Gilchrist, the candidate endorsed by the *News*, received less than 6 percent. The other seven, including former governors Folsom and Patterson, split the remaining 16 percent.

Later analysis revealed that Richmond won about 90 percent of the black vote, while Lurleen got practically none of it. The results were consistent statewide. Lurleen won all but three of Alabama's sixty-seven counties, and the three she lost, which were carried by Richmond, were in the Black Belt.[36] Albert Brewer, Speaker of the Alabama House of Representatives and a Wallace supporter, was elected lieutenant governor and would succeed to the top position if the governor died.

In several local races where whites were challenged by black candidates for the first time in the twentieth century, blacks split their vote and supported whites. So the fear of blacks voting as a block was unfounded. The only solid block voting by blacks was in support of Richmond and of Wilson Baker, who defeated Jim Clark for sheriff in Dallas County. Al Lingo, the former state Public Safety Director and militant civil rights foe, was defeated soundly in his race for sheriff of Jefferson County. A number of blacks won in other races.

For governor, the Republicans ran congressman James Martin, who had almost defeated Lister Hill in the 1962 Senate race, and they were thought to have a good chance in November. The *News* strongly endorsed Martin and pointed out over and over in its editorials the dangers of electing Wallace. In one it stated, "If George Wallace is successful in fooling a majority of voters, the limits of power which would accrue to him are indefinable."[37] The Republicans were well-organized, spent a lot of money, and ran a hard campaign. Nevertheless, in the general election in November, in which the total vote was smaller than in the Democratic primary in May, Lurleen won about 67 percent of the vote, including about half of the black vote.[38]

A Serious Miscalculation. After the fact, Richmond realized that he had made a serious miscalculation. "That was my biggest disappointment in politics," he says. "When I ran for governor, I was thoroughly confident. My polls had told me, with the black vote I was going to receive, I could win with a small percent of the whites. That's one time I was completely wrong. I took a calculated risk and lost. I thought I had it figured, but I didn't.

"I was beat in the primary badly. She won without a runoff. Of course I took second place, and third was way behind me. It wasn't just me they didn't trust. Carl Elliott was in that race and he didn't get enough votes to count. He didn't get any white vote, and he didn't get any black vote. With the black vote I killed him, but that's all I got. I guess I should have kept talking about the Southern Way of Life.

"I didn't think George could do it, and I was wrong. The progressive whites were not there. George was the king, and he elected his wife, who had terminal cancer. He might have supported me for lieutenant governor, but he was so powerful, he might have opposed me even for that. I realized then that the heavy majority of the white population of this state approved of what George Wallace did and said.

"That election is where more trouble started for me. The regular Democrats saw me absolutely control the black vote, and they were afraid of what might happen. The blacks voted for me against the wishes of the national Democratic party, and I think you could understand why. They had been paid off in years past. The leaders would make a little money, and the rest of them would say, 'We Democrats won.'"

Marshall Frady, writing in 1968, agreed that Richmond's strategy in 1966 was badly misconceived and produced grim prospects. "Richmond Flowers was obliterated along with everyone else when he ran for governor against Lurleen," Frady notes. "He conspicuously identified himself with the ambition of the newly registered Negro voters in the state and the dreams of the white liberal minority when he ran for governor. He publicly erased himself as any serious factor in future campaigns."[39]

King George. Lurleen's victory demonstrated that George Wallace was indeed king in Alabama. This was the first time that the real strength of Wallace was realized by state leaders, and it came as a surprise. They thought his loss in the succession fight weakened him, and Lurleen's candidacy was a last, desperate gamble.

Now they knew better. Wallace emerged from the succession crisis and the election miraculously revitalized. Other politicians, including Alabama's congressional delegation in Washington, now recognized the extent of his political strength.[40] Wallace was establishing himself as the most powerful politician in the history of the state, and, according to Stephan Lesher, who covered Wallace for *Newsweek* more than twenty years, he proved at the national level to be "the dominant and most important issue maker of his time."[41]

The *News* took a dim view of things. It said in an editorial just after the general election, "Alabama voters had their emotional fling Tuesday.

They 'showed em'—LBJ, Katzenbach, the beatniks, the blacks, the 'liberal' press. And they changed reality not a whit. They did create some doubt that this state is ready to stand eyeball-to-eyeball with the future and move ahead calmly to meet its challenges."[42]

"George Wallace has shown a remarkable talent for making people see reality in illusion," the paper editorialized. He had a talent for "making it appear that eternal grasping for personal power is a service to 'the people' and making the people believe he is a defender of the constitution while before their very eyes he mocks it."[43]

Lurleen was inaugurated governor in January of 1967. The following June, a lump was found in her stomach, and a recurrence of cancer was confirmed. It had spread to the lower abdominal region, including the colon. Her health continued to deteriorate through various treatments, and she died on May 7, 1968, only sixteen months after her inauguration. Albert Brewer became governor and finished the two and one-half years which remained in her term.

Indictment and Trial

Richmond completed his term as attorney general in January of 1967, and he opened a law office in Montgomery. He intended to run for governor again in 1970, and Montgomery was a desirable base for unofficial campaigning. In a bit of irony, Richmond's law office was in the same building and one floor above the Wallace national campaign headquarters.[44]

Almost from the day he began his new work, Richmond heard rumors of an investigation of his activities as attorney general. He reasoned that it would be wise to stay out of the limelight for a while. "I went to Barefoot Sanders in Washington and said, 'Barefoot, I've got to have a job,'" he recalls. "Barefoot Sanders was the assistant attorney general attached to the White House. I knew him because the president always sent him to the attorney generals meetings. I said, 'I've been sitting down here for four years supporting the Justice Department, saying they were right and we had to comply with their rulings. Now that I've lost the protection of my office, they may try to crucify me. Pull me into Washington for a while, and let things die down.'

"Barefoot got in touch later and told me there wasn't anything. He said, 'If we don't elect Hubert Humphrey, ain't any of us going to have a job.' I said, 'In other words, the only job you've got for me is to help Hubert Humphrey.' He said, 'That's about it.' After that, it wasn't any time until the investigation really opened up. That's the way they play ball. They play hardball. I stepped on toes and didn't even realize it. The president was mad because I didn't do exactly what he said do."

Richmond practiced a little more than a year in Montgomery. Then, with trouble clearly on the horizon, he decided to make a change. "My brother Paul kept insisting that I return to Dothan," Richmond says, "because his hospital was growing in leaps and bounds, and he needed help. He was administrator, and he was running the kitchen and purchasing and the surgical suite and delivery room. Finally I said, 'I'll commute for six or eight weeks to see what you need and if I can help.'

"He asked me to take over purchasing. He had a 120-bed hospital and no central purchasing office. The drug salesmen and everybody else would walk up and down the hall taking orders from nurse's stations. So he really did need help. I had such a warm feeling because I had thought Paul was just trying to help me out of a financial bind. Paul used to say that somebody asked him, 'How do you put up with Richmond?' 'Ah, me and Richmond made mud pies together. I have to put up with him.'

Richmond soon realized that the investigation of him had begun while he was still attorney general, and he learned that the Internal Revenue Service was handling it. "I had a very good friend and supporter, Oscar Hyde, who was under investigation for tax evasion. He had been battling them for years. He kept telling me, 'Richmond, they're trying to tie the two of us together.' I said, 'Well, let them tie. I haven't anything to do with your evasion. So you're my friend, so what? What is it we're supposed to have done wrong?' 'I don't know, but they're trying to trace every place there's been some money made.' I said, 'Well, Oscar, I haven't made any money.' I was confident because I knew I hadn't taken any money.

"Two IRS agents had come to see me just before I left office and asked about my financial records. I said, 'Now gentlemen, if you're special agents, I'm not going to talk to you because I don't trust a special agent. I know the way they're trained, and I know their object in life is to get information, fair or foul. Some of them are not beyond manufacturing evidence either; I've been in this office long enough to see that.' They said, 'Aw, Mr. Flowers, we're not special agents.' I made a mistake by not demanding they show me their credentials. But I thought surely a man representing the United States government wouldn't come into the office of the highest law enforcement official in the state and lie—especially since I had been working with the Justice Department hand and foot for four years and drawing the fire of the devil for doing it.

"They were both special agents. They testified against me in court and told bald-face lies, both of them. In court they said, 'We did not lie, we told him we were special agents. We showed him our credentials and told him anything he said could be held against him.'"

Oscar Hyde. Richmond's friend, Oscar Hyde, turned out to be a central figure in the investigation and later in the trial. "I met Oscar when I was fighting loan bills in the legislature," he remembers. "Every time the legislature met, bills were introduced against the so-called loan sharks. I took my father's advice on this. He was a former president of the Alabama Bankers Association and was a very solid, conservative banker. He said, 'Richmond, don't fall for all of this folderol about loan shark, loan shark. Don't you go up there and be a hero and shut down the small loan operators. In our bank, we can't lend $100. We can't lend $50. It costs us more to put it on the books and take it off than we can make on it. The man that borrows twenty and the man that borrows fifty need it just as bad as the man that borrows $2,500 and $5,000.' When I was in the legislature, I helped beat the bills.

"But under Governor Patterson the big loan companies came in, and they meant business. I was hired to lobby against their bill, which would allow them to take over from local companies. In truth, the biggies were just another crowd doing the same thing, the foreign crowd rather than the local crowd. As a former senator, I had access to the legislative floor. It was strictly a lobbying job, with legitimate legal fees. It helped pay the expenses of me traveling around making those speeches, and it kept me in the limelight so I could get the speeches.

"Oscar Hyde had several loan companies, so he was very interested. He was primarily responsible for hiring me to do the lobbying. Oscar became a close friend, and later he was the largest single contributor to my campaigns for attorney general and for governor."

Investigation. The investigation did not involve Richmond's performance as attorney general, but focused on possible misconduct in the approval of stock issues and the regulation of loan companies. At the time, the attorney general also served as state securities commissioner. He approved applications and issued licenses for the sale of securities, and he enforced the law relative to the operation of loan companies.

Wayne Greenhaw says that the securities commission was one of the worst places in the state government for possible bribes and fraud. "There was so much opportunity for this kind of stuff. The big companies tried all of the time to get their way, by whatever would work."[45]

As the investigation progressed, Richmond could see that there was big trouble ahead, and he tried to get help. "I went to U.S. Attorney General [Ramsey] Clark and told him, 'You can't turn me over to an Alabama grand jury. I tried to go along with the Democratic party and cooperated with the Justice Department in every way. If you turn me over to a bunch of George Wallace rednecks, they'll lock me up forever.' He said, 'Go on home and don't worry about it. Nothing's going to happen to you.' I got word they did not want an indictment sent up on me. Then, for some reason the Justice Department reversed themselves and said, 'Go ahead and indict him.'"

A grand jury was called in Birmingham to consider the case, and the foreman turned out to be Julian Lackey, who had been a friend of Richmond's at the University of Alabama. This was an unusual turn of events since Julian's father, Rufus, was a Birmingham millionaire who had crossed swords with Richmond in the legislature. An active 'Big Mule' in state politics, Rufus Lackey had been instrumental in getting Clarence Allgood, who was to conduct the trial, appointed as Judge of the Northern District of Alabama. As Richmond observes, there are too many connections in all of this to believe it could be accidental. "The fact that Julian Lackey was drawn for the grand jury is interesting, isn't it? Julian's father and the judge planned the case, and he was called on the grand jury and elected foreman. A grand jury is supposed to be drawn randomly out of the jury box like every other jury. It wouldn't happen like it did in a thousand years if the selections were made properly."

Grand Jury Testimony. Richmond felt he was innocent of any legal offense, and he decided on the unusual tactic of testifying before the grand jury to try to convince them. He contacted Bear Bryant, the Alabama football coach, who was a close friend of Julian Lackey and asked if Bear would help get him permission to testify. "I wanted to find out what they'd been told and straighten them out," he says.

"You have to waive your rights; otherwise, if the grand jury lets you testify in front of them, they can't indict you. Another one can, but they can't. So I waived my rights, and went in there and asked, 'Gentlemen, what is it I'm accused of? What is it I'm supposed to have done? I guarantee if you'll just tell me what it is, I can convince you that it's all a bunch of malarkey. I haven't touched a nickel. I have able support, and what little financial help I need, I get from them. Mainly its from my brother who is an extremely wealthy man. I haven't allowed anybody around me to touch a nickel. If they have, they have done it totally without my knowledge.'

"None of them would answer any questions. I turned to Lackey, and said, 'What is it Julian? You know me.' 'Well now, I've got a responsibility here to run this thing,' he answered. 'I'm not here to help you.' I never could get anything out of them. I said, 'Well, let me just say this. I heard there's talk out the street that I've been accused of telling someone the only way he could get a stock issue before the securities commission was to see Oscar Hyde. He will have to say that on the witness stand, and I'll look him in the face and tell him he's a damn liar.'"

James Fullan, one of the lawyers who represented Richmond in the trial, feels that the grand jury testimony was a mistake. "Years later," he says, "a man came into my office on some matter, and he told me that he had been on the grand jury that indicted Richmond. He said that the jurors had just about made up their minds that there was nothing to it until Richmond testified. Richmond took it on himself to appear before the grand jury. It wasn't on our advice."[46]

Indictment. A four-count indictment was returned by the grand jury on August 2, 1968. It charged that Richmond and three others violated the Hobbs Act, which makes it a federal crime to obstruct or affect interstate commerce by committing or conspiring to commit extortion. The indictment was announced in Birmingham and later the same day by U.S. Attorney General Ramsey Clark in Washington. Also indicted were Oscar Hyde, Joe Breck Gantt, and James Kelly, a business associate from Mississippi. Six others were named as co-conspirators but were not indicted.

Gantt was assistant attorney general/assistant securities commissioner when Richmond was attorney general. He was in charge of processing the requests for approval of stock issues, for granting exemptions to sell front-end stock prior to a public issue, and for licensing stock salesmen. "We were close," Richmond says. "He traveled with me some, and he appeared to be very loyal. There's a man I befriended and helped, and he turned on me to an extent. Some of his friends gave testimony which insinuated that I was in some money deals that I absolutely was not in. Joe Breck and his friends didn't stick strictly to the truth."

Jim Kelly, the other co-defendant, met Richmond when both were associated with Alabama General Insurance Company during the Folsom administration. Kelly was corporation secretary and sales manager when Richmond became president. "He was an experienced, skilled insurance salesman," Richmond says. "We got along beautifully and soon were very good friends. When the company folded, he went back to Mississippi, and I helped him buy two funeral homes. Jim supported me in my campaigns and paid some of the political bills. In the trial, they tried to make out that, if you wanted to get to Flowers, go see Jim Kelly. It looked like a natural setup. He wasn't a resident of Alabama, and seemingly, you could leave the state and do what you wanted without any problems. Strong evidence was given that Jim Kelly actually took money under the guise that he was going to give it to me. Hearing this was the biggest surprise I ever had. He denied it right up to trial time."

There was a major question about the composition of the grand jury, and in September 1968, Richmond's attorneys moved to dismiss the indictment on this account. Census data showed that about 79 percent the adult population in the Northern District of Alabama was white and 21 percent black, and that 47 percent were male and 53 percent female. The grand jury had 21 males and no females, and it had three blacks. The request to dismiss was denied. In November, a motion was filed for a hearing on the grand jury issue. This, too, was denied. On January 20, 1969, Richmond's attorneys, in a move to set up a possible appeal, took the depositions of the two court clerks on the issue of grand jury composition.

Counts. The four counts of the indictment were:

Count 1: Richmond was accused of lending the powers of his office to an extortion ring. The indictment alleged that applicants for stock sale rights would be "surreptitiously" referred to Oscar Hyde, who put propositions to the ring's victims. Hyde would demand a sum of money equal to 5 percent of the total amount of stock to be authorized. The money would be paid by the victims in the guise of legal and public relations fees.

Count 2: The four defendants were accused of conspiring to extort money from small loan companies by threatening investigation for violation of state usury laws, by seizing their records, and by false suits in the state courts. Oscar Hyde was again pictured as the contact man. The indictment alleged that the money was received by the extortion ring as public relations fees and as payment in credit life insurance premiums.

Count 3: Richmond and Oscar Hyde were charged with extorting $25,000 from Paramount Life Insurance Company in authorizing it to sell stock. They were alleged to have threatened that, if the company did not pay the money, the authorization to sell stock would not be granted.

Count 4: Flowers, Hyde, and Gantt were charged with collection of $59,438 from Century Discount Corporation on threat of interference in the company's business. Flowers and Gantt, it was alleged, seized company records and filed suit to enjoin it from operation as a small loan company. Hyde then told Century the suit would be dropped if they purchased credit life insurance and public relations services, and after the company agreed to a contract, the suit was dismissed and the records returned.

The gist of the indictment so far as Richmond was concerned was that he allowed himself to be manipulated in his job as state securities commissioner, primarily by Oscar Hyde. An indictment is, of course, a formal accusation and not a presumption of guilt. The burden of proof is on the government no matter what evidence has been presented to a grand jury, and the accused is presumed innocent until a jury finds otherwise.

Trial. The trial started on January 27, 1969. The government intended to try all four defendants together, but James Kelly had a heart attack and had to be dropped. Richmond was represented by the firm of Beddow, Embry, and Beddow, whom he had been advised were good trial lawyers who got along well with the judge.

Richmond was the highest-ranking former state constitutional officer in Alabama history to come to trial on such formidable allegations.[47] This and the publicity he had received in his civil rights actions made him a very prominent figure, and the trial attracted wide press coverage. It was carried extensively by both Birmingham papers and was regularly in the television news. Because of the effect this could have on jurors, defense attorneys requested that the jury be sequestered during the trial, but the request was denied.

Richmond's attorneys moved for trying him separately from the other defendants. "We tried our best to be tried separately," he says, "because I could not say anything about my fellow defendants. I could not accuse them. I could not make a statement such as, 'Just ask him didn't I tell him so-and-so.' If I do that it's a mistrial. The judge would go in chambers with the lawyers and say, 'Now, you're getting close to Richmond accusing these other fellows of letting him down. I mean you better not do it. I'll have to throw the case out, but I'll put you all in contempt.' He kept threatening the lawyers with contempt.

The trial lasted six weeks and was one of the longest ever conducted in federal court in Birmingham. During the first four and one-half weeks, the prosecutors proceeded painstakingly through the four counts of the indictment. Officials of two loan companies and of four corporations which had sought stock issues testified they made payoffs, through contracts for public relations, credit life insurance, or other services. A great quantity of documentary evidence was presented.[48]

All of this was accompanied by large, front-page headlines such as "Loan exec tells of $4,600 'shakedown' to avoid trouble,"[49] "$95,000 Paid for OK on Stock, Jury is Told,"[50] and "Witness: Flowers Got Pay."[51] Since jury members were not sequestered, they saw these and were free to read the reporters' interpretations of events.

The evidence left little doubt that high-pressure tactics had been used under questionable circumstances and that illegal payments had been made. However, there was only one claim that a payment had been made directly to Richmond, and this was effectively countered by his defense. The major charge against him was that he let it happen. He was the chief law enforcement officer in the state, and he had the responsibility and authority to investigate and take corrective action as needed. The judge instructed the jury that Richmond did not have to receive anything directly to be guilty of conspiracy.

The evidence presented against Richmond can be summarized in five points:

1. He let Oscar Hyde and the others extort money. He either knew about it or should have known about it.

2. He had received large campaign contributions from Hyde and, in return, he allowed himself to be unduly influenced by Hyde.

3. Hyde had paid a $50,000 debt Richmond owed as a result of the Alabama General Insurance fiasco, and Richmond was hugely indebted to him because of it.

4. Richmond signed a contract with a company, which was accused of receiving payments in the extortion scheme, for a job he was to receive after he left office.

5. He received a check for $2,500 as part of one of the schemes. This was the only claim that he took money directly.

Almost all of the testimony centered on the activities of Oscar Hyde, and the evidence against him was the most damning. There was testimony that Hyde claimed to have great influence with the attorney general and said he could get him to close any business that didn't cooperate. Several witnesses said that Hyde was quite direct and blunt in his demands. According to the testimony, Hyde spread the payments among several companies which he owned or controlled.

Oscar Hyde's prior record was not clean. He was one of six Alabamians indicted by a federal grand jury in November 1966 on charges of seeking payoffs from persons trying to get approval of applications before the Alabama Public Service Commission. He was indicted in August 1968 on two counts of tax evasion and ten counts of filing false federal and corporation tax returns.

Alabama General. Richmond had trouble previously because of his connection with Alabama General Insurance Company, and now it came back to haunt him. Shortly after he accepted the presidency of Alabama General in 1956, an audit showed the company to be in the red about $400,000. He decided to borrow $224,000 in an effort to get the company back on its feet.

The loan was with Pan American National Bank in Miami. Richmond, Jim Kelly, and two other Alabama General officers signed the papers, and Richmond put up 80,000 shares of Alabama General stock as security. After the company went into voluntary receivership, the stock wasn't any good. He and Kelly faced the entire loss of the note, Richmond testified, "because the other officials transferred their property into their wive's names." He asked bank officials not to file suit, on promise that he and Kelly would pay off the loan.

In 1963, bank officials contacted him about payment. Oscar Hyde, with the help of political friend Claude Pepper, got the bank to agree to settle for $50,000. Richmond and Kelly then obtained a loan in this amount from Hyde. The $50,000 was paid in August 1963 through a cashier's check to Oscar Hyde. To cover the $50,000, Kelly gave Hyde a note for that amount and Flowers released to Kelly all the property held jointly by the two.

The $2,500 Check. The IRS agents who had visited Richmond's office in Montgomery took copies of a bank statement from which they pulled information on a $2,500 check which had been written to Oscar Hyde and endorsed by Richmond. Richmond freely gave them this information. Later it was the basis of a charge against him.

"The only direct evidence they used against me," he says, "was this check I got to cover an overdraft. My brother Drury called me and said, 'You've got an overdraft of $2,500. We'd better get it covered.' I called Oscar, and he sent me a check for that amount. He operated half a dozen or more corporations, and I didn't pay any attention to the check. I just endorsed it and deposited it in Drury's bank. It covered my overdraft, and I thought everything was happy.

"The check was drawn on a company that had been dealing with the attorney general's office. Oscar told me it was for strictly legitimate service. But because of the nearness of time and the fact that he got the check from this particular company, the prosecution said it was a payoff to me. The truth was that I signed a note and paid it back at $200 a month. We presented evidence to prove this. It was one of those happen-sos that I can see looks bad, but there wasn't anything to it."

The Basis of Alleged Guilt. Richmond maintains that the government's testimony and evidence did not directly implicate him. "They didn't have a single witness who said, 'I talked to Richmond Flowers, and he said pay me' or that sort of thing. The judge charged the jury, 'Ladies and gentlemen, defendant Flowers has tried to make a large point of the fact that he did not receive any of the money. He doesn't have to. If his friends make money because of his influence, he is as guilty as they are.'

"I turned to my lawyer and said, 'If that's the law, they might as well start with Dick Nixon and wipe out the last justice of the peace.' Who are you going to let make money? Your enemies? As long as there are legitimate fees that somebody's going to make, you want your friends to get them.

"None of the people who had championed my cause while I was attorney general came forward during the trial. The people in Montgomery wouldn't help because they were afraid of Wallace. I didn't even have much black support. Some who could have helped were named as unindicted co-conspirators and could have been brought to trial. They were threatened, 'If you don't do this, we may indict you.' A conspiracy is like using a throw net. They just throw it over everybody and 'say what we want you to say or we'll put you on trial.' I didn't have a prayer."

Richmond was the only one of the three defendants who took the stand. According to a reporter, he acted very confident and answered his attorney's questions with crisp 'yes sirs' and 'no sirs.'[52] James Fullan recalls, "My partner examined Richmond for about an hour and went down each portion of the charges. Richmond, categorically and forthrightly and looking the jury straight in the face, denied it all. He didn't have anything to do with it. Afterwards, we sat back for the hit from the prosecution, but the hit never took place. The cross-examination was short, and it produced nothing. I remember distinctly that, after the examination and cross-examination of Richmond, several people including the judge said, 'You boys have pulled it out of the fire.'"[53]

Throughout the trial, an issue was made as to whether the alleged actions involved interstate commerce. For the Hobbs Act to be applicable, there must be a "federal nexus," that is, interstate commerce must be affected. Knowing that this was almost certain to be an issue in an appeal, both sides took particular pains with it.[54] Judge Allgood stated in his instructions to the jury that, if they found evidence of a conspiracy, the court had already determined that interstate commerce was involved and affected.[55] In other words, the jury's only concern was the conspiracy, not the federal nexus. Richmond's attorneys objected that it was not the judge's prerogative to make this determination.

Verdict and Sentence. The case went to the jury on February 27, 1969, and it deliberated less than seven hours before finding the three defendants guilty on all counts. On March 7, post-trial requests for acquittal verdicts were made to Judge Allgood and were denied. Richmond was sentenced on March 10 to eight years in prison and a $10,000 fine. Hyde was given eight years and a $20,000 fine. Gantt received a

Mary, Richmond, and Richmond, Jr., leave the federal courthouse in Birmingham after Flowers's conviction.

five-year suspended sentences on two counts and a year and a day in prison on the third count.

Richmond realizes that he made a mistake in trusting some of his close associates too much. "My attorneys said that I was loyal to my friends," he reflects, "and I was. I always said I played my politics like the country girl at a dance. I may dance every set with a different guy, but I'm going home with the feller that brung me. I favored my friends, and that's what got me into trouble.

"Oscar used my name when I was attorney general, and he used my friendship. Everyone knew we were very close, and if Oscar Hyde asked me for a favor, he'd get it because he had practically financed my campaign. To my knowledge he never said, 'I'm going to give money to Flowers.' He just said, 'If you want me to help you, you cut me in. Otherwise, why should I help you?' So they'd cut him in on part of the deal. If I was suspected of helping him make money, I had no complaints.

"Some of the others I depended on turned out to be undependable. I was being loyal to Kelly, and I was being loyal to Gantt and to Lassiter. These were folks who had helped me, and I was going to help them every way I could. It turned out that some of them were actually taking money. I told them that all I wanted to know was who we were dealing with and what their business was. I'd leave the rest up to their judgment. It was one of those mistakes where my heart was in the right place."

He also feels he would have been better off with out-of-state lawyers. "My lawyers fought a valiant fight," he says, "but I realize now I never should have used Alabama attorneys. I knew I was going to need some favorable rulings out of the judge, but I never got a single one. They couldn't strong-arm a judge they had to continue to practice under. Several times in the trial we had them right over the barrel, and the judge would say, 'Now don't mention that. I don't want to hear any more about it.' They wouldn't raise an objection because they were afraid of him."

The appeal process began immediately. On March 20, Richmond's attorneys asked the judge for a new trial, citing more than 100 errors. This was denied, and the formal appeal process began. Richmond had not believed the matter would get this far, but he still felt certain he could win in an appeal. He had friends in Washington, and he thought that, with his attempts to support the Justice Department while he was attorney general, officials there would help him.

A Plot To Convict? Richmond is convinced that the trial was part of a plot to remove him from the political scene in Alabama. He believes it began with Wallace, who had both a revenge motive and the desire to eliminate Richmond as competition later. When state charges proved insufficient, the Johnson administration lent a hand.

"George Wallace put the word out," Richmond asserts. "One of his legal advisors was appointed district attorney in Birmingham, and George told him to get me. After a time, he went back to George and said, 'You can't touch him. He hasn't done anything wrong. We can't find one damn thing, except maybe conspiracy.' In Alabama, conspiracy is just a misdemeanor with a maximum $500 fine. That's when George turned to the feds. My lawyers knew this. They got it from the DA, and they told me, 'It's not George this time; he's already tried and failed.'

"The feds were more than willing to help. When Lyndon Johnson tried to deflect the black vote from me in the governor's race and couldn't do it, it frightened them. They were afraid I would run on the national Democratic party of Alabama ticket and pull votes from the regular Democrats, and the Republicans would elect congressmen all over the state.

"The IRS started investigating me, and they continued even after they couldn't find any tax problems. Why would they do this? They handled the case, but my background and troubles were political. They had to use the Hobbs Act, which is the most vicious law. It's a dirty, rotten way to get somebody if you can't convict them on anything else."

Before the indictment, Richmond heard about a conversation involving the federal judge who tried the case. "Clarence Allgood and Rufus Lackey sat in the home of Lackey's son one night and plotted how to nail me," he relates. "His son had a visitor who heard them talking about me. They said, 'We've got about enough now to indict him. With his stand on race, they'll convict him of any charges we place.' Rufus Lackey was a big crony of Judge Allgood. The foreman of the grand jury that indicted me was Rufus Lackey's son, Julian, who was in the house that night talking with them. They were actually planning it.

"The person who heard their conversation had run a loan company one time for Oscar Hyde. He went to Oscar's bookkeeper and said, 'Shouldn't we get word to Richmond what's going on. I heard it with my own ears.' She told Oscar and Oscar told me. That's when I realized the judge was in on it, and I was in serious trouble.

"Judge Allgood wasn't qualified and, in my opinion, wasn't very capable. He never held any job close to law except refereeing bankruptcy.

He had tried a few criminal cases and couldn't handle a case of any import. The judge said he knew within two or three days that I was guilty, and there had been hardly any testimony at that point. All we'd done was argue motions. He told Guy Hardwick, a mutual friend, that he knew within three days, and Guy told me.

Richmond also feels that the jury made a fair trial impossible. "There were very few blacks on my venire when I was tried," he says, "and the government struck every one of them but two. One of them got sick after about three days and was dismissed. I was so hated that with an all-white jury, I didn't have a prayer."

Appeal

The appeal process started immediately after Richmond was sentenced and Judge Allgood had denied a motion for retrial. The case went to the Fifth Circuit Court of Appeals, which then had jurisdiction in Alabama. Ironically, the Fifth Circuit Court had made a number of the landmark decisions during the civil rights battle and had supported Richmond in several of his cases.

Appealing a Federal Conviction. In a federal criminal case, a panel of circuit court judges hears the appeal and renders a decision. If the decision is unfavorable, the defendant may approach the U.S. Supreme Court. The Supreme Court will accept jurisdiction only when the case involves a constitutional issue, when there is a conflict between rulings of different circuit courts on a particular matter, or when the case involves interpretation of a statute that has not been previously presented to the Court.[56] Thousands of petitions are filed with the Supreme Court each year, and only a small percent are granted. If the Supreme Court does not accept jurisdiction, or if it hears the case and renders a decision unfavorable to the appellant, the appeal process is ended. No other channels of relief are available.

Winning in a criminal case appeal is difficult. Because the petitioner has been convicted by a jury, the burden of proof shifts to him and is no longer on the government. The question for the appeals court is not whether the evidence was sufficient for a verdict of guilty, but whether guilt was found by a jury acting according to procedures and standards established for criminal trials in the federal court system. The defense must have objected to specific actions of the government or the presiding judge during the trial for these actions to be considered. The appellate court by tradition and by Supreme Court direction takes the view most favorable to the government in deciding whether to sustain the trial jury's verdict.[57]

Basis for the Appeal. The substance of Richmond's appeal can be summarized in eight categories, as follows.

1. The composition of the grand jury and the petit (trial) juries made a fair trial impossible. There was purposeful, systematic exclusion of blacks and women from the jury system in the Northern District of Alabama, and the court erred in denying hearings in which to challenge jury composition. In a claim of a prejudicial jury, the defendant has the burden of proving that discrimination resulted, and the focus is on composition of the list (or "jury box") from which venire is selected, rather than on the individual trial jury.

The grand jury issue revolved around a "key man" system which the court had used to select possible jury members. In 1963 the chief clerk of the court wrote to 1754 persons, so-called "key men" or "nominators," asking for possible jurors. More than 18,000 names were suggested, and the clerk sent each a questionnaire. Some 11,000 were returned, and court clerks pared this group down to 7,000, according to a set of criteria established by law and by the district judge. Among those excluded were teachers, ministers, lawyers, undertakers, druggists, doctors, nurses, and persons with physical disability, language disability, or criminal conviction. From this list, the grand jury venire was selected by lot. The defendants objected that this system was inherently biased because the key men were "leaders of the white male community" and tended to recommend friends and acquaintances who were as unrepresentative as they.

For selection of the trial jury, the court used a new plan, based on the Jury Selection and Service Act of 1968, to draw the venire from voter registration lists. The defendants objected that a much larger proportion of whites than blacks were registered voters, and therefore blacks were under-represented.

2. The judge erred in denying Richmond's motion for severance, that is, for a trial separate from that of Hyde and Gantt.

Richmond's attorneys contended that he was entitled to a separate trial because, when tried with the other two defendants, he could not properly defend himself against evidence brought against them but not applicable to him. He was prevented by trial procedure from directly challenging his co-defendants.

3. The alleged actions were bribery or attempted bribery and not extortion, so the Hobbs Act was not applicable. It could not have been extortion in Richmond's case, his attorneys argued, because regulation of loan companies and related trials against them were part of his responsibility as state securities commissioner. He was just doing his job. Richmond received no personal benefit from the alleged activities, and even if a crime occurred, he was not involved and should not have been charged with it. His lawyers moved for a directed verdict of acquittal on this bases during the trial and were denied.

4. Interstate commerce was not involved, so a requirement for the Hobbs Act was not met. This was perhaps the key issue of the appeal. The jury was improperly instructed in regard to this issue, the defendants claimed, both at the beginning of the trial and in the final instructions. Also, the prosecution relied in the case on interstate commerce facts not charged in the indictment and not considered by the grand jury.

The appellants contended that, in a Hobbs Act case, it is for the jury and not the court to determine whether the conduct of defendants affected interstate commerce, particularly when the matter has been "controverted" (challenged by the defense). The defense objected at the start of the trial to the government attorney's statement that it was the judge's duty to determine whether interstate commerce was affected and that the jury need not be concerned with it.

At the end of the trial, Judge Allgood charged the jury, "It is the duty of the Court and not the jury to determine whether the government's evidence, if believed, established that interstate commerce was affected by the conduct of the defendant.

"I instruct you that if you find from the evidence beyond a reasonable doubt that a conspiracy existed . . . the Court has found, as a matter of law, that the requirements of the Hobbs Act have been met as to interstate commerce being affected." The defense objected after the charge was given.

5. A motion for continuance based on Kelly's illness and severance was denied. The defendants sought a continuance on the basis of prejudice arising from Kelly's absence. Defense attorneys had prepared their case assuming Kelly would be present, and they needed time to take his absence into account and make appropriate changes in their strategy and plans. The trial judge denied the continuance.

6. Use of hearsay evidence by the prosecution should not have been allowed. In the trial, a great deal of hearsay evidence, or "street talk" as Richmond puts it, was allowed despite repeated objections by defense attorneys. A witness would testify as to what some third party told him, and he was not required to name the party. The court held that the purpose of this testimony was not to establish facts but to show the state of the alleged victims' minds, and it was therefore admissible. The Sixth Amendment of the U.S. Constitution states that an accused in a criminal trial has the right to confront witnesses against him.

7. The defense moved at the outset that the court sequester the jury because of the likelihood of prejudicial newspaper publicity. The trial judge denied the motion. The appellants argued that the trial involved a very prominent figure and was certain to attract wide publicity. In fact, as the trial progressed, there were many front-page headlines and stories which could have been prejudicial, and jurors were free to read them. Instead of sequestering the jury, the judge admonished its members not to look at news stories or listen to broadcasts.

8. There were a number of other improper incidents, mainly prosecution actions and voluntary statements of witnesses, that were objected to and allowed by the presiding judge, and the cumulative effect of these was to deny the defendants a fair trial.

A Fifth Circuit Panel Hears the Case. A three-man panel from the Fifth Circuit came to Montgomery to hear the case. The three were John Wisdom, an Eisenhower Republican from Louisiana; James Coleman, who had been Governor of Mississippi from 1955 to 1959; and Richard

Rives of Montgomery, who had been on the court some twenty years. Rives had been a highly successful attorney before his appointment as Fifth Circuit judge, and he was the most respected member of the court.

"John Godbold was a Fifth Circuit judge who could have been on the panel, but he recused himself," Richmond notes. "He was a freshman with me at Auburn, and we went all the way through law school together. He recused himself 'because we were such good friends,' and I hadn't seen him since we finished law school. He knew if he stayed on the panel, he couldn't go against Dick Rives, and he knew Judge Rives as senior judge was going to write the opinion.

"Allgood was lobbying all the time, begging the Fifth Circuit Court not to reverse him on this case. He was so afraid they were going to reverse him. He made errors, and they should have reversed him, but he politicked the thing through. He politicked it hard. He went personally to judges on the fifth circuit and begged them, 'Don't reverse me on this thing. It will make a laughing stock of me all over Alabama.'"

The petition for a rehearing was denied on a vote of two to one by the panel. Judges Wisdom and Coleman voted to uphold the conviction, while Judge Rives voted to reverse. Rives then filed a long dissent.

On the matter of the grand jury, the court held that the defendants did not present sufficient statistical evidence to prove deliberate discrimination, even though it agreed that the jury may not have been representative. In the process of disqualifying more than 10,000 persons, the court said, blacks and women might easily have been dropped out disproportionately in a nondiscriminatory fashion.

Hearsay evidence is accepted in a Hobbs Act trial, the court ruled, if it speaks to the state of the victim's mind. The statute does not require an explicit threat from the defendant, only that the defendant has induced his victim to part with property through the use of fear. Failure to produce or even to name a third person making a statement to the victim was no ground for objection if it related exclusively to the matter of induced fear.

On the critical issue of interstate commerce, the court ruled that the evidence was sufficient to establish federal jurisdiction under the Hobbs Act. The impact on interstate commerce need not be substantial to justify prosecution for extortion under the act, it said. The trial court was correct in determining whether the statutory requirement was met, and the jury's task was to determine whether the facts related to extortion had been proved. This ruling was the basis for the strong dissent by Judge Rives.

On sequestering, the ruling was that the newspaper stories were not shown by the appellants to have emphasized the strength of the prosecution's case or the weakness of defendants' case or to have prejudiced the defendants. In other words, the appellants did not prove their argument.

Richmond based his claim of innocence on the contention that he was not involved and did not profit by the alleged actions. The appellate court ruled that this did not matter. As state securities commissioner, it held, he personally signed orders approving sale of public issues of stock. He knew or would be presumed to have known of every application to the commission for such approval. He was responsible, in other words, whether he knew about the illegal activities or not!

The court also held that a person need receive no personal benefit to be guilty of extortion. The essential part of the complaint, it said, is that there is loss to a victim caused by some action or lack of action by the accused. Combined with the ruling that the statute did not require an explicit threat from the defendant but only an inducement of fear which could be substantiated by vague third-party statements, the appellate court made it possible for Richmond to be convicted on very flimsy evidence.

Dissent. In a strong thirteen-page dissent, Judge Rives argued that the defendants' constitutional right to due process had been violated because of trial court rulings on the interstate commerce question. In deciding the question of interference with interstate commerce, Judge Rives stated, the trial judge in effect directed a verdict of guilty on this essential element of a Hobbs Act case. In our legal system, Judge Rives pointed out, a judge in a criminal trial cannot direct a verdict of guilty, and he cannot set aside a verdict of acquittal. The rule against directed verdicts of guilt includes situations in which the judge's instructions fall short of explicitly directing a guilty verdict but which nevertheless have the effect of so doing by eliminating other relevant considerations by the jury.[58] The constitutional guarantees of due process and trial by jury require that a criminal defendant be afforded the full protection of a jury, unfettered, directly or indirectly, by actions of the court.[59]

The assistant U.S. Attorney, in his opening statement to the jury, said, "I submit to you that it is the court's function and not yours to find that interstate commerce existed and that the act involved affected, impeded, or delayed interstate commerce." The defense objected that this was an incorrect statement of law. Later in the same opening statement, the prosecution said to the jury, "You need not concern yourself with interstate commerce affected, impeded, or obstructed." There was another objection.

Judge Rives observed that "The impression which these statements of government counsel, tentatively approved by the Judge, inevitably had on the minds of the jurors was never removed throughout the six weeks trial. Was it not natural for the jurors to accept the invitation of the United States Attorney that 'you need not concern yourself' with this matter?[60]

"I submit that at the evidentiary stage of the trial, proof of the interstate commerce issue goes to the court's jurisdiction only in the same sense as proof of the other issue, extortion. That is to say, if there were no evidence whether to support either issue, the conviction of the defendants would be a violation of due process."[61]

Judge Rives added that he had strong misgivings as to the composition both of the grand jury and of the petit jury, but because he had commented so fully on the interstate commerce issue, he did not elaborate on these.

After the ruling, the defendants filed a petition with the fifth circuit for a rehearing en banc, that is, for a rehearing by all of the judges on the court and not just a panel. The judges were polled, and the denial on rehearing en banc was handed down June 23, 1971.

An attempt was then made to appeal to the U.S. Supreme Court, but the Court did not accept jurisdiction. This decision was announced in 1972, almost three years after appeal process had begun.

Searching for Help. Early in the appeal process, Richmond began searching for help in dealing with his legal difficulties, and he felt that powerful people outside of Alabama would be sympathetic. Shortly after the guilty verdict of the trial jury in the spring of 1969, he moved to Washington.

"Congressman Dan Button, the former editor of the *Albany Times Union* who was going to write a book about me, called and said, 'Come on up here. I'll give you a job, and maybe there is something we can do up here on the appeal.' I hoped it would help because I had several friends there. Ed Brooke, the black senator from Massachusetts, was one of them. He was a Republican, but he was very sympathetic to me. Several in the U.S. Senate had been state attorneys general at the same time I was. Walter Mondale was one of them. So was Thomas Eagleton, the senator from Missouri who got nominated for vice-president and had to pull out. I hoped some of them would help in the appeal and, in case we lost, in getting the Supreme Court to hear the case.

"After the Republicans got in, I had entree to John Mitchell, Nixon's attorney general. I sent word to him asking to let the Supreme Court hear the case, and John Mitchell responded, 'My God, I wish you had talked to me earlier. I made a commitment the other way just a few days ago.' A commitment the other way! They were wheeling and dealing.

"Earlier, I had asked Virginia Durr, a sister [-in-law] of Justice Hugo Black, to be a character witness at my trial. She was a very dear, sweet lady in this state, and one of the early whites to go along with civil rights. Virginia told me, 'Richmond, I'd love to, but it wouldn't be smart.' I asked, 'Why not, Virginia?' She said, 'Because if I'm in that trial, I can't open my mouth about your case to Hugo. If I'm not in it and I just know what went on, he'll listen to me. You know what Hugo will do, Richmond, he'll throw it all in their faces.' I said, 'Yes, ma'am. You won't be asked any further.' Just six weeks before my case went to Supreme Court, Hugo Black had a stroke and died, and I lost that ace in the hole. There is no doubt in my mind it would have been thrown out if Black had been around. This is another example of the breaks I got.

"I left Washington in November of 1969 because I realized that I'd done all I could. I hoped the Supreme Court would hear it, but without somebody to say, 'Gentlemen, I want to hear this,' it was not going to work out. The new man that handled this district in the Court after Hugo Black didn't know me and didn't know anything about it. I realized it was all over, and I came on home. We lost the appeal, and the Supreme Court denied certiorari, which meant that the case went back to the district court in Birmingham."

A Day Late and a Dollar Short. Richmond concedes on reflection that he came up a day late and a dollar short. "I didn't think it would go as far as it did," he says. "Even after the trial court decision, I was not concerned because I had stop gaps on the appellate levels. But all of them kept falling out. It happened that way all the way through the trial and the appeals. I didn't have a decent break anywhere in the whole thing.

"Your last chance is with the United States Supreme Court. As soon as they render a decision, they send the case back to the local court, and if you've lost, you have to report in. Finally the day came when I went to Birmingham. I came home to Dothan in November of '69, and I went off to Birmingham and to prison in '72."

A Question of Justice

Richmond Flowers was one of the most promising of Alabama politicians well into his term as attorney general. He was handsome and a great speaker, and he had a winning personality which made people like to be around him. He had played his political cards well—up to the point, at least, where events led to his decision to fight Wallace and support the civil rights movement. When he entered federal prison in 1972, his political career was ruined.

Did he receive equitable treatment under the law? Was a fair trial possible? Was he put away as the result of a conspiracy, as he claims? Many of the principal figures in the case are dead, and those who are not either have no new information or choose to remain silent. These questions are very difficult to answer more than twenty-five years after the events to which they relate.

The matter is relevant, nevertheless, to a review of Richmond Flowers's life and an estimate of his place in history. Many believe he was a martyred hero of the civil rights movement. Others still consider him a "traitor" to the Southern cause and an opportunist who took advantage of his position and was duly apprehended, tried, and convicted. At least three major topics are relevant in attempting a more informed judgment as to whether he received justice. First is the applicability of the Hobbs law. Second is the possibility of a fair trial, given the temper of the times. Third is whether Wallace and his followers were capable of carrying out the conspiracy which Richmond claims.

The Hobbs Act. One of the basic questions on use of the Hobbs Act in Richmond's case is the original intent of Congress in passing the act. The Hobbs Act was passed in 1946 as a replacement for the Anti-

Racketeering Act of 1934. The debates in Congress on the act dealt largely with union violence, and passage signified congressional intent to prohibit the use of force by unions in obtaining work for their members.[62]

Justice Scalia of the U.S. Supreme Court commented in a 1990 review of the Hobbs Act that it and its predecessor legislation were used for thirty years to fight racketeering. It was not until the 1960s, Scalia noted, that it first occurred to federal prosecutors to use the act to deal with extortion and the soliciting of bribes by state officials. Initially, he said, courts were unimpressed by this notion because it was not consistent with prior practice and because it appeared to go beyond the intent of Congress.[63]

Burke Marshall, former head of the Civil Rights Division in Washington, states that the federal courts have limited the power of prosecutors to bring criminal charges based on a statute not previously considered to apply to the particular conduct involved. Such restraint of the prosecutor is particularly appropriate, says Marshall, where the case involves possible punishment of a political opponent.[64]

A second question concerning the Hobbs Act is its use where improper influence from campaign contributions is alleged. Much of the evidence against Richmond revolved around his willingness to let some large contributors gain through his friendship. In its October 1990 term, the Supreme Court ruled that charges of wrongdoing in this type of situation have to involve the promise to perform a specific act. It overturned the conviction of a West Virginia legislator who had been convicted under the Hobbs Act for extorting campaign contributions. The defendant sponsored the legislation his contributors wanted, but he never stated explicitly that their contribution was required for his sponsorship.

Justice White wrote that, to hold that officials "commit the federal crime of extortion when they act for the benefit of constituents or support legislation furthering the interests of some of their constituents, shortly before or after campaign contributions are solicited and received from those beneficiaries, is an unrealistic assessment of what Congress could have meant by making it a crime to obtain property from another, with his consent, 'under color of official right.'

"To hold otherwise would open to prosecution not only conduct that has long been thought to be well within the law but also conduct that in a very real sense is unavoidable so long as election campaigns are financed by private contributions or expenditures, as they have been from the beginning of the nation."[65]

Still another point is use of the Hobbs Act to convict of conspiracy, as in Richmond's case. Justice Robert Jackson wrote of conspiracy as "that elastic, sprawling and pervasive offense. The unavailing protest of courts against the growing habit to indict for conspiracy in lieu of prosecuting for the substantive offense itself, or in addition thereto, suggests that loose practice as to this offense constitutes a serious threat to fairness in our administration of justice. The modern crime of conspiracy is so vague that it almost defies definition . . . the judge instructs the jury that the agreement can be implied from the most casual of circumstances . . . ."[66]

Justice Jackson continued, "The accused often is confronted with a hodgepodge of acts and statements by others which he may never have authorized or intended or even known about, but which help to persuade the jury of existence of the conspiracy itself. In other words, a conspiracy often is proved by evidence that is admissible only upon assumption that conspiracy existed. The naive assumption that prejudicial effects can be overcome by instructions to the jury, . . . all practicing lawyers know to be unmitigated fiction."[67]

A whole case can be permeated with what would normally be considered hearsay statements, untested by cross-examination of the person making them, Burke Marshall observes. "This comes about by reason of a kind of an agency theory that once persons are shown to be in a conspiracy with each other, each is responsible for anything any other one says or does."[68]

Possibility of a Fair Trial. A fair trial depends on a fair jury, and there is no question of Richmond's unpopularity in 1969 with any all-white or nearly all-white jury in Alabama. He was hated, and juries in Hayneville and elsewhere proved they could render decisions on prejudice rather than fact, particularly when race was involved.

Albert Brewer agrees that feelings against Richmond were very strong. "The change in public opinion of Richmond came as a result of the Hayneville trials," he says. "When Richmond went over to prosecute those cases, that pretty well put him on 'their' side in the public mind instead of ours. By 1966, Richmond was perceived as an integrationist, a traitor to the cause, a flaming liberal, and those sorts of things."[69]

A change of venue was not requested, says James Fullan, Richmond's chief defense attorney, because "chances of getting a change in venue in a federal trial are very slim. Also, we felt that the Northern District of Alabama had traditionally been more liberal than other locations in the Fifth Circuit. The consensus of all of the lawyers involved was that a change of venue, if we could have gotten it, would not have been an advantage."

Richmond has raised the question of the competence and fairness of the trial judge, Clarence W. Allgood. A review of the judge's background suggests at least some basis for misgiving on these points.

Allgood grew up in Birmingham, and he became interested in politics while he was in college. After finishing Birmingham Law School at night, he became a strong supporter of Senator Lister Hill and soon landed the key post of "political watchdog" for the national Democratic party in Birmingham.[70] In 1938, he was appointed Referee in Bankruptcy in the federal court in Birmingham. He worked hard in Hill's campaigns, and he stated to a friend once that when campaign funds were needed, all he had to do was call his friend Rufus Lackey, and he got them.[71]

In 1961, Allgood was appointed to the federal bench as a reward for his long service to the Democratic party. His professional qualifications for this post were questionable. Author Jack Bass says he had "an undistinguished record as a bankruptcy referee."[72] After he was nominated by President Kennedy, Allgood was initially rated as unqualified by the American Bar Association. He was approved anyway. Based on his record as judge, Bass refers to him as "a disappointing early Kennedy appointee."[73]

Allgood's greatest admirers call him a "hero of the South" in his approach to civil rights issues. A brief biography, which the authors call an "exercise of esteem and devotion to Clarence W. Allgood," refers to him as a "true Southerner in his attitudes." The authors mention the tension between his loyalty as a judicial official of the United States and his Alabama and state's rights heritage.[74] They refer to Richmond Flowers's "ultra-liberal civil rights views" and note that Richmond received a "send-em-up" sentence that showed none of the compassion usually found in Allgood's criminal verdicts.[75] To what extent did the "hero of the South" agree with most other white Alabamians that Richmond Flowers deserved punishment for his pro-civil rights and anti-Wallace activities?

Wallace and The Conspiracy Theory. Richmond speaks with great emotion about a conspiracy to get him. There is no question that the IRS and the U.S. attorneys in the Northern District of Alabama wanted him. They carried on an investigation of him for more than two years, and they worked at it "diligently."[76] Allgood's biographers relate that U.S. Attorney Macon Weaver found it difficult to gain permission from the Justice Department to seek the original indictment, but he kept trying.[77]

Wayne Greenhaw points out that a plot against Richmond did not have to be elaborate. "You know, you can set things in motion," he observed, "and its hard to stop them. Allgood didn't have to be literally trying to do a railroad job. He could have known they wanted Richmond convicted but still have done his job correctly. After something is underway, you just carry things out."[78]

If there was a conspiracy, the chief perpetrator had to have been George Wallace and his followers. Were the Wallace people capable of such behavior? Wayne Greenhaw says they were. "There is no question that Wallace and his group were capable of railroading somebody," Greenhaw asserts. "Wallace would not do it personally, but he would know who to tell and make sure it got done. There is no doubt that, if they wanted to do something like that, they were capable of it."[79] Two examples of the Wallace crowd in action against political opponents support Greenhaw's assertion.

Kenneth Hammond Loses His Career. The person whose experiences most closely resemble Richmond's is Kenneth Hammond, from Valley Head. He served in the state senate from 1963 to 1967 and was elected again in 1970. He was elected president of the Alabama Public Service Commission in 1972. In 1975, he crossed George and soon found himself in prison, his career ruined.

After Hammond entered the senate in 1962, he became disturbed by the stand Wallace was taking and the damage he was doing to the state's image. When Wallace tried to change the law so he could succeed himself as governor in 1965, Hammond was one of the leaders in the senate filibuster. In a dramatic speech on the senate floor, he accused Wallace of trying to establish a dictatorship worse than that of Huey

Long. He said Wallace had marked Alabama as "a haven for hate-mongers" and that the governor was a very dangerous man.[81]

Wallace had his revenge in 1966, the year in which his great power and his sway over the people of Alabama was first fully realized. "The word went out," Hammond says. "It went out to every branch head and every Wallace coordinator that they had decided to elect a lawyer, Dan Stone, in my place. They spent roughly $60,000 to get him elected, and in a rural race in those days, that was a lot of money."

Two years later, Wallace decided that maybe Hammond had learned his lesson. Hammond remained an attractive figure who could speak effectively to the common people in Alabama, and he would be a great asset if he would be a member of the team. Wallace called him to Montgomery for a private meeting and they came to an understanding.[82]

With Wallace support, Hammond was easily re-elected to the state senate in 1970. The next two years he voted the Wallace line consistently. In 1972, he decided the time had come to seek statewide office, and he ran for president of the Public Service Commission. Hammond campaigned statewide in the Folsom manner, speaking in every little town and making use of his natural ability to communicate. He won the election and took office in January 1973.

The Public Service Commission is responsible for regulating the big utilities and approving their rate increases. Millions of dollars are involved in its decisions, and it is rife with opportunities for skulduggery and rumors of wrongdoing. On assuming the presidency, Kenneth Hammond found that his powers to regulate were limited. The power company would request a rate increase, he says, and if it was turned down, the company would appeal to the state supreme court. Before the court acted, the company would request another increase and through this strategy would keep things in disorder and confusion. Often, the state supreme court would grant the increase, subverting the authority which was supposed to be exercised by the commission.

Hammond's fighting instinct was aroused once more, and in March 1975, he blasted Wallace in a public statement, charging that the governor was playing both sides of the issue. Hammond said he was going to tell it like he saw it "although it'll probably mean a one-way ticket back to Valley Head" in the next election.[83] On August 8, 1975, barely four months later, a Montgomery grand jury handed down an indictment which charged Hammond with the state-level crime of inciting to a felony. As in Richmond's case, there was no claim that he actually took money, only that he had incited someone to perform an act, bribery, which could result in his receiving money.

The case revolved around placement of vending machines in a Bell Telephone Company building. Hammond had urged a Bell executive to allow the machines to be placed, and a few months later, the commissioner asked that they be removed. Rex Moore, an unindicted co-conspirator and prosecution witness in Richmond's trial, was half-owner with his brother of the vending machines, and he claimed that Hammond asked him for a bribe. The state said that Hammond pressured the Moores by requesting that the Bell executive ask them to remove their vending machines. There was no evidence that Hammond promised to favor the telephone company on a future rate increase request.

Hammond was convicted and sentenced to three years in prison. He appealed to the state Court of Criminal Appeals and, when he lost there, to the state supreme court. He lost in the high court by a vote of four to two. The Court of Criminal Appeals concluded, "We have been presented with a hodgepodge of facts and are told that upon one theory or another, they substantially prove every material allegation of the indictment. It has been necessary to fit facts together like connecting pieces of a complex jigsaw puzzle." Nevertheless, the court found the evidence "to be sufficient to meet the bare minimum standards to support the verdict of the jury."[84]

In a dissent to the Alabama Supreme Court ruling, a justice stated that, in a criminal case, there must be substantial evidence to prove all the elements of the charge. "The presumption of innocence, shielding every prisoner at bar, is not overcome by a mere scintilla of evidence."[85] It was a dangerous departure from the substantial evidence rule, the justice said, and violated Hammond's constitutional rights. "Here, there was no evidence at all that Hammond was offered, promised, or given any gift, gratuity or thing of value to influence his vote on a pending rate case."[86]

Kenneth Hammond spent time in prison, and like Richmond, his political career was ruined. He notes that, "The people they set me up with were some of the same ones the federal government used to get Richmond Flowers."

Albert Brewer Meets the Destructive Force. Albert Brewer was one of the bright young men who entered the legislature in January 1955. It was an idealistic, progressive group intending to do great things for the state. Brewer was from Decatur, in the Tennessee Valley, and he had impressed people from the time he graduated from law school at the University of Alabama. Believed headed for great things, he supported George Wallace for governor in 1958 and 1962. In 1958, Brewer recalls, Wallace seemed like one of the young progressive group. By 1962, there was some concern. Brewer says, "A lot of us had reservations about comments from him, like some he made about Judge Johnson, but we thought it was just political rhetoric."[87]

Albert Brewer was speaker of the Alabama House of Representatives during Wallace's first term as governor. He was elected lieutenant governor in 1966, and when Lurleen Wallace died, he became governor. He was popular, and he thought he was in line to be elected to a full term in 1970. "Lurleen and I had been pretty close," he says, "and I worked well with her when she was governor. After she died, George indicated to me and to others that he was not going to run for governor again."[88]

By 1970, however, George had changed his mind. He ran and lost to Brewer by almost 6,000 votes in the first primary. As he faced the runoff election, he was desperate, and as Carlson notes, he abandoned any pretense at gentlemanly tactics. "Doctored photographs appeared showing Governor Brewer with prize fighter Muhammed Ali and Black Muslim chief Elijah Muhammed."[89] Wallace gained the endorsement of Klan leader Robert Shelton, and somehow 30,000 new voters registered in areas of Wallace strength before the runoff. Just before the runoff election, people were surprised to find unexpected bumper stickers on their cars which said, "I'm for Brewer and the Blacks."[90]

Brewer believes that Wallace underestimated him. "When it became apparent that things were not going like they wanted them to," he says, "they got desperate. Taylor Hardin was quoted as saying that, after the first primary when I got the most votes, they decided that their strategy would be 'Promise the moon and yell nigger.' Wallace had started some of the race thing in the primary, but he always used his code words. Wallace would say things like, 'If you elect Brewer, the niggers are going to run the state for the next fifty years.' He scared people.

"They would do anything. I know people who have paid a terrible price for getting involved with Wallace. You hear stories of people who get so powerful that they have no regard for human life or human dignity, and I can see how that would happen. Some people in national politics are reputed to be power mad. I guess that the lust for power overcomes whatever moral principles they have.

"The hate was tangible in 1970," Brewer remembers. "You could cut it with a knife. I never have understood how an individual could capture the emotions of people, and make them do things and say things like Wallace could. He was really a master at defining people's fears. His ambition overcame whatever scruples he had.

"These people were vicious, and they were hurtful. They would try to absolutely take away a person's livelihood, to reduce him to just nothing if they could. It was not enough to destroy him politically; they wanted to destroy him personally, and his family. Nastiness is one thing, but they would try to absolutely destroy a person. They hated Richmond enough to want to destroy him.

"This presidential thing got to George, I think. The idea of going to Harvard and Princeton and being on national television and meeting the press, that's pretty heady stuff. And when you're governor, everybody comes in and says how great you are, because they all want something.

"George Wallace did great harm to this state. He squelched a generation of progressive political figures and made it difficult to this day to find effective political leaders. Most of us don't have the benefit of knowing our role in history during our lifetime. Wallace is in a unique position in that he has lived to see the judgment of history on him, and it is negative."[91]

Was Justice Done? Was justice done to Richmond Flowers? Every person interviewed in this project agreed that the conspiracy theory is plausible and believable, and all agree that there were problems in finding an unbiased jury.

The available evidence suggests that Richmond did not receive any funds personally. He let certain people exert a great deal of influence in handling the affairs of the securities commission, and as the appellate court said, he should have paid more attention to it. Without question, he was negligent in this regard. But this is a judgement after the fact. As attorney general, he was extremely busy with other matters such as desegregation suits, Freedom Rides, demonstrations in Birmingham, the Selma-Montgomery march, and the Hayneville trials. Shortly after his trial, the state legislature recognized the difficulty of doing both the attorney general and securities commissioner jobs and split the two into separate offices.

His involvement with the Alabama General Insurance Company was a bad judgment. He and Jim Kelly were left holding the bag on that one, and Oscar Hyde bailed them out. Whether or not they later transferred property worth $50,000 to Oscar, this situation looked bad at Richmond's trial. After all, even the best of friends are not likely to make gifts of $50,000 to each other.

In the final analysis, it's as former governor Albert Brewer says. After twenty-five years, it is all conjecture and supposition unless someone comes forward unexpectedly with new information—and most of those who could are dead.[92] Readers must make their own judgment.

Prison

Richmond reported to the federal court in Birmingham to begin serving his sentence in April of 1972. He and Oscar Hyde had been assigned to the federal correctional institution in Texarkana, Texas.

"I had to report in to Birmingham on a Monday," he recalls. "My son was in Dothan that weekend. He took me back with him to Atlanta and put me on a plane for Birmingham. Oscar picked me up. He was staying in a hotel because we were going to leave early in the morning. We reported over at the federal courthouse.

"When we were being prepared for the trip, I was wrapped in chains and so was Oscar. This is the way they transport federal prisoners. They put chains on me, and then they put handcuffs through the chains and handcuffed me. They put us in the back of an automobile, and we went from Birmingham down to Meridian across to Jackson to Shreveport and up to Texarkana. They were riding 85 to 90 miles an hour. Its about 480 miles, and we got there in one day."

Did he think his life had come to an end? "No," he says. "I just wondered why. Why do they have to treat us this way? If they had opened the door and pushed me, I wouldn't have run. Where could I go? I had a wife and family. I can't run. I've got to put this thing behind me. Later I heard that they actually did me a favor. I was supposed to be in leg irons, too, but they didn't put them on me until I was almost in Texarkana.

"They gave me plenty of time to escape if I was going to. It's wonderful to be able to laugh about it now. Going out there, Oscar said, 'Big Red, would you believe that I was in the Republic of Panama ten days ago, and I came back to this? Ten days ago, I was in the Republic of Panama way up on top of a big high cliff having lunch at a big beautiful home and enjoying the breeze, and I left all that to come back to this?'"

Coming to Terms. Mary Flowers remembers the family's pain in having to come to terms with the fact of prison. "When Richmond had to go to Texarkana," she says, "we were living in Dothan. Richmond, Jr., didn't want me to put him on the plane, so he came over. He and his daddy played golf all day on Sunday. Then he took Richmond back to Atlanta.

"When he got on the plane in Atlanta, Richmond had to give up everything he had. He couldn't take any money or have a billfold. He started to reach into his pocket for something, and he realized here is this person who's been able to carry credit cards and identification, and he had no identification. Well, this is the one thing that absolutely threw Richmond, Jr. It was okay to put him on the plane and to say good-bye to him, but when he realized about the billfold, he called me up and said 'Mother, he has no identity.' After Richmond, Jr., put him on the plane, he broke down and cried. He was pitiful.

"The next week, he called me and said, 'Now Mother, Daddy's in Texarkana. When are you going out?' I said , 'Oh, I'm not going. He'll be home in two or three weeks, and . . .' He said, 'Mother, he's not coming home in two or three weeks. You've got to go out there.' I said, 'Oh Richmond, I can't. I simply cannot go and see him in those flannels. I just can't do it!' He said, 'Mother, you have to do it.' So I said, 'Well, what must I do?' He said, 'You come to Dallas. I've got a car, and you can drive to Texarkana to see Daddy. Then come back and spend the night and fly on back home.' Well, it was a horrible experience. I did it, and from then on, I went every single month as long as he was there. It was a thirteen-hour drive."

A lot of people were milling about when he first arrived, Richmond recalls. "We went into the receiving area, and men were all out in the halls because it was the time they were not locked in their individual cells. These men are standing all around to hear them call your name, and you have all these chains on. They knew I was coming in. I don't know how it possibly comes about, but in the prison population there is the darnedest grapevine you ever saw. They not only know who's coming in, but they know what his background is.

"If a new inmate has done anything that will put him in bad with any of the others, they have to watch him very closely and segregate him for awhile until they can get it settled, or they have to ship him out. That was why the superintendent refused me at Atlanta. He said, 'That man wouldn't last the first night here. There would be no way we could protect him. He'd have to sleep with us, and they might kill us all.'

Frightened All of the Time. Richmond was afraid the whole time he was in Texarkana. "I got all sorts of blind threats," he remembers. "That's a tough bunch out there. That is a penitentiary. They call it a federal correctional institute, but it's a penitentiary. They bring you in chains, and they lock big iron doors behind you, and you go through sections to get in and out. I was afraid because they had some mean people out there.

"A former policeman gave me the name of a man and told me to stay away from him, that he was boasting he would kill me. I asked, 'What for?' And he said, 'I have no idea.' This was when I first got there and was doing temporary jobs. I was working in the laundry, and they'd come in and ask for their clothes.

"This fellow came in, and I said to him, 'I understand you've been threatening to kill me.' He says, 'I am, buddy.' I said, 'Would you mind telling me why?' He says, 'My name's so-and-so.' I said, 'So?' 'You mean that name don't mean nothing to you?' I said, 'Not a thing in the world my friend, why should it?' 'You sent my brother to the penitentiary for robbing a bank and I'm gonna kill you for it. If he was here, he'd do it.'

"I said, 'Ask him when did I do that? The whole time I was in office I never tried any bank-robbing case, because the attorney general's office doesn't try those cases. When was it?' He said something like January of 1968. I said, 'Fellow, I went out of office in 1967. And anyway, where was it?' 'In Birmingham.' I said, 'The U.S. District Attorney is the one who tried your brother.' He said, 'Well, ain't that what you are?' I said, 'Man, no, I was the state attorney general. I didn't try criminal cases.' 'You didn't try my brother?' 'Of course not, I wasn't even in office when your brother got tried.' He said, 'Well, by God it's a good thing you told me 'cause I was going to make short work of you.'

"Someone set my bed afire one night. I knew exactly who it was. He just hated me and despised and resented me because of my reputation. It wasn't because I bothered anybody. I just minded my own business.

"One man tried to get me before he was transferred out. He was a member of a motorcycle gang that chained a woman to a tree and beat her, and the only reason he wasn't in one of the big prisons was she didn't die. He was being transferred from Texarkana to this maximum security hospital up in Missouri. He promised somebody just before he left that he was going to get me. They stopped him going into the dining room about 3:00 or 3:30 coming after me, and they had to restrain him. They put him in cuffs and shipped him out of there. That's why I stayed scared.

"After I started working in the kitchen, it was obvious that one guard wanted me. He could be talking to the food service administrator, and if I walked by, you could see his attitude change. I had to post the personnel roster for the cooks and bakers because they were on rotation. Some of them would get up early one week, and the others would get up the next. You post the roster so the guards will wake them up and have them down there. I got them reversed one morning, and they woke up the second shift instead of the first and told them to go to work. It sorta messed things up.

"That guard told me, 'If you do that again, you're going in the hole.' 'The hole' is their expression for solitary confinement. I was looking for parole, and if you got solitary confinement, you were not even going to be considered for a parole. So I went to the food service administrator and told him I'd do anything else. How about getting somebody else to do the list. He says, 'Why?' And I told him what had happened. I said, 'I'm just as sorry as I can be. The guys didn't get mad. After they got waked up, they got tickled about it and said, 'Damn you Flowers,' and they laughed at it.'

"I said, 'You know I'm trying to keep my record lily white and produce so that men like you will be able to say, 'This fellow is top-notch.' He said, 'Did he say that to you?' I said, 'He sure did.' He said, 'I'm going to see the captain.' Now that's captain of security.

"In about twenty minutes he came back and he said, 'You go ahead and make out the list. If you make another mistake, tell them you're sorry and it'll be all right.' I said, 'Are you sure?' He said, 'I went to the captain and told him I don't want that guard fooling with my men. I run that kitchen. I don't care if he is security.' The captain said, 'Why don't you go tell him?' I said, 'You mean you don't mind if I go curse him out?' He said, 'I hope you will.' 'Boy, I just polished him off.' I never did have any more trouble with him."

Just Doing a Job. "When I first got there, they asked me to take a typing test," Richmond says. "I said, 'How do you know I can type?' They said, 'Come on, we know you can type. You're taking a typing test.' I went to it with mixed emotions. But then I thought, 'Well, at least they're not going to set me out in the hot sun to type, so I'll go ahead.' I did pretty well on the test, and they assigned me to the kitchen.

"Everybody said, 'Boy, they're pouring it on him, aren't they? They made a KP out of him.' Well, it wasn't that at all. I went over to the kitchen expecting to be a KP, but the food service administrator wanted me to become what they called the poundage clerk. Every thing they eat in those institutions, they turn into poundage. It's just simple arithmetic once you learn the formula. That's the way they watch their expenses and watch their diet.

"It turned out to be the best job in the whole place, in my estimation. I worked in an air conditioned office, and I worked at my own pace. It was easy and low key. Kitchen personnel wore white clothing, and that was something because most of the inmates wore khaki. They started serving breakfast at seven o'clock. The cooks and bakers and the people who were going to serve had to be there early. So I'd just get on up and go in with them. I ate before they ever started serving breakfast.

"The head of the kitchen was an old chief petty officer, retired. He was a tough little cookie, and he was there all day long. He had been running these big navy messes, and he knew what he was doing. He'd comb his workers and comb them until he got him a good crew. He kept people he could tell what to do and they'd do it. You give him one of these fellows you have to keep telling, and he'd send him somewhere else. I did my best to make the old chief's job easy. He liked me. But how often are you going to get help that good in a place like Texarkana? So I just got along beautifully.

"I was hustling, but I was hustling for myself. There's no doubt about it. I knew I had something on the ball that not every guy down there had, so I was just using it to my advantage. I think it was smart. At least, after they put me off one year, I came out on parole a year later."

Eglin. After nine months in Texarkana, Richmond was informed that he would be transferred to the minimum security institution at Eglin Field, Florida. This was a change greatly desired, and he was anxious to make it. Just before he was to leave, he had an experience which threatened to upset his plans. "We went over to the freeze compartment in town where we kept butter," he says. "They had this regular army butter in frozen sixty-pound blocks. One of those things slipped out of my hand. Somebody asked me, 'Richmond, didn't that thing hit your foot?' I said, 'It's so durn cold, I don't know. When I get outside and begin to warm up, I can tell you.' I said that in jest, but the truth was I had knocked my toenail clean off, as they say in the cartoons. It wasn't any time after I got on the truck that my foot started pounding, and I realized my shoe was about half full of blood.

"I didn't know what to do. I thought, 'I can't work with this busted foot. They'll take me off of the list to go to Eglin.' I had some bedroom slippers, and I wore one of them. We were going to Eglin the next morning. We went in to eat before anybody else, so it was good and dark. I sat down and got my foot up under the table, and then I got on the bus. I couldn't possibly have put a shoe on. I left Texarkana with one shoe and one bedroom slipper. I figured I'd just have to worry about shoes when I got to Eglin.

"About the second day down there one of the guards said, 'Flowers, what are you doing with that? Go get your shoe on.' I said, 'Sir, I don't have one.' 'What in the hell do you mean, you don't have one?' I said, 'I don't. I don't have one because I wanted to come so badly, I was afraid they might not let me come. I figured they wouldn't send me back once I was down here.' I took the slipper off and showed him my foot. He said, 'Good lord a mercy. Go over to the sick bay and let them dress that thing. Gosh a mighty!' It was infected and big. They cleaned it up good with alcohol and peroxide. I wore that ole bedroom slipper around there until I about wore it out.

"One of the men I used to know at Texarkana, a former governor of Maryland, was in the supply, and he told me, 'I'm going to have to chisel you a pair of shoes.' I said, 'Don't get them for a little while, I can't wear them.' So he got me a new slipper. Finally, after my toe got sound enough I went over there, and he got me a brand new pair of shoes. The attorney general and the governor, we were big buddies.

"Once I got to Eglin, they didn't want me to work out on the base. They were afraid folks might want to talk to me. I didn't want to work at the base, and I didn't want anybody to talk to me. At first, I was working the grounds, and I was manicuring it like it had never been manicured. You could go over to the shop and draw any kind of tool you wanted. And boy, I trimmed those walks and put graveling around the trees, and I had it looking pretty. After a short time, I was transferred to the kitchen and was a poundage clerk again.

"It was really a pretty area. We lived in barracks-type dormitories, and they had a big beautiful mess hall. The food was excellent! We ate Air Force food, and they eat good. In fact, we drew most of our supplies from the Air Force. That place is wide open. There were no fences down there at all. You could walk off any time you wanted to. But you'd be so foolish. Walk off, and you go back to Texarkana and finish every bit of your time.

"I was never scared at Eglin. When you get to an honor camp, you're supposedly on the way out. You're really keeping your nose clean then. That place was full of moonshiners and folks that had been locked up for drugs. The drug guys were loud and boisterous, and they'd make you feel uncomfortable. You wonder why they had to be all that loud, but you never were frightened.

"I really had a good schedule there. I worked incessantly because time was so heavy on your hands. We had a huge warehouse of food all jumbled up, and every time you'd go to get something, you had to look everywhere to see if you had it. I started back in one corner of the warehouse, and I stacked and I moved. We had some old stainless steel racks that the Air Force gave us. So I put them up and put the smaller cases on them.

"One of the first jobs I had in the kitchen was to inventory that warehouse. Another man and I inventoried it, and it took two days. Before I left, I had a sheet made up where you could put counts in, and I inventoried the entire warehouse by myself in twenty minutes. In fact, when the commissioner of Bureau of Prisons out of Washington visited us one time, they showed him that warehouse. He said, 'Who did that?' and they answered, 'We could line them all up and you'd never guess.' I didn't know they were talking about me. They said, 'That's him right over there.' 'Hell, that's that Flowers, isn't it?' 'Yes, he has worked liked a beaver on this thing.'

"I'd get up in the morning, finish breakfast, go back there and work in the warehouse, and somebody would say, 'You better go change your clothes. We're getting ready for lunch.' At lunch I had to serve the officer's table, and I mean I was a waiter par excellence! Afterwards I would do my poundage work. By that time, I could do it in a couple of hours. Then they'd open the dining room, and I was through. So I'd go do my exercising until time for count, as they called it, and I'd be tired and worn out. I'd work crossword puzzles or something, and about 9:30 or 10:00, I'd just die. I'd get up and go over there every morning at 6:00.

"I never ate much at night, because I was watching my diet pretty close. I had a 32-inch waist when I left. I got in excellent shape. The grounds were surrounded by a big road in a horseshoe shape, and that's where we did our walking. Up on one end of it was a little weight room. So I'd walk a bunch of laps, then I'd go in the weight room for a little while. I really was in good shape for a fellow my age when I got out of there."

Family. Richmond feels that his term in prison was much harder on his family than it was on him. "They were the ones that suffered," he feels. "I didn't suffer, except for my loneliness. I was fighting bitterness and humiliation, but I got my head up. I knew it was a full-time job. I had to go in with my head up, and I did.

"I figured that if I allowed myself to become bitter, I would destroy myself totally and completely. Your bitterness will eat you up. So I would just not allow myself to be bitter. I knew all the sculduggery that went on behind me, all of these so-called friends that turned their backs on me and went out of their way to stick me. If you keep mulling that stuff, you're going to be a bitter, bitter old person. I said to myself ten million times, 'Get your shoulders back, get your head up and get a smile on your face, and you're going to make it. When you come out of here, nobody will ever know the difference. Those that do let it make a difference, you don't need them anyhow.'

"After I left, my wife went to work in Flowers Hospital. Paul promoted her to almost what my salary would have been, so it enabled her to live a little better. Jeff graduated from Dothan High School the next year and went to the University of Tennessee. Mary and our daughter Mary lived with my mother. That worked out beautifully because it was close to the hospital. My mother had quit driving by then and didn't leave the house, so there was somebody in the house with her."

"The first time Richmond, Jr., came to see me in Texarkana, Mary was there. He was playing with the New York Giants. He said, 'You really need to be out this time.' I said, 'For what? The Giants had been having a pitiful season.' He said, 'We're going to knock Dallas off.' I said, 'Well, you're about a 13-18 point underdog.' He said, 'We're going to beat them straight up. When the team heard I was coming by to see you, they said tell him we'll take Dallas for him.' And, by God, they beat them. That was about the only game the Giants won all year."

"It got easier on all of us when I moved to Eglin. Mary came down there every Sunday I was there. She and little Mary would leave Dothan early, and they'd always get back by 10:00 Sunday night. She'd get to Eglin about 9:30, and she'd leave there about 3:30 or 4:00. Mary would go to work the next morning. She always came down there with a smile on her face, and her attitude was as good as mine. She never complained about having a hard time. I've got a strong woman.

"When she came to Eglin she got some of the cooks at the hospital to pack a big picnic lunch. I knew all of them well, and they knew me. Mary said the only trouble she ever had was them deciding who was going to fix my picnic each week. You can imagine how big it was. So the three of us would have a big picnic lunch. In the nine months I was down there, we only had rain one time.

"Mary, the youngest child is really a chip off the old block as far as her mother is concerned. She laughs about it today. She'll say 'so-and-so happened, Daddy, when you were on vacation.' I don't believe her mother could have done it without her. And I don't think she could have done it without her mother. She was at Dothan High School, and she got some kickback from my position.

"So I'd say that my family suffered much more than I did. I'd lost my freedom, but otherwise I got along well. Any penitentiary in the world that you throw me in, I'm above the average intelligence of the people who are in there. There may be some in there smarter than I am, but the run of the mill, I can figure my way around. I can get along, and I did. I didn't have any visitors but family. I didn't want any."

Return to the Real World. Richmond was paroled in the fall of 1974, and he returned to Dothan. He had served eighteen months of his eight-year sentence. "I had what they call an A-2 sentence," he explains, "and that made me eligible for parole the day I went in. A month after I got to Texarkana I went up for parole and was put off a year. A year later I went back before the board and was paroled.

"As things turned out, the prison term may have saved my life. I was in when George Wallace was shot. There's no doubt in my mind that if they'd kill George Wallace, they'd kill me. I was dealing with underhanded, low scheming, sorry people in the Ku Klux Klan. The only reason they didn't kill me earlier was because they didn't have the nerve. They had already killed one attorney general in this state [Albert Patterson], and they felt like the people might not stand for another one. But if I'd been out and running for office, they'd have killed me just as sure as I'm a foot high. During the trial and appellate period, Bobby Kennedy and Martin Luther King and George Wallace were all shot.

"I am a religious person, though I don't run around giving testimony and all that. In thinking about it, I've become convinced that the Lord talked to me that first night in Texarkana. I was lying there saying, 'Why me, Lord? Lord, why me of all people? I tried to help the downtrodden. This happened to me because I did your business?' All of a sudden my attitude got belligerent toward myself. 'Quit. You're not a crybaby. Quit that crying.' I was thinking about the judge. I was thinking about Julian. I was thinking about all the people, and all of a sudden I said, 'Get that out of your mind! Get your head up. Get your shoulders back. You can do this thing and go back home and be happy the rest of your life.' I didn't have to hear a voice. That notion boomed in my head, and it kept booming in my head. The Lord told me, 'You're a bigger man than that.' And I said, 'That's right, Lord. I am!'

"I've had people try to hurt my feelings, and I always turn it away with a soft word. I have never had cross words with anybody about it. I don't know why it happened, but it happened and it's behind me. I don't believe any friend or associate has changed his attitude toward me because of it. Since I've been home, I can't recall a single incident where anybody shorted me or got up and left or dropped out of a conversation or had anything ugly to say.

"I'm like the old man in church. The preacher was preaching against hate. 'Can't have no hate in your heart. Can't dislike nobody. Bet 'ya there ain't nobody in here that ain't got enemies.' One old hand stuck up. 'Uncle Ben, how old are you?' 'I'm ninety-six, preacher.' 'You hadn't got an enemy?' 'Not one in the world.' 'Well, glory be. Stand up. Tell this congregation the secret of your success. Ninety-six years old and no enemies.' He says, 'Weren't nothin' to it preacher. I just outlived the sons-of-bitches.' So I've outlived all of mine.

"Anybody who was involved in my case, I'm better off today than they are. The judge is dead. The U.S. attorney was not very well regarded to begin with, and he's got a job as a magistrate which is just a reward, a pat on the head for a fellow that hung around a long time. You go right down the line to any one of them who testified against me. Rufus Lackey is dead. His son is dead. I'm better off than every one of them. So the Lord doth move in mysterious ways."

9

After the Storm

Building a New Life

When Richmond returned to Dothan after being released from the federal correctional institution at Eglin Field, he was naturally apprehensive about how he would be treated. He was also concerned about his financial status and the necessity of building a new life. He was fifty-three years old, an age when starting over is not easy.

He discovered right away that his worst fears about acceptance might be unfounded. "The first morning I was back," he recalls, "I went to the hospital, back to my old haunts where I had been working before I left. You'd have thought I was home from the army. Everybody just welcomed me, and hugged me and kissed me and shook my hand, and that made me feel great.

"I went right to work in my old job. Paul shifted things back to where they had been for me salary-wise, and he gave Mary a complimentary raise for what she had learned to do. We both had good jobs, and we got along all right. I went back to purchasing, and I ran supplies. I also ran the laundry and took charge of housekeeping. I built a snack bar, and I kept it cleaned, stocked, and supplied. I worked like a wage hand because I still had that old drive to work, work, work. Then it gradually came to me that I didn't have to break my neck. So I began to play a little golf."

His experience in the larger community was also positive. "My acceptance back in Dothan was really surprising to me," he says. "I wasn't sure what to expect, but I was anxious, you know, after all that had happened. To me, it has been remarkable. I've been asked to serve in many capacities. I've served on the administrative board of my church. I'm on the board of trustees now. I teach a men's Bible class. People in the community couldn't have been nicer. The family also helped a lot. The Flowers clan is a big one, and they're close."

Many people in Richmond's circumstances would have moved where they were not known to begin building their new life, but Richmond never gave it a serious thought. "I never considered going anywhere else," he says. "To me, Dothan was such a grand place. It wasn't what I was going to do somewhere else, it was what I was going to do in Dothan. I had some good offers, but I never considered going anywhere else."

Acceptance among family and friends in Dothan made building a new life easier and more pleasant. It did not solve the problem of finances, however, and this was serious. Richmond says that the court battle and prison sentence broke him financially. "This was one thing about it that really hurt," he recalls. "In fact, it more than broke me. If hadn't been for my brother Paul, who picked up big pieces of the expenses, I couldn't have done it. It took every dime I had."

The House. At first, Richmond did not feel like socializing. He needed time to settle in, get his thoughts straightened out, and find out how people would treat him. He did not want to brood about it, and he and Mary came up with a project that kept them occupied for several months.

"Mary and I moved into my mother's house after I returned," he recalls. "My mother had died in 1970, and my brothers didn't do anything about the house because they knew I might need it. They all had homes, and they knew I was going to have to borrow money. My oldest brother asked me, 'Richmond, do you want the house? If you do, we'll sell it to you at whatever you can afford to pay for it. Otherwise, we're going to sell it.' I got an appraisal on it, and when it came in, they cut the price almost in half. I thought, 'It will give us a place to live. It's worth more than that, and I think it's a piece of property that will sell.' So I bought the house at a very good price.

"It was downtown in an old section, and it got to looking almost spooky because there were just two of us living there. Most of the time, we stayed over on the heavy wooded side, and people wouldn't see any lights at night. It looked like a big old dark empty house, but we were there in the back.

"Mary and I completely redid the interior. The paper looked bad in some of the house, and we re-papered every room including the stairwell. In her late years, my mother's eyesight failed to an extent. She got around all right, but she didn't see dirt or dinginess. Her little path was from her chair by the television through her bedroom to the breakfast room. She'd sit down and eat her meals, and then go back in there with the TV. Upstairs it had gotten awful.

"Every afternoon we would get home from work about 4:30 or 5:00. We'd immediately put on our fatigue clothes and go to papering. I learned how to match those patterns perfectly all the way up and down and to smooth it out. We took one room at a time. Mary would first paint all the woodwork. She didn't have to be so particular because we knew we were going to paper. She could just paint all over the wall, and then we'd go in and paper over it. We painted and papered every room in that house. We were slow, but what the heck? We'd rush home every afternoon, looking forward to it, and we really had a good time. We'd work until about seven, and then we would clean up. Mary always loved the tub and I loved the shower, and both of those were in bathrooms downstairs. So, we bathed at the same time, got our robes on, and we'd have us a drink and eat something. By that time we'd shot the evening. There were trials and tribulations with it. Sometimes a glop of that stuff would fall right in your face. But it was fun, and we had a lot of laughs.

"When we finished, that house was as pretty on the inside as anything in this town. We kept the premises well, but it was grown up. It was in an old section of town, and it just wasn't attractive to look at from the outside. We spent some money to turn the big back porch into a comfortable den that opened into the kitchen. We had one of these tremendous counters that was half in the den and half in the kitchen. We stayed back there most of the time.

"We had all of mother's antique furniture, and it was plush. It was really a beautiful home, but it just got off the beaten path. It got to be sort of a rough section of town, and I didn't feel good about being down there. There were a lot of drunks roaming up and down the street at night. Every time we'd clean the shrubbery beds in the front, there would be whiskey bottles thrown up under there. Some of them were half full, and you don't know whether they hid them there or what.

"We lived there until 1983, when we built our current house. We love where we are now, but I'll tell you that old house was great for us."

Teaching at Wallace College. Richmond and Mary were getting along, but he soon realized they needed more income. "I had a decent salary at the hospital," he recalls, "but I started out broke and couldn't save a lot. I knew Phillip Hamm, the president at Wallace Community College just outside of Dothan, and after I had been back about two years, I decided to go out there and see him."

I went out there and told him, 'Phil, I need a favor, and I need it bad.' 'Well, you know, Senator, you can get it if I can help you.' I said, 'I think you can. How about letting me teach out here part time at night?' He said, 'You really want to?' I said, 'Phil, I've got to. I've got to supplement my income.' 'Well, if that's a fact, we'll set it up.' He gave me a job teaching one course from eight to ten o'clock on Tuesday and Thursday nights for $300 a month. I was glad to get it.

"Things picked up right away. A man teaching courses in psychology and sociology quit on very short notice because he got a better position. They had almost completed registration when this happened. I went to the dean and said, 'I couldn't help but overhear you say you've already got both those classes filled. How about letting me teach them? They're introductory courses, and a man who has graduated from law school and been through the practice of law and three statewide campaigns, he knows some psychology and sociology. All he's got to do is look at an introductory book and put it in the words they want.' He laughed and said, 'I don't know whether he can or not, but we're in a jam. You can do it.' That gave me three classes.

"I heard them close out a class of public speaking that met at night, and there were five or six folks standing there begging to get in. They were told the instructor said there were already too many. I asked, 'Is it Monday and Wednesday from six to eight?' This was the time I had left. They said it was, and I asked, 'Why don't you split it and let me take one section? You don't have to ask can I teach public speaking. I can make a speech better than anybody in this college, and besides, that was my major at Auburn.'

"So I ended up teaching twenty hours on a temporary part-time basis and making $800 a month. I kept teaching like that, and then it occurred to me I wasn't making enough. Even my son told me, 'Daddy, you're working for peon's wages teaching. You're supposed to make more than that.' So I went the next day and told them that I would like to be on full time if there was any opportunity. Later they advertised for someone to teach public speaking and history, and I applied for it. That was my major and minor, and I got the job.

"After I had been teaching three years full-time, I tenured. I didn't quit the hospital. I had my classes split between night and day, and I was still teaching two classes at night. I could make my day classes and still get back to the hospital. I kept working for the hospital full-time. I didn't retire from the hospital until I was seventy."

Richmond started at Wallace College in the fall of 1979 and retired in 1992. Someone has pointed out the irony of Richmond securing his financial status by teaching at George C. Wallace State Community College. It would be an interesting touch, but the fact is that the community college in Dothan was named for Wallace's father, who had been a county judge. George himself introduced the legislation in 1949 when he was a member of the legislature.

Reinstatement and Pardon. In addition to the trauma of being convicted of a felony and serving a term in federal prison, Richmond had suffered the humiliation of being disbarred in Alabama from the practice of law. Not long after his return to Dothan, he set about to reverse the damage caused by these events.

First, he applied for reinstatement to the state bar. He went before the local bar association in Dothan and was unanimously recommended for reinstatement. "I got Guy Hardwick, a former lieutenant governor, and Alto Lee, who was the immediate past president of the Alabama Bar Association, to sponsor me for reinstatement at state level," he recalls. "You went before the grievance committee of the Board of Bar Commissioners, and they assigned it to a subcommittee. The subcommittee which heard my case turned me down without giving any reason.

"Guy said, 'We'll wait until next year and apply again.' But Alto disagreed. 'No,' he said. 'I'm going to appeal it straight to the Board of Bar Commissioners and fight them head on.' Guy said, 'Well, if you're willing, I'm willing.' Every circuit has a member on that board, so it's a big organization. Guy and Alto would call these fellows and say, 'Don't just turn it down. Wait to hear what we've got to say about it.' Guy and I had a lot of friends on the board, and Alto had more than both of us because he had been so active. Guy also called some of his old legislative friends.

"I went up to the hearing with Guy and Alto and the president of the local bar association. I was going to take my local preacher, but he had exams for his doctorate at Emory that day. So Wilbur Walton, a former minister who was retired, went up and made a beautiful speech. He said, 'I've pastored him in Dothan, and I've pastored him in Montgomery.' He had come to the Montgomery church while I was there, and he was fully respected in both towns. They voted and I passed by three votes.

"One reason I wanted reinstatement was I knew it would help when I made application for pardon. I wanted to say on my application that I was accepted unanimously by my local bar association, and I was readmitted to the practice of law by the state bar association, represented at their hearing by the former lieutenant governor and the former bar association president.

"Applications for a pardon are filed with the pardon attorney of the Justice Department. He reviews it and sends it to the White House with a recommendation. It goes to the White House even if he recommends turning it down. So I wanted all that information in there.

"By that time Howell Heflin had been elected to the Senate. Howell and I were in law school together and were friends. He had been very strong in the leadership of the state Democratic party before his election to the state supreme court. I wanted to arm Howell with enough that he could say, 'Look. This man ought to be pardoned.' Nothing happened for a long time after the application was in. I finally got Howell to check, and he said, 'It went to the White House. Those things are closed, so I don't know what the recommendation is. But now I can go make my appeal.'

"I had some other help, too. Emory Solomon, who is big in the peanut business here, has been a friend since college days. Before Jimmy Carter was even in the Georgia legislature, Emory did business with him. Emory told me, 'I don't want to mess in this thing if you don't want me to, but let me tell you my possibility. I know Billy Carter on as cordial a basis as I know you. We've had a couple of conversations about you, and

Billy said, 'Wasn't that sort of a railroad?' I told him it was the worst you ever saw. I can ask Billy to put in a word with the president.' I said to Emory, 'I would appreciate anything you can do.'

"He called me back the next day and said, 'You finally got a break. I called over there for Billy. He was out of town, and his wife came on the phone. She was scheduled to talk with Rosalyn that very evening. 'I'll tell Rosalyn', she said, 'and nothing can keep her from telling Jimmy. She called me back the next day and said, 'Rosalyn said it will be called to his attention in the morning.'"

"Five days later I got a letter from Howell Heflin saying my pardon had been granted and would arrive in a few days. So I finally got a pardon, signed by Jimmy Carter. It doesn't expunge the record; it excuses it. I have strict instructions. If I am asked, 'Have you ever been convicted of a felony?' I must answer yes. I also have the authority to say, 'But I have presidential pardon.' The record shows that you were convicted, but it also shows that you have Executive Clemency. As far as I'm concerned, that wiped the slate clean.

"After I got reinstated to the bar association, I took the position of general counsel at the hospital and started practicing law. I still had the school job, of course."

The TV Movie *Unconquered*. One of the more interesting things which happened to Richmond and his family in recent years was the TV movie *Unconquered*. This was about Richmond's troubles as attorney general and about Richmond, Jr's., triumph over adversity to become an All-American football player at the University of Tennessee and a world record holder in high hurdles. *Unconquered* was shown nationally on CBS in prime time in the fall of 1979 and was repeated two years later.

Talk about a possible movie started when Martin Chipwood, an Atlanta attorney, called the Flowers residence in Dothan two years earlier and wanted to know where Richmond, Jr., was. "He said that he had been interested in making movies," Richmond remembers, "and that he and a friend had discussed the possibility of one about Richmond, Jr. He asked, 'Do you mind if I run down when he's there, and let's talk a little just see what the possibilities are?' I said, 'Absolutely not.' He came down and asked Richmond, Jr., if he would be interested in having it done. Richmond told him, 'I'm interested if there's any money in it. I don't care about doing it for free. I've had all the free accolades I need.'

Chipwood was talking at that time about making a regular movie.

"Chipwood hustled it the whole time from that. He got a contract for a screenplay with Pat Conroy, who had written *The Great Santini*. Pat Conroy told him, 'You've got a great athletic story. But you've also got another story that you can't separate because this boy's father was such an inspiration to him. Every time you ask him any questions, he attributes his success to his father's staying with him, training with him, and working with him. His mother helped him, too, and that's a great story.'

"It just worked along from that. It dragged on for a couple of years, but every now and then, they'd get a little step closer. Then they said, 'We can't raise the money to make a regular movie, because it takes three and a-half to five million dollars. We can't raise that, but we can make a television movie. CBS is interested in making the movie, and they will honor the contract for the money that you and your boy are to make.' So we said, 'Why not?' We negotiated some with Conroy and his people about the script, and then they filmed the movie in Atlanta. The filming took a little more than thirty days.

The movie predictably raised some hackles. George Wallace was in his fourth term as governor, and many of his supporters took umbrage at having the former attorney general presented as a hero. Also, Wallace was not portrayed in a very flattering way. The flap was minor, however, and died away quickly. At the least, the movie acquainted a new generation with some of the things that happened in the 1960s.

The Family and The Kids. Richmond and Mary live in a comfortable home in Dothan, and they see their children and their eight grandchildren often. Richmond, Jr., the oldest, lives in Birmingham, Alabama; Jeff lives in Washington, D.C.; and Mary, the youngest, lives in Knoxville, Tennessee.

Richmond, Jr., had a fabulous career in both football and track at the University of Tennessee. Then he went to the Dallas Cowboys to play professional football. He was there a little over two years and was traded to the New York Giants. He played in the NFL five years. Then he decided it was time to get out of football, and he got a law degree from the University of Alabama.

Richmond, Jr., practiced law for a time and then went into commodities. At present, he lives in Birmingham, Alabama. He is a division manager for Nu-Skin, a multi-marketing company, and he travels a great deal, both in the U.S. and abroad. He has three children, Lindsay, Richmond III, and Bill.

Jeff, the second child, was born about five years after Richmond. "His full name is Jefferson Hampton Flowers," Richmond says. "Jefferson is from my father, and Hampton was an old Flowers name. He had better health than Richmond, but he was loaded with allergies. Jeff developed asthma and sinus problems. Every year he would go through the same cycle. He'd start out with a little cold. It would go into bronchial asthma and then into pneumonia. We'd fight, and he'd pull around.

"Jeff was a good athlete in his own right. He followed Richmond to the University of Tennessee, and he played football one year. Finally he told me, 'You know I'm not ever going to be a superstar.' So he dropped football and just ran track." Jeff has made his career in the computer field and has done well. Today Jeff lives in the Washington, D.C., area. He works with Sysco, a large computer company. Jeff and his wife have two boys, Jeff and Tanner.

Mary, the daughter, was born three years after Jeff. She entered the second grade when Richmond and his family moved to Montgomery for his term as attorney general, and she had to deal directly with all of the trauma. Mary went to the University of Tennessee and majored in communications.

"While she was in college she got to be chairman of the teen board of this huge department store in Knoxville," Richmond recalls, "and this was a high honor for her. She matured quickly and without any bitterness. She went to work with the store full time after she graduated from college, and she worked herself into a buyers position. Then she worked for Revlon for a while.

"Mary married just the finest man, Dwight Tarwater, and we love her husband to death. He was born and raised in Knoxville and is a lawyer. They have three small children, Davis, Katherine, and Dwight, and Mary is just being Mommy now."

Philosophy of Life. Asked about his philosophy of life, Richmond answered, "I've never thought about it very much. I don't think I've had a very complicated philosophy. I've always been a great one to live and let live. I think one of my saving characteristics has been my ability always to adapt myself to whatever situation I was thrown in and to get along well in it.

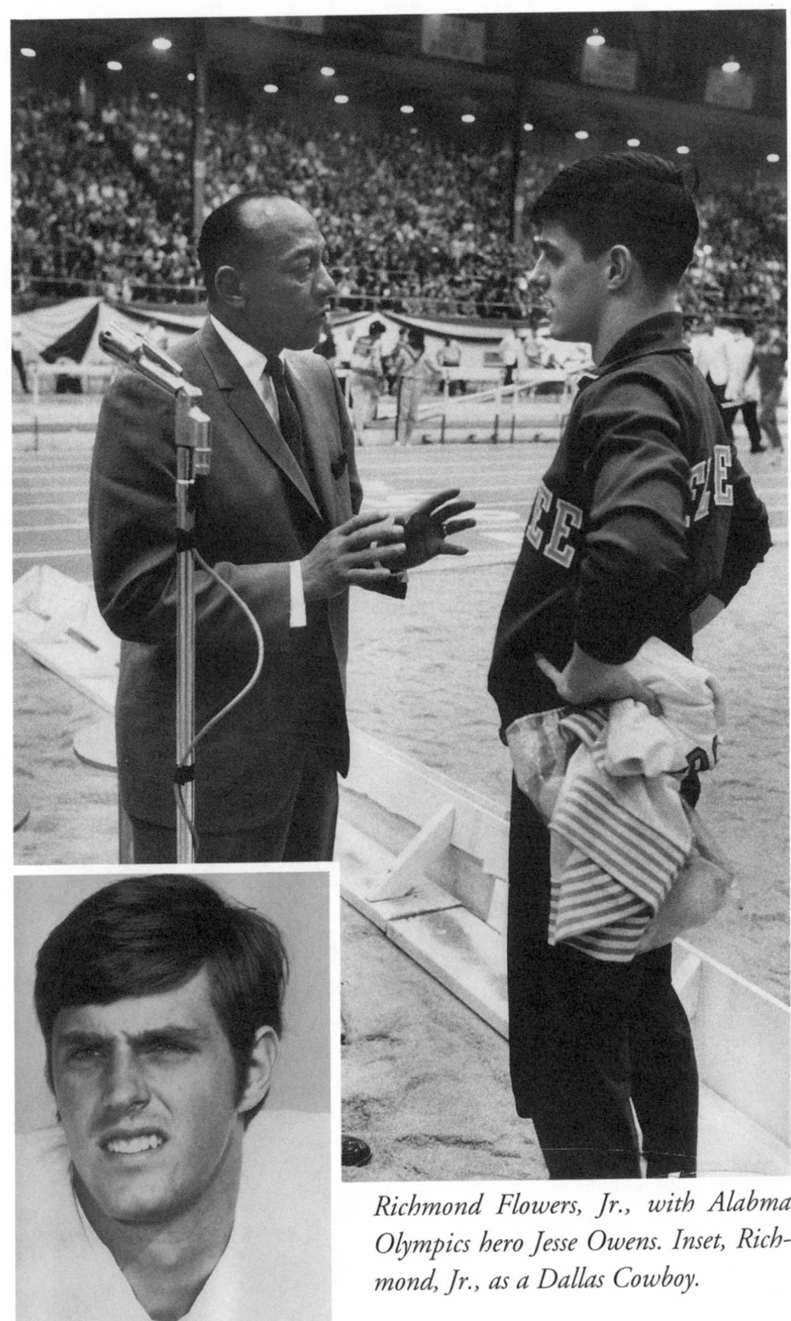

Richmond Flowers, Jr., with Alabma Olympics hero Jesse Owens. Inset, Richmond, Jr., as a Dallas Cowboy.

Above: Flowers with his younger son, Jeff. Golf was a favorite family sport. Opposite page: Daughter Mary on her wedding day, with Beulah Baines, who worked for the family for many years.

"As a child, I was very brash and aggressive. I knew as well as I knew my name and didn't want anybody else to know, I was basically very, very shy. I always feared and despised rejection. It just threw me for a loop every time I experienced it, directly or indirectly. Basically, that has to be because of shyness, timidity, or lack of self-confidence. And yet, you'd have thought I was the cockiest little rascal in the world.

"This made me a great one to achieve, I think. I've always wanted to

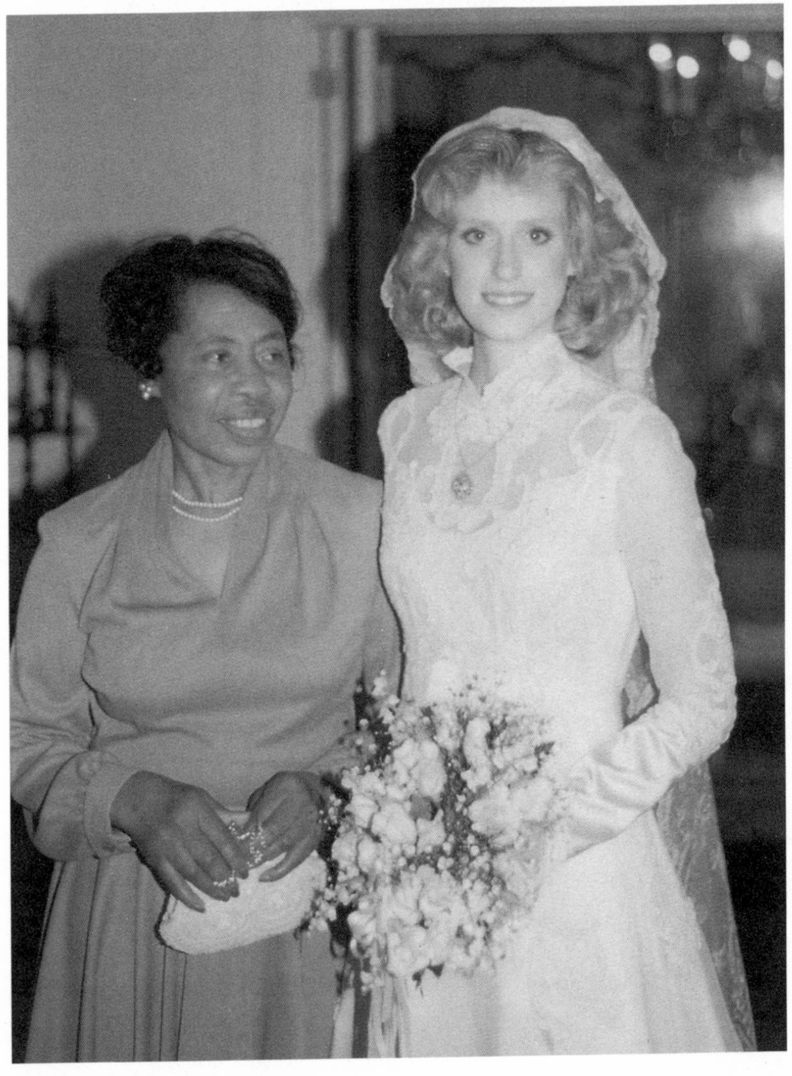

be the best. Whatever I did, I had this driving desire to be the best. I never wanted to be mediocre at anything. Yet, I knew full well I couldn't be best most of the time. If I couldn't be good at something, I had a tendency to stay away from it. I think that might have affected some of my scholastic background. I'd shy away from a subject unless I could be the best. I've always said high school chemistry kept me from being a doctor. I didn't like it. I didn't want any more chemistry, so medicine went out the window.

"By the time I was an adolescent, I had a reputation of having a fine personality and of never meeting a stranger. I've never ever been accused of being stuck-up or snobbish, even as a child. I rarely met a person I didn't like. I don't know if that is part of a philosophy or not, but it's my general nature.

"I loved people, and even when I was a very small child, I was a champion of the underdog. My mother used to say I brought home every little ragamuffin I saw at school. I always felt sorry for the little fellow who didn't have as much as I did. I always wanted to share with him, to give him some of mine.

"When I got into politics, I had never thought much about the big mules, as Jim Folsom used to call them, but I tended to agree with Big Jim about it. The big mules are going to look after themselves, so we have to be concerned about the people who don't have so much. I used to say that God didn't mean for people to suffer because they were poor. He didn't make them poor to make them suffer. Maybe he made them poor to teach them to survive."

Asked whether his attitudes had changed as a result of his experiences with the courts and the penal system, Richmond answered, "I really don't think they have. Today, because of the inheritance from my father and the fact that I have been fairly frugal and have saved, I'm in a comfortable position. I'm not wealthy, but I have no worries about the future. Everything about my situation should make me a staunch Republican, and yet I still think about the poor devil. Who is going to look after the guy who never had a chance? I'm not talking about the ne'er-do-wells, those who had all the opportunities there were and blew them all away drinking or doping or what have you. I know full well that all men are not created equal. The rich man's son just has so many advantages over the poor man's son.

The Flowers family today: from left, Richmond, Jr., and his wife, Diane, son Bill, and daughter Lindsay; Richmond and Mary; Jeff; Mary, Dwight and baby Katherine Tarwater; and, kneeling in front, Richmond III; Jeff's sons Tanner and Benjamin; and Mary's son Davis.

"I've always been a religious person. I've always felt very strongly that God has blessed me. He not only blessed me with parents that were able to put me in a comfortable position, but he blessed me with a lot of talent. I've got a good mind, and I have a talent for articulating and expressing myself. Sometime I feel that maybe I should be ashamed that I haven't done more with my talent. Maybe I oversell it. I may not have as much talent as I thought.

"I try to be candid and honest. The current secretary of the senate in Montgomery said recently to a mutual friend, 'When Richmond Flowers was in the legislature, there weren't many like him. If he gave his word, you could put the Bible on it. He would not back off. When I see these senators up here now promising one another and then wiggling out and backing off, I think about those old days when men like Richmond Flowers were up here. If he told you he'd do something, that's it, buddy.' I've always prided myself on that. If I tell you I'll do something, I'll do it. I never have shunned work. If I've got a job to do, I'll do it. I've always believed that a person should take responsibility seriously. You know the old saying, 'With freedom comes responsibility.'

"When I went into the attorney general's office, I had no idea what was going to happened. I said during the campaign, 'I'll fight them in the courts until the last letter of the law.' But things change. Between election and inauguration, Ross Barnett of Mississippi stood in the school house door, and a French reporter was killed. Federal troops showed up. Mississippi was the joke of the nation! They didn't have to stay the joke long. We in Alabama took over the jester's position.

"I was scared to death half the time. I was so proud that I had nerve enough to do it, and I knew what I stood for was right. I know today it was right! The stand I took was right in the eyes of the law and in the eyes of God. I'm glad I took it. I hold no ill feelings about what it did to me. After all, it hasn't deprived me of anything really important. Oh, I might have been bigger politically. But so what?

"People who instigate changes are the ones who get crucified. They get caught in the transition. They get trampled every time. My friends used to tell me that, but I didn't believe it. It was just exactly what happened. I learned a lot through it all, and I certainly would do some things differently if I could go over it again. But I have no regrets. I did what I believed was right."

10

Epilogue

The dust has long since settled since the civil rights revolution of the 1950s and 1960s. Richmond Flowers and his wife live peacefully and comfortably in Dothan, Alabama, their home town. They can view their past with equanimity, though Richmond muses at times on what might have been. He is naturally concerned with how history will treat him.

Thirty years have passed, and many people approaching middle age have no direct recollection of those fateful years, no sense of the intensity of feelings, of the outrage on both sides, which pervaded much of the South. With the perspective of time, what can be concluded about the central events of Richmond's term as attorney general? What about the manner in which the challenge to an entrenched system was handled? Did the upheaval, with all of its pain and suffering, make the South and the nation a better place? And what of the man whose life is the subject of this book and who found himself inadvertently playing a central role in the struggle?

A Leadership Thesis. A thesis stated several times in this book is that Alabama suffered a fundamental failure in leadership during the civil rights revolution, the period roughly from the *Brown* decision in 1954 to Martin Luther King's assassination in 1968. This failure, according to the thesis, contributed significantly to the manner in which the state responded to the demand for social change. A corollary is that the transition would have been much less disruptive and its consequences less harmful if leadership had been more insightful and prudent.

The counter-argument is that no other leadership was possible, because no one else could have been elected to major public office. The social change which was demanded was revolutionary in its scope, and strong reaction was not surprising. Richmond Flowers, who came from an affluent family, says that he grew up believing that segregation was natural and right, and almost all whites shared this outlook.[1] They were impervious to moral persuasions of the integrationists because they believed deeply that their own way was moral.

At the time of the *Brown* decision, twenty-one states and the District of Columbia permitted racial segregation in education in some form. The District of Columbia and ten states complied quickly with the requirements of *Brown*. Of the remaining eleven, North Carolina, Tennessee, and Texas ended their legal opposition by 1957. The remaining eight were Alabama, Arkansas, Florida, Georgia, Louisiana, Mississippi, South Carolina, and Virginia.

By 1960, it had become clearer that the government and the civil rights movement would persist, particularly after the election of Kennedy. A series of violent episodes, including those at the University of Alabama, Little Rock, and New Orleans, had occurred and had proved futile and degrading. The sit-ins, with their image of brutal whites attacking black youths who refused to fight back, affected the conscience of many who, like Richmond Flowers, had grown up believing that segregation was right and proper. All Deep South states except Alabama and Mississippi decided they must reach an accommodation of some sort, and they had begun taking appropriate steps. This happened even though their populations were similar to those of Alabama and Mississippi and were just as bitterly opposed to the changes which were demanded.

Peter Soderberg says that by 1964 the civil rights revolution was beginning its final phase. According to his formulation, those resisting change are subjected at such a time to heavy pressure to make concessions; if the pressure becomes great enough, they do.[2] Bitter-end resistance is unlikely when it becomes obvious that there is no choice but to change. Those who continue to resist risk losing everything,[3] and most rational people will retreat and try to cut their loses.

Alabama, however, just continued on its self-destructive course, and one reason is that leaders assured the populace that hard resistance would keep the social structure as it was and keep the blacks in "their place." Hamilton notes that Alabama voters tended to be unsophisticated and sparsely educated, and this made them susceptible to emotional, oversimplified messages.[4]

Most of the time, social change moves at an imperceptible pace, and conditions appear basically stable and nonthreatening. The populace wants this comfortable situation to continue, and they prefer "consensus" leadership. A consensus leader is like the rest of us, a "first among equals," a person whose position is usually in the center of the political spectrum and who can be counted on to keep things pretty much as they are.[5]

When something threatening happens, however, the importance of interpretation and of strong action by leaders increases. "People want to know what the problem is, why they are being asked to do certain things and how they relate to the larger picture," says Gardner.[6] If the objective reality is unclear, people depend on trusted leaders, and they are likely to believe it if they are told by their leaders that a change is threatening. As disorder and perceived threat grow, individuals tend to quit thinking for themselves and just accept what they are told.[7] They "regress to states of marked dependence" and "unquestioning submission."[8]

The individual with the greatest potential influence in a state is the governor. The governors of surrounding states—Griffin and Vandiver of Georgia, Clement and Ellington of Tennessee, and Collins of Florida—said they were for preserving segregation when they were first elected. But most urged caution and constraint when the test came, and they cooperated with local business and political leaders in effecting change and avoiding violence. In contrast, Alabama's governors encouraged lawlessness with their statements and actions. Wilma Dykeman notes that, at such times, political leaders need to be statesmen at the same time it is necessary for them to be politicians.[9]

The effective leader in such a time must have insight and the ability to see what is desirable in the long term, what is possible within the context of his or her environment, and within this, what actions can be taken to guide the system toward a desirable outcome. The first essential is to maintain social control, even if this requires strong use of the state's legal and police power for brief periods. Beyond this, the effective leader must educate and develop a consensus around needed actions. This is not easy, and as history indicates, such leadership is rare.

The Current State of Civil Rights. And what of civil rights, the issue which was so central to Richmond Flowers's life and for which, intentionally or not, he sacrificed his career?

When President Lyndon Johnson signed the Voting Rights Bill on August 6, 1965, it seemed the moment of triumph to many persons, black and white, who had worked so long to eliminate legal barriers to full participation in the society by all Americans. Jim Crow in its legal form was dead. This optimism lasted less than a week. On August 11, terrible riots broke out in the Watts section of Los Angeles, and they were among the most destructive racial violence in American history.[10] Troops had to be brought in, and it took a week to restore order. Thirty-four people, all but three of them black, were killed, and more than a thousand were injured. Hundreds of buildings were destroyed.

The Watts riots came as a profound shock to many whites.[11] Could it be that smashing Jim Crow in the South was not enough? As it turned out, Watts was only a beginning, a sign that the complex, deep-seated, persistent problem of race relations in American society would last many more decades. Among other things, Watts signaled that it was no longer a Southern problem, but a problem of the whole nation.

The civil rights movement had eliminated legal denial of rights, but it had not made blacks equal in economic standing nor in other aspects of life. This was perceived by some as a failure, a broken promise, and this aroused and unleashed violent passions. According to Woodward, things broke in the late 1960s because the civil rights struggle in the South sensitized northern blacks to their grievances and reduced their tolerance of old injustices. "It simultaneously increased their levels of expectation and shortened their patience with a white establishment that could not or would not fulfill these expectations. Hope rather than despair bred rebellion."[12]

The events of the late 1960s also proved that the black community was much more diverse than many people had previously thought. Naive liberals tended to perceive the black population as more or less a monolith. In fact, there was a wide range of opinion among blacks—from Uncle Toms, who just wanted to get along whatever the price; to full integrationist, who wanted to participate fully in the society; to separatists who wanted strict segregation, even to the point of separate regions in which to live; to revolutionaries who wanted to kill. King spoke only for a portion of the total, and so did anyone else.

The problem had not been solved, but after things settled down in the 1970s, it became clear that lasting progress had been made. Richard Arrington, Jr., a black college professor, was elected mayor of Birmingham in 1979. The son of a rural Alabama sharecropper, Arrington worked his way through college and earned a Ph.D. in vertebrate zoology from the University of Oklahoma. Under his leadership, the city experienced a renaissance of sorts.

Birmingham was listed in the February 6, 1989, issue of *Newsweek* as one of the nation's ten "hot" cities, that is, one of the best places to live and work. The article said that "Birmingham can claim to be a symbol of how much the South has changed for the better."[13] The following June, Birmingham was selected by the U.S. Conference of Mayors as America's most livable city.[14]

In November 1992, the Birmingham Civil Rights Institute was opened. It occupies ground which civil rights leaders feel "is as sacred to the country's history as Bunker Hill, Independence Hall and the Alamo."[15] The Institute is owned by the city of Birmingham. It is an impressive structure, with a large exhibit area which evokes memories of the struggle and of its sacrifices.

Great progress has been made, but recent events show that many difficult problems remain. Many black youth share the sense of alienation described as a problem nationally among minority youth. They feel no sense of ownership in the American system and do not see for themselves any stake in its future. One explanation is that full equality has still not been achieved. What is meant by "full equality," if it is more than equal treatment before the law? According to historian Joel Williamson full equality is "a fair share of the good things of American life," a proper proportion of "wealthy, educated, and prosperous individuals."[17]

"Full equality" is more than material circumstances, however. It is also an attitude, a feeling inside that one is equal and is seen as equal. It is self-esteem and self-pride. Martin Luther King, Jr., in his "Letter from a Birmingham Jail," wrote of constant humiliation, of forever fighting a degenerating sense of "nobodyness," of seeing the "ominous clouds of inferiority" forming in a child's mind.[18]

"Full equality," therefore, means participating in American society in exactly the same way as other citizens and experiencing the same rewards. This definition raises some fundamental and very difficult questions. To what extent is society responsible for redressing old wrongs, such as centuries of mistreatment of blacks? In the American democracy, is it society's obligation to guarantee equal *opportunities* or equal *outcomes*? If the answer is equal outcomes, how can this possibly be achieved in a country which limits the powers of its government, makes decisions via the ballot, and follows the free enterprise system? These are the questions faced as the nation approaches a new century, and its most perplexing problem remains unsolved.

A Concluding Statement on Richmond Flowers. Richmond Flowers remains a controversial figure in Alabama political history. There is no question that he was very successful as a state senator. He was thirty-six when he took office, and he did a great deal for the district he represented. He was one of the governor's floor leaders, an unusual position for a first-term legislator, and he handled this assignment well. The Montgomery press corps voted him the outstanding freshman senator in his class. He was considered one of the most promising of the young politicians in the state.

His problems came during his term as attorney general, and his performance then is the source of conflicting opinions about him. A critic observed that, in his interviews for this book, Richmond revealed at least three persona with regard to his stand on civil rights. First, he was the smart segregationist who knew that Wallace-style demagoguery was the least effective way to maintain the old ways. Second, he was the servant of the law who upheld his oath and did his duty even though the law changed in ways he did not welcome. Finally, he was the leader who sympathized with the underdog, realized that blacks were underdogs who had been badly mistreated, and became a convert to their cause.[19]

Which of these was the real Richmond Flowers, the critic asked? The answer depends in part on the final judgment of the man. The fact is that all three were the real Richmond Flowers. Each of us plays different roles and sees himself or herself in different ways, depending on circumstances and needs of the moment. Richmond was all three persons, though his beliefs and relative positions changed in time. He began as the segregationist, and he held this position through his term as senator and his campaigns for attorney general. As attorney general, he tried from the start to live up to his oath to uphold the law, and circumstances forced him more and more into stronger positions on this matter. Finally, as things developed, he says his experiences changed him, and he became to an extent at least a supporter of civil rights. His later behavior seemed to support this claim.

In considering his possible status as a "hero," one should remember that he did not intend to risk all for a cause and be a martyr, but neither do many men who win medals for acts of bravery on the battlefield. Richmond just meant to be moderate, but as things heated up, "moderate" came to refer to someone who remained silent and avoided commitment.[20] Events swept him along. He knew he was taking a risk, but he still thought he might win. Richmond did not realize the extent of his miscalculation until the election of 1966, and even then, he thought he might recover. He never deliberately sacrificed his career.

He was grievously wounded politically in 1966, and whether he could have come back will remain an open question because he never had the opportunity. The trial and his term in prison ended his political life. Many people still believe he was guilty of extortion, and a final assessment of him depends on the possibility this could be true. This assessment requires great care. Richmond made many enemies, and there are plenty of people ready to cast aspersions on hearsay and wishful thinking.

There is no question that Richmond made some very serious mistakes in his handling of the securities office. He allowed almost free reign to some characters who can only be described as unsavory. On reading the trial evidence and studying some of the people involved, one cannot escape the conclusion that the kickbacks and other illegal activities Richmond's associates were accused of actually occurred.

As securities commissioner, Richmond was responsible, as the court said. The question is whether he knew the details of what his friends and associates were doing and allowed it to continue anyway—or even whether he was actually a participant in it. The conclusion of the author is that Richmond was careless to the point of irresponsibility and perhaps deserved some kind of punishment, though a term in federal prison hardly seems appropriate.

I do not believe he was knowingly a direct part of any activity he believed to be illegal. First, as he says, he was extremely busy with the affairs of the attorney general's office during those fateful years. Second, he was from wealth, and while he likes to poor-mouth it about the struggle he and Mary had in the early years of their marriage, he never had any real financial problems. His parents and brothers were always ready to come to his rescue, and he knew it. He has a big ego and loves adulation, but he is not obsessed with money *per se*. Finally, he prides himself on his religious beliefs and his longtime affiliation with and active participation in the Methodist Church. Richmond is very serious about this, and when one gets to know the man well, it is impossible to believe that he is capable of teaching Sunday School and at the same time lying about and participating in serious illegal activities.

Richmond is like the rest of us—he is full of potential for both good and bad, and sometimes he has fallen short of the mark. His political success came primarily from his personality and speaking ability. It all came so easy, he thought he could have anything without having to worry about details. This made him careless, I believe. He did not want to bother with details on the securities side, and he did not. And this was the source of big trouble.

On the matter of upholding the law during the first Wallace term, he rose to the occasion. He had to face some harsh realities, and he did what he thought was right in spite of the vilification he had to endure and the warnings that he might be ruining his political career. This was heroic. The man deserves to have it remembered, and the rest of us need to be reminded of what happened. For four years, he fought the forces of evil and represented the best in our character.

Richmond Flowers reaped a bitter harvest for the stand he took on civil rights during his term as attorney general. He was hated by large numbers of his fellow citizens and literally spat upon as he tried to do his job. His promising political career was destroyed, and he spent a term in prison, part of it with hardened criminals. This would have made many men bitter and filled them with hate.

He was tempted to go in this direction, he says, and he slipped into self-pity a few times. But he determined not to do it, not to be held captive by the past and, because of bitterness, to ruin his chances for contentment and useful work. Rather, he would try to live by his religious convictions and forgive. He made many mistakes and lost many battles, but this was a battle he won.

Notes

1. Antecedents

[1]Woodward, C. Vann. *The Burden of Southern History*. Third Edition. Baton Rouge: Lousiana State University Press, 1993. p. 74.

[2]Current, Richard Nelson. *Those Terrible Carpetbaggers: A Reinterpretation*. New York: Oxford University Press, 1988. p. 323

[3]Craven, Avery. *Reconstruction: The Ending of the Civil War*. New York: Holt, Rinehart and Winston, Inc., 1969. p. iii.

[4]*Ibid.* p. 225.

[5]Ayers, Edward L. *The Promise of the New South*. New York: Oxford University Press, 1992. p. 8.

[6]Woodward, C. Vann. *Origins of the New South*. Baton Rouge: Louisiana State University Press, 1951. p. 20.

[7]*Ibid.* p. 14.

[8]Craven, Avery. *Reconstruction: The Ending of the Civil War*. New York: Holt, Rinehart and Winston, Inc., 1969. pp. 304-305.

[9]*Ibid.* pp. 3, 262.

[10]Wiggins, Sarah Woodfolk. "Alabama: Democratic Bulldozing and Republican Folly." In *Reconstruction and Redemption in the South*, Otto H. Olson, Ed. Baton Rouge, LA: Louisiana State University Press, 1980. p. 60.

[11]Craven, Avery. *Reconstruction: The Ending of the Civil War*. New York: Holt, Rinehart and Winston, Inc., 1969. p. 305.

[12]Woodward, C. Vann. *Origins of the New South*. Baton Rouge: Louisiana State University Press, 1951. pp. 28-29.

[13]Meier, August, and Elliott Rudwick. *From Plantation to Ghetto.* New York: Hill and Wang, 1970. p. 50.

[14]Current, Richard Nelson. *Those Terrible Carpetbaggers: A Reinterpretation*. New York: Oxford University Press, 1988. p. xi.

[15]Craven, Avery. *Reconstruction: The Ending of the Civil War*. New York: Holt, Rinehart and Winston, Inc., 1969. pp. 244-245.

[16]Craven, Avery. *Reconstruction: The Ending of the Civil War*. New York: Holt, Rinehart and Winston, Inc., 1969; Current, Richard Nelson. *Those Terrible Carpetbaggers: A Reinterpretation*. New York: Oxford University Press, 1988; Woodward, C. Vann. *Origins of the New South*. Baton Rouge: Louisiana State University Press, 1951.

[17]Wiggins, Sarah Woolfolk. "Alabama: Democratic Bulldozing and Republican Folly." In *Reconstruction and Redemption in the South*, Otto H. Olson, Ed. Baton Rouge, LA: Louisiana State University Press, 1980. p. 72.

[18]Woodward, C. Vann. *Origins of the New South*. Baton Rouge: Louisiana State University Press, 1951. p.

22.

[19]Williamson, Joel. *The Crucible of Race.* New York: Oxford University Press, 1984. p. 316.

[20]*Ibid.* p. 80.

[21]Ayers, Edward L. *The Promise of the New South.* New York: Oxford University Press, 1992. p. 7.

[22]*Ibid.* pp. viii.

[23]*Ibid.* p. 21.

[24]*Ibid.* pp. 124.

[25]*Ibid.* p. 59.

[26]McWilliams, Tennant S. "A New Day Coming: Alabama Since 1930."

In *Perspectives: The Alabama Heritage,* Rosemary Canfield, ed.

Troy, AL: Troy State University Press, 1978. p. 176.

[27]Woodward, C. Vann. *Origins of the New South.* Baton Rouge: Louisiana State University Press, 1951. p. 65.

[28]Ayers, Edward L. *The Promise of the New South.* New York: Oxford University Press, 1992. pp. 198-203.

[29]Current, Richard Nelson. *Those Terrible Carpetbaggers: A Reinterpretation.* New York: Oxford University Press, 1988. p. 311.

[30]Woodward, C. Vann. *Origins of the New South.* Baton Rouge: Louisiana State University Press, 1951. p. 178.

[31]Ayers, Edward L. *The Promise of the New South.* New York: Oxford University Press, 1992. pp. 98, 234.

[32]Wiggins, Sarah Wookfolk. *The Scalawags in Alabama Politics, 1865-1881.* University, AL: University of Alabama Press, 1977. p. 2.

[33]Ayers, Edward L. *The Promise of the New South.* New York: Oxford University Press, 1992. p. 35.

[34]Current, Richard Nelson. *Those Terrible Carpetbaggers: A Reinterpretation.* New York: Oxford University Press, 1988. pp. 315-319.

[35]Williamson, Joel. *The Crucible of Race.* New York: Oxford University Press, 1984. p. 85.

[36]Ayers, Edward L. *The Promise of the New South.* New York: Oxford University Press, 1992. p. 136.

[37]Williamson, Joel. *The Crucible of Race.* New York: Oxford University Press, 1984; Woodward, C. Vann. *Origins of the New South.* Baton Rouge: Louisiana State University Press, 1951. p. 178.

[38]Williamson, Joel. *The Crucible of Race.* New York: Oxford University Press, 1984. p. 111.

[39]Ayers, Edward L. *The Promise of the New South.* New York: Oxford University Press, 1992. pp. 148-149.

[40]*Ibid.* p. 132.

[41]*Ibid.* pp. 155-157.

[42]Woodward, C. Vann. *The Burden of Southern History.* Third Edition. Baton Rouge: Lousiana State University Press, 1993. p. 141.

[43]Woodward, C. Vann. *Origins of the New South.* Baton Rouge: Louisiana State University Press, 1951. p. 252.

[44]*Ibid.* p. 24.

[45]Ayers, Edward L. *The Promise of the New South.* New York: Oxford University Press, 1992. p. 418.

[46]*Ibid.* p. 203.

[47]*Ibid.* p. 304.

[48]Williamson, Joel. *The Crucible of Race.* New York: Oxford University Press, 1984. p. 249.

[49]*Ibid.* p. 95.

[50]*Ibid.* p. 181.

[51]*Ibid.* p. 179.

[52]Wiggins, Warah Woodfolk. "Alabama: Democratic Bulldozing and Republican Folly." In *Reconstruction and Redemption in the South,* Otto H. Olson, Ed. Baton Rouge, LA: Louisiana State University Press, 1980. p. 72.

[53]Williamson, Joel. *The Crucible of Race.* New York: Oxford University Press, 1984. p. 265.

[42]*Origins of the New South.* C. Vann Woodward. Baton Rouge: Louisiana State University Press, 1951. pp. 369-395.

[43]*Alabama Handbook.* Montgomery, Al: Alabama Department of Agriculture and Industry, 1919. p. 2.

[44]*The Promise of the New South.* Edward L. Ayers. New York: Oxford University Press, 1992. p. 426.

[45]*Origins of the New South.* C. Vann Woodward. Baton Rouge: Louisiana State University Press, 1951. pp. 356-359.

[46]*The Promise of the New South.* Edward L. Ayers. New York: Oxford University Press, 1992. p. 210.

[47]*Ibid.* p. 331.

[48]*Those Terrible Carpetbaggers: A Reinterpretation.* Richard Nelson Current.

New York: Oxford University Press, 1988. p. 404.

[49]*From Plantation to Ghetto.* August Meier and Elliott Rudick. New York:

Hill and Wang, 1970. p. 165.

Chapter 2. Birth and Background

[1]Flowers, P. B., Jr. *Flowers Chronicles.* Baltimore: Gateway Press, Inc., 1987. p. 289.

[2]*Ibid.* p. 357.

[3]Belches, Alan T. "Introduction." In *Devil Make a Third,* by Douglas Fields Bailey. University, AL: University of Alabama Press, 1989. p. 1.

[4]Moore, Albert B. *History of Alabama.* Tuscaloosa, AL: Alabama Book Store, 1951. p. 522.

[5]*Memorial Record of Alabama.* Volume I. Madison, WI: Brant and Fuller, 1893.

[6]Ayers, Edward L. *The Promise of the New South.* New York: Oxford University Press, 1992. p. 413.

[7]Woodward, C. Vann. *Origins of the New South.* Baton Rouge: Louisiana State University Press, 1951. pp. 369-395.

[8]*Ibid.* p. 52.

[9]Williamson, Joel. *The Crucible of Race.* New York: Oxford University Press, 1984. p. 322.

[10]Ayers, Edward L. *The Promise of the New South.* New York: Oxford University Press, 1992. p. 426.

[11]Woodward, C. Vann. *Origins of the New South.* Baton Rouge: Louisiana State University Press, 1951. pp. 356-359.

[12]Ayers, Edward L. *The Promise of the New South.* New York: Oxford University Press, 1992. p. 210.

[13]*Ibid.* p. 331.

[14]Current, Richard Nelson. *Those Terrible Carpetbaggers: A Reinterpretation.*New York: Oxford University Press, 1988. p. 404.

Chapter 3. Growing Up the Right Way

[1]Leuchtenburg, William E. *Franklin D. Roosevelt and the New Deal.* New York: Harper and Row, 1963. p. xii.

[2]*Ibid.* p. 16.

[3]*Ibid.* p. 18.

[4]*Ibid.* p. 12.

[5]*Ibid.* p. 39.

[6]Gallager, Hugh Gregory. *FDR's Splendid Deception.* New York: Dodd, Mead & Company, 1985. p. 170.

[7]Hamilton, Virginia Van der Veer. *Hugo Black: The Alabama Years.* Baton Rouge, LA: Louisiana State University Press, 1972. pp. 181-191.

[8]*Ibid.* p. 189.

[9]Blaustein, Albert P., and Robert L. Zangrando. Eds. *Civil Rights and the American Negro.* New York: Trident Press, 1968. p. 334.

[10]Helson, Bernard H. *The Fourteenth Amendment and the American Negro Since 1920.* New York: Russell and Russell, 1946. p. 16.

[11]Blaustein, Albert P., and Robert L. Zangrando. Eds. *Civil Rights and the American Negro.* New York: Trident Press, 1968. p. 346.

[12]Lytle, Andrew. *Bedford Forrest and His Critter Company.*
Seminole, FL: The Green Key Press, 1931. p. 385.

[13]Chalmers, David M. *The History of the Ku Klux Klan.* Chicago: Quadrangle Books, 1965. p. 2.

[14]*Loc. Cit.*

[15]*Ibid.* p. 31.

[16]Ginger, Ray. Ed. *William Jennings Bryan: Selections.* New York: The Bobbs-Merrill Company, Inc., 1967. p. 217.

[17]Delgar, Carl N. "A Century of the Klans." *Journal of Southern*
History. Vol. 31, No. 4. November 1965. p. 435.

[18]Hamilton, Virginia Van der Veer. *Hugo Black: The Alabama Years.* Baton Rouge, LA: Louisiana State University Press, 1972. p. 95.

[19]*Ibid.* p. 98.

[20]Chalmers, David M. *The History of the Ku Klux Klan.* Chicago: Quadrangle Books, 1965. p. 4.

Chapter 4. Maturing to Serious Pursuits

[1]Leuchtenburg, William E. *Franklin D. Roosevelt and the New Deal.* New York: Harper and Row, 1963. p. 324.

[2]*Ibid.*, p. 324.

[3]Silberman, Charles E. *Crisis in Black and White.* New York: Random House, 1964. p. 65.

[4]Blaustein, Albert P., and Robert L. Zangrando, eds. *Civil Rights and the American Negro.* New York: Trident Press, 1968. p. 273.

[5]Truman, Margaret. *Harry S. Truman.* New York: William Morrow and Company, Inc., 1973. p. 414.

Chapter 5. A Political Career Begins

[1]*The Birmingham Post-Herald.* April 12, 1954.

[2]*Montgomery Advertiser.* October 29, 1954.

[3]Gilliam, Thomas J. "The Second Folsom Administration: The Destruction of Alabama Liberalism, 1953-58." Ph.D. dissertation, Auburn University, 1975. p. 57.

[4]Bass, Jack. *Unlikely Heroes.* Tuscaloosa, AL: University of Alabama Press, 1981. p. 64.

[5]Frady, Marshal. *Wallace.* New York: New American Library, 1968. p. 103.

[6]Lord, Walter. *The Past That Would Not Die.* New York: Harper & Row, Publishers, 1965. p. 69; Sims, George E. *The Little Man's Big Friend.* Tuscaloosa, AL: University of Alabama Press, 1985. p. 177.

[7]Goldfield, David R. *Black, White, and Southern.* Baton Rouge, LA: Louisiana State University Press, 1990. p. 104.

[8]*Ibid.* p. 102.

[9]Bass, Jack. *Unlikely Heroes.* Tuscaloosa, AL: University of Alabama Press, 1981. p. 59.

[10]Woodward, C. Vann. *The Strange Career of Jim Crow.* Third Revised Edition. New York: Oxford University Press, 1974. p. 9.

[11]Grafton, Carl and Anne Permaloff. *Big Mules and Branchheads.* Athens: University of Georgia Press, 1985. p. 166.

[12]*Alabama Journal.* January 18, 1954.

[13]*Alabama Journal.* January 12, 1955.

[14]*Alabama Journal.* November 15, 1954.

[15]Woodward, C. Vann. *The Strange Career of Jim Crow.* Third Revised Edition. New York: Oxford University Press, 1974. p. 152.

[16]*Montgomery Advertiser.* June 1, 1955.

[17]Woodward, C. Vann. *The Strange Career of Jim Crow.* Third Revised Edition. New York: Oxford University Press, 1974. p. 154.

[18]Frady, Marshal. *Wallace.* New York: New American Library, 1968. p. 103.

[19]*Ibid.* p. 127.

[20]Woodward, C. Vann. *The Strange Career of Jim Crow.* Third Revised Edition. New York: Oxford University Press, 1974. p. 155.

[21]Lord, Walter. *The Past That Would Not Die.* New York: Harper & Row, Publishers, 1965. pp. 74, 78-80.

[22]Plowledge, Fred. *Free at Last?* Boston: Little, Brown and Company, 1991. p. 183.

[23]Sims, George E. *The Little Man's Big Friend.* Tuscaloosa, AL: University of Alabama Press, 1985. p. 175.

[24]*Ibid.* p. 186.

[25]Woodward, C. Vann. *The Burden of Southern History.* Third Edition. Baton Rouge, LA: Louisiana State University Press, 1993. pp. 240-241.

[26]Hamilton, Virginia Van der Veer. *Lister Hill.* Chapel Hill: University of North Carolina Press, 1987. p. 233.

[27]Coles, Robert. *Children of Crisis: A Study of Courage and Fear.* Boston: Little, Brown and Company, 1965. pp. 268-271.

[28]Woodward, C. Vann. *The Strange Career of Jim Crow.* Third Revised Edition. New York: Oxford Uni-

versity Press, 1974. p. 153.

[29]Lesher, Stephan. *George Wallace, American Populist*. New York: Addision-Wesley Publishing Company, 1994. pp. 124-125.

[30]*Montgomery Advertiser*. Issues from April 15 to April 30, 1958.

[31]Lesher, Stephen. *George Wallace, American Populist*. New York: Addision-Wesley Publishing Company, 1994. p. 123.

Chapter 6. Four Years of Campaigning

[1]Interview with Francis Speaks, member of the Alabama House of Representatives during the second Folsom administration and friend of John Patterson, July 22, 1992.

[2]Taylor, James S. "John M. Patterson and the 1958 Alabama Guvernatorial Race." *The Alabama Review*. 23:3 (July 1970) p. 227.

[3]Gilliam, Thomas J. "The Second Folwom Administration: The Destruction of Alabama Liberalism, 1954-58." Ph.D. dissertation, Auburn University, 1975.

[4]Sims, George E. *The Little Man's Big Friend*. Tuscaloosa, AL: University of Alabama Press, 1985.

[5]Nunnelley, William A. *Bull Connor*. Tuscaloosa, AL: University of Alabama Press, 1991. p. 86.

[6]*New York Times*. January 20, 1959.

[7]*New York Times*. September 9, 1959.

[8]*New York Times*. November 14, 1959.

[9]Grafton, Carl, and Anne Permaloff. *Big Mules and Branchheads*. Athens, GA: University of Georgia Press, 1985. p. 226.

[10]*Birmingham News*. November 6, 1960.

[11]*New York Times*. February 7, 1959.

[12]*New York Times*. May 18, 1959.

[13]D'Emilio, John. *The Civil Rights Struggle: Leaders in Profile*. New York: Facts on File, 1979. p. 114.

[14]*New York Times*. July 24, 1959.

[15]*New York Times*. March 14, 1959.

[16]*New York Times*. January 21, 1961.

[17]*New York Times*. March 14, 1959.

[18]*New York Times*. July 5, 1962.

[19]*New York Times*. November 15, 1960.

[20]Bass, Jack. *Unlikely Heroes*. Tuscaloosa, AL: University of Alabama Press, 1981. p. 107.

[21]Nunnelley, William A. *Bull Connor*. Tuscaloosa, AL: University of Alabama Press, 1991. p. 82.

[22]*New York Times*. November 15, 1962.

[23]Grafton, Carl, and Anna Permaloff. *Big Mules and Branchheads*. Athens, GA: University of Georgia Press, 1985. p. 229.

[24]Frady, Marshall. *Wallace*. New York: New American Library, 1968. p. 125.

[25]*Loc. Cit.*

[26]Nunnelley, William A. *Bull Connor*. Tuscaloosa, AL: University of Alabama Press, 1991. p. 87.

[27]Stewart, John Craig. *The Governors of Alabama*. Gretna, LA: Pelican Publishing Company, 1975. p. 201.

[28]*Birmingham News*. May 21, 1961.

[29]Speaks interview.

[30]Taylor, James S. "John M. Patterson and the 1958 Alabama Guvernatorial Race." *The Alabama Review*. 23:3 (July 1970) p. 226.

[31]Frady, Marshall. *Wallace*. New York:

New American Library, 1968. p. 125.

[32]Woodward, C. Vann. *The Strange Career of Jim Crow*. Third Revised Edition. New York: Oxford University Press, 1974. p. 168.

[33]Nunnelley, William A. *Bull Connor*. Tuscaloosa, AL: University of Alabama Press, 1991. p. 86.

[34]D'Emilio, John. *The Civil Rights Struggle: Leaders in Profile*. New York: Facts on File, 1979. p. 7.

[35]Meier, August, and Elliott Rudwick. *From Plantation to Ghetto*. New York: Hill and Wang, 1966. p. 225.

[36]Williamson, Joel. *The Crucible of Race*. New York: Oxford University Press, 1984. p. 7.

[37]D'Emilio, John. *The Civil Rights Struggle: Leaders in Profile*. New York: Facts on File, 1979. p. 13.

[38]Nunnelley, William A. *Bull Connor*. Tuscaloosa, AL: University of Alabama Press, 1991. p. 84.

[39]Woodward, C. Vann. *The Strange Career of Jim Crow*. Third Revised Edition. New York: Oxford University Press, 1974. p. 169.

[40]Meier, August, and Elliott Rudwick. *From Plantation to Ghetto*. New York: Hill and Wang, 1966. p. 257.

[41]Blaustein, Albert P., and Robert L. Zangrando, eds. *Civil Rights and the American Negro*. New York: Trident Press, 1968.

[42]Bass, Jack. *Unlikely Heroes*. Tuscaloosa, AL: University of Alabama Press, 1981. p. 267.

[43]Meier, August, and Elliott Rudwick. *From Plantation to Ghetto*. New York: Hill and Wang, 1966. p. 258.

[44]Bass, Jack. *Unlikely Heroes*. Tuscaloosa, AL: University of Alabama Press, 1981. p. 267.

[45]*Loc. Cit.*

[46]Goldfield, David R. *Black, White, and Southern*. Baton Rouge, LA: Louisiana State University Press, 1990. p. 111.

[47]Woodward, C. Vann. *The Strange Career of Jim Crow*. Third Revised Edition. New York: Oxford University Press, 1974. p. 172.

[48]Bass, Jack. *Unlikely Heroes*. Tuscaloosa, AL: University of Alabama Press, 1981. p. 183.

[49]Nunnelley, William A. *Bull Connor*. Tuscaloosa, AL: University of Alabama Press, 1991. p. 1.

[50]Goldfield, David R. *Black, White, and Southern*. Baton Rouge, LA: Louisiana State University Press, 1990. p. 131.

[51]Nunnelley, William A. *Bull Connor*. Tuscaloosa, AL: University of Alabama Press, 1991. p. 129.

[52]Sikora, Frank. *The Judge*. Montgomery, AL: The Black Belt Press, 1992. p. 103.

[53]*New York Times*. May 4, 1961.

[54]Meier, August, and Elliott Rudwick. *From Plantation to Ghetto*. New York: Hill and Wang, 1966. p. 100.

[55]Sikora, Frank. *The Judge*. Montgomery, AL: The Black Belt Press, 1992. p. 104.

[56]*Loc. Cit.*

[57]*Birmingham Post-Herald*. May 15, 1961.

[58]Sikora, Frank. *The Judge*. Montgom-

ery, AL: The Black Belt Press, 1992. p. 106.

[59]*Birmingham Post-Herald.* May 15, 1961.

[60]Sikora, Frank. *The Judge.* Montgomery, AL: The Black Belt Press, 1992. p. 107.

[61]*Ibid.* p. 170.

[62]*New York Times.* May 21, 1961.

[63]Sikora, Frank. *The Judge.* Montgomery, AL: The Black Belt Press, 1992. p. 109.

[64]*Loc. Cit.*

[65]*Ibid.* p. 110.

[66]Powledge, Fred. *Free at Last?* Boston: Little, Brown and Company, 1991.p. 279.

[67]*New York Times.* May 26, 1961.

[68]*New York Times.* May 17, 1961.

[69]*Birmingham Post-Herald.* May 15, 1962.

[70]*Birmingham Post-Herald.* May 3, 1962.

[71]*Birmingham Post-Herald.* May 3, 1962.

[72]*Birmingham Post-Herald.* May 1, 1962.

[73]*Birmingham Post-Herald.* May 10, 1962.

[74]*Birmingham Post-Herald.* May 9, 1962.

[75]*Birmingham Post-Herald.* May 10, 1962.

[76]*Birmingham Post-Herald.* May 9, 1962.

[77]Speaks interview.

[78]*Birmingham Post-Herald.* May 9, 1962.

[79]*Birmingham News.* May 17, 1962.

[80]*Birmingham News.* May 30, 1962.

[81]*Birmingham News.* May 27, 1962.

[82]*Birmingham Post-Herald.* May 10, 1962.

[83]*Birmingham Post-Herald.* November 2, 1962.

Chapter 7. Strange Bedfellows

[1]Frady, Marshall. *Wallace.* New York: New American Library, 1968.

[2]*Montgomery Journal-Advertiser.* June 5, 1983.

[3]*Loc. Cit.*

[4]Blaustein, Albert P., and Robert L. Zangrando, eds. *Civil Rights and the American Negro.* New York: Trident Press, 1968.

[5]*Montgomery Journal-Advertiser.* June 5, 1983. Also Greenhaw, Wayne. *Watch Out for George Wallace.* Englewood Cliffs, NJ: Prentice-Hall, Inc., 1976.

[6]*Montgomery Journal-Advertiser.* June 5, 1983.

[7]Coleman, Stephen, Jr., and Stephen Coleman, Sr. *Judge Clarence Allgood.* Birmingham, AL: Birmingham Historical Society, 1991.

[8]*Birmingham Post-Herald.* February 28, 1965.

[9]Goldfield, David R. *Black, White, and Southern.* Baton Rouge, LA: Louisiana State University Press, 1990.

[10]Dowe, Kelley. "Richard Arrington, Birmingham." *Southern Exposure.* 12:1. 1984. pp. 76-78.

[11]Hampton, Harry, and Steve Fayer. *Voices of Freedom.* New York: Bantam Books, 1990. p. 124.

[12]*Birmingham News.* November 15, 1992.

[13]*Birmingham News.* May 4, 1960.

[14]*Birmingham News.* May 19, 1961.

[15]*Birmingham News.* May 17, 1961.

[16]*Birmingham News.* May 19, 1961.

[17]Nunnelley, William A. *Bull Connor.* Tuscaloosa, AL: University of Alabama Press, 1991. p. 185.

[18]*Birmingham News.* May 16, 1961.

[19]Nunnelley, William A. *Bull Connor.* Tuscaloosa, AL: University of Alabama Press, 1991. p. 109.

[20]Hampton, Harry, and Steve Fayer. *Voices of Freedom.* New York: Bantam Books, 1990. pp. 124-126; Blumberg, Ronda Lois. *Civil Rights: The 1960s Freedom Struggle.* Boston: G. K. Hall, 1984. p. 103.

[21]Hampton, Harry, and Steve Fayer. *Voices of Freedom.* New York: Bantam Books, 1990. p. 125.

[22]Nunnelley, William A. *Bull Connor.* Tuscaloosa, AL: University of Alabama Press, 1991. p. 132.

[23]Hampton, Harry, and Steve Fayer. *Voices of Freedom.* New York: Bantam Books, 1990. p. 125.

[24]King, Martin Luther, Jr. *Why We Can't Wait.* New York: Signet Books, 1964. p. 57.

[25]Nunnelley, William A. *Bull Connor.* Tuscaloosa, AL: University of Alabama Press, 1991. p. 140.

[26]Hampton, Harry, and Steve Fayer. *Voices of Freedom.* New York: Bantam Books, 1990. p. 128.

[27]Nunnelley, William A. *Bull Connor.* Tuscaloosa, AL: University of Alabama Press, 1991. p. 147.

[28]King, Martin Luther, Jr. *Why We Can't Wait.* New York: Signet Books, 1964. p. 100.

[29]*Ibid.* p. 104.

[30]Hampton, Harry, and Steve Fayer. *Voices of Freedom.* New York: Bantam Books, 1990. p. 133.

[31]Nunnelley, William A. *Bull Connor.* Tuscaloosa, AL: University of Alabama Press, 1991. p. 150.

[32]*Ibid.* p. 162.

[33]Garrow, David J. *Bearing the Cross: Martin Luther King, Jr. and the Southern Christian Leadership Conference.* New York: William Morrow and Company, 1986. p. 264.

[34]King, Martin Luther, Jr. *Why We Can't Wait.* New York: Signet Books, 1964. p. 100.

[35]Meier, August, and Elliott Rudwick. *CORE.* New York: Oxford University Press, 1973. p. 225.

[36]Nunnelley, William A. *Bull Connor.* Tuscaloosa, AL: University of Alabama Press, 1991. p. 4.

[37]*Ibid.* p. 6.

[38]*Ibid.* p. 5.

[39]Blumberg, Ronda Lois. *Civil Rights: The 1960s Freedom Struggle.* Boston: G. K. Hall, 1984. p. 106.

[40]Personal note: When I was visiting Lomé, Togo, in 1990, I met a friendly young man who wanted to act as a guide. During our walks, he sang a little song about Abraham Lincoln and Martin Luther King.

[41]*Newsweek.* November 8, 1965. p. 33.

[42]Abernathy, Ralph David. *And the Walls Came Tumbling Down.* New York: Harper and Roe, 1989. p. 303.

[43]*New York Times.* January 2, 1965.

[44]Abernathy, Ralph David. *And the Walls Came Tumbling Down.* New York: Harper and Roe, 1989. p. 304.

[45]*Loc. Cit.*

[46]*New York Times*. January 23, 1965.

[47]Abernathy, Ralph David. *And the Walls Came Tumbling Down*. New York: Harper and Roe, 1989. p. 320.

[48]*New York Times*. February 4, 1965.

[49]*New York Times*. February 5, 1965.

[50]Bass, Jack. *Unlikely Heroes*. Tuscaloosa, AL: University of Alabama Press, 1981. p. 260.

[51]*New York Times*. March 12, 1965.

[52]*New York Times*. March 14, 1965.

[53]*New York Times*. March 19, 1965.

[54]Clark, James G. *The Jim Clark Story*. Selma, AL: Selma Enterprises, Inc., 1966. p. 43.

[55]*New York Times*. April 28, 1965.

[56]*New York Times*. March 27, 1965.

[57]Woodward, C. Vann. *The Strange Career of Jim Crow*. Third Revised Edition. New York: Oxford University Press, 1974. p. 185.

[58]Bass, Jack. *Unlikely Heroes*. Tuscaloosa, AL: University of Alabama Press, 1981. p. 262.

[59]*Ibid*. p. 263.

[60]Woodward, C. Vann. *The Strange Career of Jim Crow*. Third Revised Edition.New York: Oxford University Press, 1974. p. 186.

[61]*New York Times*. October 18, 1965.

[62]*Newsweek*. November 8, 1965. p. 33.

[63]Hampton, Harry, and Steve Fayer. *Voices of Freedom*. New York: Bantam Books, 1990. p. 272.

[64]*New York Times*. September 16, 1965.

[65]*New York Times*. October 1, 1965.

[66]*Loc. Cit.*

[67]*New York Times*. March 27, 1965.

[68]*New York Times*. May 10, 1965.

[69]*New York Times*. May 9, 1965.

[70]*Birmingham News*. July 12, 1948.

[71]*Birmingham News*. July 15, 1948.

[72]Stewart, John Craig. *The Governors of Alabama*. Gretna, LA: Pelican Publishing Company, 1975. p. 213.

[73]Greenhaw, Wayne. *Watch Out for George Wallace*. Englewood Cliffs, NJ: Prentice-Hall, Inc., 1976. p. 146.

[74]"Preliminary Results of Investigation. United Klans of America, Incorporated, Knights of the Ku Klux Klan, and Other Klan Organizations." Report published by the office of the attorney general of Alabama. October 18, 1965.

[75]*Loc. Cit.*

[76]*Ibid*. p. 13.

[77]*Look*. May 3, 1966. p. 37.

[78]Press Release from the office of the attorney general of Alabama. June 11,1965.

[79]*Look*. November 16, 1965. p. 46.

[80]Frady, Marshall. *Wallace*. New York: New American Library, 1968. p. 180.

[80]*Ibid*. p. 183.

[82]*New York Times*. March 28, 1966.

Chapter 8. Vengence Wreaked

[1]*Birmingham News*. January 13, 1966.

[2]*Birmingham News*. February 10, 1966.

[3]*Birmingham Post-Herald*. January 22, 1966.

[4]*Birmingham News*. January 22, 1966.

[5]*New York Times*. January 30, 1966.

[6]Frady, Marshall. *Wallace*. New York: New American Library, 1968. p. 191.

[7]*New York Times*. February 25, 1966.

[8]*Birmingham Post-Herald.* February 19, 1966.

[9]*New York Times.* February 26, 1966.

[10]*Birmingham News.* Jananuary 9, 1966.

[11]*Birmingham News.* March 3, 1966.

[12]*Birmingham News.* January 11, 1966.

[13]*New York Times.* January 23, 1966.

[14]*New York Times.* March 3, 1966.

[15]*New York Times.* March 16, 1966.

[16]Smith, Anita. *The Intimate Story of Lurleen Wallace.* Montgomery, AL: Communications Unlimited, Inc., 1969. p. 83.

[17]*Birmingham News.* January 10, 1966.

[18]*New York Times.* February 25, 1966.

[19]Lesher, Stephan. *George Wallace, American Populist.* New York: Addison-Wesley Publishing Company, 1994. pp. 116-118, 143.

[20]Frady, Marshall. *Wallace.* New York: New American Library, 1968. p. 189.

[21]Smith, Anita. *The Intimate Story of Lurleen Wallace.* Montgomery, AL: Communications Unlimited, Inc., 1969. p. 78.

[22]*Birmingham News.* March 22, 1966.

[23]*Birmingham News.* March 27, 1966.

[24]*Birmingham News.* April 4, 1966.

[25]*New York Times.* February 11, 1966.

[26]*New York Times.* February 21, 1966.

[27]*Birmigham News.* March 27, 1966.

[28]*Birmingham News.* March 27, 1966.

[29]*Birmingham News.* April 8, 1966.

[30]Interview with Wayne Greenhaw, former reporter and editorial writer for the*Montgomery Advertiser*, conducted April 8, 1993.

[31]*Birmingham News.* May 1, 1966.

[32]*Birmingham News.* April 13, 1966.

[33]*Birmingham News.* April 10, 1966.

[34]*New York Times.* April 14, 1966.

[35]*Birmingham News.* May 1, 1966.

[36]*New York Times.* May 4, 1966.

[37]*Birmingham News.* May 6, 1966.

[38]*New York Times.* November 10, 1966.

[39]Frady, Marshall. *Wallace.* New York: New American Library, 1968. p. 206.

[40]Lesher, Stephan. *George Wallace, American Populist.* New York: Addison-Wesley Publishing Company, 1994. p. 366.

[41]*Ibid.* p. xiii.

[42]*Birmingham News.* May 5, 1966.

[43]*Birmingham News.* May 6, 1966.

[44]Frady, Marshall. *Wallace.* New York: New American Library, 1968. p. 206.

[45]Greenhaw interview.

[46]Interview with James M. Fullan, Jr., defense attorney during the trial of Richmond Flowers, conducted May 25, 1993.

[47]*Birmingham News.* February 23, 1969.

[48]*Post-Herald.* February 26, 1969.

[49]*Birmingham News.* February 8, 1969.

[50]*Post-Herald.* February 1, 1969.

[51]*Post-Herald.* February 14, 1969.

[52]*Post-Herald.* February 25, 1966.

[53]Fullan interview.

[54]*Birmingham News.* February 15, 1969.

[55]*Post-Herald.* February 27, 1969.

[56]Smith, Edward Conrad, editor. *The Constitution of the United States.* New York: Harper and Row, 1972. p. 70.

[57]*Federal Reporter.* "United States v. Hyde." 2nd Series 448. 448 F. 2nd

815.1971. p 851.

[58]*Federal Reporter*. p. 852.

[59]*Federal Reporter*. p. 855.

[60]*Federal Reporter*. p. 856.

[61]*Federal Reporter*. p. 857.

[62]"Labor Violence and the Hobbs Act." Hearings Before the Committee on the Judiciary, United States Senate, Ninety-eighth Congress. Washington, DC: Government Printing Office, 1984.

[63]*Supreme Court Reports*. "McCormick v. United States." 112 Lawyers Edition.Second Series 14. 111 S. Ct. 37 (1990). p. 1818.

[64]Raines, John C., Editor. *Conspiracy*. New York: Harper and Row, 1974. p. 143.

[65]*Supreme Court Reports*. p. 1816.

[66]Raines, John C., Editor. *Conspiracy*. New York: Harper and Row, 1974. p. 153.

[67]*Ibid*. p. 155.

[68]*Ibid*. p. 154.

[69]Interview with Albert Brewer, former governor of Alabama, conducted July 20, 1993.

[70]Coleman, Stephen, Jr., and Stephen Coleman, Sr. *Judge Clarence Allgood*. Birmingham, AL: Birmingham Historical Society, 1991. p. 18; Hamilton, Virginia Van der Veer. *Lister Hill*. Chapel Hill, NC: University of North Carolina Press, 1987. p. 168.

[71]*Ibid*. p. 16.

[72]Bass, Jack. *Unlikely Heroes*. Tuscaloosa: University of Alabama Press, 1981. p. 169.

[73]*Ibid*. p. 168.

[74]Coleman, Stephen, Jr., and Stephen Coleman, Sr. *Judge Clarence Allgood*. Birmingham, AL: Birmingham Historical Society, 1991. p. 4.

[75]*Ibid*. p. 40.

[76]*Ibid*. p. 43.

[77]*Ibid*. p. 40.

[78]Greenhaw interview.

[79]Greenhaw interview.

[80]Frady, Marshall. *Wallace*. New York: New American Library, 1968. p. 204.

[81]*Ibid*. p. 205.

[82]Interview with Kenneth Hammond, former state senator and former president

of the Alabama Public Service Commission, conducted April 16, 1993.

[83]*Gadsden Times*. March 26, 1975.

[84]*Southern Reporter*. "Kenneth Hammond v. State." 354 Southern Reporter, Second Series. 3 Div. 444. p. 2.

[85]*Southern Reporter*. p. 4.

[86]*Ibid*.

[87]Brewer interview.

[88]Brewer interview.

[89]Carlson, Jody. *George C. Wallace and the Politics of Powerlessness*. New Brunswich, NJ: Transaction Books, Inc., 1981. p. 135.

[90]*Ibid*. p. 136.

[91]Brewer interview.

[92]Brewer interview.

Epilogue

[1]Coleman, K. *A History of Georgia*. Second Edition. Athens, GA: University of Georgia Press, 1991. p. 369.

[2]Soderberg, Peter A. "The Negro Revolution and the Year of Decision: 1963-1964." *Social Science*. 40:2.

April 1965. p. 91.

[3]*Ibid.* p. 90.

[4]Hamilton, Virginia Van der Veer. *Lister Hill.* Chapel Hill: University of North Carolina Press, 1987. p. 247.

[5]Zaleznik, Abraham. "Charismatic and Concensus Leaders: A Psychological Comparison." In *Contemporary Issues in Leadership*. William E. Rosenbach and Robert L. Taylors, eds. Boulder, CO: Westview Press, 1989. p. 102.

[6]Gardner, John W. "The Tasks of Leadership." In *Contemporary Issues in Leadership*. William E. Rosenbach and Robert L. Taylor, eds. Boulder, CO: Westview Press, 1989. p. 29.

[7]Cartwright, Dorwin, and Alvin Zander. *Group Dynamics*. Evanston, IL: Row, Peterson and Company, 1953. p. 59.

[8]*Ibid.* p. 60.

[9]Dykeman, Wilma. *Tennessee: A Bicentennial History*. New York: W. W. Norton & Company, Inc., 1975. p. 115.

[10]Woodward, C. Vann. *The Strange Career of Jim Crow*. New York: Oxford University Press, 1974. p. 189.

[11]*Ibid.* p. 191.

[12]*Loc. Cit.*

[13]"America's Hot Cities." *Newsweek*. February 6, 1989. p. 44.

[14]*Birmingham News.* June 21, 1989.

[15]*Birmingham News.* November 15, 1992.

[16]*Birmingham News.* November 29, 1993.

[17]Williamson, Joel. *The Crucible of Race*. New York: Oxford University Press, 1984. p. 509.

[18]King, Martin Luther, Jr. *Why We Can't Wait*. New York: Signet Books, 1964. pp. 81-82.

[19]Williamson, Joel. *The Crucible of Race*. New York: Oxford University Press, 1984. p. 522.

[20]Tilove, Jonathan. "Scars of Slavery." *Birmingham News*. July 24, 1994. p. C1.

[21]*Loc. Cit.*

[22]Williamson, Joel. *The Crucible of Race*. New York: Oxford University Press, 1984. p. 289.

[23]King, Martin Luther, Jr. *Why We Can't Wait*. New York: Signet Books, 1964. p. 77.

[24]Critique of the first draft of the text

[25]Martin, Harold H. *Ralph McGill, Reporter*. Boston: Little, Brown and Company, 1972. p 196.

BIBLIOGRAPHY

Abernathy, Ralph David. *And the Walls Came Tumbling Down*. New York: Harper and Roe, 1989.

Alabama Handbook. Montgomery, AL: Alabama Department of Agriculture and Industry, 1919

Alexander, Charles C. *Holding the Line: The Eisenhower Era, 1952-1961*. Bloomington, IN: Indiana University Press, 1975.

Allen, Frederick Lewis. *Only Yesterday*. New York: Bantam Books, 1931.

Awoonor, Kofi Nyidevu. *Ghana: A Political History*. Accra, Ghana: Sedco Publishing Limited, 1990.

Ayers, Edward L. *The Promise of the New South*. New York: Oxford University Press, 1992

Bass, Jack. *Unlikely Heroes*. Tuscaloosa, AL: University of Alabama Press, 1981.

Belsches, Alan T. "Introduction." In *Devil Make a Third* by Douglas Fields Bailey. Tuscaloosa, AL: University of Alabama Press, 1989.

Biles, Roger. "A Bittersweet Victory: Public School Desegregation in Memphis." *Journal of Negro Education*. 55:4. Fall 1986. 470-483.

Blaustein, Albert P., and Robert L. Zangrando, editors. *Civil Rights and the American Negro*. New York: Trident Press, 1968.

Blumberg, Lois Ronda. *Civil Rights: The 1960's Freedom Struggle*. Boston: G. K. Hall, 1984.

Brewer, Albert P. "Famous Filibusters: High Drama in the Alabama Legislature." *The Alabama Review*. 43:2. April 1990. 83-97.

Carlson, Jody. *George C. Wallace and the Politics of Powerlessness*. New Brunswich, NJ: Transaction Books, Inc., 1981.

Carrison, Webb. *The Legacy of Atlanta*. Atlanta: Peachtree Publishers, Ltd., 1987.

Cartwright, Dorwin, and Alvin Zander. *Group Dynamics*. Evanston, IL: Row, Peterson and Company, 1953.

Chalmers, David M. *The History of the Ku Klux Klan*. Chicago, IL: Quadrangle Books, 1965.

Clark, James G. *The Jim Clark Story*. Selma, AL: Selma Enterprises, Inc., 1966.

Colburn, David R., and Richard K. Scher. "Race Relations and Gubernatorial Politics." *The Florida Historical Quarterly*. 55:2. October 1976. 154-160.

Coles, Robert. *Children of Crisis: A Study of Courage and Fear.* Boston: Little, Brown and Company, 1964

Coleman, Kenneth, editor. *A History of Georgia.* Second Edition. Athens, GA: University of Georgia Press, 1991.

Coleman, Stephen, Jr., and Stephen Coleman, Sr. *Judge Clarence Allgood.* Birmingham, AL: Birmingham Historical Society, 1991.

Craven, Avery. *Reconstruction: The Ending of the Civil War.* New York: Hold, Rinehart and Winston, Inc., 1969

Current, Richard Nelson. *Those Terrible Carpetbaggers: A Reinterpretation.* New York: Oxford University Press, 1988

Delgar, Carl N. "A Century of the Klans." *Journal of Southern History.* 31:4. November 1965. 435-443.

D'Emilio, John. *The Civil Rights Struggle: Leaders in Profile.* New York: Facts on File, 1979.

Dowe, Kelley. "Richard Arrington, Birmingham." *Southern Exposure.* 12:1. 1984. 76-78.

Dykeman, Wilma. *Tennessee: A Bicentennial History.* New York: W. W. Norton & Company, Inc., 1975.

Fleming, Cynthia Griggs. "White Lunch Counters and Black Consciousness: The Story of the Knoxville Sit-Ins." *Tennessee Historical Quarterly.* 49:1. Spring 1990. 40-52.

Flowers, Paul B., Jr. *Flowers Chronicles.* Baltimore: Gateway Press, Inc., 1987.

Frady, Marshall. *Wallace.* New York: New American Library, 1968.

Gallager, Hugh Gregory. *FDR's Splendid Deception.* New York: Dodd, Mead & Company, 1985.

Gardner, John W. "The Tasks of Leadership." In *Contemporary Issues in Leadership.* William E. Rosenbach and Robert L. Taylor, editors. Boulder, CO: Westview Press, 1989.

Garrow, David J. *Bearing the Cross: Martin Luther King, Jr., and the Southern Christian Leadership Conference.* New York: William Morrow and Company, 1986

Geier, W. A. "Nashville Sit-Ins." *Christian Century.* 77:17. April 27, 1960. 525-526.

Geier, W. A. "Slow Integration." *Christian Century.* 76:39. September 30, 1959. 1124-1126.

Ginger, Ray, editor. *William Jennings Bryan: Selections.* New York: The Bobbs-Merrill Company, Inc., 1967.

Goldfield, David R. *Black, White, and Southern.* Baton Rouge, LA: Louisiana State University Press, 1990

Graham, Hugh Davis. *Crisis in Print.* Nashville, TN: Vanderbilt University Press, 1967.

Grafton, Carl and Anna Permaloff. *Big Mules and Branchheads.* Athens: University of Georgia Press, 1985.

Greenhaw, Wayne. *Watch Out for George Wallace*. Englewood Cliffs, NJ: Prentice-Hall, Inc., 1976.
Griffith, Lucille. *Alabama: A Documentary History to 1900*. Tuscaloosa, AL: University of Alabama Press, 1972.
Halberstam, David. *The Best and the Brightest*. New York: Random House, 1972.
Hamilton, Virginia Van der Veer. *Hugo Black: The Alabama Years*. Baton Rouge, LA: Louisiana State University Press, 1972.
Hamilton, Virginia Van der Veer. *Lister Hill*. Chapel Hill, NC: University of North Carolina Press, 1987.
Hampton, Harry, and Steve Fayer. *Voices of Freedom*. New York: Bantam Books, 1990.
Helson, Bernard H. *The Fourteenth Amendment and the Negro since 1920*. New York: Russell and Russell, 1946.
Hobson, Fred. "Introduction." In *The Fighting South* by John Temple Graves. Tuscaloosa, AL: University of Alabama Press, 1985.
Hollis, David Webster, III. *An Alabama Newspaper Tradition*. Tuscaloosa, AL: University of Alabama Press, 1983.
Jasper, Thomas. "The Second Folsom Administration: The Destruction of Alabama Liberalisn, 1954-58." Ph.D. dissertation, Auburn University, 1957.
"Kenneth Hammond v. State." *354 Southern Reporter*. 2nd Series. 3 Div. 444.
King, Martin Luther, Jr. *Why We Can't Wait*. New York: Signet Books, 1964
"Labor Violence and the Hobbs Act: Hearings before the Committee on the Judiciary, United States Senate, Ninety-eighth Congress." Washington, DC: U.S. Government Printing Office, 1984.
Lassey, William R., and Marshall Sashkin, editors. *Leadership and Social Change*. San Diego, CA: University Associates, Inc., 1983.
Lesher, Stephan. *George Wallace, American Populist*. New York: Addison-Wesley Publishing Company, 1994
Leuchtenburg, William E. *Franklin D. Roosevelt and the New Deal*. New York: Harper and Row, 1963.
Lewis, Dan A., and Greta Salem. *Fear of Crime*. New Brunswick, NJ: Transaction, Inc., 1986.
Lewis, W. David. "Preface: The South in Transition." In *The Southern Mystique*. W. David Lewis and B. Eugene Griessman, editors. Tuscaloosa, AL: University of Alabama Press, 1977.
Lichtman, Allan. "The Federal Assault against Voting Distrimination in the Deep South: 1957-1967." *Journal of Negro History*. 54:4. 1969. 346-367.
Lomax, Lewis E. *The Negro Revolt*. New York: Harper and Brothers, 1962.
Lord, Walter. *The Past That Wouldn't Die*. New York: Harper & Row, Publishers, 1966
Lytle, Andrew. *Bedford Forrest and His Critter Company*. Seminole, FL: The Green Key Press, 1984.

Manchester, William. *The Last Lion*. New York: Dell Publishing, 1983.
Martin, Harold H. *Ralph McGill, Reporter*. Boston: Little, Brown and Company, 1973.
"McCormick v. United States." *U.S. Supreme Court Reports*. Second Series. 484 U.S. 846. 112 L. Ed. 2nd 14 (1990).
McMillen, Neil R. "Organized Resistance to School Desegregation in Tennessee." *Tennessee Historical Quarterly*. 30:3. Fall 1971. 315-320.
McWilliams, Tennant S. "A New Day Coming: Alabama Since 1930." In *Perspectives: The Alabama Heritage*. Rosemary Canfield, editor. Troy, AL: Troy State University Press, 1978.
Memorial Record of Alabama. Volume I. Madison, WI: Brant and Fuller, 1893.
Meier, August, and Elliott Rudwick. *CORE*. New York: Oxford University Press, 1973.
Meier, August, and Elliott Rudwick. *From Plantation to Ghetto*. New York: Hill and Wang, 1970.
Mills, C. Wright. *Power, Politics and People*. New York: Oxford University Press, 1963.
Moore, Albert B. *History of Alabama*. Tuscaloosa, AL: Alabama Book Store, 1951.
Muir, Donal E., and C. Donald McGlamery. "Trends in Integration Attitudes on a Deep-South Campus During the First Two Decades of Desegregation." *Social Forces*. 62:4. June 1984. 963-972.
Nunnelley, William A. *Bull Connor*. Tuscaloosa, AL: University of Alabama Press, 1991.
Olson, Otto H. "Introduction." In *Reconstruction and Redemption in the South*. Olson, Otto H., editor. Baton Rouge, LA: Louisiana State University Press, 1980.
Permaloff, Anna, and Carl Grafton. "The Chop-Up Bill and the Big Mule Alliance." *The Alabama Review*. 43:4. October 1990. 243-269.
Perry, John A., and Erna K. Perry. *The Social Web*. New York: Harper and Row, 1988.
Powledge, Fred. *Free at Last?* Boston: Little, Brown and Company, 1991.
"Preliminary Results of Investigation. United Klans of America, Incorporated, Knights of the Ku Klux Klan, and Other Klan Organizations." Report published by the office of the attorney general of Alabama. October 18, 1965.
Pritchett, C. Herman. "Equal Protection and the Urban Majority." *The American Political Science Review*. 58:4. December 1964. 869-875.
Rabby, Glenda Alice. "Out of the Past: The Civil Rights Movement in Tallahassee, Florida." Ph.D. Dissertation, The Florida State University, 1984.
Raines, John C., editor. *Conspiracy*. New York: Harper and Row, 1974.
Ricks, John. "Martin Luther King's Mistakes in Albany, Georgia, 1961-62."

Proceedings and Papers of the Georgia Association of Historians. Volume 9. 1988. 169-176.

Roland, Charlles P. *The Improbably Era: The South Since World War II*. Lexington, KY: The University Press of Kentucky, 1975.

Rosenbach, William E., and Robert L. Taylor, editors. *Contemporary Issues in Leadership*. Boulder, CO: Westview Press, Inc., 1989.

"S. 613, A Bill to Amend the Hobbs Act: Hearings Before the Subcommittee on Criminal Law of the Committee on the Judiciary, United States Senate, Ninety-seventh Congress." Washington, DC: U.S. Government Printing Office, 1982

Shofner, Jerrell H. "Custom, Law, and History: The Enduring Influence of Florida's 'Black Code.'" *The Florida Historical Quarterly*. 55:3. January 1977. pp. 277-298.

Sikora, Frank. *The Judge*. Montgomery, AL: The Black Belt Press, 1992.

Silberman, Charles E. *Crisis in Black and White*. New York: Random House, 1964.

Simpson, Lewis. "Introduction." In *Perspectives: The Alabama Heritage*. Rosemary Canfield, editor. Troy, AL: Troy State University Press, 1978.

Sims, George E. *The Little Man's Big Friend*. Tuscaloosa, AL: University of Alabama Press, 1985.

Smith, Anita. *The Intimate Story of Lurleen Wallace*. Montgomery, AL: Communications Unlimited, Inc., 1969.

Smith, Edward C., editor. *The Constitution of the United States*. New York: Harper and Roe, 1972.

Smith, Stanley. H. "A Case Study on Socio-Political Change." *Phylon*. 29:4. 1968. 380-387.

Smith, Steven A. *Myth, Media, and the Southern Mind*. Fayetteville, AR: University of Arkansas Press, 1985.

Soderbergh, Peter A. "The Negro Revolution and the Year of Decision: 1963-1964." *Social Science*. 40:2 April 1965. 86-93.

Stern, Mark. "Lyndon Johnson and Richard Russell: Institutions, Ambitions and Civil Rights." *Presidential Studies Quarterly*. 21:4. 1991. 687-704.

Stewart, John Craig. *The Governors of Alabama*. Gretna, LA: Pelican Publishing Company, 1975.

Taylor, James S. "John M. Patterson and the 1958 Alabama Gubernatorial Race." *The Alabama Review*. 23:3. July 1970. 226-234.

The Alabama Opportunity. Montgomery, AL: Alabama Department of Agriculture and Industries, 1906

Thorton, J. Mills III. *From Civil War to Civil Rights*. Tuscaloosa, AL: University of Alabama Press, 1987.

Tomberlin, Joseph A. "Florida Whites and the *Brown* Decision of 1954." *The Florida Historical Quarterly*. 51:1. July 1972. 22-36.

Truman, Margaret. *Harry S. Truman*. New York: William Morrow and Com-

pany, Inc., 1973.
"Union Violence and the Hobbs Act: Hearing Before the Subcommittee on Separation of Powers of the Committee on the Judiciary, United States Senate, Ninety-eighth Congress." Washington, DC: U.S. Government Printing Office, 1983
"United States v. Hyde." *Federal Reporter*. 2nd Series 448 448 F. 2nd 815 (1971).
Wagy, Thomas R. "Governor LeRoy Collins of Florida and the Little Rock Crisis of 1957." *Arkansas Historical Quarterly*. 38:2. Summer 1979. 95-115.
Wiggins, Sarah Woolfolk. "Alabama: Democratic Bulldozing and Republican Folly." In *Reconstruction and Redemption in the South*. Otto H. Olson, editor. Baton Rouge, LA: Louisiana State University Press, 1980.
Wiggins, Sara Woolfolk. *The Scalawags in Alabama Politics, 1865 -1881*. Tuscaloosa, AL: University of Alabama Press, 1977.
Williamson, Joel. *The Crucible of Race*. New York: Oxford University Press, 1984
Woodward, C. Vann. "Lewis H. Blair, Prophet Without Honor." Introduction to *A Southern Prophecy: The Prosperity of the South Dependent on the Elevation of the Negro*. Lewis H. Blair. Boston: Little, Brown and Company, 1964.
Woodward, C. Vann. *Origins of the New South*. Baton Rouge: Louisiana State University Press, 1951
Woodward, C. Vann. *The Burden of Southern History*. Third
Edition. Baton Rough: Louisiana State University Press, 1993
Woodward, C. Vann. *The Strange Career of Jim Crow*. Third Revised Edition. New York: Oxford University Press, 1974.
Wynn, Linta T. "The Dawning of a New Day: the Nashville Sit-Ins, February 14-May 10, 1960." *Tennessee Historical Quarterly*. 50:1. Spring 1991. 42-54.
Yarbrough, Tinsley E. *Judge Frank Johnson and Human Rights in Alabama*. Tuscaloosa, AL: University of Alabama Press, 1981.
Zaleznik, Abraham. "Charismatic and Consensus Leaders: A Psychological Comparison." In *Contemporary Issues in Leadership*. William E. Rosenbach and Robert L. Taylors, editors. Boulder, CO: Westview Press, 1989.

Index

C

D

G

H

I

J

K

L

M

N

O

P

R

S

Y

About the Author

John Hayman is a former college teacher who from 1991 to 1994 directed a study of information technology in African universities for the International Association of Universities. He has a B.S. degree from the University of Alabama, an M.A. from Syracuse University, and a Ph. D. from Stanford. Prior to *Bitter Harvest*, he published three books and more than sixty articles. He was editor of *Teaching and Learning With Computers* and served sixteen years as a consulting editor for the *Journal of Educational Research*. His paper, "Culture, the Self-Fulfilling Prophecy, and Quality of Life in the Black Belt Region of the Southeast United States," won a special award for at the 1980 International Congress on Applied Systems Research. Mr. Hayman lives in Birmingham, Alabama, with his wife, Clara Ruth.